Close-up

COMPANION C2

Liz Gardiner

NATIONAL GEOGRAPHIC
LEARNING

Australia · Brazil · Mexico · Singapore · United Kingdom · United States

NATIONAL GEOGRAPHIC
L E A R N I N G

Close-up C2 Companion
Liz Gardiner

Executive Editor: Sian Mavor

Editorial Manager: Claire Merchant

Commissioning Editor: Kayleigh Buller

Editor: Nicola Foufouti

Head of Production: Celia Jones

Content Project Manager: Melissa Beavis

Manufacturing Manager: Eyvett Davis

Cover Designer: MPS Limited

Compositor: Wild Apple Design Ltd

For product information and technology assistance, contact us at
Cengage Learning Customer & Sales Support, cengage.com/contact
For permission to use material from this text or product,
submit all requests online at **cengage.com/permissions**
Further permissions questions can be emailed to
permissionrequest@cengage.com

ISBN: 978-1-4080-9844-8

National Geographic Learning
Cheriton House, North Way, Andover, Hampshire,
SP10 5BE United Kingdom

National Geographic Learning, a Cengage Learning Company, has a mission to bring the world to the classroom and the classroom to life. With our English language programs, students learn about their world by experiencing it. Through our partnerships with National Geographic and TED Talks, they develop the language and skills they need to be successful global citizens and leaders.

Locate your local office at **international.cengage.com/region**

Visit National Geographic Learning online at **NGL.cengage.com/Closeup**

Visit our corporate website at **www.cengage.com**

Photo credits

Cover image: MalcolmC/Shutterstock Inc

Student Access: to access the Close-up C2 Companion audio, please visit the Student Online Zone at
NGL.Cengage.com/closeup

Teacher Access: to access the Grammar and Vocabulary Answer Keys, please visit the Teacher Online Zone at
NGL.Cengage.com/closeup and use the password provided in the Teacher's Book

Printed in the United Kingdom by CPI Antony Rowe
Print number 08 Print year 2023

MIX
Paper | Supporting
responsible forestry
FSC® C013604

Contents

Note to Teachers

Close-up C2 Companion provides students with everything they need to understand the vocabulary and grammar in the *Close-up C2 Student's Book*.

In the vocabulary section, words and phrases are listed in order of appearance together with their parts of speech and IPA. Each entry includes a clear explanation of the headword, an example sentence, derivatives (appropriate for the level) and the Greek translation of the word or phrase as it is used in the context of the Student's Book. For some entries there are special notes. These include antonyms, synonyms and expressions. At the end of the word lists for most sections, there are word sets that help students learn related words or phrases more easily. There are also *Look!* boxes with notes on usage. The vocabulary section ends with a variety of tasks that practise many of the new words and phrases of that unit.

In the grammar section, there are comprehensive grammar explanations in Greek with plenty of topic-related example sentences. The grammar section ends with tasks that practise the grammar of that unit. Each unit of the Companion ends with a C2 *(Proficiency)* exam-style task, which is based on the grammar and vocabulary of the unit.

At the back of the book, there is a complete list of all the words and phrases in the Companion in alphabetical order with their entry number. This helps teachers and students to locate words easily, for example, if they want to refer to a word they learnt in another unit, or if they come across any difficulties.

Finally, *Close-up C2 Companion* is accompanied by audio, which contains the accurate pronunciation of each headword. You can find the audio here: ngl.cengage.com

Terms & Abbreviations

Terms / Abbreviations		Όροι / Συντομεύσεις
n	noun	ουσιαστικό
v	verb	ρήμα
phr v	phrasal verb	περιφραστικό ρήμα
adj	adjective	επίθετο
adv	adverb	επίρρημα
det	determiner	προσδιοριστικό
pron	pronoun	αντωνυμία
prep	preposition	πρόθεση
conj	conjunction	σύνδεσμος
expr	expression	έκφραση
excl	exclamation	επιφώνημα
Opp	opposite	αντίθετο
Syn	synonym	συνώνυμο
abbr	abbreviation	συντόμευση

Key to pronunciation and phonetic symbols

Consonants					
p	pen	/pen/	tʃ	chain	/tʃeɪn/
b	bad	/bæd/	dʒ	jam	/dʒæm/
t	tea	/tiː/	f	fall	/fɔːl/
d	did	/dɪd/	v	van	/væn/
k	cat	/kæt/	θ	thin	/θɪn/
g	get	/get/	ð	this	/ðɪs/

Vowels and diphthongs					
iː	see	/siː/	ɜː	fur	/fɜː/
i	happy	/ˈhæpi/	ə	about	/əˈbaʊt/
ɪ	sit	/sɪt/	eɪ	say	/seɪ/
e	ten	/ten/	əʊ	go	/gəʊ/
æ	cat	/kæt/	aɪ	my	/maɪ/
ɑː	father	/ˈfɑːðə/	ɔɪ	boy	/bɔɪ/
ɒ	got	/gɒt/	aʊ	now	/naʊ/
ɔː	saw	/sɔː/	ɪə	near	/nɪə/
ʊ	put	/pʊt/	eə	hair	/heə/
u	actual	/ˈæktʃuəl/	ʊə	pure	/pjʊə/
uː	too	/tuː/	ʌ	cup	/kʌp/

1 Do You Mind?

page 5

1.1 **gelada** (n) /gəlˈɑdɑ/
a rare species of monkey native to Ethiopia
• *Unlike other monkeys, geladas spend most of their time eating grass in the meadows of Ethiopia.* ❖ σπάνιο είδος μαϊμούς-μπαμπουίνου της Αιθιοπίας

1.2 **bare** (v) /beə(r)/
uncover sth so that it is visible • *The burglar took to his heels when the large family dog bared its teeth and growled at him.*
➢ bareness (n), bare (adj), barely (adv)
❖ ξεγυμνώνω, αποκαλύπτω

Reading

pages 6-7

1.3 **interaction** (n) /ˌɪntərˈækʃn/
the act of communicating with or reacting to others • *Teachers are under pressure to create positive interactions between local children and immigrant students.* ➢ interact (v), interactive (adj), interactively (adv)
❖ διάδραση

1.4 **individual** (n) /ˌɪndɪˈvɪdʒuəl/
a particular person who behaves in a unique way • *Our genetic code is what makes us all individuals so no two people are quite the same.* ➢ individuality (n), individually (adv)
❖ άτομο

1.5 **unbeknown (to sb)** (adv) /ˌʌnbɪˈnəʊn tuː ˈsʌmbədi/
without sb knowing • *Unbeknown to us, the boss had heard our entire conversation.*
❖ άγνωστο (σε κάποιον)

1.6 **sustain** (v) /səˈsteɪn/
experience or suffer sth unpleasant • *Lance sustained a severe leg injury when he fell off his bike.* ➢ sustainability (n), sustainable (adj)
❖ υφίσταμαι

1.7 **neuroscience** (n) /ˈnjʊərəʊsaɪəns/
the science of studying the brain and nervous system • *As research methods in neuroscience develop, there is more evidence to explain how people experience different emotions.* ➢ neuroscientist (n)
❖ νευροεπιστήμη

1.8 **miraculous** (adj) /mɪˈrækjələs/
extraordinary and unexpected • *The patient made a miraculous recovery and was back to work long before anyone expected.* ➢ miracle (n), miraculously (adv) ❖ θαυματουργός

1.9 **foreman** (n) /ˈfɔːmən/
a worker who is responsible for leading a group of other workers, especially in construction or factory work • *The factory foreman told the workers to take a break while the machines were being serviced.*
❖ επιστάτης / αρχιεργάτης

1.10 **dynamite** (n) /ˈdaɪnəmaɪt/
a highly explosive substance • *Several sticks of dynamite were used to blow up the old block of flats.* ➢ dynamite (v) ❖ δυναμίτης / δυναμίτιδα

1.11 **blast** (v) /blɑːst/
destroy sth by using explosives • *The explosion had blasted a hole in the side of the building.* ➢ blast (n) ❖ ανατινάζω

1.12 **rod** (n) /rɒd/
a long thin straight pole • *Ted lost his balance and fell off the ladder when he was putting up the new curtains on the rod.* ❖ ράβδος, βέργα

1.13 **compact** (v) /kəmˈpækt/
compress the parts of sth closely together into a more solid state or into a smaller space • *After the household waste is collected, it is compacted into large blocks to take up less space.* ➢ compact (n), compact (adj)
❖ συμπτήσσω

1.14 **ignite** (v) /ɪgˈnaɪt/
cause sth to start burning • *The heat of the sun through broken glass can be enough to ignite dry grass and cause a wildfire.*
➢ ignition (n) ❖ αναφλέγω

1.15 **subsequent** (adj) /ˈsʌbsɪkwənt/
coming after sth else • *The cause of the accident was unknown until the subsequent enquiry was conducted.* ➢ subsequently (adv)
❖ μεταγενέστερος

1.16 **propel** (v) /prəˈpel/
push sth/sb forward usually causing rapid movement • *The strong current propelled the raft towards the rocks.* ➢ propeller (n), propellant (n), propulsion (n) ❖ προωθώ

1.17 **exit** (v) /ˈeksɪt/
leave; go out • *James exited the room without saying goodbye.* ➢ exit (n) ❖ εξέρχομαι

1.18 **skull** (n) /skʌl/
the bone that gives structure to the head and protects the brain • *Wearing a motorcycle helmet reduces the risk of injury to the skull in the event of an accident.* ❖ κρανίο

1.19 against all odds (expr)
/əˈgenst ɔːl ɒdz/
despite seeming impossible • *Against all odds, the climbing team made it to the top of K2.*
❖ ενάντια σε όλες τις πιθανότητες

1.20 initially (adv) /ɪˈnɪʃəli/
at first • *Paul's parents were initially surprised at his decision to leave home, but they soon came round to the idea.* ➤ initial (n), initial (adj)
❖ αρχικά

1.21 semicomatose (adj)
/ˈsemi ˈkəʊmətəʊs/
almost unconscious • *Gwen was still semicomatose when we saw her after her operation, so she didn't seem to realise where she was.* ❖ ημικωματώδης

1.22 physically (adv) /ˈfɪzɪkli/
involving the body rather than the mind
• *Robin still found cycling physically challenging months after breaking his ankle.*
➤ physical (adj) ❖ σωματικά

1.23 mentally (adv) /ˈmentəli/
involving the mind rather than the body
• *Solving crosswords and other puzzles can be mentally stimulating.* ➤ mentality (n), mental (adj) ❖ διανοητικά

1.24 inappropriate (adj) /ˌɪnəˈprəʊpriət/
not suitable • *I hadn't realised it would be a formal dinner, so my jeans and T-shirt were quite inappropriate for the occasion.*
➤ inappropriateness (n), inappropriately (adv)
❖ ακατάλληλος

1.25 acquaintance (n) /əˈkweɪntəns/
sb you know but are not close friends with
• *Laura has a large number of acquaintances on social media sites, most of whom she has never met personally.* ➤ acquaint (v)
❖ γνωριμία

1.26 hold down (phr v) /həʊld daʊn/
manage to keep a job • *John had difficulty in holding down two jobs at once as he was utterly exhausted.* ❖ διατηρώ

1.27 epileptic (adj) /ˌepɪˈleptɪk/
related to epilepsy, an illness affecting the brain • *Tom became epileptic as a result of a head injury.* ➤ epilepsy (n) ❖ επιληπτικός

1.28 seizure (n) /ˈsiːʒə(r)/
an attack of an illness that strikes suddenly
• *Aunt Hilda was admitted to hospital after her heart seizure.* ➤ seize (v) ❖ κρίση, αποπληξία

1.29 post-traumatic (adj) /ˌpəʊst.trɔːˈmæt.ɪk/
as a result of a serious shock or injury, especially to the brain • *Naser suffered from post-traumatic stress after his town was bombed.* ❖ μετατραυματικό

1.30 disinhibition (n) /ˌdɪsɪnhɪˈbɪʃn/
the state of having no feeling of embarrassment or shyness to restrict behaviour • *Certain drugs, which have caused people to experience sudden social disinhibition and lead to self-destructive behaviour, are banned in Australia.* ➤ disinhibit (v) ❖ έλλειψη αυτοσυγκράτησης
✎ Opp: inhibition ❖ αυτοσυγκράτηση

1.31 frontal lobe (n) /ˈfrʌnˌtəl ləʊb/
one of the two parts of the brain which control behaviour, personality, etc. • *In the past, mental illness was treated by removing all or part of the frontal lobes.* ➤ lobotomy (n), lobotomise (v) ❖ πρόσθιος λοβός

1.32 cognitive (adj) /ˈkɒgnətɪv/
related to the processes of thinking and understanding • *It's amazing how children's cognitive development varies according to their upbringing.* ❖ γνωστικός

1.33 inhibit (v) /ɪnˈhɪbɪt/
restrict sb's actions by causing them to feel shy or embarrassed • *Students felt that their new teacher inhibited them from learning with her strict manner.* ➤ inhibition (n)
❖ αναστέλλω

1.34 self-awareness (n) /self əˈweənəs/
a sense of understanding your own behaviour and who you are • *Watching how you behave on video can lead to a greater sense of self-awareness.* ➤ self-aware (adj) ❖ αυτογνωσία

1.35 solid (adj) /ˈsɒlɪd/
certain • *Though Ken was the prime suspect in the murder investigation, the police had no solid proof to arrest him.* ➤ solidify (v), solidly (adv) ❖ ατράνταχτος

1.36 trauma (n) /ˈtrɔːmə/
the effect of a serious shock or injury, especially on the brain • *Alex needed the help of a psychologist to help him through the trauma of his parents' divorce.* ➤ traumatise (v), traumatic (adj), traumatically (adv)
❖ τραύμα

1.37 introductory (adj) /ˌɪntrəˈdʌktəri/
intended to introduce you to a subject or activity • *The college offers a range of short introductory courses for foreign students.*
➤ introduce (v), introduction (n) ❖ εισαγωγικός

1.38 sought-out (adj) /sɔːt aʊt/
desired; wanted • *The most sought-out paintings fetched a good price at the auction.*
➤ seek (v), seeker (n) ❖ δημοφιλής

1.39 ground-breaking (adj) /ˈgraʊndbreɪkɪŋ/
making a new and important discovery
• *Before the ground-breaking discovery of antibiotics, people used to die from infections that are now curable.* ➤ groundbreaker (n)
❖ πρωτοπόρος
✎ Also: groundbreaking

1.40 **temperament** (n) /ˈtemprəmənt/
your manner of behaving or reacting towards others ● *Lucy's calm temperament makes her an ideal school counsellor.* ➣ temperamental (adj), temperamentally (adv) ❖ ταμπεραμέντο

1.41 **track** (v) /træk/
follow the progress of sth/sb ● *Our tutor gives us monthly tests to track our academic progress.* ➣ tracker (n) ❖ παρακολουθώ

1.42 **well-being** (n) /wel ˈbiːɪŋ/
the state of good physical and psychological health ● *Having enough sleep is as important as diet and exercise for your overall well-being.* ❖ ευεξία

1.43 **infancy** (n) /ˈɪnfənsi/
the stage of life from birth to early childhood ● *Children's psychological development depends greatly on the stimulus they receive during their infancy.* ➣ infant (n), infantile (adj) ❖ νηπιακή ηλικία

1.44 **invaluable** (adj) /ɪnˈvæljuəbl/
very useful ● *The internet has become such an invaluable source of information that we now feel quite deprived if we cannot get online.* ➣ value (v), value (n) ❖ πολύτιμος

Look!

Θυμηθείτε ότι η λέξη **invaluable** σημαίνει πολύτιμος, και **δεν** είναι το αντίθετο της **valuable**.

Mind and Body

Nouns	Adjectives
adolescence	adolescent
contagion	epileptic
frontal lobe	innate
gesture	post-traumatic
infancy	semicomatose
neuroscience	physically
posture	mentally
seizure	cognitive
skull	
trauma	
well-being	

1.45 **intricate** (adj) /ˈɪntrɪkət/
finely-detailed and complex ● *The neutral shade of the curtains went well with the intricate floral pattern of the carpet.* ➣ intricacy (n), intricately (adv) ❖ πολύπλοκος

1.46 **mosaic** (n) /məʊˈzeɪɪk/
a pattern or image made with many small parts put together ● *The path leading to the mansion was a mosaic of broken tiles and pebbles.* ➣ mosaic (adj) ❖ μωσαϊκό

1.47 **keenly** (adv) /ˈkiːnli/
enthusiastically; deeply ● *Visitors to the zoo keenly observed the young panda's behaviour.* ➣ keenness (v), keen (adj) ❖ ένθερμα, έντονα

1.48 **devoted** (adj) /dɪˈvəʊtɪd/
completely loyal and loving ● *Barbara is utterly devoted to her grandchildren and adores spending time with them.* ➣ devote (v), devotion (n), devotee (n), devotedly (adv) ❖ αφοσιωμένος

1.49 **optimal** (adj) /ˈɒptɪməl/
to the maximum or best possible extent ● *The car reaches its optimal fuel efficiency at an average speed of around 50 miles per hour.* ➣ optimum (adj) ❖ άριστος

1.50 **attribute** (n) /ˈætrɪbjuːt/
a quality or characteristic ● *Modesty is one of Malcolm's greatest attributes as he's rather quiet about his own successes.* ➣ attribute (v), attributable (adj) ❖ ιδιότητα

1.51 **ethically** (adv) /ˈeθɪkli/
in a morally acceptable way ● *In some cultures, it is considered ethically correct to eat certain insects.* ➣ ethic (n), ethical (adj) ❖ ηθικά

1.52 **empathetic** (adj) /ˌempəˈθet̩ɪk/
showing understanding for sb's feelings ● *Good teachers have to be both patient and empathetic towards their students' needs.* ➣ empathise (v), empathy (n), empathetically (adv) ❖ συμπονετικός

1.53 **determinant** (n) /dɪˈtɜːmɪnənt/
a deciding factor ● *Qualifications may not be the sole determinant in securing a job, but they can give you an advantage over other candidates.* ➣ determine (v), determined (adj), determining (adj) ❖ καθοριστικός, αποφασιστικός παράγοντας

1.54 **adolescent** (n) /ˌædəˈlesnt/
a teenager; sb going through the stage of life between childhood and adulthood ● *Ms Jones refused to take her class on a three-day excursion as she did not wish to be held responsible for a group of adolescents.* ➣ adolescence (n), adolescent (adj) ❖ έφηβος

1.55 **adolescence** (n) /ˌædəˈlesns/
the stage of life between childhood and adulthood ● *Teenagers go through major physical and emotional changes during adolescence.* ➣ adolescent (n), adolescent (adj) ❖ εφηβεία

1.56 **peer** (n) /pɪə(r)/
sb of the same age or in the same social position as another ● *Sophie gets along well with most of her peers in her class at college.* ❖ συνομίληκος / ισάξιος

1.57 **flourish** (v) /ˈflʌrɪʃ/
develop and do well • *Andrew's self-confidence began to flourish when his parents sent him to music school.* ❖ ευημερώ
✎ Syn: thrive

1.58 **limitations** (n) /ˌlɪmɪˈteɪʃnz/
sth that limits sb/sth from achieving more or being better • *It isn't a bad camera, but it has its limitations in close-up photography.* ➤ limit (v), limit (n), limited (adj) ❖ όριο / περιορισμοί

1.59 **infer** (v) /ɪnˈfɜː(r)/
make an educated guess or develop an opinion about sth based on the information given • *From the author's overall tone, we can infer that she must have had a difficult childhood.* ➤ inference (n) ❖ συνάγω

1.60 **fascination** (n) /ˌfæsɪˈneɪʃn/
a strong interest in sth • *Thelma's fascination with archaeology led her to write a book on Minoan art.* ➤ fascinate (v), fascinated (adj), fascinating (adj) ❖ γοητεία, έντονο ενδιαφέρον

1.61 **baffle** (v) /ˈbæfl/
confuse • *Grace's decision to resign from her comfortable job completely baffled her colleagues.* ➤ baffling (adj) ❖ μπερδεύω, προκαλώ απορία

1.62 **troubled** (adj) /ˈtrʌbld/
worried • *I knew all was not well when I saw Tom's troubled expression.* ➤ trouble (v), trouble (n), troublesome (adj) ❖ ταραγμένος

1.63 **authority** (n) /ɔːˈθɒrəti/
the power to make decisions and tell others how to behave • *My neighbours appear to have no authority over their kids, who are unacceptably noisy.* ➤ authorise (v), authoritative (adj), authoritative (adv) ❖ εξουσία

1.64 **eliminate** (v) /ɪˈlɪmɪneɪt/
rule out; remove • *John is likely to win the singing contest as the judges have eliminated most of the other contestants.* ➤ elimination (n) ❖ εξαλείφω, αποκλείω

1.65 **encompass** (v) /ɪnˈkʌmpəs/
include • *Make sure your essay encompasses all the relevant points.* ❖ συμπεριλαμβάνω

1.66 **multitude** (n) /ˈmʌltɪtjuːd/
large number of people or things together • *There are a multitude of expressions to describe different types of human behaviour.* ➤ multitudinous (adj) ❖ πληθώρα

1.67 **interrelated** (adj) /ˌɪntərɪˈleɪtɪd/
connected together; bearing a relation to each other • *Our states of physical and emotional health are closely interrelated.* ➤ interrelate (v), interrelationship (n) ❖ αλληλοσυνδεόμενος

Vocabulary pages 8-9-10

1.68 **misspent** (adj) /ˌmɪsˈspent/
used in a careless or wasteful way • *Despite her misspent teenage years when she hardly studied at all, Elaine passed her university degree with flying colours.* ➤ misspend (v) ❖ σπαταληθέντα

1.69 **pleasurable** (adj) /ˈpleʒərəbl/
enjoyable • *My holiday at the spa was a most pleasurable experience which left me feeling refreshed and relaxed.* ➤ please (v), pleasure (n), pleasurably (adv) ❖ ευχάριστος

1.70 **dysfunctional** (adj) /dɪsˈfʌŋkʃənl/
not functioning normally • *Dysfunctional relationships between couples are generally due to incompatible interests and desires.* ➤ dysfunction (n) ❖ δυσλειτουργικός

1.71 **neglect** (n) /nɪˈglekt/
lack of care or attention • *In the UK, parents who leave underage children alone at home can be imprisoned for child neglect.* ➤ neglect (v), neglected (adj) ❖ παραμέληση

1.72 **maladjusted** (adj) /ˌmæləˈdʒʌstɪd/
with emotional problems that prevent sb behaving in a socially acceptable way • *Those who bully others often tend to be maladjusted as a result of their upbringing.* ➤ maladjustment (n) ❖ απροσάρμοστος

1.73 **at a loss** (expr) /æt ə lɒs/
not knowing what to say • *Roxanne was at a loss to explain why her husband had left her.* ❖ σε αδυναμία να

1.74 **aberrant** (adj) /æˈberənt/
antisocial • *Mike was expelled from school as a result of his repeated aberrant behaviour in class.* ➤ aberration (n) ❖ παρεκκλίνων, αποκλίνων

1.75 **abnormal** (adj) /æbˈnɔːml/
not normal; unnatural • *Having lost an abnormal amount of weight during her illness, Ellen is on a special diet to regain her strength.* ➤ abnormality (n), abnormally (adv) ❖ αφύσικος, ανώμαλος

1.76 **misanthrope** (n) /ˈmɪsənθrəʊp/
sb who does not like other people and avoids human company • *Although Sue enjoys spending time alone with her books, it doesn't mean that she's a complete misanthrope; she actually has a wide circle of friends.* ➤ misanthropy (n), misanthropic (adj) ❖ μισάνθρωπος

1.77 **adamant** (adj) /ˈædəmənt/
having a fixed opinion about sth • *The parliamentary spokesperson was adamant that the tax increases were justified and no amount of public protest would change the decision.* ➤ adamantly (adv) ❖ αμετάπειστος

1.78 **cynical** (adj) /ˈsɪnɪkl/
not believing that sth is done for good or unselfish reasons; negatively thinking ● *Stop being so cynical! You have just as much chance of getting the job as anyone else.* ➣ cynic (n), cynicism (n), cynically (adv) ❖ κυνικός

1.79 **inflexible** (adj) /ɪnˈfleksəbl/
not willing to change your mind; difficult to change or bend ● *Colin's inflexible attitude towards his teenage daughter made her want to leave home.* ➣ inflexibility (n), inflexibly (adv) ❖ άκαμπτος

1.80 **obstinate** (adj) /ˈɒbstɪnət/
stubborn; sticking to your opinion ● *Jane is so obstinate that she refuses to follow her parents' advice.* ➣ obstinacy (n), obstinately (adv) ❖ πεισματάρης

1.81 **elated** (adj) /iˈleɪtɪd/
joyful and very excited ● *We were elated at the referee's decision to award our team a penalty.* ➣ elation (n) ❖ συνεπαρμένος

1.82 **jubilant** (adj) /ˈdʒuːbɪlənt/
very happy because of a successful result ● *The jubilant fans cheered loudly after the final whistle.* ➣ jubilation (n), jubilantly (adv) ❖ περιχαρής, ενθουσιώδης

1.83 **overjoyed** (adj) /ˌəʊvəˈdʒɔɪd/
extremely pleased ● *Irene's grandmother was overjoyed to see her when she returned from Canada.* ❖ περιχαρής

1.84 **meticulous** (adj) /məˈtɪkjələs/
with great attention to detail; thorough ● *Lynne keeps a meticulous record of the company accounts.* ➣ meticulously (adv) ❖ προσεκτικός, λεπτολόγος

1.85 **apathetic** (adj) /ˌæpəˈθetɪk/
lacking interest or unwilling to take action ● *If voters hadn't been so apathetic, there would have been a better turnout for the election.* ➣ apathy (n), apathetically (adv) ❖ απαθής

1.86 **dispassionate** (adj) /dɪsˈpæʃənəti/
clear-thinking because of lack of emotional involvement ● *To a dispassionate observer, United clearly did not deserve to win, though the fans would never admit it.* ➣ dispassionately (adv) ❖ ψύχραιμος

1.87 **uneasy** (adj) /ʌnˈiːzi/
worried or unconfident ● *They had an uneasy feeling that they were being followed.* ➣ uneasiness (n), uneasily (adv) ❖ άβολος

1.88 **withdrawn** (adj) /wɪðˈdrɔːn/
quiet and introverted; not outgoing ● *Mabel had become even more shy and withdrawn as she found it hard to fit in at her new school.* ➣ withdraw (v) ❖ αποτραβηγμένος

1.89 **compulsive** (adj) /kəmˈpʌlsɪv/
unable to stop doing sth ● *Nobody takes Bill seriously since he's known to be a compulsive liar.* ➣ compulsion (n), compulsively (adv) ❖ παθολογικός

1.90 **neurotic** (adj) /njʊəˈrɒtɪk/
behaving nervously or unreasonably ● *Mr Templar became neurotic about home security after the burglary and had cameras fitted in every room.* ➣ neurosis (n), neurotically (adv) ❖ νευρωτικός

1.91 **obsessive** (adj) /əbˈsesɪv/
focussed on one person or thing to an abnormal extent ● *Greg has become so obsessive about his new project that he never has time for his friends or family.* ➣ obsess (v), obsession (n), obsessively (adv) ❖ έμμονος

1.92 **obnoxious** (adj) /əbˈnɒkʃəs/
horrible; offensive ● *What an obnoxious manner he has! It's small wonder he has no friends.* ➣ obnoxiously (adv) ❖ αποκρουστικός, απεχθής

1.93 **amiable** (adj) /ˈeɪmiəbl/
likeable; good-natured ● *Ian took his clients out to dinner to create a more amiable atmosphere for discussion.* ➣ amiability (n), amiably (adv) ❖ αρεστός, αγαπητός

1.94 **impassive** (adj) /ɪmˈpæsɪv/
showing no sign of emotion ● *From her impassive expression, you can never tell what our teacher is thinking.* ➣ impassively (adv) ❖ απαθής

1.95 **poised** (adj) /pɔɪzd/
with a calm and confident manner; not moving but ready to do so ● *The cat stood poised for action as she waited for the bird to land on the lawn.* ➣ poise (v), poise (n) ❖ σε ετοιμότητα

1.96 **serene** (adj) /səˈriːn/
peaceful and not worried ● *The serene smile on Da Vinci's Mona Lisa has become legendary.* ➣ serenity (n), serenely (adv) ❖ γαλήνιος

1.97 **eloquent** (adj) /ˈeləkwənt/
able to express opinions well in a clear and confident way, especially in public ● *The most eloquent speaker was chosen to represent the team in the debate.* ➣ eloquence (n), eloquently (adv) ❖ εύγλωττος

1.98 **principled** (adj) /ˈprɪnsəpld/
having strong moral beliefs ● *Beth has a principled approach towards helping students who cannot afford to pay fees.* ➣ principle (n) ❖ με αρχές
✎ Opp: unprincipled ❖ χωρίς αρχές

1.99 **scrupulous** (adj) /'skruːpjələs/
honest; giving careful attention to detail
• *The detectives made a scrupulous search of the crime scene.* ➢ scruple (v), scruple (n), scrupulously (adv) ❖ ευσυνείδητος, ακριβολόγος
✎ Opp: unscrupulous ❖ ασυνείδητος

1.100 **upright** (adj) /'ʌpraɪt/
behaving honestly and ethically • *I couldn't believe such an apparently upright citizen could have committed murder.* ➢ upright (n), upright (adv) ❖ έντιμος

1.101 **distrustful** (adj) /dɪs'trʌstfl/
not trusting sb/sth easily • *Granddad is extremely distrustful of all politicians.* ➢ distrust (v), distrust (n) ❖ φιλύποπτος, καχύποπτος

1.102 **arouse** (v) /ə'raʊz/
excite or awaken particular feelings in sb • *The referendum aroused a great deal of disagreement even between friends.* ➢ arousal (n), arousing (adj) ❖ εξεγείρω

1.103 **assert** (v) /ə'sɜːt/
state confidently • *After his arrest, the prisoner asserted his right to call a lawyer.* ➢ assertion (n), assertive (adj), assertively (adv) ❖ διαβεβαιώνω, υποστηρίζω

1.104 **grudge** (n) /grʌdʒ/
a bad feeling or strong dislike for sb because of sth they did in the past • *You beat me fair and square in the tennis match, so I bear no grudge against you.* ➢ grudge (v), grudging (adj), grudgingly (adv) ❖ μνησικακία

1.105 **breed** (v) /briːd/
cause sth to happen • *Tina's promotion bred a feeling of resentment amongst her colleagues, who had also applied for the position.* ➢ breed (n) ❖ προκαλώ

1.106 **conduct yourself** (v) /kən'dʌkt jɔː'self/
behave in a certain way • *The sales assistant conducted herself in a highly unprofessional manner when she lost her temper with the customer.* ➢ conduct (n) ❖ συμπεριφέρομαι

1.107 **exert** (v) /ɪg'zɜːt/
use effort, such as strength or influence to achieve a result • *Parents often exert too much pressure on their children to achieve success from an early age.* ➢ exertion (n) ❖ εξασκώ

1.108 **swallow (sth)** (v) /'swɒləʊ 'sʌmθɪŋ/
hold (sth) back; not reveal or express sth • *Linda tried to swallow her emotions as she broke the bad news to her friend.* ➢ swallow (n) ❖ καταπίνω

1.109 **vent** (v) /vent/
express strongly • *Alex hit the ball hard into the net to vent his frustration at losing the match.* ➢ vent (n) ❖ εκτονώνω

1.110 **familiarity** (n) /fə,mɪli'ærəti/
the feeling of closeness through knowing sth/sb well • *He felt a sense of familiarity as he approached his birthplace for the first time in 20 years.* ➢ familiarise (v), familiar (adj) ❖ οικειότητα

1.111 **contempt** (n) /kən'tempt/
the feeling of looking down on or showing disrespect for sb/sth you believe to be inferior • *The islanders viewed the boatloads of immigrants with contempt and suspicion at first.* ➢ contemptible (adj), contemptuous (adj), contemptibly (adv), contemptuously (adv) ❖ περιφρόνηση

1.112 **appallingly** (adv) /ə'pɔːlɪŋli/
in a shocking way • *The court case was appallingly handled; the verdict was so unfair!* ➢ appal (v), appalled (adj), appalling (adj) ❖ απαίσια, τρομερά

1.113 **peer pressure** (n) /pɪə(r) 'preʃə(r)/
the pressure from people your own age or social status to do the same as they do so as to be accepted • *Tracy dresses exactly as she pleases and refuses to give in to peer pressure to wear certain brands of clothing.* ❖ πίεση από τον κοινωνικό περίγυρο

1.114 **gullible** (adj) /'gʌləbl/
easy to deceive; liable to believe what other say without question • *How could you be so gullible as to buy that old heap of a car?* ➢ gullibility (n) ❖ εύπιστος

1.115 **vulnerable** (adj) /'vʌlnərəbl/
easy to hurt or damage emotionally or physically • *Adolescents are particularly vulnerable to criticism from their peers.* ➢ vulnerability (n) ❖ ευάλωτος

1.116 **distant** (adj) /'dɪstənt/
related by family, but not closely • *I have a distant cousin – possibly a granddaughter of my grandma's cousin – living somewhere in this area, but we've never managed to meet yet.* ➢ distance (v), distance (n), distantly (adv) ❖ απομακρυσμένος

1.117 **reciprocal** (adj) /rɪ'sɪprəkl/
that is done or given by both people involved; mutual • *The ceasefire took place under a reciprocal agreement.* ➢ reciprocate (v), reciprocally (adv) ❖ αμοιβαία

1.118 **companionable** (adj) /kəm'pæniənəbl/
friendly and good to be in the company of • *My uncle is a companionable character, who is always the life and soul of the party.* ➢ companion (n), company (n), companionship (n) ❖ κοινωνικός, συντροφικός

1.119 compatible (adj) /kəmˈpætəbl/
able to get on well together through having similar or matching characteristics or interests and needs ● *Our musical tastes are not compatible as I really can't stand jazz.*
➢ compatibility (n), compatibly (adv)
❖ συμβατός
✎ Opp: incompatible ❖ ασύμβατος

1.120 inseparable (adj) /ɪnˈseprəbl/
that can't be separated; having a very friendly close relationship ● *Nancy and Robert have been absolutely inseparable from the year they met.* ➢ inseparably (adv) ❖ αχώριστος

1.121 philosophical (adj) /ˌfɪləˈsɒfɪkl/
accepting a negative situation with a calm, understanding reaction ● *Mum was quite philosophical about losing her job as she said she might now consider starting her own business.* ➢ philosophy (n), philosopher (n), philosophically (adv) ❖ φιλοσοφικός

1.122 platonic (adj) /pləˈtɒnɪk/
having a friendly, but not sexual relationship ● *Steve's insists that his friendship with Margo is purely platonic and they aren't romantically involved.* ❖ πλατωνικός

1.123 condition (v) /kənˈdɪʃn/
train a person or animal to behave in a particular way or accept sth ● *Army recruits are conditioned to follow orders from their superiors.* ➢ conditioning (n), conditioned (adj) ❖ εκπαίδευση

1.124 unconditional (adj) /ˌʌnkənˈdɪʃənl/
unlimited; without expecting sth in return ● *Fiona is a true friend who is always prepared to offer unconditional help whenever necessary.* ➢ unconditionally (adv) ❖ άνευ όρων

Positive adjectives

amiable	outright
companionable	overjoyed
compatible	philosophical
devoted	platonic
dispassionate	pleasurable
elated	poised
eloquent	principled
empathetic	reciprocal
ground-breaking	scrupulous
inseparable	serene
intricate	solid
invaluable	sought-out
jubilant	tender
meticulous	unconditional
miraculous	upright
non-confrontational	withdrawn
optimal	

1.125 come between (phr v) /kʌm bɪˈtwiːn/
cause to separate; harm a relationship ● *They've been utterly devoted to each other for years and nothing can come between them.* ❖ μπαίνω ανάμεσα

1.126 drift apart (phr v) /drɪft əˈpaːt/
gradually become less friendly with sb ● *We were best friends at school, but we drifted apart over the years when we went off to study at different universities.* ➢ drift (n), drifter (n) ❖ ψυχραίνομαι με

1.127 fit in (phr v) /fɪt/
feel accepted and have a sense of belonging in a group, team, etc. ● *Language and cultural barriers made it hard for Omar to fit in with Greek society.* ❖ ταιριάζω με και ανήκω σε ομάδα με κοινά χαρακτηριστικά

1.128 go back (phr v) /gəʊ bæk/
know each other from a time in the past ● *Angela and I go back 15 years; we used to work together.* ❖ γνωρίζομαι με κάποιον για μεγάλο χρονικό διάστημα

1.129 lead (sb) on (phr v) /liːd ˈsʌmbədi ɒn/
make sb believe an untrue situation ● *The caller had no intention of buying my bike; he was just leading me on to gain personal information about where I live.* ❖ παραπλανώ

1.130 settle down (phr v) /ˈsetl daʊn/
stop moving around and start living in one place to develop a steady lifestyle ● *After years of working on cargo ships, Paul found it difficult to settle down and live in a city apartment.* ➢ settler (n), settled (adj) ❖ καταλαγιάζω, νοικοκυρεύομαι

1.131 stick up for (phr v) /stɪk ʌp fə(r)/
support sb/sth ● *Liz always sticks up for her little brother if he gets into trouble in the school playground.* ❖ υποστηρίζω, προστατεύω

1.132 work up (phr v) /wɜːk ʌp/
cause a feeling or idea to develop ● *Vince held an exhibition of his artwork to work up some interest from potential customers.* ❖ προκαλώ, καλλιεργώ

1.133 do sb's head in (expr) /duː ˈsʌmbədiz hed ɪn/
annoy or confuse sb intensely ● *Please turn off that music! It's doing my head in and I can't concentrate.* ❖ μου τη δίνει

1.134 urge (v) /ɜːdʒ/
encourage or strongly advise sb to do sth ● *Jeff wanted to study art, but his parents were urging him to leave school and get a job to earn a living.* ➢ urge (n), urging (n), urgent (adj) ❖ παροτρύνω, παρακινώ

1.135 egg (sb) on (phr v) /eg ˈsʌmbədi ɒn/
encourage or provoke sb to do sth ● *As the boys egged each other on to dive off the high rocks into the sea, two of them ended up in hospital.* ❖ προκαλώ κάποιον να κάνει κάτι

1.136 **tease** (v) /tiːz/
make fun of sb in a friendly way as a joke, or to embarrass them • *Patrick got used to being teased about his red hair and freckled complexion as a child.* ➢ tease (n), teaser (n) ❖ πειράζω

1.137 **wind (sb) up** (phr v) /waɪnd 'sʌmbədi ʌp/
annoy sb; say sth that is not true to annoy sb • *Don't take George seriously; he's just winding you up.* ➢ wind-up (n), wound-up (adj) ❖ ενοχλώ, πειράζω

1.138 **stress (sb) out** (phr v) /stres 'sʌmbədi aʊt/
cause sb to feel very anxious • *The pressure of studying for exams was stressing him out completely.* ➢ stressed-out (adj) ❖ προκαλώ άγχος / αγχώνομαι

1.139 **put sb down** (phr v) /pʊt 'sʌmbədi daʊn/
make sb feel inferior or stupid • *Not having strong enough policies of their own, the electoral candidates resorted to putting each other down in the debate.* ➢ put-down (n) ❖ μειώνω

1.140 **slap** (n) /slæp/
a hit with an open hand • *Fred gave his friend a friendly slap on the back.* ➢ slap (v) ❖ σφαλιάρα, φάπα

1.141 **a slap in the face** (expr) /slæp ɪn ðə feɪs/
an insulting or disappointing action or event • *It was a real slap in the face for Rita when she got turned down for promotion after all her hard work.* ❖ προσβολή, απόρριψη

1.142 **ego** (n) /'iːɡəʊ/
the sense of self worth • *Getting elected as class president was a boost for Diana's ego since she was actually quite shy.* ➢ egotist (n), egoism (n), egotistic (adj) ❖ εγωισμός

1.143 **at arm's length** (expr) /ət ɑːmz leŋθ/
at a safe distance • *Tracy keeps her neighbours at arm's length as she prefer to keep her personal business private.* ❖ σε απόσταση

1.144 **have a chip on your shoulder** (expr) /hæv ə tʃɪp ɒn jɔː(r) 'ʃəʊldə(r)/
feel easily offended about sth because of a past experience • *As Morag is from Inverness, she has a chip on her shoulder about being called English.* ❖ παρεξηγούμαι, θίγομαι εύκολα

1.145 **confide in** (phr v) /kən'faɪd ɪn/
trust sb with your private thoughts or problems • *Do you confide your secrets to a friend or family member?* ➢ confidence (n), confidential (adj), confidentially (adv) ❖ εμπιστεύομαι

1.146 **get sth off your chest** (expr) /get 'sʌmθɪŋ ɒf jɔː(r) tʃest/
reveal what is worrying you; talk openly about a problem • *What's up with you? I'm all ears if it would help to get it off your chest.* ❖ το βγάζω από μέσα μου

1.147 **keep a cool head** (expr) /kiːp ə kuːl hed/
remain calm • *Don't worry so much about your interview; just keep a cool head and do your best.* ❖ μένω ψύχραιμος

1.148 **behind sb's back** (expr) /bɪ'haɪnd 'sʌmbədiz bæk/
without sb knowing or against their wishes • *Carol fell out with her colleague when she found out he'd been talking about her behind her back.* ❖ πίσω από την πλάτη

1.149 **bite your tongue** (expr) /baɪt jɔː(r) tʌŋ/
hold yourself back from saying sth that might upset sb • *I knew my teacher had made a mistake, but I didn't know whether to tell her or just bite my tongue.* ❖ σιωπώ

1.150 **put your foot in it** (expr) /pʊt jɔː(r) fʊt ɪn ɪt/
say sth inappropriate in a certain situation that upsets sb • *It was supposed to be a surprise party. You've really put your foot in it now!* ❖ λέω κάτι σε ακατάλληλη στιγμή που απογοητεύει κάποιον

1.151 **give sb the elbow** (expr) /gɪv 'sʌmbədi ðə 'elbəʊ/
reject sb; tell sb to leave because they are no longer needed or wanted • *Harry gave his so-called friend the elbow when he realised he'd been using him to advance his own career.* ❖ παρατάω, διώχνω (κάποιον)

Body-related expressions

a slap in the face	give sb the elbow
at arm's length	have a chip on your
at heart	shoulder
behind sb's back	keep a cool head
bite your tongue	put your foot in it
do sb's head in	rear its (ugly) head
get sth off your chest	

1.152 **a pain in the neck** (expr) /ə peɪn ɪn ðə nek/
an annoyance • *My little sister is always trying to listen in on my phone calls; she can be a real pain in the neck at times.* ❖ ενοχλητικός

1.153 **be in tune with** (expr) /bi ɪn tjuː wɪθ/
have the same ideas as sb; accord with sb's way of thinking • *Jack isn't quite in tune with the rest of the staff as he's a bit of a loner and prefers to do his own thing.* ❖ στο ίδιο μήκος κύματος

1.154 **be beside yourself** (expr) /bi bɪ'saɪd jɔː'self/
be overcome by an emotion • *Dad was beside himself with happiness when I told him I'd got my scholarship.* ❖ εκτός εαυτού από χαρά

1.155 **be on good terms** (expr) /bi ɒn gʊd tɜːmz/
have a friendly relationship • *Jerry is an amicable student who is on good terms with most of his teachers.* ❖ τα έχω καλά (με κάποιον)

1.156 **be in sb's bad books** (expr) /bi ɪn ˈsʌmbədiz bæd bʊks/
be out of favour with sb because of having done sth to displease them ● *Nick had another argument with the boss, so he's in her bad books again.* ❖ είμαι στα «μαύρα κατάστιχα» κάποιου

1.157 **at heart** (expr) /ət hɑːt/
essentially, sometimes underneath an outward appearance ● *Debbie can sound abrupt over the phone despite being a warm and friendly person at heart.* ❖ κατά βάθος

1.158 **be on the same wavelength** (expr) /bi ɒn ðə seɪm ˈweɪvleŋθ/
have similar ideas; share the same opinion ● *We're on the same wavelength when it comes to animal welfare as neither of us can stand seeing animals suffer.* ❖ στο ίδιο μήκος κύματος

1.159 **against your will** (expr) /əˈgenst jɔː(r) wɪl/
although you don't want to do so ● *Stuart had to leave the country against his will when his visitor's permit expired.* ❖ ενάντια στη θέληση

1.160 **in a rut** (expr) /ɪn ə rʌt/
in a routine (often boring) situation that is hard to change ● *I wish I could find a more exciting job instead of being stuck in a rut as a bank clerk.* ❖ είμαι «σε λούκι»

1.161 **on cloud nine** (expr) /ɒn klaʊd naɪn/
extremely happy ● *Tracy was on cloud nine when she heard the unexpected good news.* ❖ «στον έβδομο ουρανό»

1.162 **at ease** (expr) /ət iːz/
confident and relaxed ● *She is much too shy to feel at ease in the company of strangers.* ❖ χαλαρά, άνετα

1.163 **on edge** (expr) /ɒn edʒ/
nervous; easily upset ● *Most parents tend to be a bit on edge when they are unsure of their teenage children's whereabouts.* ❖ «σε αναμμένα κάρβουνα»

1.164 **out of character** (expr) /aʊt əv ˈkærəktə(r)/
in a way that is different from sb's usual personality ● *How strange that Mandy lost her temper last night – it was so out of character!* ❖ μη συμβατό με το χαρακτήρα κάποιου, εκτός χαρακτήρα

1.165 **associate** (v) /əˈsəʊʃieɪt/
mentally link sth/sb with (sth/sb else); have a connection with ● *Ian always associates Cornwall with his childhood memories of summer.* ➢ association (n), associate (n), associated (adj) ❖ συνδέω

1.166 **attribute** (v) /əˈtrɪbjuːt/
say that sb/sth is the cause of sth ● *Sam attributed his success in business to a lot of hard work and a little luck.* ➢ attribute (n), attributable (adj) ❖ αποδίδω

1.167 **clan** (n) /klæn/
a large extended family group with a common surname ● *My Scottish ancestors were members of the Gordon clan.* ➢ ❖ πατριά, φυλή

1.168 **mob** (n) /mɒb/
a large crowd of people who may behave violently ● *An angry mob protested outside the town hall.* ➢ mob (v) ❖ όχλος

1.169 **clique** (n) /kliːk/
a small close-knit group which excludes others ● *I'm afraid the school students' committee has become a bit of a clique who are doing whatever they feel like whilst ignoring their classmates' views.* ➢ cliquey (adj) ❖ κλίκα

1.170 **self-content** (n) /self ˈkɒntent/
the sense of being happy with the way you are ● *Despite having lived in a city most of her life, Karen had a feeling of self-content settling down in her small country house.* ➢ self-content (adj) ❖ ικανοποίηση με τον εαυτό μου

1.171 **self-satisfaction** (n) /self ˌsætɪsˈfækʃn/
the sense of being pleased or satisfied with sth you have done ● *Having received so much praise for her project, Kate felt a sense of self-satisfaction.* ➢ self-satisfied (adj) ❖ ικανοποίηση με τις πράξεις μου

1.172 **self-esteem** (n) /self ɪˈstiːm/
the sense of feeling valued or important ● *Constant criticism from teachers and parents can lower a child's self-esteem.* ❖ αυτοεκτίμηση

1.173 **self-sufficiency** (n) /self səˈfɪʃnsi/
the state of having enough resources without needing anything from others ● *Moving to another country requires a great deal of self-sufficiency as it could be difficult to build support networks.* ➢ self-sufficient (adj) ❖ αυτάρκεια

1.174 **back sb up** (phr v) /bæk ˈsʌmbədi ʌp/
say that what sb says is true ● *Your alibi sounds unlikely. Is there any witness who can back you up?* ➢ back-up (n) ❖ υποστηρίζω

1.175 **look sb up** (phr v) /lʊk ˈsʌmbədi ʌp/
contact or visit sb when you are in their area ● *Next time you're in London, look me up and we can get together.* ❖ έλα σε επαφή μαζί μου / πάρε με τηλέφωνο

1.176 **crack sb up** (phr v) /kræk ˈsʌmbədi ʌp/
say sth that amuses sb very much ● *Billy's live performance was so funny it cracked us all up. We couldn't stop laughing!* ❖ κάνω κάποιον να ξεκαρδιστεί

1.177 **outburst** (n) /ˈaʊtbɜːst/
an unexpected expression of strong emotion ● *The centre forward was sent off due to his outburst of violence during the match.* ❖ ξέσπασμα

1.178 **prone (to)** (adj) /prəʊn (tə)/
likely to do sth or suffer sth • *Our old teacher was prone to falling asleep in the middle of a exam.* ❖ επιρρεπής

1.179 **bitterly** (adv) /ˈbɪtəli/
in an extremely bad way; acutely • *I was bitterly disappointed at his dreadful attitude.* ➤ bitterness (n), bitter (adj) ❖ βαθειά

1.180 **steer clear of sb/sth** (expr) /stɪə(r) klɪə(r) əvˈsʌmbədi/ˈsʌmθɪŋ/
stay out of the way of sb/sth that might be problematic • *You'd better steer clear of Tommy; he's in a foul mood today.* ❖ αποφεύγω

1.181 **outsider** (n) /ˌaʊtˈsaɪdə(r)/
sb who is not an accepted member of a community group • *Although Penny spends a month on the island every year, she is still regarded as an outsider as she is not a permanent resident.* ➤ outside (adj), outside (adv) ❖ ξένος

1.182 **intruder** (n) /ɪnˈtruːdə(r)/
sb who enters a place illegally or when they are not wanted • *With three fierce guard dogs in pursuit, the intruders climbed swiftly back over the wall.* ➤ intrude (v), intrusion (n), intrusive (adj), intrusively (adv) ❖ παρείσακτος, εισβολέας

1.183 **novice** (n) /ˈnɒvɪs/
sb who is new to doing sth and has little experience • *Lia is a complete novice at playing the violin; she sounds terrible!* ❖ αρχάριος, πρωτάρης

Phrasal verbs

back sb up	engage in sth	settle down
come	fit in	stick up for
between	go back	stress (sb)
confide in	hold down	out
crack sb up	lead (sb) on	wind (sb) up
drift apart	look sb up	work up
egg (sb) on	put sb down	

Grammar   pages 11-12-13

1.184 **gathering** (n) /ˈɡæðərɪŋ/
a meeting of people • *Greek name days are always a great excuse for a family gathering.* ➤ gather (v), gatherer (n) ❖ συγκέντρωση

1.185 **annoyance** (n) /əˈnɔɪəns/
sth that is annoying; the feeling of being annoyed • *Olga could not hide her annoyance at the interruption.* ➤ annoy (v), annoying (adj), annoyingly (adv) ❖ ενόχληση

Feelings

annoyance	self-content
contempt	self-esteem
disinhibition	self-satisfaction
distress	self-sufficiency
fascination	sorrow
self-awareness	

Relationships & Groups

acquaintance	misanthrope
clan	mob
clique	outsider
gathering	peer
intruder	

Listening   page 14

1.186 **leave sb cold** (expr) /liːv ˈsʌmbədi kəʊld/
fail to arouse any interest or excitement for sb • *The idea of a night at the opera leaves Daniel cold.* ❖ με αφήνει παγερά αδιάφορο

1.187 **overwhelm** (v) /ˌəʊvəˈwelm/
have an overpowering effect on • *Sarah was overwhelmed by the beauty of the island.* ➤ overwhelming (adj), overwhelmingly (adv) ❖ κατακλύζομαι, κατακλύζω

1.188 **mistaken** (adj) /mɪˈsteɪkən/
incorrect in a belief; based on an incorrect belief or assumption • *I was under the mistaken impression that he came from a poor family.* ➤ mistake (v), mistake (n), mistakenly (adv) ❖ λανθασμένος

1.189 **extrovert** (n) /ˈekstrəvɜːt/
an outgoing confident person • *Although Gary appears so confident when performing in the band, he's not such an extrovert and is rather shy offstage.* ➤ extroverted (adj) ❖ εξωστρεφής

1.190 **introvert** (n) /ˈɪntrəvɜːt/
a quiet person who doesn't make friends easily • *Nigel prefers to express his thoughts in writing as he's too much of an introvert to speak up in public.* ➤ introverted (adj) ❖ εσωστρεφής

1.191 **contagion** (n) /kənˈteɪdʒən/
the quick spread of sth, such as disease or a negative idea • *The sudden influx of immigrants has led to the contagion of racism throughout Europe.* ➤ contagious (adj), contagiously (adv) ❖ μετάδοση, μόλυνση

1.192 convergence (n) /kənˈvɜːdʒəns/
the action of two or more things meeting and joining together, then becoming similar • *The new Acropolis Museum is a prime example of the convergence of ancient and modern architecture.* ➣ converge (v), convergent (adj) ❖ σύγκλιση

1.193 trait (n) /treɪt/
a characteristic • *Unfortunately, Simon had always been a fraud and honesty was not a trait of his character.* ❖ γνώρισμα, χαρακτηριστικό

1.194 conform (v) /kənˈfɔːm/
behave according to the accepted rules of a society; be in agreement with or follow the same pattern as sth/sb • *Neil moved out of the university hall of residence in first year as he couldn't conform with the idea of communal living.* ➣ conformity (n) ❖ συμμορφώνομαι

Behaviour

Verbs	Nouns
assert	ego
associate	extrovert
baffle	familiarity
breed	humanity
captivate	interaction
conform	introvert
grudge	neglect
infer	outburst
overwhelm	peer pressure
repulse	temperament
ridicule	trait
tease	
urge	

Speaking   page 15

1.195 innate (adj) /ɪˈneɪt/
that you were born with • *Do you believe that musical talent is innate or is it learned?* ➣ innately (adv) ❖ έμφυτος

Writing   pages 16-17

1.196 discursive (adj) /dɪsˈkɜːsɪv/
used to describe writing or spoken discussion involving different opinions on sth • *We were asked to write a discursive essay on the pros and cons of technological advances.* ❖ λόγος ή γραφή που συνθέτουν διαφορετικές απόψεις

1.197 susceptible (adj) /səˈseptəbl/
likely to be affected by sth/sb or suffer from sth • *As a teenager, Mike was highly susceptible to criticism from his peers and took it all very personally.* ➣ susceptibility (n) ❖ ευαίσθητος

1.198 beneficially (adv) /ˌbenɪˈfɪʃəli/
in a way that is helpful or useful • *I'm sure a few days' break will affect you beneficially and you'll come back to work feeling refreshed.* ➣ benefit (v), benefit (n), beneficial (adj) ❖ ευεργετικά

1.199 adversely (adv) /ˈædvɜːsli/
in a way that has an opposite or undesired effect • *The recession has adversely affected our plans to develop our business and we've lost most of our customers lately.* ➣ adversity (n), adverse (adj) ❖ δυσμενώς

1.200 undue (adj) /ˌʌnˈdjuː/
unnecessary or more than acceptable • *Working from home put undue stress on Annie's family relationships.* ❖ υπερβολικός, άδικος
✎ Opp: due ❖ αναμενόμενος, αρμοστός

1.201 excessive (adj) /ɪkˈsesɪv/
much more than necessary • *Working in front of a computer for an excessive period of time can lead to eye strain and backache.* ➣ exceed (v), excess (n), excessively (adv) ❖ υπέρμετρος, υπερβολικός

1.202 engage in sth (phr v) /ɪnˈgeɪdʒ ɪn ˈsʌmθɪŋ/
participate in sth • *Some children may engage in bullying at school as a result of problems within their family environment.* ➣ engagement (n), engaged (adj), engaging (adj), engagingly (adv) ❖ μπλέκομαι με

1.203 ridicule (v) /ˈrɪdɪkjuːl/
make fun of • *Hamish's peers ridiculed him because of his Scottish accent when he moved to York.* ➣ ridicule (n), ridiculous (adj), ridiculously (adv) ❖ γελοιοποιώ

1.204 draw the line (expr) /drɔː ðə laɪn/
set a limit; be unwilling to do sth • *Kate's parents are generally very tolerant, but they draw the line at letting her stay out all night unless they are sure of her whereabouts.* ❖ τραβάω τη γραμμή, οριοθετώ

1.205 core (adj) /kɔː(r)/
central and basic • *All staff are expected to support the core values of the company: integrity and quality service.* ➣ core (n) ❖ κεντρικός

1.206 let yourself in for sth (expr) /let jɔːˈself ɪn fə(r)ˈsʌmθɪŋ/
get involved in sth that may be a difficult experience • *Before you sign the contract with the company, make sure you know what you're letting yourself in for.* ❖ εμπλέκομαι με κάτι που μπορεί να αποδειχθεί δύσκολο ή δυσάρεστο

1.207 distress (n) /dɪˈstres/
anxiety or suffering • *Mark is always willing to help a friend in distress.* ➣ distress (v), distressed (adj), distressing (adj) ❖ απελπισία, θλίψη

1.208 **non-confrontational** (adj)
/ˈnɒnˌkɒnfrʌnˈteɪʃənl/
in a way that avoids causing an argument
• *At times, even the most understanding
parents find it hard to bite their tongues and
remain calm and non-confrontational with
their teenage children.* ❖ που δεν έρχεται σε
σύγκρουση, αντίθεση

1.209 **boundary** (n) /ˈbaʊndri/
a point that marks the limit of sth • *Teachers
have to set boundaries for student behaviour
within the classroom environment.* ❖ όριο

1.210 **rear its (ugly) head** (expr) /rɪə(r) ɪts ˈʌgli
hed/
appear or occur • *When the possibility of
losing his job reared its ugly head, George
thought of becoming self-employed.*
❖ κάνει την εμφάνισή του (κάτι αρνητικό)

1.211 **stand your ground** (expr) /stænd jɔː(r)
graʊnd/
refuse to back down or give up; stick to your
opinion • *Julie stood her ground and refused
to work any unpaid overtime.* ❖ δεν κάνω
πίσω, δεν υποχωρώ
✎ Also: hold your ground

Negative adjectives

aberrant	maladjusted
abnormal	misspent
apathetic	mistaken
compulsive	neurotic
cynical	obnoxious
distrustful	obsessive
dysfunctional	obstinate
excessive	troubled
gullible	undue
impassive	uneasy
inappropriate	vulnerable
inflexible	

Other useful expressions

against all odds	be in sb's bad books
against your will	be in tune with
at a loss	be on good terms
at ease	be on the same
in a rut	wavelength
on cloud nine	steer clear of sb/sth
on edge	draw the line
out of character	let yourself in for sth
be beside yourself	stand your ground

Video I: From the Same Family
page 18

1.212 **gesture** (n) /ˈdʒestʃə(r)/
a non-verbal movement to show a certain
feeling or meaning • *When travelling abroad,
it's wise to avoid making certain gestures
in case they're considered rude in another
culture.* ➢ gesture (v) ❖ χειρονομία

1.213 **captivate** (v) /ˈkæptɪveɪt/
attract and hold sb's close attention • *The
audience were captivated by his stunning
performance.* ➢ captive (n), captivating (adj)
❖ σαγηνεύω

1.214 **repel** (v) /rɪˈpel/
cause sth/sb to move away or avoid you
• *The combined Athenian and Platean forces
repelled the Persian invaders at the Battle
of Marathon.* ➢ repellent (n), repulsive (adj),
repulsively (adv) ❖ αποκρούω

1.215 **outright** (adj) /ˈaʊtraɪt/
absolute • *Her new book was an outright
success and has been nominated for several
awards.* ➢ outright (adv) ❖ απόλυτος,
ξεκάθαρος

1.216 **tender** (adj) /ˈtendə(r)/
gentle and caring • *The tender words in his
letter moved me to tears.* ➢ tenderness (n),
tenderly (adv) ❖ τρυφερός

1.217 **redefine** (v) /ˌriːdɪˈfaɪn/
give sth a new meaning; move the limits of sth
• *Technology has redefined the art of written
communication.* ➢ redefinition (n) ❖ αλλάζω
τον ορισμό, επαναπροσδιορίζω

1.218 **complex** (adj) /ˈkɒmpleks/
not simple • *It's amazing to think that ancient
Greeks had the knowledge to devise complex
mathematical formulae.* ➢ complexity (n)
❖ σύνθετος

1.219 **grasp** (n) /ækt'ɪvəti/
ability to reach or achieve • *Having eaten
all the leaves that were within its grasp, the
panda lay down for a snooze.* ➢ grasp (v)
❖ που μπορώ να πιάσω

1.220 **sorrow** (n) /ˈsɒrəʊ/
a strong feeling of sadness • *A look of sorrow
swept across his face when he heard the bad
news.* ➢ sorrowful (adj), sorrowfully (adv)
❖ λύπη

1.221 **glimpse** (v) /glɪmps/
briefly notice sth/sb • *We just glimpsed the
tail of lizard before it disappeared into the
undergrowth.* ❖ βλέπω φευγαλέα

1.222 **repulse** (v) /rɪˈpʌls/
stop sb/sth coming close to you; reject sb's
help or attention • *Any attempt the keeper
made to get close to the lion was repulsed with
an angry roar.* ➢ repulsive (adj), repulsively
(adv) ❖ αποκρούω

1.223 **posture** (n) /ˈpɒstʃə(r)/
the manner you position your body when you
stand or sit • *Wearing uncomfortable shoes
will do nothing for your posture and may cause
severe back problems.* ❖ στάση του σώματος

1.224 **humanity** (n) /hjuːˈmænəti/
the quality of showing kindness and
compassion towards others; the state of being
human • *If the new supervisor hopes to win
the respect of the staff, she'd better loosen up
and start showing some humanity.*
➢ humanitarian (adj), humanitarianism (n)
❖ ανθρωπιά

1.225 **resemblance** (n) /rɪˈzembləns/
the fact of having a similar appearance to sth
• *The sequel bears no resemblance to his
original novel in the series.* ➢ resemble (v)
❖ ομοιότητα

> **Verbs of movement**
>
> | | |
> |---|---|
> | bare | propel |
> | blast | swallow |
> | compact | track |
> | exert | grasp |
> | exit | repel |

Vocabulary Exercises

A Complete the sentences with the correct form of the words.

1 Sue was _____ to learn that she had passed her exams. **JOY**

2 He comes from a(n) _____ family, so it was no surprise to anyone when he turned to crime. **FUNCTION**

3 John is not only my teacher, he is my mentor; participating in his classes has offered me _____ knowledge and experience. **VALUE**

4 A good reporter should be able to offer a(n) _____ account of the news. **PASSION**

5 The children of immigrant families are often _____ students as they have problems coping with the new language and the unfamiliar environment. **ADJUST**

6 Her _____ behaviour in the office is likely to cost her her job. **ERRANT**

7 You can try talking to him, but I don't think it will do any good; he is a very stubborn and _____ man and he will never admit he was wrong. **FLEXIBILITY**

8 He comes from a good family, but has ended up alone and homeless as a result of his _____ youth. **SPEND**

9 The defendant managed to keep his face _____ as he listened to the witnesses making false allegations against him. **PASSIVE**

10 The new mayoral candidate is a(n) _____ man; I'm sure he will benefit the town greatly if he is elected. **RIGHT**

B Complete the sentences with these words.

arm's   back   character   chest   elbow   face   foot   head   heart   tongue   neck   shoulder

1 I really put my _____ in it when I asked the boss's wife if she was his mother!

2 It was a slap in the _____ to find out that my best friend had betrayed me.

3 If Kathy ever finds out you've been lying to her, she's likely to give you the _____.

4 It was completely out of _____ for Tom to blame his colleague for his own mistake.

5 I know you'll do fine in the interview, as long as you keep a cool _____.

6 Mark can be a real pain in the _____; I honestly don't know why you hang out with him.

7 Jenny tries to appear tough, but she's really sensitive at _____.

8 I can't believe Tom would go behind my _____ the way he did, to get the job I was after.

9 No matter how hard I've tried to get close to Simon, he seems determined to keep me at _____ length, and I really don't understand why.

17

10 Don't ask Stella about her studies because she's got a real chip on her _____ about not having got a university degree.

11 Anna got so upset when I mentioned she had put on weight; why didn't I just bite my _____?

12 I'm always here for you if you need to get something off your _____. You know you can talk to me about anything.

C Circle the correct words.

1 Dean and I have a mutual / reciprocal respect for each other.

2 Penny is a caring mother, who is really devoted / dependent to her children.

3 Nick is so vulnerable / gullible he'll believe anything you tell him.

4 Dan reflects / resembles his father in so many ways; it's almost as if they are the same person!

5 How could you say such a thing about Lena? It was an open / outright lie and you know it!

6 Mark and Stacey are distant / remote relatives.

7 If you want your relationship to work, you need to find someone you are companionable / compatible with.

8 If you take in a stray animal, your biggest reward is the conditioned / unconditional love it gives you in return.

9 The two sisters have always been very close; in fact, they are virtually inseparable / unified.

10 Tina is very expressive and makes a lot of postures / gestures when she speaks.

11 The lecturer was such a charismatic speaker that everyone in the audience sat transformed / transfixed throughout the entire lecture.

12 It was so heartwarming to see the cat's tender / total affection as she nursed her new-born kittens.

D Choose the best answer.

1 Maria and I used to be close friends, but we just ___ apart when we moved to different towns to study.
    a drifted   b fell   c came

2 I'm afraid I have been in the teacher's bad ___ since I played that trick on her.
    a books   b side   c opinion

3 Thank you for giving me a second chance; I won't let you ___ again.
    a up   b over   c down

4 A true friend is someone who will stand ___ you no matter what.
    a over to   b up to   c up for

5 Jessie and I seem to be on the ___ wavelength when it comes to our work.
    a same   b proper   c current

6 Arthur has been trying to ___ up the courage to ask Sylvia to marry him.
    a get   b work   c follow

7 Tina's parents are always egging her ___ to finish her studies, but she just isn't interested.
    a over   b in   c on

8 Martin really enjoys ___ Gina up about the way she dresses.
    a teasing   b winding   c pulling

9 Kevin was on ___ nine when he heard he had won the scholarship.
    a sky   b cloud   c star

10 Don't let anyone force you to do something ___ your will.
    a against   b opposite   c contrary to

1 Grammar

1.1 Present Simple

Χρησιμοποιούμε τον Present Simple για:
γεγονότα ή γενικές αλήθειες.
→ The brain **controls** the central nervous system.
ρουτίνες ή συνήθειες (συχνά με επιρρήματα συχνότητας).
→ Lynne seldom **goes** to social gatherings.
μόνιμες καταστάσεις.
→ He **is** a school counsellor.
προγράμματα, ώρες έναρξης/λήξης/άφιξης/αναχώρησης στο μέλλον.
→ The flight **departs** at 6 am tomorrow.
αφηγήσεις (μια ιστορία, ένα ανέκδοτο, μια πλοκή, μια αθλητική αναμετάδοση κλπ.).
→ Murray **leaps** forward and **smashes** the ball across the net.
τίτλους ειδήσεων
→ Man **bites** fellow passenger during flight!
Μετά από the last time για να δείξουμε ενόχληση ή ότι μετανιώσαμε για κάτι που συνέβη στο παρελθόν
→ What a bore he turned out to be! That's the last time I **try** online dating!

Σημείωση: Κάποιες συνηθισμένες χρονικές εκφράσεις που χρησιμοποιούνται συχνά με τον Present Simple είναι
every day/week/month/spring, every other day, once a week, twice a month, in the morning/afternoon/evening, at
night, at the weekend, in July, on Fridays, on Tuesday mornings κλπ.
→ I chat with my classmates **every day**.

Θυμήσου: Χρησιμοποιούμε συχνά adverbs of frequency (επιρρήματα συχνότητας) με τον Present Simple. Μας
εξηγούν πόσο συχνά γίνεται κάτι. Μπαίνουν πριν από το κύριο ρήμα, αλλά μετά από το ρήμα be.
→ She **often** helps out at the youth club.
→ Scientists are **never** in complete agreement with each other.
→ I **rarely** take part in festivals.

Συνηθισμένα adverbs of frequency είναι always, usually, often, sometimes, rarely, hardly ever, seldom και never.

1.2 Present Continuous

Χρησιμοποιούμε τον Present Continuous για:
πράξεις που συμβαίνουν την ώρα που μιλάμε.
→ They **are having** a meeting right now.
πράξεις που εξελίσσονται γύρω από την ώρα που μιλάμε, αλλά όχι αυτή τη στιγμή.
→ I'm **researching** the reasons behind juvenile crime.
καταστάσεις που είναι προσωρινές.
→ He **is filming** the match live from the sidelines now.
ενοχλητικές συνήθειες (συχνά με τα always, continually, constantly και forever).
→ Our neighbours **are always using** noisy tools in their garden.
να περιγράψουμε μια εικόνα.
→ Clearly, the crowd **are waiting** for the band to appear.
σχέδια και ό,τι έχουμε κανονίσει για το μέλλον.
→ We **are holding** a press conference on Friday.
καταστάσεις που μεταβάλλονται ή εξελίσσονται στο παρόν.
→ Social change **is occurring** as a result of cultural diversity.
πράξεις που ενοχλούν στο παρόν (συνήθως με τα always, continually, constantly, forever κλπ.).
→ Why **are you always looking** at your phone?

Σημείωση: Κάποιες συνηθισμένες χρονικές φράσεις που χρησιμοποιούνται συχνά με τον Present Continuous είναι:
at the moment, now, for the time being, this morning/afternoon/evening/week/month/year, today κλπ.
→ **At the moment**, he's studying neurology.

1 Grammar

Θυμήσου

Τα stative verbs συνήθως δε χρησιμοποιούνται στους χρόνους διαρκείας (continuous) διότι περιγράφουν καταστάσεις (states) και όχι πράξεις. Για να μιλήσουμε για το παρόν, χρησιμοποιούμε τα ρήματα αυτά στον Present Simple.

→ *Eric **doesn't seem** terribly amused.*
→ *I **detest** TV soap operas.*

1.3 Present Perfect Simple

Χρησιμοποιούμε τον Present Perfect Simple:

για κάτι που ξεκίνησε στο παρελθόν και συνεχίζεται ως τώρα.
→ *I**'ve known** Amanda and Bob for six years.*

για κάτι που έγινε στο παρελθόν αλλά δε γνωρίζουμε ή δεν αναφέρουμε ακριβώς πότε.
→ *She**'s bought** a new car.*

για κάτι που έγινε στο παρελθόν και το αποτέλεσμα επηρεάζει το παρόν.
→ *Martin **has won** a talent contest. That's why he looks so pleased with himself.*

για πράξεις που έχουν μόλις τελειώσει.
→ *I**'ve just sent** the invitations by email.*

για εμπειρίες και επιτεύγματα.
→ *Janine **has had** several years of training as a specialist.*

για κάτι που έγινε αρκετές φορές, ή επανειλημμένα στο παρελθόν.
→ *She **has competed** in quite a few tournaments, but has never reached the finals.*

με τον υπερθετικό των επιθέτων (superlatives), και με τις φράσεις *the first time/the second time* κλπ.
→ *It's the first time I**'ve ever heard** such an interesting speaker.*

Σημείωση: Κάποιες συνηθισμένες χρονικές εκφράσεις που χρησιμοποιούνται με τον Present Perfect Simple είναι *already, ever, for, for a long time, for ages, just, never, once, recently, since 2009/October, so far, twice, seven times, until now, yet* κλπ.
→ *We haven't seen the Wilsons **for ages**.*

Θυμήσου: Χρησιμοποιούμε *have been* όταν κάποιος έχει πάει κάπου και έχει επιστρέψει. Χρησιμοποιούμε *have gone* όταν κάποιος έχει πάει κάπου και βρίσκεται ακόμα εκεί.
→ *Ted **has been** to the post office, but he's on the way back now.*
→ *Ted **has gone** to the post office and he'll be back later.*

1.4 Present Perfect Continuous

Χρησιμοποιούμε τον Present Perfect Continuous για:

πράξεις που ξεκίνησαν στο παρελθόν και είναι ακόμα σε εξέλιξη ή που έχουν συμβεί επανειλημμένα ως τώρα.
→ *We **have been receiving** a lot of enquiries about the new course.*

πράξεις που έγιναν πολλές φορές στο παρελθόν και έχουν ολοκληρωθεί πρόσφατα, αλλά έχουν αποτελέσματα που επηρεάζουν το παρόν.
→ *I'm exhausted because I**'ve been working** non-stop all day.*

να τονίσουμε τη διάρκεια μιας πράξης.
→ *Harry **has been considering** a career move for quite some time.*

μια πράξη που είναι πρόσφατη ή που δεν έχει ολοκληρωθεί.
→ *I**'ve been looking** up some old friends on Facebook.*

Σημείωση: Κάποιες συνηθισμένες χρονικές εκφράσεις που χρησιμοποιούνται συχνά με τον Present Perfect Continuous είναι *all day/night/week, for years, for a long time, for ages, lately, recently, since*. Μπορούμε να χρησιμοποιήσουμε *How long ...?* με τον Present Perfect Continuous σε ερωτήσεις, και *for (very) long* σε ερωτήσεις και αρνητικές προτάσεις.
→ *Tracy's been following that series **for years**.*
→ ***How long** have you been staying in the student hostel?*

1.5 Past Simple

Χρησιμοποιούμε τον Past Simple για:
κάτι που ξεκίνησε και τελείωσε στο παρελθόν.
→ He **won** a Nobel Prize for Chemistry in 1999.
ρουτίνες και συνήθειες που είχαμε στο παρελθόν (συχνά με adverbs of frequency).
→ In his youth, my father often **went** fishing.
καταστάσεις του παρελθόντος.
→ Life **wasn't** always so complicated.
πράξεις που έγιναν η μία μετά την άλλη στο παρελθόν, για παράδειγμα όταν λέμε μία ιστορία.
→ Betty **walked** to the corner and **caught** a taxi into town.

Σημείωση: Κάποιες συνηθισμένες χρονικές εκφράσεις που χρησιμοποιούνται συχνά με τον Past Simple είναι
yesterday, last night/week/month/summer, a week/month/year ago, twice a day, three times a month, at the weekend,
in March, in the morning/afternoon/evening, at night, on Saturdays, on Sunday evenings κλπ.
→ They broke up **five months ago**.

1.6 Past Continuous

Χρησιμοποιούμε τον Past Continuous για:
πράξεις που ήταν σε εξέλιξη σε συγκεκριμένη χρονική στιγμή στο παρελθόν.
→ Anna **was watching** a documentary on TV last night.
δύο ή περισσότερες πράξεις που ήταν σε εξέλιξη την ίδια χρονική στιγμή στο παρελθόν.
→ We **were listening** to the radio while we **were having** dinner.
να δώσουμε το σκηνικό μιας ιστορίας.
→ They **were preparing** to go on stage and the audience **were getting** agitated.
μια πράξη που ενώ ήταν σε εξέλιξη στο παρελθόν, διακόπηκε από μια άλλη.
→ He **was trying** to reboot his phone when the internet connection stopped.
προσωρινές καταστάσεις στο παρελθόν.
→ I **was doing** a weekend job to earn some pocket money back then.

Σημείωση: Κάποιες συνηθισμένες χρονικές εκφράσεις που χρησιμοποιούνται συχνά με τον Past Continuous είναι
while, as, all day/week/month/year, at eight o'clock last night, last Tuesday/week/month/year, this afternoon κλπ.
→ We were studying on the same course **all year**.

1.7 Past Perfect Simple

Χρησιμοποιούμε τον Past Perfect Simple για μια πράξη ή κατάσταση που τελείωσε πριν από κάποια άλλη πράξη ή
κατάσταση στο παρελθόν.
→ He **had taken** his test three times before he succeeded.
→ By the time the rain stopped, the vegetable patch **had disappeared** in a pool of mud.

Σημείωση: Κάποιες συνηθισμένες χρονικές εκφράσεις που χρησιμοποιούνται συχνά με τον Past Perfect Simple είναι
before, after, when, already, for, for a long time, for ages, just, never, once, since 2011/September, so far, yet κλπ.
→ She had **never** been good at horticulture.

1.8 Past Perfect Continuous

Χρησιμοποιούμε τον Past Perfect Continuous για:
πράξεις που ξεκίνησαν στο παρελθόν και ήταν ακόμα σε εξέλιξη όταν ξεκίνησε μια άλλη πράξη ή όταν έγινε κάτι.
→ Kate **had been living** in Germany for years before she finally learnt the language.
πράξεις που ήταν σε εξέλιξη στο παρελθόν και επηρέασαν μια μεταγενέστερη πράξη.
→ Adam was tired as he **had been lying** awake all night worrying about the meeting.

1 Grammar

Σημείωση: Κάποιες συνηθισμένες χρονικές εκφράσεις που χρησιμοποιούνται συχνά με τον Past Perfect Continuous είναι *all day/night/week, for years, for a long time, for ages, since.* Μπορούμε επίσης να χρησιμοποιήσουμε *How long ...?* σε ερωτήσεις με τον Past Perfect Continuous και *for (very) long* σε ερωτήσεις και αρνητικές προτάσεις.
→ *He hadn't been working **for very long** when we realised he was the boss's son.*

1.9 *Used to, Would & Will*

Χρησιμοποιούμε *used to* + bare infinitive (απαρέμφατο χωρίς *to*) για:
πράξεις που κάναμε συχνά στο παρελθόν, αλλά δεν κάνουμε τώρα πια.
→ *He **used to write** long letters home when he was a student.*
καταστάσεις που υπήρχαν στο παρελθόν αλλά δεν υπάρχουν τώρα.
→ *She **used to be** a neurologist, but now she's retired.*

Σημείωση: Χρησιμοποιούμε *would* + bare infinitive (απαρέμφατο χωρίς *to*) για πράξεις που κάναμε συχνά στο παρελθόν, αλλά δεν κάνουμε τώρα πια. Δεν το χρησιμοποιούμε για καταστάσεις.
→ *In the past, tourists **would usually send** postcards to their friends while they were on holiday.*
→ *As children, we **would make** our own costumes for fancy dress parties.*

1.10 Auxiliaries

Συχνά μπορούμε να χρησιμοποιούμε μόνο το auxiliary (βοηθητικό ρήμα) αντί να επαναλαμβάνουμε το κύριο ρήμα όταν αυτό εννοείται από τα συμφραζόμενα.
→ *Tessa enjoys swimming, and so **does** her brother.*
→ *He never appeared to let things get him down, but I'm sure he **did** when he was alone.*
→ *I rarely shop online, but when I **do**, I only use a trusted site.*
Σε αυτές τις περιπτώσεις, το auxiliary μπορεί επίσης να είναι σε διαφορετικό χρόνο από το κύριο ρήμα.
→ *We finally tried eating snails and after we **had**, we swore never to do it again.*
Μπορούμε επίσης να προσθέσουμε το auxiliary πριν το κύριο ρήμα για να δώσουμε έμφαση.
→ *He **did** try very hard to make new friends when he changed schools.*

Grammar Exercises

A Choose the correct answers.

1 The behaviour of patients who have sustained brain injuries sometimes ___ dramatically.
  a has changed   **b** changes   **c** is changing   **d** has been changing

2 Josh ___ a really obnoxious streak of character since he was passed over for promotion.
  a has exhibited   **b** is exhibiting   **c** exhibits   **d** has been exhibiting

3 When I ___ to borrow the car, my father was adamant in his refusal.
  a was asking   **b** had been asked   **c** asked   **d** have asked

4 In the last few years, Martha ___ a habit to encourage gullible men to give her presents.
  a is making it   **b** makes it   **c** has been making it   **d** has made it

5 Although most people ___ the need for change, few were willing to take the necessary steps towards that direction.
  a recognise   **b** recognised   **c** were recognising   **d** are recognising

6 Sue is my best friend and I ___ her since we were ten years old.
  a know   **b** have been knowing   **c** knew   **d** have known

7 Doing some strenuous exercise after a busy work day ___ pent-up energy.
  a releases   **b** is releasing   **c** has released   **d** has been releasing

8 Monica really ___ her foot in her mouth when she told her boss the latest gossip.
  a puts   **b** is putting   **c** has put   **d** put

B Complete the sentences with the verbs in brackets. Use the correct form of the Past Simple, Past Continuous, Past Perfect Simple or Past Perfect Continuous.

1 Scientists _____ (attribute) the sudden change in the subjects' behaviour to external factors.
2 The spy _____ (swallow) the pill before anyone could do anything to stop her.
3 The two partners _____ (drift) apart for years when they eventually decided to split up.
4 Jennifer _____ (infer) the hidden meaning of the announcement without difficulty.
5 As a child, Bob had a chip on his shoulder and _____ (always/pick) fights with his peers.
6 Jasmine _____ (work) very hard all year to secure the scholarship, so it came as no surprise when she got it.
7 The bullies _____ (tease) Henry all the time during the lesson, and he eventually snapped.
8 Paul _____ (dare) Nick to jump into the river, but he chickened out.

C Circle the correct words.

1 As a child, Donna would / used to adore playing with her dolls and dressing them up.
2 He would swear / swore unconditional love to her, only to dump her a few months later.
3 When I first took on this project, I used to / would be overwhelmed by the sheer volume of the work.
4 My grandad told such funny jokes he would crack / was cracking me up every time!
5 The children would play together / like each other when they were younger.
6 Who would you / did you use to hang around with as a teenager?
7 My parents would never / never used to help me with my homework. I had to do it all alone.
8 There wouldn't / didn't use to be such wide variety of consumer goods 40 years ago.

D Read the article about anger and aggression and think of a word which best fits each space. Use only one word in each space.

Your brain is programmed to act fast.

According to Douglas Fields, a neurobiologist, our brains are programmed to react quickly against threats. There are several stressful and potentially life-threatening situations that people may experience, and when they (**1**) _____ , they react violently.

This phenomenon is not new, but so far it (**2**) _____ been considered abnormal, a mental and moral defect on the part of the person who snaps. However, in his new book, *Why We Snap: Understanding the Rage Circuit in Your Brain*, Fields shows that far from being abnormal, snapping (**3**) _____ in fact, quite a healthy reaction of the brain: violent behaviour is often the result of the clash between the modern world we live in and the parts of our brains, which have not evolved since primeval times.

Fields explains that our brains, like those of other animals (**4**) _____ , have a large part, called the hypothalamic attack region, allocated to threat detection. Its role is to constantly evaluate situations for potential threats. In experiments, scientists stimulated that part of the brain with electrodes. When they (**5**) _____ , the guinea pigs in the study became aggressive and attacked other test animals in the cage.

Aggression is considered to be gender influenced, and so (**6**) _____ heroism. Almost 90% of all people locked up in prison for violent crimes are men. But respectively, 90% of the people who have been awarded medals for heroism (**7**) _____ men as well. Their brains are hard-wired differently, which comes from our different roles during evolution, when the brain was formed. Men had a role of being aggressive, whereas women (**8**) _____ not. So 'snapping' as a mental function is both good and bad –depending on the use we put it to.

1 Grammar

For questions **1–6,** complete the second sentence so that it has a similar meaning to the first sentence, using the word given. **Do not change the word given.** You must use between **three** and **eight** words, including the word given.

1 We were childhood friends, but we have drifted apart in recent years.

   be

   Although we _____ childhood, we have drifted apart in recent years.

2 Janine and her husband have been together for over 20 years.

   back

   Janine and her husband _____ years.

3 Henry was bullied relentlessly at school until he snapped.

   had

   Henry snapped _____ relentlessly at school.

4 Darren hasn't forgiven Kate for her harsh words.

   grudge

   Darren still _____ her harsh words.

5 Zeya took up painting two years ago in an effort to become more creative.

   for

   Zeya _____ now, in an effort to become more creative.

6 He's very absent-minded and keeps misplacing his reading glasses.

   always

   Being very absent-minded, _____ reading glasses.

2 Bright Ideas

Reading

pages 20-21

2.1 **pixel** (n) /ˈpɪksl/
a unit that is the smallest individual part of a picture on a digital screen • *One small photograph can contain a million pixels.* ➣ pixelate (v) ❖ πίξελ, εικονοκύτταρο

2.2 **heart rate monitor** (n) /hɑːt reɪt ˈmɒnɪtə(r)/
a piece of equipment used to check the pace of your heart • *From the movements on the heart rate monitor, it was clear that the unconscious patient was beginning to recover.* ❖ καρδιακός παλμογράφος

2.3 **hideously** (adv) /ˈhɪdiəsli/
in a disgusting or extremely unpleasant way • *The restaurant was hideously decorated with plastic Santas and glittery red streamers.* ➣ hideous (adj) ❖ φριχτά

2.4 **cheap and nasty** (expr) /tʃiːp ənd ˈnɑːsti/
not costing much, but of poor quality • *On the website these boots seemed to be a great bargain, but they turned out to be just a cheap and nasty disappointment.* ❖ φτηνιάρικο

2.5 **minimalist** (adj) /ˈmɪnɪməlɪst/
in a style that uses simple ideas or not using any more than what is absolutely necessary • *The play was staged on a minimalist set with a simple wooden frame and black background, which carried a powerful sense of tragedy.* ➣ minimalism (n), minimal (adj), minimally (adv) ❖ μινιμαλιστικός

2.6 **slew** (n) /sluː/
a great number or amount • *The government was subject to a slew of criticism over the proposed changes to the education system.* ❖ μεγάλος αριθμός / πληθώρα

2.7 **sleek** (adj) /sliːk/
smooth, shiny and seemingly elegant • *Gwyneth wore a sleek black dress which made her look even more elegant than usual.* ➣ sleek back/down (v), sleekness (n), sleekly (adv) ❖ κομψός

2.8 **radical** (adj) /ˈrædɪkl/
completely different and new • *Jean hardly recognised her old school friend due to the radical change in her appearance.* ➣ radical (n) ❖ ριζικός

2.9 **render** (v) /ˈrendə(r)/
cause sth to be in a certain state • *The latest update on this program has rendered it totally useless. I must find a way to revert to the earlier version.* ❖ καθιστώ

2.10 **generic** (adj) /dʒəˈnerɪk/
common to a group or a range of things rather than specific • *The word 'device' is a generic term for any piece of equipment designed for a specific job.* ➣ generically (adv) ❖ γενικός

2.11 **flattery** (n) /ˈflætəri/
the act of giving excessive compliments or praise, often in order to gain sth from sb • *Flattery will get you everywhere with Professor Huggins; he just loves being praised for his work!* ➣ flatter (v), flattering (adj) ❖ κολακεία

2.12 **seminal** (adj) /ˈsemɪnl/
very important and having a major influence on developments • *Lesley played a seminal role in forming the company.* ❖ επιδραστικός

2.13 **downfall** (n) /ˈdaʊnfɔːl/
the cause of the end of sth being in a powerful position • *The years of plague were a major factor in the downfall of ancient Athens.* ❖ πτώση

2.14 **hanker** (v) /ˈhæŋkə(r)/
strongly desire sth • *No matter how many gadgets Eric has, he's constantly hankering for more.* ➣ hankering (n) ❖ λαχταρώ

2.15 **mind you** (expr) /maɪnd juː/
used informally to add a detail what you already said • *Andrea's just locked herself out of her email account. Mind you, I'm not surprised – she can never remember passwords.* ❖ «εδώ που τα λέμε»

2.16 **diehard** (adj) /ˈdaɪhɑːd/
with a fixed belief or goal; stubborn • *Even diehard gamers will find the new version of WipeOut really challenging.* ➣ diehard (n) ❖ σκληροπυρηνικός

2.17 **iconic** (adj) /aɪˈkɒnɪk/
symbolising a particular ideal or concept; famous • *Mark Zuckerburg has reached iconic status with the success of Facebook.* ➣ icon (n) ❖ εικονικός

2.18 **not be fussed (about sth)** (expr) /nɒt biː fʌst əˈbaʊt ˈsʌmθɪŋ/
not be bothered about sth; not much interested in sth • *I'm not fussed about which brand name the phone is, so long as it functions efficiently.* ➣ fuss (v), fuss (n), fussy (adj) ❖ δεν με νοιάζει, δεν με ενδιαφέρει

2.19 **brim** (v) /brɪm/
be full of sth • *Brimming with enthusiasm, Antonia waited for her new tablet to arrive in the post.* ➣ brim (n) ❖ ξεχειλίζω

2.20 **sport** (v) /spɔːt/
wear sth proudly; show off a possession you're proud of • *People who go around sporting their new smartphones in public places are prime targets for thieves.* ❖ επιδεικνύω

2.21 **zeitgeist** (n) /'zaɪtgaɪst/
the common spirit or prevailing attitude typical of a particular period in history • *The book perfectly captured the zeitgeist of early 20th century Ireland.* ❖ το πνεύμα της εποχής

2.22 **genie pants** (n) /'dʒiːni pænts/
type of loose-fitting wide trousers • *The head teacher does not approve of students wearing baggy genie pants to school.* ❖ είδος φαρδιού παντελονιού

2.23 **beanie** (n) /'biːni/
a type of small brimless hat • *Don't forget to wear your scarf and beanie; it's freezing out there!* ❖ είδος σκούφου

2.24 **testament** (n) /'testəmənt/
sth that proves sth else is true or exists • *A statue of the dog was erected in Edinburgh as a testament to his loyalty to his master.* ❖ μαρτυρία

2.25 **measure up** (phr v) /'meʒə(r) ʌp/
be as good as expected • *The new printer didn't quite measure up to what we expected, given the rave reviews.* ➢ measurement (n) ❖ ανταποκρίνομαι, επιβεβαιώνω (δικαιώνω) προσμονές

2.26 **demographic** (n) /ˌdemə'græfɪk/
a group of customers within a particular age group, gender, interest group • *The website aims to appeal to the fifty-something demographic.* ➢ demographic (adj) ❖ πληθυσμιακή ομάδα

2.27 **spec** (n) /spek/
a specification; a detail of the design or materials used in sth • *Just tell us what you want and we can build a new PC according to your specs.* ➢ spec (v) ❖ τεχνική προδιαγραφή

2.28 **overexpose** (v) /ˌəʊvərɪk'spəʊz/
affect the quality of an image by using a camera setting that lets too much light in • *It took some practice to master the phone's camera settings so as not to overexpose the photos.* ➢ overexposure (n) ❖ υπερεκθέτω

2.29 **asking price** (n) /'aːskɪŋ praɪs/
the starting price decided by the seller • *In my opinion, the house isn't worth the asking price; perhaps they would accept a lower offer.* ❖ αρχική τιμή

2.30 **underwhelming** (adj) /ˌʌndə'welmɪŋ/
not likely to impress or excite • *Despite the overwhelming cost of the tickets, I'm afraid the band's actual performance was disappointingly underwhelming.* ➢ underwhelm (v) ❖ απογοητευτικός
✎ Opp: overwhelming ❖ συντριπτικός

2.31 **deviate** (v) /'diːvieɪt/
change or do sth differently from normal • *Whilst J. K. Rowling deviated from her usual style to write adult fiction, Jo Nesbo has deviated in the opposite direction, moving from crime fiction to children's stories.* ➢ deviation (n), deviant (adj) ❖ παρεκκλίνω

2.32 **incorporate** (v) /ɪn'kɔːpəreɪt/
bring sth in to make it a part of sth else • *An unbreakable screen has been incorporated in the tablet's design.* ➢ incorporation (n) ❖ ενσωματώνω

2.33 **element** (n) /'elɪmənt/
a necessary part or a quality of sth • *Front-facing cameras have become an essential element of phones for selfie addicts.* ➢ elementary (adj) ❖ στοιχείο, χαρακτηριστικό

2.34 **precede** (v) /prɪ'siːd/
occur or exist before sth else • *Months of trial and error on the part of the research team preceded the launch of the smartwatch.* ➢ precedent (n) ❖ προηγούμαι

2.35 **scoff** (v) /skɒf/
talk in a mocking way about sth that you consider stupid • *In the past, the idea of a horseless carriage was scoffed at in the way people recently scoffed at driverless vehicles.* ❖ χλευάζω

2.36 **sold on sth** (expr) /səʊld ɒn 'sʌmθɪŋ/
enthusiastic about; convinced that sth is useful/desirable • *Pavlos is sold on the idea of getting a 3D printer. Now all he needs is the cash to buy one.* ❖ πεπεισμένος για την αξία (χρησιμότητα) κάποιου πράγματος, ενθουσιώδης

2.37 **hefty** (adj) /'hefti/
larger than normal • *It's not surprising you got such a hefty fine since you had parked all day in front of the police station.* ❖ βαρύς, μεγάλος

2.38 **fork out** (phr v) /fɔːk aʊt/
pay a lot for sth • *Few parents are wealthy enough to fork out for all the latest gadgets their children demand.* ❖ πληρώνω πολλά χρήματα

2.39 **jam** (v) /dʒæm/
become unable to operate or move • *We returned the printer within a day of buying it because the paper was constantly jamming.* ❖ φρακάρω

2.40 tinge (n) /tɪndʒ/
a small amount of a particular colour
• *Something was wrong with the colour setting on the camera, so all the prints came out with a greenish tinge.* ➢ tinge (v) ❖ χροιά

2.41 the last straw (expr) /ðə lɑːst strɔː/
the final setback after a series of them, that makes sth impossible to deal with or accept
• *We've been having problems with our new neighbours, but the last straw came when they tried to install a satellite dish and it fell on top of our car.* ❖ «η σταγόνα που ξεχείλισε το ποτήρι»

2.42 durable (adj) /ˈdjʊərəbl/
made to be strong and long-lasting • *The smartphone cover was made of durable plastic that protected it from accidental damage.* ➢ durability (n) ❖ ανθεκτικός

2.43 withstand (v) /wɪðˈstænd/
be strong enough to remain unharmed through an extreme condition • *Liz was so relieved that her glasses managed to withstand being driven over after she had dropped them on the road.* ❖ αντέχω

2.44 outweigh (v) /ˌaʊtˈweɪ/
be more important than sth else • *The convenience of having a dual sim phone outweighs the costs.* ❖ υπερτερώ

2.45 furnace (n) /ˈfɜːnɪs/
a piece of equipment enclosed by walls on all sides and closed on top that is heated to a high enough temperature to melt hard materials, such as metal or glass • *Until now, furnaces for melting iron ore have been heated by fossil fuels.* ❖ κάμινος, κλίβανος

2.46 aviation (n) /ˌeɪviˈeɪʃn/
the practical business of designing and building aircraft • *The modern age of aviation began with the design of hot air balloons in the 18th century.* ➢ aviator (n) ❖ αεροπορία

Compound nouns

asking price	heart rate monitor
carbon dioxide	micro-organism
computer literacy	quantum theory
cybernetic implant	test tube
genie pants	

Vocabulary
pages 22-23-24

2.47 deduce (v) /dɪˈdjuːs/
reach a conclusion about sth on the basis of existing evidence • *Judging from the tyre tracks at the scene of the accident, the police deduced that the driver had been exceeding the speed limit.* ➢ deduction (n), deducible (adj) ❖ συμπεραίνω

2.48 deduct (v) /dɪˈdʌkt/
take sth away from a total amount • *A small transaction fee will be deducted from the payment into your bank account.* ➢ deduction (n), deductible (adj) ❖ αφαιρώ

2.49 eminent (adj) /ˈemɪnənt/
respected and important, often within a certain profession • *An eminent underwater photographer produced the unique images for the magazine.* ➢ eminence (n), eminently (adv) ❖ διαπρεπής

2.50 imminent (adj) /ˈɪmɪnənt/
seemingly about to happen • *Seeing the rapidly gathering clouds, we realised a storm was imminent.* ➢ imminence (n), imminently (adv) ❖ επικείμενος

2.51 emit (v) /iˈmɪt/
give off; send out • *The whale emitted a high-pitched sound before disappearing under the surface.* ➢ emission (n) ❖ εκπέμπω

2.52 melatonin (n) /ˌmeləˈtəʊnɪn/
a chemical substance that affects skin colour in the body • *Melatonin is an essential hormone which affects our sleep patterns.* ❖ μελατονίνη

2.53 causality (n) /kɔːˈzæləti/
the scientific principle that everything has a cause • *Causality is simply the basic relationship between the cause of something and its effect.* ➢ causal (adj) ❖ αιτιότητα

2.54 infrared (adj) /ˌɪnfrəˈred/
using invisible electromagnetic waves longer than those of visible light • *Infrared radiation is used in scientific and medical applications.* ❖ υπέρυθρος

2.55 censor (n) /ˈsensə(r)/
sb who checks the content of books, films, and other media to remove parts considered unsuitable for a particular audience • *As the film contained some violent scenes, the censor had rated it unsuitable for young children.* ➢ censor (v), censorship (n) ❖ λογοκριτής

2.56 sensor (n) /ˈsensə(r)/
a piece of equipment that reacts to sound, light or movement, etc. to cause a device to operate or show sth • *The light above our front door is triggered by a sensor that detects movement.* ➢ sensory (adj) ❖ αισθητήρας

2.57 erode (v) /ɪˈrəʊd/
wear away the surface of sth • *The sides of the riverbank had been eroded dramatically by the heavy rains.* ➢ erosion (n) ❖ διαβρώνω

2.58 eradicate (v) /ɪˈrædɪkeɪt/
get rid of • *Insect-borne diseases are not easy to eradicate, especially in a humid climate.* ➢ eradication (n) ❖ εξαλείφω, εξαφανίζω

2.59 polio (n) /ˈpəʊliəʊ/
the disease poliomyelitis, which affects the
central nervous system • *Polio has become
rare in the UK since the introduction of child
inoculation programmes.* ❖ πολιομυελίτιδα

2.60 fission (n) /ˈfɪʃn/
the act of splitting the central part of an atom
• *The discovery of nuclear fission opened
radical new possibilities in the field of electric
power generation as well as the creation of
atomic weapons.* ❖ σχάση, διάσπαση

2.61 fusion (n) /ˈfjuːʒn/
the act of combining two or more things
together to form one • *The artistic fusion of
sound and light gave the restaurant a relaxing
atmosphere.* ❖ συνδυασμός, συγχώνευση

2.62 entail (v) /ɪnˈteɪl/
involve • *If you tell us what exactly the project
entails, we can give an accurate estimate for
the job.* ❖ συνεπάγομαι

2.63 uranium (n) /juˈreɪniəm/
a heavy, silver-coloured metal • *Uranium is
used in the production of nuclear energy.*
❖ ουράνιο

2.64 ingenuous (adj) /ɪnˈdʒenjuəs/
honest and blindly trusting • *I'd advise you
not to be so ingenuous but to consider his
proposal very carefully before you accept.*
➢ ingenuously (adv) ❖ ευκολόπιστος

2.65 ingenious (adj) /ɪnˈdʒiːniəs/
very clever • *Virtual clouds are an ingenious
way to save or share data.* ➢ ingenuity (n),
ingeniously (adv) ❖ ευφυής

2.66 decompose (v) /ˌdiːkəmˈpəʊz/
slowly break down or become destroyed
naturally • *If you don't eat those grapes soon,
they'll start to decompose.* ➢ decomposition
(n) ❖ αποσυνθέτω

2.67 disintegrate (v) /dɪsˈɪntɪgreɪt/
break up into very small pieces • *The dress
was so old that its fabric had begun to
disintegrate.* ➢ disintegration (n) ❖ διασπώ

2.68 dissolve (v) /dɪˈzɒlv/
make sth solid become part of a liquid
• *The honey dissolved quickly in the hot tea.*
❖ διαλύω

2.69 hurtle (v) /ˈhɜːtl/
move very quickly • *The spaceship began
to break up as it hurtled through the Earth's
atmosphere.* ❖ κινούμαι με μεγάλη ταχύτητα

2.70 micro-organism (n) /ˌmaɪkrəʊˈɔːɡənɪz(ə)m/
a tiny living thing • *Steve looked into the
microscope to examine the micro-organisms in
the piece of wood.* ❖ μικροοργανισμός

2.71 radioactivity (n) /ˌreɪdiəʊækˈtɪvəti/
the dangerous radiation sent out as a result
of nuclear fission • *Dangerous levels of
radioactivity were recorded across the country
when the nuclear reactor exploded.*
➢ radioactive (adj) ❖ ραδιενέργεια

2.72 circumference (n) /səˈkʌmfərəns/
the measurement straight around a circle or
a curved object • *The circumference of the
Moon is almost 11,000 km.* ❖ περιφέρεια

2.73 obsolete (adj) /ˈɒbsəliːt/
no longer produced, often due to being
replaced by sth new • *I doubt if it's possible to
repair your ten-year-old printer as it's probably
obsolete by now and you'll never find new
parts.* ➢ obsolescence (n) ❖ απαρχαιωμένος

2.74 outdated (adj) /ˌaʊtˈdeɪtɪd/
old-fashioned, therefore, not useful
• *Unfortunately, our school's computers are so
outdated that they keep breaking down.*
❖ απαρχαιωμένος, παρωχημένος

2.75 utilitarian (adj) /ˌjuːtɪlɪˈteəriən/
made for a practical purpose rather than for
appearance • *Kate hated wearing her dull
grey school uniform, denouncing it as an
utterly utilitarian style.* ➢ utilitarianism (n)
❖ χρηστικός

2.76 aesthetically (adv) /iːsˈθetɪkli/
in a way related to the look of sth • *The
garden offered an aesthetically pleasing
riot of colour in spring.* ➢ aesthetic (adj),
aestheticism (n) ❖ αισθητικά

2.77 unorthodox (adj) /ʌnˈɔːθədɒks/
unconventional; different from what is normally
done • *Her unorthodox teaching methods
were questioned at first, but they have shown
positive results.* ➢ unorthodoxly (adv)
❖ ανορθόδοξος
✎ Opp: orthodox ❖ ορθόδοξος

2.78 painstaking (adj) /ˈpeɪnzteɪkɪŋ/
with great care and effort • *With painstaking
attention to detail, the technician removed and
replaced the faulty hardware.* ➢ painstakingly
(adv) ❖ επιμελέστατος

2.79 tangible (adj) /ˈtændʒəbl/
able to be seen and touched • *Detectives are
pretty certain that he is the thief, but he can't
be charged without tangible evidence.*
➢ tangibly (adv) ❖ απτός
✎ Opp: intangible ❖ ακαθόριστος, άυλος

2.80 scrutiny (n) /ˈskruːtəni/
close examination • *The politician's personal
emails have become subject to public scrutiny.*
➢ scrutinize (v) ❖ λεπτομερής έλεγχος

2.81 **breach** (n) /briːtʃ/
a break in a system or agreement which causes it to fail • *Pete was fired from the company as a result of his breach of confidentiality.* ➢ breach (v) ❖ αθέτηση, ρήξη

2.82 **computer literacy** (n) /kəmˈpjuːtə(r) ˈlɪtərəsi/
the ability to use and understand computers well • *Vincent's level of computer literacy isn't proficient enough for him to design his own website.* ➢ literate (adj) ❖ βαθμός εκπαίδευσης και κατοχής γνώσεων υπολογιστών

2.83 **spreadsheet** (n) /ˈspredʃiːt/
a computer program in which data is recorded in rows and columns for calculations or plans, etc. • *All our financial accounts are recorded on monthly spreadsheets, which are backed up on the cloud.* ❖ υπολογιστικό φύλλο

2.84 **mimic** (v) /ˈmɪmɪk/
copy the way sb/sth acts or speaks • *The anti-virus scan detected a potential threat which was simply a harmless program that mimicked the pattern of phishing bug.* ➢ mimic (n), mimicry (n) ❖ μιμούμαι

2.85 **at your fingertips** (expr) /æt jɔːr ˈfɪŋgətɪps/
get and use sth very easily • *Ben made sure he had all the data at his fingertips before submitting his proposal.* ❖ στη διάθεσή μου

2.86 **up and running** (expr) /ʌp ənd ˈrʌnɪŋ/
functioning correctly • *A few delays held up the start of the project, but it's now up and running on schedule.* ❖ σε καλή λειτουργία

2.87 **think outside the box** (expr) /θɪŋk ˌaʊtˈsaɪd ðə bɒks/
have imaginative and original ideas • *If humans were incapable of thinking outside the box, they wouldn't have survived past the Stone Age.* ❖ πρωτότυπη και πρωτοπόρα σκέψη

2.88 **ghastly** (adj) /ˈgɑːstli/
terrrible • *Are you feeling okay? You look absolutely ghastly.* ❖ φρικτός, απαίσιος

2.89 **quantum theory** (n) /ˈkwɒntəm ˈθɪəri/
the theory of physics around the idea that energy exists in indivisible units • *I don't know anyone at all who understands quantum theory!* ❖ κβαντική θεωρία

2.90 **ahead of the curve** (phr) /əˈhed əv ðə kɜːv/
more advanced than a current trend • *Instead of copying other companies' products, it's better to develop original ideas to keep ahead of the curve.* ➢ curve (v) ❖ έχω πρωτοπορία / πρωτοτυπία

2.91 **advent** (n) /ˈædvent/
the arrival of a new invention • *Before the advent of email, we had to wait days or weeks to receive letters.* ❖ έλευση

2.92 **negligence** (n) /ˈneglɪdʒəns/
not giving enough care and attention • *The car wasn't so much old as falling apart due to the owner's negligence.* ➢ negligent (adj), negligently (adv) ❖ αμέλεια

2.93 **centenarian** (n) /ˌsentɪˈneəriən/
sb who is 100 years old or more • *It's amazing how many centenarians are still alive and well on the island.* ❖ εκατοντάχρονος

2.94 **precedent** (n) /ˈpresɪdənt/
an action or decision in the past which was the same or similar to one that happened later • *Such devastating storms are without precedent in this part of the country; we've never seen anything like it!* ➢ precede (v), precedence (n) ❖ προηγούμενο

2.95 **persevere** (v) /ˌpɜːsɪˈvɪə(r)/
keep on trying despite adverse conditions • *Despite the high fees, Martin decided to persevere with the course until he completed his masters degree.* ➢ perseverance (n), persevering (adj) ❖ επιμένω

2.96 **carbon dioxide** (n) /ˌkɑːbən daɪˈɒksaɪd/
the gas emitted when people or animals breathe out, by plants or by burning • *Plants and trees take in carbon dioxide in the daylight and emit it at night.* ❖ διοξείδιο του άνθρακα

2.97 **back and forth** (expr) /bæk ənd fɔːθ/
from own side to another and back again • *Jerry walked back and forth, impatiently waiting for the train.* ❖ πέρα δώθε

2.98 **back to front** (expr) /bæk tə frʌnt/
with the wrong side facing • *I got dressed in such a rush after swimming that I put on my sweater back to front and didn't notice till I was on the bus.* ❖ ανάποδα

2.99 **little by little** (expr) /ˈlɪtl baɪ ˈlɪtl/
in slow and steady steps • *Little by little, the sea level is rising along our coast.* ❖ σιγά σιγά

2.100 **more or less** (expr) /mɔː(r) ɔː les/
approximately; nearly • *Rabies is more or less non-existent in our country, thanks to immunisation.* ❖ λίγο-πολύ, σχεδόν

2.101 **safe and sound** (expr) /seɪf ənd saʊnd/
out of danger; not harmed • *It was a rough flight through the storm clouds, but we landed safe and sound at the airport.* ❖ σώος και αβλαβής

2.102 **time after time** (expr) /taɪm ˈɑːftə(r) taɪm/
repeatedly; regularly • *Time after time, our head teacher has warned us not to bring mobile phones into the classroom.* ❖ επανειλημμένα

2.103 **touch and go** (expr) /tʌtʃ ənd gəʊ/
a difficult situation that may have an unpleasant outcome • *I was confident about taking the exam, but it was touch and go on the day when I realised how hard it actually was.* ❖ οριακό λόγω δυσκολιών

2.104 **wear and tear** (expr) /weə(r) ənd teə(r)/
damage to things from normal everyday use
● *Most modern phones are not designed to last through years of wear and tear.* ❖ φθορά λόγω χρήσης

2.105 **hitch** (n) /hɪtʃ/
a minor problem or delay ● *Frank managed to install the new program without a hitch by following the step-by-step guide.* ❖ μικρή αναποδιά, κώλυμα

2.106 **grain** (n) /greɪn/
a small seed of a plant such as rice; a small hard piece or amount of sth ● *Nura took a few grains of rice and planted them to grow food for her family.* ➢ grainy (adj) ❖ κόκκος

2.107 **fungi** (n) /ˈfʌŋgiː/
plural of fungus; organisms like a plant without leaves that grows on othe plants or trees and in damp areas ● *The north side of the tree was covered in fungi.* ➢ fungal (adj) ❖ μύκητες

2.108 **progenitor** (n) /prəʊˈdʒenɪtə(r)/
an ancestor ● *The ancient calculating device found in the Antikythera shipwreck is regarded as a progenitor of the computer.* ➢ progeny (n) ❖ πρόγονος

2.109 **genome** (n) /ˈdʒiːnəʊm/
the genetic material of a living thing ● *A human genome fits into a cell nucleus that's just the size of a pinpoint.* ➢ genomics (n) ❖ γονιδίωμα

2.110 **mutation** (n) /mjuːˈteɪʃn/
a change in the structure of sth; a genetic variation ● *The city's population was affected by a deadly mutation of the flu virus.* ➢ mutate (v), mutant (adj) ❖ μετάλλαξη

2.111 **spring** (v) /sprɪŋ/
move suddenly and quickly ● *George sprang to his feet as soon as the phone rang.* ➢ spring (n) ❖ αναπηδώ

2.112 **proceed** (v) /prəˈsiːd/
continue to do sth; go on (to do sth after doing sth else) ● *After reading the instructions, Mavis proceeded to connect the new router.* ➢ proceedings (n) ❖ προχωρώ, ενεργώ

2.113 **originate** (v) /əˈrɪdʒɪneɪt/
come from a particular place/source ● *The game of chess is thought to have originated in Asia or the Middle East.* ➢ originator (n) ❖ προέρχομαι

2.114 **crucial** (adj) /ˈkruːʃl/
of critical importance ● *Regular back-ups are crucial to avoid losing important data.* ➢ crucially (adv) ❖ σημαντικότατος, κρίσιμος

2.115 **shed light on** (expr) /ʃed laɪt ɒn/
give a clue to explain the cause of sth ● *If you could shed some light on exactly what the job involves, we could give you an estimate for the costs.* ❖ διαφωτίζω

2.116 **sift** (v) /sɪft/
examine sth in detail ● *Jason had to sift through years of paperwork to find his birth certificate.* ➢ sifter (n) ❖ κοσκινίζω

Research & Science verbs

anticipate	hanker
brim	hurtle
decompose	incorporate
deduce	jam
deteriorate	mimic
deviate	originate
disintegrate	overexpose
dissolve	persevere
emit	precede
entail	proceed
envisage	render
eradicate	scoff
erode	sift
exceed	unveil
flag	withstand

Grammar   pages 25-26-27

2.117 **flag** (v) /flæg/
put a mark on sth that needs future attention ● *Lulu skimmed through the mass of emails in her in box and flagged up the ones which were urgent.* ➢ flag (n) ❖ σημειώνω

2.118 **exponentially** (adv) /ˌekspəˈnenʃəli/
in a way that increases progressively faster ● *Air pollution over the city increases exponentially with the burning of fossil fuels upon the onset of winter.* ➢ exponent (n), exponential (adj) ❖ εκθετικά

2.119 **deteriorate** (v) /dɪˈtɪəriəreɪt/
become worse ● *John decided to emigrate after his hopes of finding work deteriorated rapidly as local businesses closed.* ➢ deterioration (v), deteriorated (adj) ❖ χειροτερεύω

2.120 **test tube** (n) /test tjuːb/
a glass tube used in scientific experiments and medical tests ● *An array of test tubes filled with strange liquids were perched on the rack next to his microscope.* ❖ δοκιμαστικός σωλήνας

2.121 **frontier** (n) /ˈfrʌntɪə(r)/
a limit ● *Alexander Fleming broke the frontiers of medical science when he discovered penicillin in 1928.* ❖ σύνορα

2.122 **loom** (v) /luːm/
appear suddenly, often in a manner that is threatening ● *A huge dark shape loomed in the doorway.* ❖ διαγράφομαι

2.123 brew (v) /bruː/
slowly begin to form; seem likely to happen
• *Trouble had been brewing on the borders long before war finally broke out.* ➢ brew (n), brewery (n) ❖ ετοιμάζω

2.124 literary (adj) /ˈlɪtərəri/
to do with literature • *Gwen wrote her thesis on the literary works of 19th century female authors.* ➢ literature (n) ❖ λογοτεχνικός

2.125 envisage (v) /ɪnˈvɪzɪdʒ/
imagine • *I cannot envisage having a robot to clean the house.* ❖ φαντάζομαι, εικονίζω

2.126 dread (v) /dred/
have a fear that sth terrible will happen
• *I dread to think what would happen if there was an accident on the metro line.* ➢ dread (n), dreadful (adj), dreadfully (adv) ❖ φοβάμαι πολύ

2.127 resounding (adj) /rɪˈzaʊndɪŋ/
loud or great • *Anna's first novel was a resounding failure, but her second had more sales.* ➢ resoundingly (adv) ❖ ηχηρός

2.128 in the pipeline (expr) /ɪn ðə ˈpaɪpˌlaɪn/
scheduled or planned for the future
❖ προγραμματισμένο, επερχόμενο

2.129 unveil (v) /ˌʌnˈveɪl/
reveal sth that has been covered • *The prince's official portrait was unveiled at a special ceremony.* ❖ αποκαλύπτω

2.130 on the cards (expr) /ɒn ðə kaːdz/
likely to happen; predictable • *Your promotion was always on the cards as you've been working so hard all these years.* ❖ επικείμενος, ενδεχόμενος

2.131 keep sb posted (expr) /kiːp ˈsʌmbədi ˈpəʊstɪd/
give sb regular information on a situation
• *Keep me posted on how things go after your operation.* ❖ διατηρώ ενήμερο

2.132 upcoming (adj) /ˈʌpkʌmɪŋ/
planned to happen soon • *Walter was feeling a bit nervous about his upcoming driving test.* ❖ επερχόμενος

2.133 anticipate (n) /ænˈtɪsɪpeɪt/
expect an outcome and prepare for it; look forward to sth that's about to happen • *Try to anticipate what type of questions you'll be asked in the interview.* ➢ anticipation (n) ❖ αναμένω, προβλέπω

2.134 warehouse (n) /ˈweəhaʊs/
a store where goods are kept before being sold or sent to shop • *Our lost cat was found sleeping in a furniture warehouse near our home.* ❖ αποθήκη

2.135 likelihood (n) /ˈlaɪklihʊd/
possibility • *In all likelihood, driverless buses will soon be a common sight in our cities.* ➢ likely (adj) ❖ πιθανότητα

2.136 nanofibre (n) /ˈnænəʊfaɪbə(r)/
a light flexible fabric made using nano-technology • *These nanofibre climbing boots are incredible light and waterproof.* ❖ νανονήματα, νήματα φτιαγμένα με νανοτεχνολογία

2.137 cybernetic implant (n) /ˌsaɪbəˈnetɪk ɪmˈplaːnt/
an implant made to enhance human abilities using cybernetics (the study of how machines communicate information compared with how the human brain communicates information)
• *Cybernetic implants could be used to help patients with physical disabilities.*
❖ κυβερνητικό εμφύτευμα

2.138 exceed (v) /ɪkˈsiːd/
go beyond what is expected • *His generous offer exceeded our expectations.* ➢ excess (n), excessive (adj), excessively (adv) ❖ ξεπερνώ, υπερβαίνω

2.139 doom (n) /duːm/
an inevitable unpleasant event • *A sense of doom hung over the dull graffiti-covered boarded-up shops and empty marketplace.* ➢ doom (v) ❖ καταστροφή, χαμός

2.140 forthcoming (adj) /ˌfɔːθˈkʌmɪŋ/
willing to give help or information; upcoming
• *Tom wasn't very forthcoming about his research. It all seems highlt confidential.* ❖ ανοιχτός, πρόθυμος

2.141 in the offing (expr) /ɪn ðə ˈɒfɪŋ/
likely to happen in the near future • *The company has a revolutionary new design in the offing which they hope to present at the next car exhibition.* ❖ επικείμενος

2.142 impending (adj) /ɪmˈpendɪŋ/
about to happen (usually for sth negative)
• *As the tremors increased, the villlagers evacuated to escape the impending volcanic eruption.* ❖ επικείμενος

Useful expressions

Adverbial & Adjectival	Expressions with Verbs
ahead of the curve	keep sb posted
back and forth	put sth into
back to front	perspective
in the offing	shed light on
in the pipeline	think outside the box
little by little	not be fussed about
more or less	
on the cards	**Phrasal Verbs**
safe and sound	measure up
sold on sth	fork out
the last straw	
time after time	
touch and go	
up and running	
wear and tear	

Speaking

2.143 **automated** (adj) /ˈɔːtəmeɪtɪd/
made to operate by a machine to reduce
human labour • *The process of car
manufacturing has become almost entirely
automated, cutting the need for factory
workers.* ➢ automate (v), automation (n),
automatic (adj), automatically (adv)
❖ αυτοματοποιημένος

2.144 **striking** (adj) /ˈstraɪkɪŋ/
noticeable and interesting; atrractive in an
unusual way • *There was a striking similarity
between the girls, although they were not
related.* ➢ strike (v), strikingly (adv)
❖ εκπληκτικός, εντυπωσιακός

Writing

pages 30-31

2.145 **reluctantly** (adv) /rɪˈlʌktəntli/
unwillingly • *Reluctantly, we bid our friendly
hosts goodbye and headed for the airport to
catch our homebound flight.* ➢ reluctant (adj),
reluctance (n) ❖ απρόθυμα

2.146 **techie** (n) /ˈteki/
a computer expert or enthusiast • *My internet
connection simply froze, and I had to call the
techie on the 24-hour helpline to get back
online again.* ➢ technical (adj), technically
(adv) ❖ ειδικός ή χομπίστας τεχνολογίας,
κυρίως σε υπολογιστές

2.147 **drone** (n) /drəʊn/
a small remote-controlled aircraft used for
aerial photography or for military purposes
• *Eric used his drone to take some
spectacular aerial photos of the lake.* ❖ drone,
μη επανδρωμένο αεροσκάφος

2.148 **thought-provoking** (adj) /θɔːt prəˈvəʊkɪŋ/
inspiring serious thoughts about sth • *While
some 20th century works of science fiction
were pure fantasy in their time, it's quite
thought-provoking how close they've come to
reality.* ❖ προκαλεί σκέψη, μελέτη και ανάλυση

2.149 **put sth into perspective** (expr) /pʊt ˈsʌmθɪŋ
ˈɪntə pəˈspektɪv/
compare things to make a reasoned
judgement about sth • *When you see people
living on the streets, it puts our idea of home
comforts into perspective.* ❖ θέτω κάτι στη
σωστή του διάσταση

Technology

Nouns

advent	mutation
aviation	nanofibre
biofluorescence	neon
breach	pixel
causality	precedent
circumference	progenitor
drone	radioactivity
element	scrutiny
fission	sensor
frontier	spec
furnace	spreadsheet
fusion	techie
genome	tinge
hitch	uranium
likelihood	

Video 2: Neon Seas

page 32

2.150 **neon** (n) /ˈniːɒn/
a gas that gives a bright light when electricity
goes through it • *A bright green neon sign was
flashing continuously outside the hotel window,
making it impossible for me to sleep.* ❖ νέον
(αέριο χημικό στοιχείο)

2.151 **biofluorescence** (n) /ˌbaɪəʊˌflɔːˈresns/
the naturally ability to absorb light and
transform it to a different colour • *The
biofluorescence of fish and other creatures
makes the sea bed a colourful place.*
➢ biofluorescent (adj) ❖ βιο-φθορισμός

2.152 **cartilaginous** (adj) /ˌkaːtɪˈlædʒɪnəs/
with a skeleton made of cartilage (strong white
tissue) • *Sharks are an example of huge
cartilaginous animals* ➢ cartilage (n)
❖ φτιαγμένο από χόνδρο

2.153 **serenity** (n) /səˈrenəti/
peaceful calmness • *The soft lighting created
an atmosphere of serenity.* ➢ serene (adj),
serenely (adv) ❖ ηρεμία

2.154 **eel** (n) /iːl/
a snakelike fish • *The sight of the long wriggly
eels was enough to put me off swimming in
the lake.* ❖ χέλι

2.155 **stingray** (n) /ˈstɪŋreɪ/
a large flat fish with a long tail that has a
dangerous sting • *As he was scuba diving,
Marios almost stood on a stingray which was
lying on the sea bed.* ❖ είδος σαλαχίου με
κεντρί

2.156 **physiologically** (adv) /ˌfɪziəˈlɒdʒɪkli/
in a way connected with how a living
thing functions ● *Human beings' organs
are physiologically similar to many other
mammals.* ➤ physiology (n), physiologist (n),
physiological (adj) ❖ φυσιολογικά

2.157 **surreal** (adj) /səˈriːəl/
more dreamlike rather than realistic
● *Swimming close to the dolphins was a
surreal experience.* ➤ surrealism (n), surrealist
(n) ❖ σουρεαλιστικός

Adjectives	
automated	obsolete
cartilaginous	outdated
crucial	painstaking
eminent	radical
forthcoming	seminal
generic	sleek
iconic	surreal
imminent	tangible
impending	thought-provoking
infrared	unorthodox
ingenuous	upcoming
ingenious	utilitarian
minimalist	

Vocabulary Exercises

A Circle the correct words.

1 Farmers use ingenious / ingenuous methods which will continue to be subject to technological innovation such as accelerated freezing and irradiation in order to preserve food for longer periods.

2 Whilst nuclear power stations could provide the world's energy needs instead of fossil fuels, minimalist / radical safeguards need to be in place to avoid radioactive leaks.

3 Cleaner renewable sources of energy, such as solar, wind or wave energy may become viable alternatives to minimise the harmful effects of carbon dioxide / uranium emissions.

4 Driverless cars will have electronic and infrared censors / sensors to calculate distances of objects and so enhance safety while driving.

5 If you are doing a presentation, it is handy to use a laser pen, which is a small battery-powered gadget that omits / emits a narrow low power beam of red light.

6 Some companies have deliberately made certain manufactured products such as light bulbs and cars outdated / obsolete so as to maximise their profit margins based on the fickle and changing tastes of consumers.

7 Not only do smartphones appear to be aesthetically pleasing to look at, but they also have to be utilitarian / functional.

8 Nuclear fission / fusion is the process that releases huge amounts of energy for electricity by splitting the atom.

B Complete the sentences with the verbs in the correct form.

decompose   deduce   deduct   disintegrate   dissolve   emit   erode   eradicate   entail   hurtle   mimic   persevere

1 Maths is often used to _____ the statistical probability of weather patterns.

2 The science museum shop _____ fifty pence off the price of the little electromagnet.

3 The old coal-fired power stations _____ huge amounts of carbon dioxide into the atmosphere.

4 The strange geological rock formations were _____ over millions of years.

5 On impact with the surface of the Earth the meteorite _____ into thousands of pieces.

6 Can artificial intelligence _____ the human brain and speech patterns?

7 The dreaded smallpox disease was finally _____ globally in the 1970s.

8 The implementation of this experiment _____ thorough and painstaking attention to detail.

9 If you add salt to hot water it _____ more quickly than if you add it to cold water.

10 The meteorite _____ through the atmosphere at an incredible speed.

11 When rotten leaves or vegetation _____ in a humid environment, they turn into compost.

12 The PhD student _____ for five years and finally completed her thesis, proving her initial theoretical assumptions.

C Complete the sentences with these expressions.

> back and forth   back to front   little by little   more or less
> safe and sound   time after time   touch and go   wear and tear

1 _____ his boss warned him to install anti-virus software on his computer to protect his files.

2 If a city with poor infrastructure has roads with potholes, the constantly bumpy ride may result in _____ on the tyres of vehicles.

3 It's a worrying trend that some parents prefer that their children are _____ at home, communicating with their friends online via social networking sites, rather than socialising out of doors and engaging in sporting activities.

4 In the near future, driverless trailer trucks will _____ lead to a change in the global workforce.

5 Due to a technical delay it was _____ as to whether the aircraft would depart on time.

6 The salesman moved _____ arranging the new smartphones on the display stand.

7 _____ humankind is exploring and conquering new frontiers in space and hopefully soon a manned mission will be sent to Mars.

8 Virtual schools using computer programmes may assist dyslexic students who often reverse letters and write _____.

D Complete the sentences with the correct form of the words.

1 Scientists can't always explain why certain disorders arise from genes that have _____. **MUTANT**

2 There have been great strides towards improving computer _____ across all age groups. **LITERATE**

3 Global warming has led to a greater _____ of extreme weather patterns and droughts which were previously unheard of. **LIKELY**

4 The profligate burning of fossil fuels has increased the _____ of noxious gases into the atmosphere. **EMIT**

5 After the disastrous earthquake in Japan, the Fukushima nuclear power plant released _____ into the atmosphere and the ocean, encompassing a 30 mile radius. **RADIOACTIVE**

6 Copernicus made an _____ breakthrough, observing that the Earth and the other planets in our solar system rotate around the Sun. **ICON**

7 Galileo's views were considered unconventional and _____ at the time. **GENIUS**

8 Microbes and other microorganisms as well as earthworms facilitate the _____ of rotten vegetation or leaves on the ground. **DECOMPOSE**

9 The WHO is aiming for the _____ of polio worldwide through comprehensive immunisation programmes. **ERADICATE**

10 _____ to greenhouse gases in urban areas may cause city dwellers to develop allergic responses and breathing difficulties. **OVEREXPOSE**

2 Grammar

2.1 Future Simple

Χρησιμοποιούμε τον Future Simple για:
αποφάσεις που παίρνουμε την ώρα που μιλάμε.
→ My phone battery is low so **I'll put** it on to charge for a while.
προβλέψεις.
→ Communication systems **will continue** to evolve in the future.
υποσχέσεις.
→ **I'll help** you finish your project.
απειλές.
→ Stop posting annoying comments or **I'll take** you off my friend list.
να μιλήσουμε για μελλοντικά γεγονότα.
→ The download **will be** over soon.
να προσφέρουμε να κάνουμε κάτι για κάποιον.
→ **I'll clean** your keyboard for you.
να ζητήσουμε από κάποιον να κάνει κάτι.
→ **Will** you **show** me how to build a website?

2.2 *Be going to*

Χρησιμοποιούμε *be going to*:
για μελλοντικά σχέδια.
→ He**'s going to install** a new hard-drive today.
για προβλέψεις για το κοντινό μέλλον που στηρίζονται σε τωρινές καταστάσεις ή στοιχεία.
→ My laptop **isn't going to last** much longer at this rate. It keeps crashing.

Σημείωση: Κάποιες συνηθισμένες χρονικές εκφράσεις που χρησιμοποιούνται συχνά με τον Future Simple και το *be going to* είναι *this week/month/summer, tonight, this evening, tomorrow, tomorrow morning/afternoon/evening/ night, next week/month/year, at the weekend, in March, in a few minutes/days/hours, on Thursday, on Wednesday morning* κλπ.
→ I'll get a new laptop **next month**.

2.3 Future Continuous

Χρησιμοποιούμε τον Future Continuous για:
πράξεις που θα βρίσκονται σε εξέλιξη σε συγκεκριμένη χρονική στιγμή στο μέλλον.
→ **I'll be catching up** on my emails at seven o'clock tonight.
σχέδια και πράγματα που έχουμε κανονίσει για το μέλλον.
→ They **will be opening** the factory next year.

Σημείωση: Κάποιες συνηθισμένες χρονικές εκφράσεις που χρησιμοποιούνται συχνά με τον Future Continuous είναι *this time next week/month/summer, this time tomorrow morning/afternoon/night* κλπ.
→ **This time next month,** we'll be having our online conference.

2.4 Future Perfect Simple

Χρησιμοποιούμε τον Future Perfect Simple για να μιλήσουμε για:
κάτι που θα έχει ολοκληρωθεί ως ή πριν από μια συγκεκριμένη χρονική στιγμή στο μέλλον.
→ The files **will have uploaded** by four o'clock this afternoon.
τη διάρκεια μιας πράξης ως κάποια χρονική στιγμή στο μέλλον.
→ By 2022, he**'ll have worked** as a programmer for six years.

Σημείωση: Κάποιες συνηθισμένες χρονικές εκφράσεις που χρησιμοποιούνται συχνά με τον Future Perfect Simple είναι *by the end of the week/month/year, by this time tomorrow, by tomorrow evening/seven o'clock/2025* κλπ.
→ By 2050, our education system **will have changed** completely.

2 Grammar

2.5 Future Perfect Continuous

Χρησιμοποιούμε τον Future Perfect Continuous για:
να δείξουμε ότι κάτι θα συνεχίζεται ως ένα συγκεκριμένο γεγονός ή χρονική στιγμή στο μέλλον.
→ *I **will have been using** this program for four years when I finish my studies.*
πράξεις που θα βρίσκονται σε εξέλιξη στο μέλλον και θα επηρεάσουν μια άλλη πράξη.
→ *He will have backache because he **will have been sitting** in the same position for days.*

2.6 *Shall*

Χρησιμοποιούμε *shall* όταν θέλουμε να:
προτείνουμε ή να προσφέρουμε κάτι.
→ ***Shall** I adjust the screen for you?*
δείξουμε αποφασιστικότητα.
→ *I **shall** do the best I can to complete the assignment on time.*
δηλώσουμε προθέσεις.
→ *We **shan't** bother to do business with them again.*

2.7 Other ways to express the future

Χρησιμοποιούμε *to be (just) about to* για να μιλήσουμε για το άμεσο μέλλον.
→ *Could we talk later? I**'m just about to go** out.*
Χρησιμοποιούμε *to be (just) on the point/brink/verge of* για να μιλήσουμε για το άμεσο μέλλον.
→ *The company **is on the brink of** releasing a new antivirus program.*
Χρησιμοποιούμε *to be due to* για να μιλήσουμε για επίσημα σχέδια.
→ *The factory **is due to** open next month.*
Χρησιμοποιούμε *to be to* για να μιλήσουμε για επίσημα
→ *The government **is to** raise taxes again soon.*
→ *You **are not to** touch the engine while it's running.*

2.8 Time expressions (temporals)

Χρησιμοποιούμε χρονικές εκφράσεις όπως *when, before, after, until, once, by the time* κλπ. για να μιλήσουμε για το μέλλοντα. Σ' αυτή την περίπτωση, χρησιμοποιούμε Present Simple ή Present Perfect, και δε χρησιμοποιούμε future. Όταν χρονικές εκφράσεις αναφέρουν το Future in the Past (το μέλλον στο παρελθόν) χρησιμοποιούμε Past Simple ή Past Perfect.
→ ***Once I send** the emails, I'll ring you to confirm.*
→ *I won't switch off the pc **until I have backed up** everything.*
→ *He knew that **when** he **decided** to start a business that I would help him promote it online.*

2.9 Verbs with a future implication

Χρησιμοποιούμε ρήματα όπως *foresee, envisage, plan, anticipate, expect, look forward to, count on, hope, fear, dread,* κτλ. για να:
αναφερθούμε στο μέλλον.
→ *He **hopes** to pursue a career in design engineering.*
αναφερθούμε στο μέλλον και να δώσουμε πληροφορίες για το γεγονός (αν είναι κάτι θετικό ή αρνητικό κλπ.).
→ *We**'re looking forward to** moving to the new office.*
→ *She **anticipates** a favourable result in the next election.*
→ *I **dread** opening my online tax statement which is sure to be fatally high.*

2.10 Adjectives and phrases in the future

Χρησιμοποιούμε μερικές φράσεις και επίθετα για να κάνουμε αναφορά στο μέλλον. Αυτές συμπεριλαμβάνουν:
ουδέτερες εκφράσεις όπως *in the offing, in the pipeline, on the horizon, on the way, forthcoming, upcoming, imminent, ahead* κλπ.

→ *A merger involving one of their former competitors **is in the offing**.*
→ *Striking developments are **imminent** in internet technology.*

εκφράσεις και επίθετα που δείχνουν ότι το γεγονός θα συμβεί πολύ σύντομα όπως *upon us, on the verge of* (δείτε 2.7), *fast approaching*.

→ *Our final exams are **fast approaching/upon us**.*
→ *He's **on the verge of** handing in his resignation.*

εκφράσεις που δείχνουν ότι ένα γεγονός είναι πολύ πιθανό όπως *on the cards, be bound/certain/sure to* κλπ.

→ *There's **bound/certain/sure to** be a new version of the phone released before the end of the year.*
→ *A new version of the phone is **on the cards**.*

in store για να δείξουμε ότι δεν ξέρουμε τι να περιμένουμε.

→ *Who knows what's **in store** for us this time next year?*

εκφράσεις και επίθετα για να δείξουμε ότι πρόκειται για κάτι αρνητικό όπως *be looming, be brewing, impending*.

→ *Trouble **is looming/brewing** in the halls of power.*
→ *I sensed an air of **impending** doom as I opened the envelope.*

2.11 Future in the Past

Χρησιμοποιούμε Future in the Past για να εκφράσουμε την ιδέα ότι στο παρελθόν σκεφτήκαμε πως κάτι θα συνέβαινε στο μέλλον. Για να εκφράσουμε το μέλλον από μια άποψη στο παρελθόν, χρησιμοποιούμε το σχετικό past tense *would* για να μιλήσουμε για προσφορές ή υποσχέσεις.

→ *You said you **would help** me install the software.*

was/were going to για να μιλήσουμε για σχέδια.

→ *She couldn't decide which course she **was going to apply** for.*

would και *was/were going to* για να μιλήσουμε για προβλέψεις.

→ *He knew it **would be** a challenging project.*
→ *We were convinced that the advertising campaign **wasn't going to gain** any support.*

Grammar Exercises

A Choose the correct answers.

It is doubtful the inventors of the mobile phone had any idea how important this (1) ___ become in our everyday lives. Despite its usefulness, all etiquette seems to (2) ___ out the window when it comes to using mobile phones in public.

For those who find it hard to make do without their mobile phone, first of all, it is advisable to put it on silent mode when meeting friends or in a classroom. If it (3) ___ – as phones (4) ___ – you might consider excusing yourself. Of course, you should make all calls as brief as possible when this (5) ___ . By the way, you really shouldn't take it with you when you (6) ___ into bed at night. It's likely you'll have problems sleeping.

That said, there are some innovations coming up, one being nano-batteries, which (7) ___ so small that they can be printed in 3D and charged within minutes. Also, by 2020, super speeds of up to 70 times faster than today will be able to download a film in less than three minutes. There will also be screens that unfurl to allow you to play a game or watch something on a bigger screen, so maybe we shouldn't (8) ___ about phone etiquette since we'll all be even more preoccupied with our phones and totally ignoring each other anyway.

1	**a** will	**b** would	**c** are	**d** had
2	**a** go	**b** have gone	**c** be	**d** be going
3	**a** is ringing	**b** rings	**c** will ring	**d** will have rung
4	**a** do	**b** are doing	**c** will do	**d** would
5	**a** will happen	**b** is happening	**c** happens	**d** should happen
6	**a** will have got	**b** will be getting	**c** would get	**d** get
7	**a** are	**b** will have been	**c** would	**d** will be
8	**a** be bothered	**b** bothered	**c** bothering	**d** have bothered

2 Grammar

B Circle the correct answer.

1 If you don't hurry up, the conference will finish / will have finished before we even get there.

2 Sorry, but I've already made plans for Friday night. I will / am going to wash my hair.

3 All electronic devices are to be / will be switched off before the performance.

4 The internet was first used by the military in the early 80s but would / is to be widely used by the public in the future.

5 He is bound to / going to be late. It's such an annoying habit!

6 I won't even think about turning on my computer in the morning until I will have / have had some quiet time by myself.

7 Since you're going to the centre, will / shall you please post this letter for me?

8 Henry is about / due to arrive on the 9 a.m. flight today if all goes according to plan.

9 You had better take an umbrella because the weatherman said it will / is going to rain later on.

10 Many teenagers hope / foresee robots will be able to clean their rooms in the near future.

C Complete each second sentence so that it has the same meaning as the first, using the word given.

1 It seems highly unlikely there will be much traffic at that time in the morning.

anticipate

I _____ much traffic at that time in the morning.

2 Their flight to London is scheduled to arrive at six this evening.

be

They _____ in London at six this evening.

3 Scientists must register for the conference by the end of June or they will not be allowed to present their findings.

are

Registrations for the conference _____ submitted before the end of June or presentations will not be allowed.

4 They are celebrating their 25th anniversary this September.

will

By this September, they _____ for 25 years.

5 The subject of ethics in science will be under discussion in the upcoming forum.

be

They _____ the subject of ethics in science in the upcoming forum.

6 Don't bother calling her at the lab. She usually leaves a three.

have

In all probability, she _____ at three so I wouldn't bother calling her at the lab.

7 It was only a matter of time before they cloned a human being.

bound

The cloning of a human _____ sooner or later.

8 Supposedly, artificial intelligence will cause a lot of unemployment by the end of this century.

will

Many people think most jobs _____ artificial intelligence by the end of this century.

D Read the paragraph and decide whether the verbs in bold are correct. Write the correct form if they are wrong.

Donald Quack, who is now seven years old, is determined to become a scientist when he (1) **grows** _____ up. He has always been interested in rain and has decided to spend his life studying it. Being a bit of a control freak, he seems to have mapped out his future for the next 25 years. He reckons he (2) **is getting** _____ into Harvard University by the age of 16 and (3) **will have finished** _____ his PhD by the age of 21. Then, he plans on getting a job at Cern. He's not so sure if it (4) **is going to rain** _____ enough in Switzerland, but he would like to study atmospheric aerosols and their effect on clouds. Not only (5) **he will have solved** _____ this problem that has been puzzling scientists in this field for years, but he assumes he will have been awarded the Nobel Prize in physics by the time he (6) **is** _____ 30.

However, it (7) **is not being** _____ all work for our young Mr Quack. Once he (8) **is turning** _____ 27, he will meet the woman of his dreams and get married and have two children; a boy and a girl. They will be named Cirrus and Cumulus respectively, but Mark is not sure if his future wife (9) **is agreeing** _____ to this.

We (10) **are wishing** _____ him all the best.

Exam Task

For questions 1–8, read the text below and decide which answer (A, B, C or D) best fits each gap.

Computers and creativity

Futurists purport that computers will (1) ___ replace humans in most mundane, every day jobs. They (2) ___ the day in the near future that robots will be driving buses and lorries and operating heavy machinery; in short, they'll be doing all run-of-the-mill jobs that don't require human initiative and creativity. They're (3) ___ to take over in factories and farms and anywhere else that human inventiveness, inspiration and interaction are not prerequisites for the job to get done. So (4) ___ we've been reassured that certain qualities humankind possesses, such as imagination, (5) ___ and vision will never be replicated by artificial intelligence, right?

And yet, here comes a group of scientists who have programs on computer perception and creativity (6) ___, and who've already managed to create computer programs which can 'see' structures and objects in clouds – just like humans when they're gazing up at the sky! The same scientists have used another program to make computers write poetry based on images a photographer has taken. The computer produced poetry is (7) ___ pleasing, too!

If computers can write poetry and be creative, perhaps they can learn in other ways, too. Is this the end of an era? Is our end (8) ___? Is artificial intelligence to take over from us?

1	**a** likely	**b** eventually	**c** possible	**d** already
2	**a** foresee	**b** look forward to	**c** hope	**d** are looming
3	**a** sure	**b** possible	**c** bound	**d** brewing
4	**a** much	**b** long	**c** well	**d** far
5	**a** resourcefulness	**b** resources	**c** invention	**d** brain
6	**a** on hold	**b** in the pipeline	**c** at will	**d** at large
7	**a** predominantly	**b** concretely	**c** deniably	**d** aesthetically
8	**a** emitted	**b** eminent	**c** imminent	**d** ingenuous

3 Right On!

page 35

3.1 **snare** (n) /sneə(r)/
a small, usually metal, trap used for catching animals ● *Lee released the rabbit whose foot had got trapped in the snare.* ➢ snare, ensnare (v) ❖ παγίδα, δόκανο

Reading

pages 36-37

3.2 **NGO** (abbrev) /ˌen dʒiː ˈəʊ/
a non-governmental organisation; a charity or other non-profit organisation not controlled by governments ● *Several new NGOs were formed to offer aid to economic immigrants.* ❖ ΜΚΟ (Μη Κυβερνητική Οργάνωση)

3.3 **relief** (n) /rɪˈliːf/
practical emergency aid, such as food, clothes or medical supplies ● *Relief workers have been doing their best to support the earthquake victims.* ➢ relieve (v), relieved (adj) ❖ περίθαλψη, βοήθεια

3.4 **humanitarian** (adj) /hjuːˌmænɪˈteəriən/
related to supporting and improving conditions for people in need ● *The mass influx of illegal immigrants has created an unmanageable humanitarian crisis.* ➢ humanitarian, humanitarianism (n) ❖ ανθρωπιστικός

3.5 **sponsorship** (n) /ˈspɒnsəʃɪp/
financial support, often given in return for advertising ● *Our local marine wildlife support group depends on sponsorship from a mobile phone provider to fund the new rescue centre.* ➢ sponsor (v), sponsor (n) ❖ αιγίδα

3.6 **food bank** (n) /fuːd bæŋk/
a place where free food is given to people in need ● *It's shocking to think that there is a need to feed people through community food banks in so many countries.* ❖ τράπεζα τροφίμων (φιλανθρωπική δομή)

3.7 **soup kitchen** (n) /suːp ˈkɪtʃɪn/
a place where soup or other cooked food is served to destitute people ● *Living on the streets since she lost her home, Tracy waits in line for a plate of food at the soup kitchen every day.* ❖ δημόσιο συσσίτιο

3.8 **run-down** (adj) /ˈrʌnˌdaʊn/
in a neglected poor condition ● *Central Glasgow has been transformed since the run-down old slums were replaced by modern buildings and pedestrianised shopping areas.* ❖ υποβαθμισμένος

3.9 **pocket** (n) /ˈpɒkɪt/
a small separate part of a larger area ● *Allied forces had taken control of most of the country, but met with a few pockets of resistance in the east.* ❖ θύλακας

3.10 **façade** (n) /fəˈsɑːd/
the outward appearance of sth/sb, which may be different to the inner character ● *Despite his brave façade, Kevin tends to get easily upset at the sight of suffering.* ❖ πρόσοψη

3.11 **bunch** (n) /bʌntʃ/
a (disorganised) group of people ● *An assorted bunch of volunteers, from teenagers to elderly, turned up to help out at the bazaar.* ➢ bunch (v) ❖ ανοργάνωτη ομάδα ατόμων

3.12 **heavenwards** (adv) /ˈhevnwədz/
towards the sky ● *When asked where she was intending to find cash for the project, Jean simply raised her eyes heavenwards and shrugged.* ❖ προς τον ουρανό

3.13 **pretence** (n) /prɪˈtens/
the act of pretending that sth is true ● *The Smiths dropped their pretence of wealth when the banks cancelled their credit cards.* ➢ pretend (v), pretender (n), pretend (adj) ❖ προσποίηση

3.14 **ladle** (v) /ˈleɪdl/
to serve food using a large deep spoon ● *Tony ladled the delicious sauce on top of the pasta.* ➢ ladle (n) ❖ βάζω με κουτάλα

3.15 **shawl** (n) /ʃɔːl/
an item of clothing worn around the shoulders or covering the head ● *Liana knitted some warm shawls for the women at the homeless shelter.* ❖ σάλι

3.16 **humbling** (adj) /ˈhʌmblɪŋ/
that makes you feel not as good as you believed you were ● *It was a humbling experience for Bill to see how happy the children were despite their poverty.* ➢ humble (v), humbleness (n) ❖ ταπεινωτικό

3.17 **turn your back on sb/sth** (expr) /tɜːn jɔː(r) bæk ɒn ˈsʌmbədi/ˈsʌmθɪŋ/
ignore or reject sb/sth ● *When George went to prison for fraud, even his close family turned their back on him.* ❖ απορρίπτω

3.18 **in earnest** (phr) /ɪn ˈɜːnɪst/
seriously and sincerely ● *The tears in his eyes showed he was speaking in earnest as he described his wartime experience.* ➢ earnestly (adv) ❖ σοβαρά

3.19 **sentiment** (n) /ˈsentɪmənt/
a strong feeling • *I completely agree with your sentiments on this issue.* ➢ sentimental (adj), sentimentally (adv) ❖ συναίσθημα

3.20 **selfless** (adj) /ˈselfləs/
caring more about the needs of others than your own • *In an utterly selfless fashion, Helen always helps anyone in need without a second thought.* ➢ selflessness (n), selflessly (adv) ❖ ανιδιοτελής

3.21 **austerity** (n) /ɒˈsterəti/
a situation where people have to make do with very little money due to poor economic conditions • *Faced with the prospect of raising their family in austerity in Greece, they opted to emigrate to Australia for a more secure future.* ➢ austere (adj), austerely (adv) ❖ λιτότητα

3.22 **middleman** (n) /ˈmɪdlmæn/
a person who liaises or negotiates between people or companies • *Charles acts as a middleman between job seekers and employers.* ❖ μεσάζων

3.23 **donor** (n) /ˈdəʊnə(r)/
a person who gives sth freely to help others • *A new children's hospital was built following a generous contribution from an anonymous donor.* ➢ donate (v), donation (n) ❖ δωρητής

3.24 **recipient** (n) /rɪˈsɪpiənt/
sb who receives sth • *Although the company sends out hundreds of emails every day, most recipients ignore them, so they only get a handful of responses.* ➢ receive (v) ❖ παραλήπτης

3.25 **orphanage** (n) /ˈɔːfənɪdʒ/
an institution for children whose parents are dead • *Candice grew up in an orphanage after her grandparents died in the war.* ➢ orphan (v), orphan (n) ❖ ορφανοτροφείο

3.26 **mutually** (adv) /ˈmjuːtʃuəli/
felt to an equal extent by all involved • *Let's find a mutually convenient venue to meet in.* ➢ mutual (adj) ❖ αμοιβαία

3.27 **redistribution** (n) /ˌriːdɪstrɪˈbjuːʃn/
sharing out sth in a different way than it was previously • *The opposition party has called for the redistribution of public money from defence into the education sector.* ➢ redistribute (v) ❖ ανακατανομή

3.28 **sustenance** (n) /ˈsʌstənəns/
the nourishment we need to stay alive and healthy • *The country's minimum wage level is hardly enough to provide daily sustenance for a small family.* ➢ sustain (v), sustainability (n), sustainable (adj), sustainably (adv) ❖ τροφή, διατήρηση

3.29 **stigma** (n) /ˈstɪgmə/
sth that causes a feeling of disapproval or prejudice • *There's no longer any stigma about being unemployed since so many people have been in the same position.* ➢ stigmatise (v) ❖ στίγμα

3.30 **traumatic** (adj) /trɔːˈmætɪk/
extremely difficult and causing great stress • *The most traumatic experience I ever had as a child was when our dog went missing for a week.* ➢ traumatise (v), trauma (n), traumatically (adv) ❖ τραυματικός

3.31 **dignity** (n) /ˈdɪgnəti/
a sense of honour and self-respect • *After years of unemployment, Fred felt a sense of dignity when he started working for this firm.* ➢ dignify (v) ❖ αξιοπρέπεια

3.32 **soul-crushing** (adj) /səʊl ˈkrʌʃɪŋ/
confidence-destroying; extremely disappointing • *Being questioned in front of the judge in court was a soul-crushing experience.* ❖ συντριπτικός

3.33 **tally** (n) /ˈtæli/
a count of the total or amount of sth • *Alison kept a tally of the number of homeless who arrived at the shelter every night.* ➢ tally (v) ❖ καταμέτρηση

3.34 **prominently** (adv) /ˈprɒmɪnəntli/
mainly • *When we reached the restaurant, a sign was prominently displayed in the window informing us that it was closed for repairs.* ➢ prominence (n), prominent (adj) ❖ σε περίοπτη θέση

3.35 **signee** (n) /ˌsaɪˈniː/
sb who signs their name on sth • *According to the group's Facebook page, the petition has attracted 30,000 signees so far.* ➢ sign (v) ❖ υπογεγραμμένος

3.36 **philanthropist** (n) /fɪˈlænθrəpɪst/
sb wealthy who helps people in need, usually by making donations • *Donating £5.00 per year to your favourite cause does not make you a philanthropist.* ➢ philanthropy (n), philanthropic (adj) ❖ φιλάνθρωπος

3.37 **hashtag** (n) /ˈhæʃtæg/
a key word or phrase with the hash symbol '#' in front of it, used as a search tool on social media • *After experimenting with different hashtags, Kate began to reach a wider audience through her Twitter account.* ❖ «χάσταγκ», δίεση #

3.38 **activism** (n) /ˈæktɪvɪz(ə)m/
the practice of working towards social change, often collectively • *Brenda felt it was time to get involved in environmental activism when she saw the state of her local beach.* ➢ activist (n), active (adj), actively (adv) ❖ ακτιβισμός

3.39 narcissism (n) /ˈnɑːsɪsɪz(ə)m/
the tendency to admire yourself and your appearance to an extreme extent • *Is the selfie craze purely down to narcissism, or is it simply a cry for approval to cover insecurity?* ➢ narcissistic (adj) ❖ ναρκισσισμός

3.40 mask (v) /mɑːsk/
disguise; cover sth up to hide it • *We all managed to mask our feelings until the last moment, so Melinda had no idea about the surprise party.* ➢ mask (n), masked (adj) ❖ αποκρύπτω

3.41 altruism (n) /ˈæltruɪz(ə)m/
the fact of caring selflessly about other people's needs • *It was questionable whether the celebrity's support for the cause was motivated by altruism or to stay in the limelight.* ➢ altruistic (adj) ❖ αλτρουϊσμός

3.42 prevalent (adj) /ˈprevələnt/
widespread or common at a particular time or place • *Taking advantage of the prevalent sympathy towards the disaster victims, the uploaded video caught the eye of millions of viewers and earned a fortune from clicks on ads.* ➢ prevail (v), prevalence (n) ❖ επικρατών

3.43 surplus (adj) /ˈsɜːpləs/
in excess of what you need • *Any more donations of clothes for the bazaar would be surplus to requirements as we already have more than we can store.* ➢ surplus (n) ❖ πλεονασματικός

3.44 straitened (adj) /ˈstreɪtnd/
short of money or having less than you had before • *Following their redundancy upon the closure of the company, the former staff are now living in straitened circumstances.* ➢ strait (n) ❖ δυσχερής

3.45 legendary (adj) /ˈledʒəndri/
famous and often mentioned • *Fans were devastated at the death of the legendary David Bowie in 2016.* ➢ legend (n) ❖ θρυλικός

3.46 irony (n) /ˈaɪrəni/
a situation where sth has an opposite or contrasting result to what is intended • *The irony was that the new Minister for Health and Sport was an overweight heavy smoker who never walked the length of himself.* ➢ ironic (adj), ironically (adv) ❖ ειρωνία

3.47 address (v) /əˈdres/
deal with • *It's time our government addressed the problem of youth unemployment.* ➢ address (n) ❖ αντιμετωπίζω

3.48 foremost (adj) /ˈfɔːməʊst/
most important or urgent • *The issue of heating allowances for the elderly should be foremost on the agenda.* ➢ foremost (adv) ❖ πρώτιστος

3.49 reap the benefit (expr) /riːp ðə ˈbenɪfɪt/
have the advantage of the positive results of sth • *Studying for her masters in Law was no picnic, but now she's got her own practice and is starting to reap the benefits.* ❖ δράττω τα ωφέλη

3.50 band together (phr v) /bænd təˈgeðə(r)/
form a group to work collectively • *The parents and teachers banded together to organise the school fair.* ❖ ενώνω τις δυνάμεις μου

3.51 destitute (adj) /ˈdestɪtjuːt/
without any money or source of income • *Finding himself destitute, Vidalis wandered the streets in search of work.* ➢ destitution (n) ❖ άπορος

3.52 prep (v) /prep/
prepare • *Have you prepped your opening speech yet?* ➢ prep (n) ❖ προετοιμάζομαι

3.53 round up (phr v) /raʊnd ʌp/
find people or animals and bring them together in a group • *Irene has rounded up a few friends to help with the kids' party.* ➢ round-up (n) ❖ μαζεύω

3.54 unsightly (adj) /ʌnˈsaɪtli/
ugly; unpleasant looking • *The unsightly figures of the homeless sleeping in city centre doorways are often a source of concern among passers-by.* ❖ άσχημος

3.55 fictitious (adj) /fɪkˈtɪʃəs/
made-up and not real or true • *His plot is based on a real situation, but all the characters have fictitious names.* ➢ fiction (n), fictitiously (adv) ❖ πλασματικός

3.56 intermediary (adj) /ˌɪntəˈmiːdiəri/
sb who helps to negotiate an agreement between two or more groups or organisations • *Websites such as eBay™ offer an intermediary platform between buyers and sellers.* ➢ intermediate (adj) ❖ ενδιάμεσος, μεσολαβητικός

3.57 benefactor (n) /ˈbenɪfæktə(r)/
sb who donates money or goods, etc. to help individuals or charities • *The new hospital wing is to be named after the benefactor who funded the construction.* ❖ ευεργέτης

3.58 solely (adv) /ˈsəʊlli/
only; exclusively • *The hostel provides shelter solely for abused women and their children.* ➢ sole (adj) ❖ αποκλειστικά

3.59 redeem (v) /rɪˈdiːm/
exchange sth for sth else • *During the Second World War, British families were given vouchers which they redeemed to claim their food rations.* ➢ redemption (n) ❖ εξαργυρώνω

3.60 **beneficiary** (n) /ˌbenɪˈfɪʃəri/
sb who is entitled to receive a donation or other benefit • *All potential beneficiaries have to give some proof of identity at the community centre before receiving any food vouchers.* ➣ benefit (v, n), beneficial (adj), beneficially (adv) ❖ δικαιούχος

3.61 **impoverished** (adj) /ɪmˈpɒvərɪʃt/
very poor • *Crime rates are high in the most impoverished areas of the city.* ➣ impoverish (v), impoverishment (n) ❖ φτωχός, ξεπεσμένος

3.62 **harrowing** (adj) /ˈhærəʊɪŋ/
frightening or very upsetting • *Getting to the bomb shelter when the air-raid warning sounded was a harrowing experience.* ➣ harrow (v) ❖ οδυνηρός

3.63 **chasten** (v) /ˈtʃeɪsn/
make sb feel sorry for doing sth • *Our visit to the long-term care unit in the children's hospital was a chastening experience.* ➣ chastely (adv) ❖ τιμωρώ, ταπεινώνω

3.64 **altruistic** (adj) /ˌæltruˈɪstɪk/
putting other people's needs before your own • *A plethora of electronic petitions are generated daily seemingly on altruistic grounds.* ➣ altruism (n), altruistically (adv) ❖ αλτρουϊστικός

Charity work: nouns

activism	orphanage
altruism	redistribution
austerity	relief
food bank	soup kitchen
humanitarian	sponsorship
NGO	sustenance

Vocabulary   pages 38-39-40

3.65 **conscious** (adj) /ˈkɒnʃəs/
deliberate; determined • *Ben always makes a conscious effort to help those less fortunate than he is.* ➣ consciousness (n), consciously (adv) ❖ συνειδητός
✎ Opp: unconscious ❖ αναίσθητος, λιπόθυμος

3.66 **conscience** (n) /ˈkɒnʃəns/
the sense that makes you feel guilty if you do sth wrong • *How can you cheat your customers with a clear conscience? Don't you care at all?* ➣ conscientious (adj), conscienciously (adv) ❖ συνείδηση

3.67 **revolt** (v) /rɪˈvəʊlt/
react against sth/sb you feel is wrong or bad • *The majority of Scots revolted against the UK's decision to leave the European Union.* ➣ revolution (v), revolutionary (adj) ❖ επαναστατώ

3.68 **oppress** (v) /əˈpres/
treat sb unfairly by denying their rights and freedom; restrict sb's development • *Laws which oppress the rights of women are still sadly prevalent in many countries.* ➣ oppression (n), oppressor (n), oppressive (adj), oppressively (adv) ❖ καταπιέζω

3.69 **suppress** (v) /səˈpres/
restrain sth; stop sth from developing • *The attempt at a military coup was suppressed overnight.* ➣ suppression, suppressant (n) ❖ καταστέλλω

3.70 **uprising** (n) /ˈʌpraɪzɪŋ/
a revolt against people in power • *The uprising which began against Ottoman rule in 1821 led to the establishment of an independent Greek nation.* ❖ εξέγερση

3.71 **persecute** (v) /ˈpɜːsɪkjuːt/
treat sb unfairly or cruelly because of their beliefs, race, etc. • *Janet discovered that her ancestors had fled from France to Scotland in 1685 because they were being persecuted for their religious beliefs.* ➣ persecution (n) ❖ καταδιώκω

3.72 **prosecute** (v) /ˈprɒsɪkjuːt/
charge sb in court for committing a crime • *The police decided not to prosecute the homeless woman for stealing food from the dustbin.* ➣ prosecution, prosecutor (n) ❖ διώκω

3.73 **affluent** (adj) /ˈæfluənt/
very wealthy with a comfortable living standard • *After the civil war, many Greek families emigrated to more affluent countries, such as Australia.* ➣ affluence (n) ❖ πλούσιος

3.74 **effluent** (n) /ˈefluənt/
sewage or other liquid waste • *Due to a blockage in the drains, there was a disgusting smell of effluent in the street.* ❖ λύματα

3.75 **disburse** (v) /dɪsˈbɜːs/
pay out sums of money from an amount collected to different people or groups • *The college disburses scholarships to up to 100 students every year.* ➣ disbursement (n) ❖ εκταμιεύω

3.76 **disperse** (v) /dɪˈspɜːs/
make sth/sb spread out and move away in different directions; scatter • *We need a good shower of rain to disperse some of the smoke polluting the city.* ➣ dispersion (n), dispersal (n) ❖ διασκορπίζω

3.77 **emigrate** (v) /ˈemɪɡreɪt/
leave your country to go to live in another one • *Many families emigrated from Europe to the USA in the 17th century.* ➣ emigrant, emigration (n) ❖ αποδημώ, μεταναστεύω

3.78 **immigrate** (v) /ˈɪmɪɡreɪt/
move to a country to live there after leaving your homeland ● *Millions of Asians and Africans have immigrated to Europe in recent years.* ➢ immigrant (n), immigration (n) ❖ μεταναστεύω

3.79 **empathy** (n) /ˈempəθi/
the ability to relate to or understand sb else's feelings ● *Rod developed a sense of empathy with the villagers after spending the harsh winter with them.* ➢ empathise (v), empathetic (adj), empathetically (adv) ❖ κατανόηση, συμπόνοια

3.80 **condemn** (v) /kənˈdem/
express strong disapproval for sth you feel is wrong ● *Animal welfare groups throughout the world condemned the mass poisoning of strays.* ➢ condemnation (n) ❖ καταδικάζω

3.81 **condone** (n) /kənˈdəʊn/
accept or show approval for immoral behaviour ● *Violence against innocent people or animals should never be condoned.* ❖ συγχωρώ, παραβλέπω

3.82 **advocate** (v) /ˈædvəkeɪt/
support and recommend sth ● *The organisation strongly advocates the provision of more homeless shelters in the city centre.* ➢ advocate (n) ❖ υποστηρίζω, συνηγορώ

3.83 **blatantly** (adv) /ˈbleɪtəntli/
openly and frankly without caring how others are affected ● *It is blatantly obvious that the state is unable or unwilling to provide adequate welfare support.* ➢ blatant (adj) ❖ κατάφωρα

3.84 **disregard** (v) /ˌdɪsrɪˈɡɑːd/
ignore ● *The fact that Tom was a war hero was disregarded when he was out of work.* ➢ disregard (n) ❖ παραβλέπω

3.85 **alarm** (v) /əˈlɑːm/
cause sb to feel worried or afraid ● *I don't want to alarm you, but isn't that smoke coming from your flat?* ➢ alarm (n), alarming (adj), alarmingly (adv) ❖ τρομάζω

3.86 **assault** (v) /əˈsɔːlt/
affect sth negatively and unpleasantly ● *It could be argued that extreme political correctness assaults the rights to freedom of speech.* ➢ assault (n) ❖ προσβάλλω, επιτίθεμαι

3.87 **abuse** (v) /əˈbjuːs/
treat sth/sb in a way that harms them ● *In our country, strict punishments are imposed on people who abuse children.* ➢ abuse (n), abusive (adj), abusively (adv) ❖ κακοποιώ

3.88 **boycott** (v) /ˈbɔɪkɒt/
refuse to buy or use sth from a particular source as a form of protest ● *Activists are encouraging the public to boycott companies which are damaging the environment.* ➢ boycott (n) ❖ μπουϊκοτάρω

3.89 **mount** (v) /maʊnt/
organise and carry out ● *The school mounted a photographic exhibition to raise awareness on social isues.* ❖ οργανώνω, εκτελώ

3.90 **occupy** (v) /ˈɒkjupaɪ/
take control of an area or country, etc. ● *Greece as we know it was occupied over the centuries by numerous forces, including Romans, Goths, Franks, Venetians, Turks and Germans.* ➢ occupation (n) ❖ κατέχω

3.91 **picket** (v) /ˈpɪkɪt/
stand outside a workplace to protest and try to persuade others to join a strike ● *Flights were disrupted for weeks when striking workers picketed the airport.* ➢ picket (n) ❖ μπλοκάρω, κλείνω

3.92 **stage** (v) /steɪdʒ/
organise and participate in sth ● *Campaigners staged a protest march during the presidential visit.* ➢ stage (n) ❖ οργανώνω, εκτελώ

3.93 **rally** (n) /ˈræli/
a large organised public protest meeting ● *The word spread rapidly throughout social media, ensuring a mass turnout at the rally against education cuts.* ➢ rally (v) ❖ συλλαλητήριο

3.94 **human chain** (n) /ˈhjuːmən tʃeɪn/
a long line of people linked together either by holding hands, or to complete a task jointly ● *Local residents formed a human chain to carry the buckets of water up the hill to put out the wildfire.* ❖ ανθρώπινη αλυσίδα

3.95 **apathetic** (adj) /ˌæpəˈθetɪk/
disinterested or not caring ● *How can you be so apathetic about people who are starving? Why don't you care?* ➢ apathy (n), apathetically (adv) ❖ απαθής

3.96 **callous** (adj) /ˈkæləs/
unkind and without sympathy or feeling for others ● *Patrick was offended by his colleagues callous remarks about the Irish.* ➢ callousness (n), callously (adv) ❖ αναίσθητος, σκληρός

3.97 **just** (adj) /dʒʌst/
fair and morally correct ● *Mrs Jones had just cause to complain about illegally parked cars blocking the wheelchair ramp.* ➢ justice (n), justly (adv) ❖ δίκαιος
✎ Opp: unjust ❖ άδικος

3.98 **benevolent** (adj) /bəˈnevələnt/
willing to help and be generous towards others ● *The centre receives financial support from a benevolent local businessman.* ➢ benevolence (n) ❖ φιλανθρωπικός

3.99 **corrupt** (adj) /kəˈrʌpt/
dishonestly using your position to get money or some advantage ● *Democracy is under threat from corrupt political practices.* ➢ corrupt (v), corruption (n), corruptible (adj) ❖ διεφθαρμένος

3.100 merciful (adj) /ˈmɜːsɪfl/
willing to be kind to and forgive people in your
power • *Henry VIII could hardly be considered
a merciful ruler when he had his own wives
executed.* ➢ mercy (n), mercifuly (adv)
❖ εύσπλαχνος, ελεήμων
✎ Opp: merciless ❖ άσπλαχνος

3.101 brutal (adj) /ˈbruːtl/
cruel, violent and without feeling • *He was
sentenced to life imprisonment for the brutal
attack on the school.* ➢ brutalise (v), brute (n),
brutality (n), brutally (adv) ❖ κτηνώδης

3.102 humane (adj) /hjuːˈmeɪn/
showing compassion and kindness to people
and animals • *Private care home should be
regulated to ensure the elderly are living in
humane conditions.* ➢ humanity (n), humanely
(adv) ❖ ανθρώπινος, με ανθρωπισμό
✎ Opp: inhumane ❖ απάνθρωπος

3.103 prejudiced (adj) /ˈpredʒədɪst/
having an unreasonable hatred of a particular
group of people • *Fear and ignorance can
often lead to prejudiced views against other
nationalities.* ➢ prejudice (n)
❖ προκατειλημμένος

3.104 catch sb red-handed (expr) /kætʃ ˈsʌmbədi
ˌredˈhændɪd/
catch sb in the act of doing sth wrong • *The
bank cashier was fired when she was caught
red-handed stealing cash as she loaded the
ATM.* ❖ «πιάνω στα πράσσα»

3.105 fall back on (phr v) /fɔːl bæk ɒn/
use as a source of support • *Living on a
minimum wage, Jimmy had no savings to fall
back on when his car needed repairs.*
❖ στρέφομαι

3.106 run up against (phr v) /rʌn ʌp əˈgenst/
encounter; face • *When the area was
designated as a refugee camp, the authorities
ran up against complaints from the local
community.* ❖ αντιμετωπίζω

3.107 come down to (phr v) /kʌm daʊn tuː/
be dependent on • *Whether he stays in the
country or not all comes down to whether he
can make a decent living here.* ❖ εξαρτάται

3.108 do away with (phr v) /du əˈweɪ wɪθ/
put an end to • *There was a public outcry at
the government's decision to do away with
some popular TV channels.* ❖ καταργώ

Phrasal verbs

band together	run up against
round up	come down to
fall back on	do away with

3.109 confront (v) /kənˈfrʌnt/
face up to and deal with directly • *Confronted
by a line of police, the hooligans following
the peaceful demonstration retreated into the
back streets.* ➢ confrontation (n) ❖ έρχομαι
αντιμέτωπος

3.110 jump on the bandwagon (expr) /dʒʌmp ɒn
ðə ˈbændwægən/
join others doing sth that is currently
fashionable to be seen to do so • *Anna had
never really cared about animals; she was just
jumping on the vegetarian bandwagon to seek
approval from her new boyfriend.* ❖ ακολουθώ
τη μόδα

3.111 bury your head in the sand (expr) /ˈberi
jɔː(r) hed ɪn ðə sænd/
ignore a problem and refuse to admit it is there
• *If politicians continue to bury their heads in
the sand regarding violence among football
fans, the problem will only get worse.*
❖ προσποιούμαι ότι δεν βλέπω

3.112 bring out the best in sb (expr) /brɪŋ aʊt ðə
best ɪn ˈsʌmbədi/
cause sb to show their best qualities
• *A few days' work at the homeless shelter has
brought out the best in Maria.* ❖ αναδεικνύω

3.113 fall on deaf ears (expr) /fɔːl ɒn def ɪəz/
be ignored • *Although several storm warnings
were issued, the advice fell on deaf ears and
motorists got trapped in snowdrifts.* ❖ «πέφτω
στο κενό»

3.114 get behind sth (expr) /get bɪˈhaɪnd ˈsʌmθɪŋ/
support sth • *If the United Nations doesn't get
behind the immigration crisis, our country will
never be able to deal with it alone.*
❖ υποστηρίζω, συνεισφέρω

3.115 spare no effort (expr) /speə(r) nəʊ ˈefət/
do as much as possible to achieve sth
• *The firefighter spared no effort and rescued
the puppy from the bottom of the well.*
❖ δεν φείδομαι προσπάθειας

3.116 obedience (n) /əˈbiːdiəns/
willingness to follow orders and behave are
you are told to • *As Julie's dog wouldn't listen
to a word she said, she had to send it to
obedience training.* ➢ obey (v), obedient (adj),
obediently (adv) ❖ υπακοή
✎ Opp: disobedience ❖ ανυπακοή

3.117 biased (adj) /ˈbaɪəst/
tending to favour one thing over another • *In
view of the referee's unfair decision, he was
clearly biased towards the home team.* ➢ bias
(n) ❖ προκατειλημμένος
✎ Opp: unbiased ❖ αμερόληπτος

3.118 privileged (adj) /ˈprɪvəlɪdʒd/
having more rights or opportunities than others
• *Until a few decades ago, only privileged
families had the luxury of travelling abroad on
holiday.* ➢ privilege (n) ❖ προνομιούχος
✎ Opp: underprivileged ❖ αυτός που
μειονεκτεί

3.119 **whistle-blower** (n) /ˈwɪsl ˈbləʊə(r)/
a person who alerts people to the fact that a company or person in power is doing sth illegal • *The politician's downfall was due to a whistle-blower's press release.* ❖ «καρφί», πληροφοριοδότης

People

asylum seeker	feminist
benefactor	human chain
beneficiary	middleman
breadwinner	philanthropist
bunch	recipient
coastguard	signee
donor	whistle-blower

Grammar   pages 41-42-43

3.120 **polling station** (n) /ˈpəʊlɪŋ ˈsteɪʃn/
a place where people go to cast their vote in an election • *On election day, our local primary schools are used as polling stations.* ❖ εκλογικό κέντρο

3.121 **abolition** (n) /ˌæbəˈlɪʃn/
the end of a law; the end of sth by order of a law • *Human rights groups are pushing for the abolition of the death penalty in countries where it still exists.* ➣ abolish (v) ❖ κατάργηση

3.122 **abolish** (v) /əˈbɒlɪʃ/
end sth officially, by order of law • *The death penalty was completely abolished in the UK in 1998.* ➣ abolition (n) ❖ καταργώ

3.123 **corruption** (n) /kəˈrʌpʃn/
illegal behaviour by sb who exploits their position of power for personal gain • *A special force was set up to clamp down on corruption among tax officials.* ➣ corrupt (v), corrupt (adj), corruptible (adj) ❖ διαφθορά

3.124 **obliterate** (v) /əˈblɪtəreɪt/
destroy or remove all evidence of sth • *The rain had obliterated the tell-tale tyre marks from the crash scene.* ➣ obliteration (n) ❖ εξαλείφω, σβήνω

3.125 **feminist** (n) /ˈfemənɪst/
sb who believes in and supports that women's and men's rights and opportunities should be equal • *Not everyone seems to have grasped that feminists stand up for equality of men's rights as well as women's.* ➣ feminism (n), feminist (adj) ❖ φεμινιστής

3.126 **breadwinner** (n) /ˈbredwɪnə(r)/
the main wage-earner of a household • *When Dad lost his job, Mum became the sole breadwinner who had to support all of us.* ❖ βιοπαλαιστής, βιοποριστής

3.127 **aftershock** (n) /ˈɑːftəʃɒk/
an earthquake that follows as a consequence of a (usually) larger one • *After the 6.5 Richter earthquake, the townspeople spent the night in the park, fearing further damage by aftershocks.* ❖ μετασεισμός

3.128 **asylum seeker** (n) /əˈsaɪləm ˈsiːkə(r)/
sb who requests permission to stay safely in another country after being forced to leave their own in danger of their lives • *Amongst the crowd of immigrants at the port were a number of asylum seekers waiting to have their passports and documents checked.* ❖ αιτών άσυλο

3.129 **coastguard** (n) /ˈkəʊstgɑːd/
the organisation responsible for policing activities at sea near the coastline and rescuing ships in trouble • *Realising we would never make it to shore without the engine, we sent up a distress flare which was seen by the coastguard.* ❖ ακτοφυλακή

3.130 **ordeal** (n) /ɔːˈdiːl/
a very difficult experience • *My first day at work after leaving school was quite an ordeal.* ❖ δοκιμασία

3.131 **monsoon** (n) /ˌmɒnˈsuːn/
a seasonal period of heavy rains in southern Asia • *Low-lying villages in Bangladesh are liable to flooding during the monsoon season.* ❖ μουσώνας

3.132 **fake** (adj) /feɪk/
made to appear to sth else; not real • *He was arrested at the Australian border for trying to enter the country with a fake identity.* ➣ fake (v), fake (n) ❖ ψεύτικο, πλαστό

3.133 **solidarity** (n) /ˌsɒlɪˈdærəti/
support for one group by another who share the same values • *Several other public services were striking in solidarity with the hospital staff.* ❖ αλληλεγγύη, συναδελφικότητα

3.134 **abstain** (v) /əbˈsteɪn/
choose not to do sth which you might normally do • *Alistair abstained from voting in the election as he could agree with either of the candidates.* ➣ abstention (n), abstinence (n) ❖ απέχω

Speaking   page 45

3.135 **underprivileged** (adj) /ˌʌndəˈprɪvəlɪdʒd/
with less money or opportunities than others • *What support is there for underprivileged families?* ❖ στερούμενος προνομίων, αδικημένος
✎ Opp: privileged ❖ προνομιούχος

Feelings: adjectives

altruistic	impoverished
apathetic	just
benevolent	matter-of-fact
biased	merciful
brutal	prejudiced
callous	selfless
conscious	soul-crushing
corrupt	straitened
harrowing	traumatic
humane	underprivileged
humbling	

Writing

pages 46-47

3.136 huddle (v) /ˈhʌdl/
sit with your arms and legs close to your body for protection or warmth; sit or stand close together with others • *We all huddled round the campfire and told ghost stories.* ➤ huddle (n) ❖ κουρνιάζω

3.137 matter-of-fact (adj) /ˈmætə(r) əv fækt/
plain-speaking and practical without expression of emotion • *She was remarkably matter-of-fact about having fled the horrors of war.* ❖ πραγματικός, ψύχραιμος

3.138 stature (n) /ˈstætʃə(r)/
height • *For one so large in stature, he was rather a coward.* ❖ ανάστημα

3.139 commend (v) /kəˈmend/
praise sb for doing sth • *The group were commended for their successful fundraising efforts.* ➤ commendation (n), commendable (adj), commendably (adv) ❖ επαινώ, επιδοκιμάζω

3.140 no big deal (expr) /nəʊ bɪg diːl/
sth that is unimportant or not a problem • *Sure, I'll look after your pets when your away; it's no big deal.* ❖ «σιγά το πράγμα»

3.141 twist sb's arm (expr) /twɪstˈsʌmbədiz ɑːm/
persuade sb who is reluctant • *If you twist Joe's arm, I'm sure he'll give you a lift to the station.* ❖ πείθω

3.142 needless to say (expr) /ˈniːdləs tə seɪ/
as is already understood • *Needless to say, none of us had even read the book before we saw the film.* ❖ περιττό να πω

3.143 mainstream (adj) /ˈmeɪnstriːm/
broadly accepted as normal by the majority • *Michele prefers obscure indie films to mainstream Hollywood culture.* ➤ mainstream (n) ❖ κυρίαρχο ρεύμα / επικρατούσα τάση

3.144 marginalise (v) /ˈmɑːdʒɪnəlaɪz/
make sb feel insignificant and not part of a group • *We made sure the new student was invited to the party so that she wouldn't feel marginalised.* ➤ margin (n), marginal (adj), marginally (adv) ❖ περιθωριοποιώ

3.145 inspirational (adj) /ˌɪnspəˈreɪʃənl/
that gives inspiration • *The president's opening speech was truly inspirational.* ➤ inspire (v), inspiration (n) ❖ που προκαλεί έμπνευση

3.146 follow in sb's footsteps (expr) /ˈfɒləʊ ɪn ˈsʌmbədiz ˈfʊtstep/
choose the same job or the same way of life as sb else, usually a family member, did or does • *Ruth surprised us all by studying art when she was expected to follow in her parents' footsteps and run the family hotel.* ❖ ακολουθώ τα βήματα

3.147 make your mark (expr) /meɪk jɔː(r) mɑːk/
have an important effect on sth • *You have to be particularly talented or well-connected to make your mark in society.* ❖ αφήνω το σημάδι μου

3.148 enrich (v) /ɪnˈrɪtʃ/
improve the quality of sth • *She hoped that her children's books would enrich the lives of their readers.* ➤ enrichment (n) ❖ εμπλουτίζω

Expressions

bring out the best in sb
bury your head in the sand
catch sb red-handed
fall on deaf ears
follow in sb's footsteps
get behind sth
jump on the bandwagon
make your mark
needless to say
no big deal
reap the benefit
spare no effort
turn your back on sb/sth
twist sb's arm

Video 3: Dirty Energy
page 48

3.149 power plant (n) /ˈpaʊə(r) plɑːnt/
a building where electric power is produced • *Residents living near the coal-fired power plant have complained of health problems due to pollution.* ❖ εργοστάσιο παραγωγής ηλεκτρικής ενέργειας

3.150 **injustice** (n) /ɪnˈdʒʌstɪs/
unfairness or an unfair act ● *19th century novelists drew attention to the social injustices of the time.* ❖ αδικία
✎ Opp: justice ❖ δικαιοσύνη

3.151 **outrage** (n) /ˈaʊtreɪdʒ/
sth very shocking which angers people
● *Environmental groups said the plans to build the runway across the country park were an outrage.* ➢ outrageous (adj), outrageously (adv) ❖ αίσχος, ντροπή

3.152 **banner** (n) /ˈbænə(r/
a large piece of fabric or paper with a message written on it showing support for a cause
● *Demonstrators carried banners outside the court calling for the woman's release.* ❖ πανώ

3.153 **slogan** (n) /ˈsləʊgən/
a catchphrase designed to attract attention and get a message across quickly ● *Protesters carried banners bearing anti-war slogans outside parliament.* ❖ σύνθημα, σλόγκαν

3.154 **roadblock** (n) /ˈrəʊdblɒk/
an obstacle that stops a plan progressing
● *We're facing so many legal roadblocks that I don't think we'll ever manage to open our restaurant.* ❖ οδόφραγμα, εμπόδιο

Places/Locations

pocket	power plant
polling station	

Feelings: nouns

conscience	obedience
dignity	outrage
injustice	sentiment
narcissism	stigma

Vocabulary Exercises

A Choose the best answer.

1 As public relations officer for the charity organisation, it is Kelly's job to find celebrities who will agree to get ___ the cause and offer their support.
   a in front of   **b** behind   **c** above   **d** under

2 The workers have been trying to negotiate better working conditions with the management, but their requests have ___ on deaf ears.
   a fallen   **b** landed   **c** settled   **d** dropped

3 He is a great philanthropist and will ___ no expense or effort to help the children in need.
   a suffer   **b** spend   **c** save   **d** spare

4 How can you possibly ___ your back on a child begging in the street?
   a show   **b** point   **c** turn   **d** give

5 You can't just ___ your head in the sand and hope the problem will go away; you need to do something about it now.
   a put   **b** bury   **c** keep   **d** shove

6 Kevin's father was a great man, and he hopes one day to ___ in his footsteps.
   a follow   **b** walk   **c** step   **d** stride

7 As a doctor who treats the less privileged patients for free, Tracy has really made her ___ in the community.
   a sign   **b** point   **c** difference   **d** mark

8 Mark was happy to volunteer in the community centre; we didn't need to ___ his arm.
   a twist   **b** turn   **c** pull   **d** push

9 You need to make an effort yourself; you can't just sit back and wait for someone to ___ to the rescue every time.
   a arrive   **b** land   **c** come   **d** show

10 Sally is always the first to ___ on the bandwagon whenever there is a need for volunteers.
   a climb   **b** step   **c** jump   **d** run

11 She is an inspiring leader, who has a gift for ___ out the best in her team.
   a seeking   **b** taking   **c** sending   **d** bringing

12 Jerry was ___ red-handed trying to steal money from the fund.
   a caught   **b** captured   **c** arrested   **d** assaulted

B Replace the phrases in bold with these words or phrases in the correct form.

address   band together   commend   come down to   do away with
fall back on   huddle   redeem   round up   run up against

1   I have a little money in the bank that I can **use for help** in an emergency.   _____

2   When the police tried to stop the protesters they **were confronted with** strong resistance.   _____

3   The mayor **praised** Dean for his contribution to the local community.   _____

4   It was so cold in the draughty old house that the children all **sat close** together to keep warm. _____

5   With the help of the social media, they managed to **gather** enough volunteers to clean all the beaches on the island in just one weekend.   _____

6   With the problems the national health system is facing today, unfortunately, when it comes to your health it all **depends on** how much money you can afford to spend.   _____

7   When the new cutbacks were announced the workers decided to **form a group** and organise a strike.   _____

8   The protestors felt that the new tax was unjust, and wanted the government to **put an end to** it.   _____

9   The government needs to **deal with** the problem of unemployment immediately.   _____

10 The homeless were given coupons, which they could **exchange** for a hot meal in a local restaurant.   _____

C Complete the sentences with the correct form of the words.

The Smile of the Child

The Smile of the Child is a non-profit organisation in Greece that helps (1) _____ children   **PRIVILEGE**
of all races and ethnic groups, by offering them a chance for a better life. This organisation was
set up by a father wishing to fulfill the dream of his ten-year-old son, Andreas, who wrote in
his diary about finding a way to fight (2) _____ and to keep all the children safe and off   **JUSTICE**
the streets. Just weeks before he passed away, this (3) _____ young boy was invited on   **SELF**
a prominent television show to present his idea. It was (4) _____ to watch this little boy,   **HUMBLE**
diagnosed with cancer himself, with complete (5) _____ to his own problems, speaking   **REGARD**
out with so much passion about the rights of all the children. He ended his (6) _____
speech by saying that "everyone knows about the children in the streets but nobody does   **INSPIRE**
anything about it. It's time to bring a smile to the face of every child."

Today The Smile of the Child is one of the largest charities in Greece and it offers much
needed (7) _____ in a country that has been one of the hardest to be hit by Europe's   **RELIEVE**
(8) _____ measures. It is run mainly by volunteers, who offer their time freely, and   **AUSTERE**
relies (9) _____ on the contribution of the people as well as on the help of several   **SOLE**
(10) _____, to meet its day-to-day expenses.   **BENEFIT**

D Circle the correct word.

1   After several months of unsuccessfully trying to find a job in his country, Jack decided to emigrate / immigrate in the hope of finding a better future elsewhere.

2   Coming from an effluent / affluent background, Kelly couldn't deal with the consequences of the recession.

3   Lara is an avid philanthropist, who has great empathy / sympathy for those suffering around her.

4   I don't understand people who abandon their pets can live with their conscious / conscience.

5   They are planning to picket / mount a rally against the proposed legislation.

6   It is a disgrace that even today people are still prosecuted / persecuted for their religious beliefs.

7   The management of the factory called in the police to disperse / disburse the strikers who were blocking the gates.

8   A democratic government should never oppress / suppress its people.

9   Activists / Advocates of the new tax law claim it will greatly benefit the unemployed.

10 All the political parties condoned / condemned the acts of violence carried out by a small group of protestors in last night's rally, and denied that they had any part in them.

11 The proposed straightened / sustenance programme is expected to offer great relief to the poor.

12 The protesters demanded that the government should abolish / obliterate some of the harsher measures.

3 Grammar

3.1 The Passive Voice

Χρησιμοποιούμε την passive voice (παθητική φωνή) όταν:
η πράξη είναι πιο σημαντική από αυτόν ή αυτό που την κάνει (agent/ποιητικό αίτιο).
→ They **were stopped** at border control.
δεν γνωρίζουμε το ποιητικό αίτιο (agent), ή δεν είναι σημαντικό.
→ The stadium **was vandalised** last night.

Σημείωση: Όταν είναι σημαντικό να αναφέρουμε το ποιητικό αίτιο (agent) στην παθητική πρόταση, χρησιμοποιούμε τη λέξη *by*. Όταν θέλουμε να αναφέρουμε το εργαλείο ή το υλικό με το οποίο έγινε κάτι, χρησιμοποιούμε τη λέξη *with*.
→ The grounds **were patrolled by** a squad of security guards.
→ He **was tied up with** a rope.
Σχηματίζουμε την passive voice με το ρήμα be και past participle (παθητική μετοχή). Προσοχή! Οι ενεργητικοί τύποι του ρήματος (active verbs) μετατρέπονται σε παθητικούς τύπους ρήματος (passive verbs).

Σημείωση: Μερικές φορές μπορούμε να χρησιμοποιήσουμε *get/have* + αντικείμενο + past participle. Αυτή η σύνταξη είναι πιο συνηθισμένη στον προφορικό λόγο.
→ I **got/had** a new alarm **installed** just to be on the safe side.

Tense / Χρόνος	Active / Ενεργητική	Passive / Παθητική
Present Simple	take/takes	am/are/is taken
Present Continuous	am/are/is taking	am/are/is being taken
Past Simple	took	was/were taken
Past Continuous	was/were taking	was/were being taken
Present Perfect Simple	have/has taken	have/has been taken
Past Perfect Simple	had taken	had been taken
Future Simple	will take	will be taken

Μετατρέπουμε μια ενεργητική πρόταση σε παθητική με τον παρακάτω τρόπο:
Το αντικείμενο του ρήματος της ενεργητικής πρότασης γίνεται υποκείμενο του ρήματος της παθητικής πρότασης. Το ρήμα be χρησιμοποιείται στον ίδιο χρόνο με το κύριο ρήμα της ενεργητικής πρότασης, μαζί με την παθητική μετοχή (past participle) του κυρίου ρήματος της ενεργητικής πρότασης.
→ She **was showing** them what to do. They **were being shown** what to do.
Όταν θέλουμε να μετατρέψουμε μια πρόταση με δύο αντικείμενα στην παθητική, τότε το ένα αντικείμενο γίνεται υποκείμενο της παθητικής πρότασης και το άλλο παραμένει αντικείμενο. Επιλέγουμε το υποκείμενο της παθητικής πρότασης ανάλογα με το ποιό θέλουμε να τονίσουμε. Αν το προσωπικό αντικείμενο (personal object) παραμένει αντικείμενο στην παθητική πρόταση, χρησιμοποιούμε και την κατάλληλη πρόθεση (to, for κλπ.).
→ He offered **us** a large **donation**.
→ **We** were offered a large **donation**.
→ A large **donation** was offered to us.

3.2 Passive Voice: Gerunds, Infinitives & Modal Verbs

(Γερούνδια, Απαρέμφατα, Modal Verbs)

Tense / Χρόνος	Active / Ενεργητική	Passive / Παθητική
Gerund / Γερούνδιο	taking	being taken
Bare Infinitive / Απαρέμφατο χωρίς *to*	take	be taken
Full Infinitive / *to* + Απαρέμφατο	to take	to be taken
Modal verb	may take	may be taken

→ He looked forward to **being given** a hot meal.
→ These animal are to **be fed** twice a day.
→ She wanted **to be relocated** to his hometown.
→ The suspect **should be kept** in police custody.

Σημείωση: Κάποια ρήματα έχουν και αντίστοιχο ουσιαστικό που μπορεί να χρησιμοποιηθεί ως υποκείμενο της παθητικής πρότασης με ένα διαφορετικό παθητικό ρήμα.
➔ **They're training** the volunteers this week.
➔ The volunteers **are being trained** this week.
➔ The volunteers' **training will be completed** by the end of this week.

3.3 Reporting with Passive Verbs

Συχνά χρησιμοποιούμε ρήματα όπως *believe, consider, know, expect, say, suppose* και *think* για να αναφέρουμε κάτι στην παθητική φωνή. Μπορούν να χρησιμοποιηθούν με απρόσωπη ή με προσωπική σύνταξη (impersonal or personal structure).
Η απρόσωπη παθητική σύνταξη (impersonal passive structure) σχηματίζεται με *it* + παθητικό ρήμα (passive verb) + *that* + πρόταση.
➔ **It is claimed that** the number of homeless is rising.
Η προσωπική σύνταξη σχηματίζεται με ουσιαστικό + παθητικό ρήμα (passive verb) + απαρέμφατο με *to* (full infinitive).
➔ **Petitions are believed to be** an effective form of protest.

3.4 Transitive and Intransitive Verbs

Τα ρήματα είναι transitive (μεταβατικά) όταν ακολουθούνται από αντικείμενο, και είναι intransitive (αμετάβατα) αν δεν παίρνουν αντικείμενο. Μερικά ρήματα χρησιμοποιούνται ως μεταβατικά και αμετάβατα. Στο παθητικό σχηματισμό, το αντικείμενο του ενεργετικού ρήματος γίνεται το υποκείμενο του παθητικού ρήματος. Επομένως, μόνο τα μεταβατικά ρήματα μπορούν να χρησιμοποιηθούν στον παθητικό τύπο. Τα αμετάβατα ρήματα όπως *die, seem, go, laugh, occur, swim, wait* κλπ. δεν χρησιμοποιούνται στον παθητικό τύπο. Υπάρχουν επίσης κάποια μεταβατικά ρήματα που δεν χρησιμοποιούνται στον παθητικό τύπο: *escape, elude, flee, get, have, like, resemble.*

3.5 Avoiding the passive

Σημείωση: Γενικά, δεν υπάρχει παθητικός τύπος για τους χρόνους Future Continuous, Present Perfect Continuous και Past Perfect Continuous.
Το παράδειγμα: *The petition content **has been being debated** for days.* είναι γραμματικά σωστό, αλλά δεν ακούγεται σωστό. Perfect Continuous τύπους χρησιμοποιούνται μερικές φορές στην παθητική, αλλά πρέπει να τους αποφεύγουμε. Ακούγεται πιο σωστό να πούμε: *The petition content has been **under debate** for days.* Άλλες εκφράσεις που είναι χρήσιμες είναι *under review, under construction, in progress, under suspicion, under scrutiny, under surveillance, under investigation* και *under arrest.*

Στο γραπτό λόγο, συχνά χρησιμοποιούμε ένα ουσιαστικό αντί για τον παθητικό σχηματισμό.
➔ We discussed the possible **construction** of a homeless shelter.
➔ We discussed the possibility of a homeless shelter **being constructed**.

3.6 Passive Causative

Χρησιμοποιούμε causative για να πούμε ότι:
κάποιος έχει αναθέσει μια δουλειά σε κάποιον άλλο.
➔ They **had** all the food parcels **distributed**.
κάτι δυσάρεστο συνέβη σε κάποιον.
➔ We **had** our luggage **stolen** at the airport.
Σχηματίζουμε την causative με το ρήμα *have* + αντικείμενο + past participle (παθητική μετοχή). Μπορεί να χρησιμοποιηθεί σε πολλούς χρόνους. Όταν θέλουμε να αναφέρουμε το ποιητικό αίτιο (agent), χρησιμοποιούμε τη λέξη *by*.
➔ They **had** a new shelter **constructed**.
➔ We **used to have** food **delivered** every day.
➔ I'm **having** all my correspondence **checked by** a volunteer.
Μπορούμε να χρησιμοποιήσουμε *get* + αντικείμενο + past participle. Αυτή η σύνταξη είναι είναι λιγότερη επίσημη.
➔ They **got** the dogs **vaccinated** yesterday.
Μπορούμε να χρησιμοποιήσουμε *get somebody to do something* και *have somebody do something* όταν βάζουμε κάποιον άλλον να κάνει κάτι.
➔ He **got** the helpers **to hand out** the food.

3 Grammar

➜ *He **had** the helpers **hand out** the food.*
Χρησιμοποιούμε *get something done* με την έννοια ότι τελειώσαμε κάτι.
➜ *He **got** all the leaflets **sent out**.*
Χρησιμοποιούμε *have something/somebody doing* με την έννοια ότι κάνουμε κάτι ή κάποιον να ξεκινήσει κάτι.
➜ *The rumours of a price rise **had** everyone **running** to fill their tanks.*
Μπορούμε να σχηματίσουμε και άλλους passive causative τύπους χρησιμοποιώντας *need/prefer/want/would like* + αντικείμενο + past ή present participle (παθητική ή ενεργητική μετοχή).
➜ *He **wants** the notes to be **written** today.*
➜ *We **prefer** the alarm to be **installed** soon.*
➜ *I **need** the packages (to be) **labelled**, please.*
➜ *The printer **needs servicing** so I'll call the technician today.*

Grammar Exercises

A Circle the correct words.

1 While dinner was cooked / was being cooked at the soup kitchen, some volunteers helped out with other tasks.

2 As the government seems to be unable to address the issue, a few NGOs have called / have been called in.

3 No provisions have been making / have been made for those left destitute after the disaster.

4 This token can redeem / be redeemed at any of the local branches of the restaurant chain.

5 Having been persecuted / Being persecuted for their beliefs in the past, the inhabitants of the village were very cautious with the strangers.

6 She gave / was given a petition to sign.

7 Any protesters breaking the law will arrest / will be arrested instantly.

8 He was believed to escape / have escaped after the war.

9 The opposition party leader disappeared / was disappeared one day before the elections.

10 We ran into several difficulties / Several difficulties were run into by us during the implementation of the project.

B Complete the sentences with the verbs in brackets. Use the correct form of the passive voice.

1 At this pace, not much progress _____ (make) by the end of the month.

2 The government is alleged _____ (consider) stricter measures against demonstrators.

3 Several activists may _____ (injure) in the clashes with the police, but the news is contradictory.

4 In order for the dam to _____ (build), the inhabitants of entire villages will have to be relocated.

5 We have been assured that all our needs _____ (meet) in a few days' time.

6 The refugees _____ (welcome) into the country and _____ (give) all the support they needed.

7 After _____ (catch) red-handed, the criminal was placed under police custody.

8 The school _____ (accuse) of being prejudiced against immigrant children and a number of parents are protesting against its policies.

9 Many people are believed _____ (leave) homeless after the earthquake.

10 Indigenous people in the Amazon _____ (marginalise) even as we speak. We must act immediately!

C Choose the correct answers.

1 It was thought ___ good interpersonal skills.
   a that the leader should have   b the leader to have had   c to have the leader
   d that should have the leader

2 The manager ___ out the letters.
   a had his secretary type   b had typed   c had his secretary typed   d had his secretary to type

3 Pauline is expected ___ the career ladder quite fast.
   a that she'll climb   b will climb   c to climb   d that she should climb

4 Don't forget to ___.

   a have renewed your passport   **b** renewed your passport   **c** get renewed your passport
   d get your passport renewed

5 She asked for the report ___ before the arrival of the managing director.

   a to get complete   **b** to be completed   **c** to have completed   **d** completed

6 Maria got all her friends ___ in the demonstration against animal cruelty.

   a take   **b** taken   **c** taking   **d** to take part

7 We ___ closer to the location of the disaster.

   a are getting moved our headquarters   **b** are moving our headquarters
   c are having our headquarters moved   **d** are getting our headquarters to move

8 The money ___ before the end of the month.

   a had better pay   **b** had better be paid   **c** had better been paid   **d** had better to be paid

9 Volunteers in animal welfare organisations ___ suffer from depression at times.

   a believe they   **b** it is believed they   **c** are believed to   **d** are believed that they

10 Food rescue organisations ___ to those who need it.

   a get food to redistribute   **b** have to redistribute food   **c** get food redistributing
   d have food redistributed

D Rewrite the sentences starting with the words given.

1 It was thought that the celebrity endorsement would help the cause.

The celebrity endorsement _____.

2 The NGO have been constructing a new bridge to connect the remote village to the nearest town.

A bridge connecting the remote village _____.

3 All the windows of the soup kitchen have been vandalised.

The soup kitchen _____.

4 We are asking all our volunteers to help us replace the windows.

We are having _____.

5 The government have been discussing the abolition of the outdated and unfair law for some time now.

The abolition of the outdated and unfair law _____.

6 Thieves broke into our offices last week.

We _____.

7 He's very popular and he managed to persuade everyone to sign the petition.

He's very popular and he's _____.

8 The food needs to be sorted out into perishables and non-perishables.

We need the food _____.

3 Grammar

For questions **1–8**, read the text below. Use the word given in capitals at the end of some of the lines to form a word that fits in the space in the same line.

Dystopia

Most sci-fi films describe (**1**) _____, dystopian futures for humankind, but I'm afraid we already live there. The human population is constantly increasing (**2**) _____ and uncontrolled, drawing on our ever-diminishing resources. There's a (**3**) _____ gap between the wealthy minority and the overwhelmingly (**4**) _____ majority on the planet, making the effort to bridge the rift an (**5**) _____.

PLEASE
CHECK
WIDE
PRIVILEGE
POSSIBLE

Extreme poverty brings along a resounding lack of human rights and (**6**) _____, as it's painfully obvious that the legal systems everywhere on the planet are designed to benefit the affluent rather than ensure a fair trial to all.

JUST

To make matters worse, the only tool which could help to ameliorate the situation, education, is (**7**) _____ to those who need it most; the millions of (**8**) _____ people in developing countries.

AVAILABLE
POVERTY

54

4 Express Yourself

Reading
pages 50-51

4.1 branding (n) /'brændɪŋ/
promoting an attractive name and an image
for a product or service to attract customers
• *Clever branding should attract customers
without pushy marketing techniques.* ➤ brand
(v), brand (n) ❖ branding, πρωωθώ ένα όνομα
και μία εικόνα για ένα προϊόν

4.2 host (n)) /həʊst/
a large number of things/people • *Our website
features a host of electronic goods at down-to-
earth prices.* ➤ host (v) ❖ πλήθος

4.3 goatherd (n) /'gəʊthɜːd/
sb whose job it is to look after a herd of goats
• *Alex dreams of living a simple life as a
goatherd tending his herd in the mountains.*
❖ βοσκός, αιγοβοσκός

4.4 conceivably (adv) /kən'siːvəbli/
imaginably; seemingly possible • *It was
conceivably the worst film I've ever seen.*
➤ conceive (v), conceivable (adj) ❖ πιθανώς

4.5 mind-boggling (adj) /maɪnd 'bɒglɪŋ/
very surprising; hard to imagine • *Using
clever hashtags, Sharon has collected a mind-
boggling number of followers on social media.*
❖ ασύλληπτος

4.6 entertain (v) /ˌentə'teɪn/
consider • *Until a few years ago, most
people would never entertain the thought of
'chatting' to strangers online.* ➤ entertainer (n),
entertaining (adj) ❖ διανοούμαι

4.7 lay the foundation for (expr) /leɪ ðə
faʊn'deɪʃn fɔː(r)/
create the ideas and basic structures to
develop a larger initiative • *Ancient Greeks
laid the foundations for democracy.* ❖ βάζω τις
βάσεις, θεμελιώνω

4.8 empirical (adj) /ɪm'pɪrɪkl/
based on observations or experience • *Only
through accurate and qualitative research
can scientists collect empirical data to prove
or disprove a theory.* ➤ empiricism (n),
empirically (adv) ❖ εμπειρικός

4.9 randomly (adv) /'rændəmli/
by chance; in no special order • *The practice
of randomly targeting potential clients by
phone must be the most annoying form of
marketing.* ➤ random (adj) ❖ τυχαία

4.10 popularise (v) /'pɒpjələraɪz/
make sth popular • *The interactive exhibition
was designed to popularise museums by using
state-of-the-art technology.* ➤ popularity (n),
popular (adj) ❖ καθιστώ δημοφιλές

4.11 parlour game (n) /'paːlə(r) geɪm/
a word game or miming game, etc. played at
home • *It's fun to put away the tablets and
have an evening playing parlour games with
friends occasionally.* ❖ επιτραπέζιο παιχνίδι
κυρίως με λέξεις ή παντομίμα

4.12 precursor (n) /priː'kɜːsə(r)/
sth/sb that preceded sth/sb else and affects its
progress • *The teachings of Pythagoras were
a precursor to European culture.* ❖ πρόδρομος

4.13 to all intents and purposes (expr) /tə ɔːl
ɪn'tents ənd 'pɜːpəsiz/
more or less; almost entirely • *Like it or not,
Facebook has become, to all intents and
purposes, a major communication platform.*
❖ ουσιαστικά

4.14 applicable (adj) /ə'plɪkəbl/
that applies to or affects sb/sth; relevant (to
sb/sth) • *Despite being applicable to all public
places, the non-smoking laws seem to be
ignored in many cafes and restaurants.*
➤ apply (v), application (n), applicant (n)
❖ εφαρμόσιμος

4.15 elaborate (v) /ɪ'læbəreɪt/
expand on a point by going into details • *Tania
simply announced her resignation and refused
to elaborate on her reasons.* ➤ elaboration (n),
elaborate (adj), elaborately (adv) ❖ αναλύω,
επεξεργάζομαι

4.16 inherent (adj) /ɪn'hɪərənt/
that is an intrinsic part of sth, therefore can't
be taken out of it • *Politeness was an inherent
part of Robert's upbringing.* ➤ inhere (v),
inherently (adv) ❖ έμφυτος

4.17 mentality (n) /men'tæləti/
the general way of thinking of an individual or
group • *I was utterly appalled at the mentality
of the villagers regarding animals.* ➤ mental
(adj), mentally (adv) ❖ νοοτροπία

4.18 intrigued (adj) /ɪn'triːgd/
so interested that you want to find out more
about sth • *I was intrigued to know how
Francis had set up his website so quickly.*
➤ intrigue (v), intrigue (n), intriguing (adj),
intriguingly (adv) ❖ περίεργος να μάθω

4.19 commodity (n) /kə'mɒdəti/
sth that is produced for sale • *How can we
put a price on our time when it's our most
irreplaceable commodity?* ❖ αγαθό

4.20 cheerily (adv) /'tʃɪərili/
happily; in a cheerful way • *Smiling cheerily,
Paul announced that he was dropping out
of university to travel the world.* ➤ cheer (v),
cheer (n), cheery (adj) ❖ χαρωπά

4.21 **connectedness** (n) /kəˈnektɪdnəs/
the sense of having a connection with others
and being a part of a group • *Social media
may offer a sense of connectedness to
people living in remote areas.* ➢ connect (v),
connection (n) ❖ διασύνδεση

4.22 **dissimilar** (adj) /dɪˈsɪmɪlə(r)/
not similiar • *Katie was finding it hard to settle
down in China as the culture was so dissimilar
to that of Wales.* ➢ dissimilarity (n) ❖ ανόμοιος
✎ Opp: similar ❖ παρόμοιος

4.23 **transmittable** (adj) /trænzˈmɪtəˌbəl/
that can be passed on or transmitted from
sb/sth to sb/sth else • *The common cold is
caused by highly transmittable infections.*
➢ transmit (v), transmission (n) ❖ μεταδόσιμος

4.24 **intrinsic** (adj) /ɪnˈtrɪnsɪk/
that is a basic part of sth/sb which can't be
taken out • *Email has become an intrinsic part
of business communications.* ➢ intrinsically
(adv) ❖ αναπόσπαστος, εγγενής

4.25 **essence** (n) /ˈesns/
the important basic quality central to what
or how sth is • *In essence, people not using
social media find it increasingly difficult to stay
informed about certain events.* ➢ essential
(adj), essentially (adv) ❖ ουσία

Vocabulary   pages 52-53-54

4.26 **kin** (n) /kɪn/
people you are related to; family members
• *Police are trying to trace the victim's next of
kin.* ➢ kinship (n), kindred (adj) ❖ συγγενείς

4.27 **board** (n) /bɔːd/
an official decision-making group in a company
or organisation • *The staffing cuts will be
discussed at the next meeting of the board of
directors.* ❖ επιτροπή

4.28 **cabinet** (n) /ˈkæbɪnət/
a team of members of parliament chosen to
make decisions on policy • *The Prime Minister
is meeting with the cabinet ministers to discuss
tax reforms.* ❖ υπουργικό συμβούλιο

4.29 **faction** (n) /ˈfækʃn/
a small part of a group whose beliefs or aims
differ from those of the wider group • *Trouble
broke out between rival factions in the stadium
after the match.* ➢ factional (adj) ❖ φατρία

4.30 **lobby** (n) /ˈlɒbi/
a pressure group who try to influence decision
makers on a particular issue • *Community
groups organised a lobby against the closure
of the local school.* ➢ lobby (v), lobbyist (n)
❖ λόμπυ

4.31 **brigade** (n) /brɪˈɡeɪd/
a group of people who share a common
opinion; a unit of soldiers in an army
• *Desmond finally gave up cigarettes under
pressure from the anti-smoking brigade at
work.* ❖ σώμα, ταξιαρχία

4.32 **entourage** (n) /ˈɒntuɑːʒ/
a group of people who travel with or follow an
important person • *The actor entered the hotel
surrounded by his entourage of security staff.*
❖ συνοδεία

4.33 **fraternity** (n) /frəˈtɜːnəti /
a close-knit group formed around a particular
ideal or shared experience • *Dramatic
fluctuations in currency rates have raised
concerns among the banking fraternity.*
❖ αδελφότητα

4.34 **squad** (n) /skwɒd/
a group of police or soldiers working together
on a specific task; a large group of players
from which a team is selected • *The rowdy
demonstrators were turned back by the riot
squad.* ❖ διμοιρία

4.35 **cartel** (n) /kɑːˈtel/
a group of companies who agree to price fixing
to maximise profits • *The dairy cartel has
ensured that milk prices are much the same
across all the supermarkets.* ❖ καρτέλ

4.36 **syndicate** (n) /ˈsɪndɪkət/
a group of companies or people who work
together towards a particular objective • *The
politician had links with the largest crime
syndicate in Mexico.* ❖ συνδικάτο, συντεχνία

4.37 **union** (n) /ˈjuːniən/
an organisation established to protect workers
needs and negotiate improved conditions
• *Flights were delayed due to a strike by the
baggage handlers' union.* ➢ unite (v), unify (v),
unionise (v), unionisation (n) ❖ συντεχνιακή
ένωση

4.38 **dynasty** (n) /ˈdɪnəsti/
a long line of rulers from the same family
group • *The Tudor dynasty ruled England for
centuries.* ➢ dynastic (adj) ❖ δυναστεία

4.39 **platoon** (n) /pləˈtuːn/
a small group of 10-12 soldiers that is part of a
larger group • *Two platoons advanced on the
enemy camp in the middle of the night.*
❖ διμοιρία

4.40 **diaspora** (n) /daɪˈæspərə/
the movement of people from one ethnic group
to another country • *The annual Notting Hill
festival brings out the music and spirit of the
Jamaican diaspora.* ❖ διασπορά

4.41 **horde** (n) /hɔːd/
a huge crowd of people • *Miltiades gave
the command to charge upon the horde
of Persians advancing across the plain of
Marathon.* ❖ ορδή, πλήθος

4.42 troupe (n) /truːp/
a team of performers • *The troupe of acrobats gave a breathtaking performance.* ➣ trouper (n) ❖ θίασος

4.43 posse (n) /ˈpɒsi/
a small group of people with a similar purpose or interest • *Eagerly awaiting the star's arrival, a small posse of photographers stood outside the theatre.* ❖ ομάδα, απόσπασμα

4.44 throng (n) /θrɒŋ/
a large crowd • *Throngs of people lined the streets to watch the parade.* ➣ throng (v) ❖ πλήθος

Groups

brigade	faction	posse
cabinet	fraternity	squad
cartel	horde	syndicate
cluster	host	throng
diaspora	kin	troupe
dynasty	lobby	union
entourage	platoon	

4.45 be thick as thieves (expr) /bi θɪk əz θiːvz/
be extremely friendly with each other, often in a conspiratorial way • *Beth and Judy are thick as thieves; anything you say to one always gets back to the other.* ❖ αχώριστοι, κολλητοί

4.46 get along famously (expr) /get əˈlɒŋ ˈfeɪməsli/
have a very good relationship • *Though a little worried about meeting her new colleagues, Christine got on famously with them from the first day.* ❖ τα πάω με κάποιον περίφημα

4.47 have a nodding acquaintance with sb (expr) /həv ə ˈnɒdɪŋ əˈkweɪntəns wɪθ ˈsʌmbədi/
know sb very casually and not closely • *We have a nodding acquaintance with most of our neighbours, but only know a few of them by name.* ❖ γνωρίζω φατσικά, εξ όψεως

4.48 one-sided (adj) /wʌn ˈsaɪˌdɪd/
that only involves or benefits one person • *The match was entirely one-sided as United had no chance of winning with two players sent off in the first half.* ❖ μονομερής

4.49 avatar (n) /ˈævətɑː(r)/
an image of a person of animal, etc. that represents a user on a website or game • *Vicky uses a photo of her favourite pet as an avatar on social media.* ❖ άβαταρ

4.50 bio (n) /ˈbaɪəʊ/
a record of your qualifications and work experience; a CV • *Colin had sent copies of his bio to over 20 companies before he received even one job offer.* ❖ βιογραφικό σημείωμα

4.51 clickbait (n) /ˈklɪkbeɪt/
images and words, etc. on the internet which attract users to open links to particular sites • *It may be hard to ignore those cute kitty videos, but most of them are purely clickbait from advertisers.* ❖ 'παγίδες' στο ίντερνετ που προκαλούν μεγαλύτερη επισκεψιμότητα σε ιστιοσελίδες

4.52 crowdfunding (n) /ˈkraʊdfʌndɪŋ/
the act of raising money for a project by attracting large numbers of small donations, usually through social media sites • *Valerie used crowdfunding to pay for her awareness-raising documentary about the children's home.* ➣ crowdfund (v) ❖ crowdfunding, χρηματοδότηση μέσω μεγάλου αριθμού μικρών συνεισφορών, κυρίως με χρήση μέσων κοινωνικής δικτύωσης

4.53 emoticon (n) /ɪˈməʊtɪkɒn/
a set of symbols used in text messages to represent a facial expression or feeling • *It is inadvisable to include smileys and other emoticons in a business email.* ❖ εικονίδια χρησιμοποιούμενα για την αναπαράσταση συναισθημάτων σε γραπτά μηνύματα

4.54 meme (n) /miːm/
an image or saying that is transmitted quickly on internet and adapted to various situations to make it funny • *While some memes can be funny, most tend to lack originality, so I usually delete them – and never share such trivia!* ❖ meme

4.55 tag (v) /tæg/
add a link with a user's name to a photo on social media • *Kindly ask my permission before tagging me on a photo next time; my friends thought I was in Rome with you.* ➣ tag (n) ❖ βάζω ετικέτα, tag

4.56 trend (v) /trend/
be a popular subject of discussion currently on social media • *Though her family have requested privacy, the singer's death is currently trending on social media.* ➣ trend (n), trendy (adj) ❖ γίνομαι δημοφιλής, trend

4.57 analogy (n) /əˈnælədʒi/
a comparison of sth with sth else that is similar to give an example • *Our biology teacher drew an analogy between the human body and a machine.* ➣ analogous (adj) ❖ αναλογία

4.58 contradict (v) /ˌkɒntrəˈdɪkt/
say sth that is the opposite of what has been said to correct sb or show disagreement • *It was obvious they were about to break up when they were constantly contradicting each other.* ➣ contradiction (n), contradictory (adj) ❖ έρχομαι σε αντίθεση

4.59 **detract from sth** (phr v) /dɪˈtrækt frəm ˈsʌmθɪŋ/
take away from the enjoyment of sth ● *The unsightly forest of wind turbines detracted from the beauty of the island.* ➤ detractor (n)
❖ μειώνω, αφαιρώ

4.60 **diversify** (v) /daɪˈvɜːsɪfaɪ/
begin to include a wider range of things to become more varied ● *The lifestyle of the islanders has diversified over the year through the influence of foreign tourists.* ➤ diversity (n), diversification (n), diverse (adj), diversely (adv) ❖ διαφοροποιούμαι

4.61 **homogenize** (v) /həˈmɒdʒənaɪz/
change sth so that all its features blend and become similar ● *The spread of chain stores has homogenized shopping centres across the UK so they are almost all identical.* ➤ homogenization (n), homegeneity (n), homogenous (adj), homogenized (adj)
❖ ομογενοποιώ

4.62 **proximate** (adj) /ˈprɒksɪmət/
closest in distance or time ● *Brake failure was the proximate cause of the accident.*
➤ proximity (n) ❖ άμεσος, εγγύτατος

4.63 **shrinkage** (n) /ˈʃrɪŋkɪdʒ/
the process of getting smaller; the extent to which sth reduces in size ● *Due to shrinkage in the wash, my new sweater was too small to wear.* ➤ shrink (v), shrunken (adj), shrinking (adj) ❖ συρρίκνωση, συστολή

4.64 **telecommunications** (n) /ˌtelikəˌmjuːnɪˈkeɪʃnz/
the communications between people using technological means ● *Advances in telecommunications have meant that we can now get in touch with people almost anywhere at anytime.* ❖ τηλεπικοινωνίες

4.65 **globalisation** (n) /ˌgləʊbəlaɪˈzeɪʃn/
the worldwide spread of trade and production of the same goods and services in many countries ● *Traditional craftsmen blame the increase in globalisation for their loss of business.* ➤ globalise (v), global (adj), globally (adv) ❖ παγκοσμιοποίηση

4.66 **connectivity** (n) /ˌkɒnekˈtɪvɪti/
the state of being connected ● *Before you buy that country house, check the internet connectivity in the area.* ➤ connect (v), connection (n) ❖ σύνδεση

4.67 **get hold of sb** (expr) /get həʊld əvˈsʌmbədi/
manage to contact sb ● *I couldn't get hold of Nigel this morning; he was in meetings for hours.* ❖ έρχομαι σε επαφή

4.68 **in the loop** (expr) /ɪn ðə luːp/
involved in a group dealing with or sharing information about a particular issue ● *Peter attends all the board meetings so he keeps in the loop with management decisions.* ❖ μένω ενήμερος
✎ Opp: out of the loop ❖ ανενημέρωτος

4.69 **touch base (with sb)** (expr) /tʌtʃ baɪs wɪθˈsʌmbədi/
make contact with sb, often after being out of touch ● *David hadn't heard from his brother in months, so he decided to phone to touch base with him.* ❖ έρχομαι σε επαφή

4.70 **disassemble** (v) /ˌdɪsəˈsembl/
take sth to pieces; spread apart in different directions ● *The technician disassembled the laptop to pinpoint the problem.*
➤ disassembler (n) ❖ αποσυναρμολογώ

4.71 **deactivate** (v) /ˌdiːˈæktɪveɪt/
cause sth to stop functioning ● *If you use the incorrect PIN number too often, the bank will deactivate your card.* ➤ deactivation (n)
❖ απενεργοποιώ

4.72 **discontinue** (v) /ˌdɪskənˈtɪnjuː/
stop manufacturing a product; stop doing sth
● *Sales of the phone have been discontinued following vast numbers of customer complaints.* ➤ discontinuity (n), discontinuous (adj) ❖ διακόπτω

4.73 **caption** (n) /ˈkæpʃn/
words written on or below an image ● *Cynthia always inserts hilarious captions on her Instagram photos.* ➤ caption (v) ❖ λεζάντα

4.74 **communal** (adj) /kəˈmjuːnl/
shared by a number of people ● *As a student, Anita rented a room in a flat and shared a communal kitchen and bathroom.*
➤ communalism (n), communally (adv)
❖ κοινόχρηστος

4.75 **cultivate** (v) /ˈkʌltɪveɪt/
develop sth, such as support, friendship, etc.
● *We aim to cultivate loyalty and trust with our clients.* ➤ cultivation (n), cultivated (adj)
❖ καλλιεργώ

4.76 **nourish** (v) /ˈnʌrɪʃ/
help sth to grow or develop; keep sth/sb alive and healthy by feeding them ● *Face-to-face communications beats virtual contact when it comes to nourishing a relationship.*
➤ nourishment (n), nourishing (adj) ❖ τρέφω

4.77 **comrade** (n) /ˈkɒmreɪd/
sb that you serve together with in a military group or fellow member of a socialist or communist party ● *Granddad gets together with his old army comrades every year on Remembrance Day.* ➤ comradeship (n), comradely (adj) ❖ σύντροφος

4.78 **confidant** (n) /'kɒnfɪdænt/
sb that you trust with your personal secrets
• *Robert has been my closest friend and confidant for years.* ➢ confide (v) ❖ έμπιστος φίλος
✎ Also: confidante

4.79 **confederate** (n) /kənˈfedərət/
sb who helps or conspires with sb to do sth
• *Police have arrested one of the terrorists, but his confederates are still at large.*
➢ confederate (adj) ❖ σύμμαχος

4.80 **counsellor** (n) /'kaʊnsələ(r)/
sb who offers specialist advice to others
• *Meg and Tom sought the advice of a guidance counsellor in an effort to save their marriage.* ➢ counsel (v), counselling (n)
❖ σύμβουλος

4.81 **overhaul** (n) /'əʊvəhɔːl/
a review of a system to assess and repair or change it • *Our country's education system is outmoded and needs a complete overhaul.*
➢ overhaul (v) ❖ επανασυγκρότηση

4.82 **infrastructure** (n) /'ɪnfrəstrʌktʃə(r)/
the basic networks, such as roads, power, water supply, hospitals, schools, etc. that help a country or organisation function • *The complex infrastructure of the multi-national giant means that any new plans take months to implement.* ➢ infrastructural (adj)
❖ υποδομή

4.83 **framework** (n) /'freɪmwɜːk/
the basic ideas or structure that a system is built around • *Discussions are underway regarding the legal framework for environmental protection.* ❖ πλαίσιο, σκελετός

4.84 **underpinning** (n) /ˌʌndəˈpɪnɪŋ/
sth that supports the basis of an idea or building • *Though I disagree with him, the underpinnings of his theory are quite logical.*
➢ underpin (v) ❖ βάση

Expressions

be thick as thieves
get along famously
get hold of sb
going forward
have a nodding acquaintance with sb
in the loop
lay the foundation for
to all intents and purposes
touch base (with sb)

Grammar pages 55-56-57

4.85 **viral** (adj) /'vaɪrəl/
that is spread rapidly over the internet • *News of the bombing went viral within minutes on Twitter.* ❖ που διαδίδεται γρήγορα μέσω του διαδικτύου, viral

4.86 **small talk** (n) /smɔːl tɔːk/
polite conversation about trivial everyday subjects • *After half an hour of small talk, Stan realised he had very little common with his new colleague.* ❖ ψιλοκουβέντα

4.87 **trolling** (n) /trɒlˌɪŋ/
writing offensive or annoying messages on an online discussion • *She was quite upset by the trolling attack that followed her objective comment on Facebook.* ➢ troll (v), troll (n)
❖ τρολάρισμα

4.88 **far-reaching** (adj) /fɑː ˈriːtʃˌɪŋ/
with long-term consequences • *Mass immigration of people from different cultures will have far-reaching consequences for our society.* ❖ εκτεταμένος

4.89 **embrace** (v) /ɪmˈbreɪs/
include within sth • *'Copyright' embraces legal rights related to books, films, plays and music.*
➢ embrace (n) ❖ περιλαμβάνω, περικλείω

4.90 **formative** (adj) /'fɔːmətɪv/
affecting the development of sth • *Oliver spent his formative years in an orphanage.*
➢ form (v), formation (n) ❖ διαμορφωτικός, διαπλαστικός

4.91 **monocultural** (adj) /ˌmɒnəˈkʌltʃərəl/
having only a single belief system, way of life, etc. • *Having never left her hometown in Ireland, Siobhan had a completely monocultural upbringing.* ➢ monoculture (n)
❖ μονο-πολιτισμικός

Networking: nouns

attention-seeking	framework
avatar	globalisation
bio	infrastructure
branding	medium
caption	meme
clickbait	mentality
commodity	newsfeed
confederate	norm
confidant	overhaul
connectedness	small talk
connectivity	telecommunications
counsellor	trolling
crowdfunding	underpinning
emoticon	vehicle
encounter	

Listening

4.92 **notoriously** (adv) /nəʊˈtɔːriəsli/
well-known for negative reasons • *My internet
provider is notoriously unreliable.* ➢ notoriety
(n), notorious (adj) ❖ εμφανώς (με αρνητική
έννοια)

4.93 **incidentally** (adv) /ˌɪnsɪˈdentli/
by the way; used to add extra information
in passing • *Incidentally, I notice we have
a common acquaintance in Canada on
Facebook.* ➢ incidental (adj) ❖ τυχαία,
παρεμπιπτόντως

4.94 **non-verbal** (adj) /nɒn ˈvɜːbl/
without spoken words • *You can often tell if
someone is lying by their non-verbal signals.*
❖ μη-λεκτικός

Adverbs

cheerily	notoriously
conceivably	randomly
incidentally	

Writing

4.95 **blatant** (adj) /ˈbleɪtnt/
frank and open, without regard to what others
feel or think • *He made a blatant attempt to
win the boss's favour.* ➢ blatantly (adv)
❖ κραυγαλέος

4.96 **attention-seeking** (n) /əˈtenʃn ˈsiːkˌɪŋ/
doing sth in order to receive recognition from
others • *Constantly posting new selfies is the
most irritating form of attention-seeking.*
❖ επιδίωξη προσοχής

4.97 **medium** (n) /ˈmiːdiəm/
way or means of expressing sth • *Television
is rapidly becoming the least credible news
medium.* ❖ μέσον
✎ Plural: media

4.98 **vehicle** (n) /ˈviːəkl/
means of achieving or expressing sth
• *Clever memes are used as a vehicle to
attract potential customers to her online shop.*
❖ μέσο (έκφρασης)

4.99 **bombard** (v) /bɒmˈbaːd/
give large amounts of sth at once • *The
moment she signed the online petition she was
bombarded by spam emails.* ➢ bombardment
(n) ❖ βομβαρδίζω

4.100 **newsfeed** (n) /ˈnjuːz ˌfiːd/
a constant updating list of stories, comments,
photos, etc. on social media sites • *I had to
block notifications from my daily newsfeed as
there was too much repetition of information to
bother with.* ❖ ροή ειδήσεων

4.101 **self-absorbed** (adj) /self əbˈzɔːbd/
only interested in yourself • *The morning train
was filled with self-absorbed commuters wired
up to their personal listening devices.*
➢ self-absorption (n) ❖ απορροφημένος στις
σκέψεις του

4.102 **narcissistic** (adj) /ˌnaːsɪˈsɪstɪk/
being too preoccupied with admiring your
own appearance • *The band's performance
would have been fantastic were it not for the
overacting of the narcissistic lead singer.*
➢ narcissism (n), narcissist (n)
❖ ναρκισσιστικός

4.103 **inflated** (adj) /ɪnˈfleɪtɪd/
exaggerated; made to seem more important
than is really the case • *Ivan has an inflated
view of his own importance, but is no better
than any other group member.* ➢ inflate (v),
inflation (n) ❖ παραφουσκωμένος

4.104 **norm** (n) /nɔːm/
usual or accepted standard of behaviour
• *Multicultural classrooms are becoming
the norm in some societies.* ➢ normality (n),
normal (adj), normally (adv) ❖ το σύνηθες, η
νόρμα

4.105 **shudder** (v) /ˈʃʌdə(r)/
shake because of a strong feeling • *Nick
shuddered at the thought of the amount of
work he still had to do.* ➢ shudder (n)
❖ τρέμω, ανατριχιάζω

4.106 **skew** (v) /skjuː/
cause sth to change so that it becomes
distorted or wrong • *The journalist skewed the
witness's account of the incident so that it bore
no resemblance to what had happened.*
❖ διαστρεβλώνω

4.107 **colloquial** (adj) /kəˈləʊkwiəl/
slang way of speaking, common to a local
area • *Visitors to Newcastle often have
problems understanding the colloquial slang
which differs widely from that of its Scottish
neighbours.* ➢ colloquialism (n) ❖ λαϊκός, της
καθομιλουμένης

4.108 **emotive** (adj) /iˈməʊtɪv/
full of or inspiring emotion • *He wrote an
emotive account of his ordeal.* ➢ emotion (n),
emotional (adj), emotionless (adj), emotionally
(adv) ❖ υποβλητικός

4.109 **going forward** (expr) /ˈgəʊɪŋ ˈfɔːwəd/
as from now; looking ahead • *Going forward,
we expect a gradual improvement in the
company's performance.* ❖ στο μέλλον,
κοιτώντας μπροστά

Verbs

bombard	embrace
contradict	entertain
cultivate	homogenize
deactivate	nourish
detract from sth	popularise
disassemble	shudder
discontinue	skew
diversify	tag
elaborate	trend

Video 4: Elephant Alert

page 62

4.110 alert (n) /ə'lɜːt/
a warning signal of impending danger
● *Smelling smoke when he woke up, the farmer raised the alert and called the fire brigade.* ➢ alert (v), alertness (n), alert (adj)
❖ συναγερμός

4.111 encounter (n) /ɪn'kaʊntə(r)/
an unexpected meeting ● *I'll never forget my first encounter with a snake; it was more scared than I was and disappeared fast.*
➢ encounter (v) ❖ απρόσμενη συνάντηση

4.112 cluster (n) /'klʌstə(r)/
a small group of similar things or people in one place ● *A cluster of local children were feeding the elephants bathe.* ➢ cluster (v)
❖ ομάδα

4.113 plantation (n) /plɑːn'teɪʃn/
a large field where a particular crop is grown
● *Travelling through Nepal, we saw vast tea plantations on the hillsides.* ➢ plant (v), planter (n) ❖ φυτεία

4.114 bulk (n) /bʌlk/
a large number or amount of similar things; size or quantity of sth ● *The bulk of demand for their products comes from northern Europe.* ➢ bulky (adj) ❖ ο κύριος όγκος

4.115 cautious (adj) /'kɔːʃəs/
careful not to take risks ● *We kept a cautious eye on the weather forecast before setting off on our hiking trip.* ➢ caution (v), caution (n), cautiously (adv) ❖ προσεκτικός

4.116 primary (adj) /'praɪməri/
basic; main ● *Their primary concern was how to keep the animals out of danger.* ➢ primarily (adv) ❖ πρωταρχικός

4.117 vicinity (n) /və'sɪnəti/
the surrounding area ● *There was no phone signal in the vicinity, so we walked for miles to find help.* ❖ στην περιοχή

Adjectives

applicable	intrigued
blatant	intrinsic
cautious	mind-boggling
colloquial	monocultural
communal	narcissistic
dissimilar	non-verbal
emotive	one-sided
empirical	primary
far-reaching	proximate
formative	self-absorbed
inflated	transmittable
inherent	viral

Vocabulary Exercises

A Complete the sentences with the words.

> communal connectedness contradict cultivating embraced
> entourage foundation commodity underpin viral

1 At university students can pool their _____ resources in order to facilitate sharing access to information concerning research data or projects.

2 While bloggers can use the internet as a platform to air their views democratically; readers should be aware of ideological beliefs expressed that may _____ their own subjective views.

3 Self-absorbed people tend to seek out websites that _____ their own narcissistic views or lifestyles.

4 When millions of users express their likes or dislikes concerning views that are trending online, simultaneously linking chains of acquaintances, the information goes _____.

5 Frequent users of social networking sites are sometimes oblivious of the fact that their data is exploited as a _____ by companies in order to generate revenues for corporations.

6 Political and business leaders are frequently accompanied by a(n) _____ of advisors to promote trade and collaboration with their counterparts overseas.

7 Once local residents develop a sense of initiative to actively include marginalised minority groups in community projects, this will lay the _____ for an inherent change in social attitudes.

8 Many young people play strategic problem-solving types of interactive games which intrigue and stimulate creative thinking as well as a sense of _____ with like-minded team players.

9 Online professional networking sites can bring together people with varied sets of skills and experience, thereby _____ an innovative work culture.

10 Young unemployed graduates have _____ crowdfunding as a source of finance to enable their start-up companies to get off the ground.

B Match the words with the definitions.

1 avatar ☐
2 bio ☐
3 crowdfunding ☐
4 clickbait ☐
5 emoticon ☐
6 meme ☐
7 norm ☐
8 branding ☐

a an image or saying that is transmitted quickly on the internet and adapted to various situations to make it funny

b the act of raising money for a project by attracting large numbers of small donations through social media

c an image of a person of animal, etc. that represents a user on a website or game

d a record of your qualifications and work experience; a CV

e images and words, etc. which attract users to open links to particular sites

f promoting a name and image for a product or service to attract customers

g a set of symbols used in text messages to represent a facial expression or feeling

h usual or accepted standard of behaviour

C Complete the sentences with words from B.

1 The advent of the smartphone was a striking departure from the _____ of basic telephony.

2 Celebrities often display an appealing _____ on their online profile which depicts their best features.

3 Young entrepreneurs often utilise _____ websites to secure enough investment for their start-up companies.

4 _____ have become a widespread phenomenon of the online landscape as more and more people use them to express humour or sarcasm.

5 Some famous people stream their activities online, thus encouraging a herd mentality, having millions of followers who emulate their style and personal _____.

6 _____ have become popular nowadays to express feelings on text messages or emails.

7 _____ techniques are used to create sensationalist headlines, so that readers are enticed to read more of the article and in so doing generate increased advertising revenues.

8 On her professional website she included a short succinct _____ that listed her past accomplishments, varied interests and current projects.

D Complete the sentences with these expressions.

be kept in the loop   get along famously   get hold of
have a nodding acquaintance with   thick as thieves   touch base with

1 Young children are _____ during their formative years, however as they mature and get older their interests diversify and they move apart.

2 Although they came from different and varied cultural backgrounds, the two girls _____ with each other.

3 In urban high rise areas most people tend to prefer anonymity and only _____ their neighbours.

4 Owing to pressures of modern living, it isn't always easy to _____ your friends.

5 We can _____ friends that we haven't seen for a long time.

6 We can use social networking sites to _____ concerning new developments in people's lives.

E **Complete the sentences with the verbs in the correct form.**

bombard   deactivate   detract   disassemble   discontinue   diversify   homogenise   shudder

1 Using the same social media service tends to _____ the population in terms of their interests and lifestyles.
2 The fledgling start-up company tried to _____ its operations too soon and now it is in financial difficulty.
3 The online service provider was _____ due to lack of interest by users.
4 Helen's online account was _____ after three months due to non-usage of her account.
5 The extensive usage of the social media _____ them from their studies.
6 John _____ the router in order to find out what the problem with it was.
7 I _____ to think what I would do if all the ebooks and other data in my cloud disappeared.
8 As the prime minister left the conference, reporters _____ her with questions.

4 Grammar

4.1 Modal Verbs

Modal	Use
can	για να μιλήσουμε για γενική ικανότητα στο παρόν και στο μέλλον για να ζητήσουμε άδεια να κάνουμε κάτι για να δώσουμε την άδεια μας
can't	για να δείξουμε πως είμαστε σίγουροι ότι κάτι δεν ισχύει
could	για να μιλήσουμε για γενική ικανότητα στο παρελθόν (αόριστος του can) για να μιλήσουμε για μια πιθανότητα για να ζητήσουμε κάτι ευγενικά για να προτείνουμε κάτι
may	για να μιλήσουμε για μια πιθανότητα στο μέλλον για να ζητήσουμε κάτι ευγενικά
may as well	για να προτείνουμε κάτι ή να δώσουμε συμβουλή όταν δεν υπάρχει καλύτερη λύση
might	για να μιλήσουμε για μια πιθανότητα στο μέλλον ως αόριστο του may
might as well	για να προτείνουμε κάτι ή να δώσουμε συμβουλή όταν δεν υπάρχει καλύτερη λύση
must	για να πούμε ότι κάτι είναι απαραίτητο για να μιλήσουμε για κάτι που είναι υποχρεωτικό για να εκφράσουμε βεβαιότητα ότι κάτι ισχύει για να προτείνουμε κάτι
mustn't	για να μιλήσουμε για κάτι που δεν επιτρέπεται
should	για να δώσουμε συμβουλή για να ζητήσουμε συμβουλή
would	για πράξεις που κάναμε συχνά στο παρελθόν αλλά δεν κάνουμε πια για να ζητήσουμε κάτι ευγενικά
needn't	για να πούμε ότι κάτι δεν είναι απαραίτητο
be able to	για να μιλήσουμε για γενική ικανότητα για να μιλήσουμε για μια συγκεκριμένη ικανότητα στο παρελθόν
have to	για να πούμε ότι κάτι είναι απαραίτητο για να μιλήσουμε για υποχρέωση
mustn't & don't have to	Χρησιμοποιούμε mustn't για να πούμε ότι κάτι δεν επιτρέπεται, ενώ χρησιμοποιούμε don't have to για να πούμε ότι δεν υπάρχει υποχρέωση ή ότι κάτι δεν είναι απαραίτητο να γίνει

Σημειώσεις:
Με τα modal verbs που εκφράζουν πιθανότητα, η πιθανότητα αυξάνεται όταν προσθέτουμε well. Έτσι may well, might well, could well δείχνουν ότι κάτι είναι πιο πιθανό από might ή could σκέτο.
Το may/might well έχει διαφορετική χρήση από το may/might as well το οποίο σημαίνει ότι δεν έχουμε τίποτα να χάσουμε αν κάνουμε κάτι.

→ She **can** install software efficiently.
→ **Can** you text me later?
→ Yes you **can** use my tablet.
→ That **can't** be his father. He looks far too young.
→ My old cat **could** switch on the laptop with her paw.
→ That comment **could** have unpleasant consequences.
→ **Could** you explain how to log on to the site?
→ You **could** close your account if you don't use it.
→ She **may well** be able to help us out.
→ **May** I use your phone?
→ Yes, you **may** borrow my phone.
→ Mum **might** get a new desktop PC with a huge screen.
→ Andy **might as well** close his Twitter account as he never looks at it.
→ We **must** try to help people in need.

→ Your project **must be finished** by tomorrow.
→ Sharing an office with your boss **must** be really oppressive.
→ You **must** clear your cookies regularly.
→ We **mustn't** open spam emails.
→ You **should** plant herbs in your garden.
→ **Should** I try to reboot when the screen freezes?
→ She **would** always reply to emails within a day, but now she's too busy to read them all.
→ **Would** you give this note to my teacher, please?
→ You **needn't** bring your laptop, you can use mine.
→ He **is able to** download files more quickly since he installed the new hard drive.
→ The techie **wasn't able to** identify the source of the fault.
→ They **have to** book a place for the seminar.
→ We **have to** protect our system from hackers.
→ I **mustn't** forget to do another backup.
→ You **don't have to** read all the posts that appear, just take a quick glance at the interesting ones.

Σημειώσεις:
Μπορούμε να χρησιμοποιήσουμε και το *ought to* για να δώσουμε μια συμβουλή, αλλά δε συνηθίζεται σε ερωτήσεις.
→ Users **ought to be protected** from cybercrime.

4.2 Perfect Modal Verbs

Perfect Modal	Meaning
must have + past participle	Είμαστε βέβαιοι ότι κάτι έγινε στο παρελθόν.
can't have + past participle	Είμαστε βέβαιοι ότι κάτι αποκλείεται να έγινε στο παρελθόν.
may/might/could have + past participle	Είναι πιθανό κάτι να έγινε στο παρελθόν, αλλά δεν είμαστε σίγουροι.
could/might have + past participle	Υπήρχε πιθανότητα να γίνει κάτι στο παρελθόν, αλλά δεν έγινε.
should/ought to have + past participle	Ήταν σωστό να γίνει κάτι, αλλά δεν το κάναμε. Περιμέναμε να γίνει κάτι, αλλά δεν έγινε.
would have + past participle	Σκοπεύαμε να κάνουμε κάτι, αλλά δεν το κάναμε.
needn't have + past participle	Δεν ήταν απαραίτητο να κάνουμε κάτι, αλλά το κάναμε.

→ The storm **must have caused** the line to short circuit.
→ The email **can't have vanished** into thin air. It was on screen a moment ago.
→ They **may have left** the office already, but I'm not sure.
→ We **could have used** Skype, but the connection isn't so good.
→ They **should have dealt with** all the complaints by now.
→ She **would have spoken** directly to the manager, but the line must have got cut off.
→ You **needn't have brought** all those files; I've got access to them in the cloud.

4.3 Expressing probability/possibility without modals

Για να εκφράσουμε πιθανότητα, μπορούμε να χρησιμοποιήσουμε τις φράσεις *in all likelihood/probability, the chances are that, there's every chance/likelihood that, there's a (good) chance that, it's (quite) probable/likely/possible that, sth is likely to happen, sth will probably happen* κλπ.
Για να εκφράσουμε πιθανότητα, μπορούμε να χρησιμοποιήσουμε τις φράσεις *there's little/no chance/likelihood that, it's just possible/very unlikely/quite unlikely/doubtful/inconceivable that sth will happen, sth is (very) unlikely to happen* κλπ.
→ **In all probability**, the ebook will be a resounding success.
→ **The chances are** that we'll miss the deadline the way things are going.
→ **It's doubtful** whether they will find out who their ancestors were on that website.

4 Grammar

4.4 Modals in clauses of concession

Μπορούμε να χρησιμοποιήσουμε modals σε συγκεκριμένες αντιθέσεις, μερικές φορές με αντιστροφή.

→ **Try as he might**, he can't get rid of the virus. (however hard he tries/although she tries hard)

→ **Hard though it may be**, you have to get out and socialise more often. (although it is hard)

→ **Strange as it may seem**, Dad found his classmates on Facebook 30 years after their graduation. (although it seems strange)

→ The internet connection is very poor here, **be that as it may**, we can still receive and send emails. (although this is true, it doesn't change the fact that)

4.6 *Need* and *Dare*

Μπορούμε να χρησιμοποιήσουμε *need* σαν modal κυρίως στους αρνητικούς και ερωτηματικούς τύπους.

→ **Need** you be so rude?

→ You **needn't ask** so many personal questions!

→ She **needn't have been** so downright pushy!

→ She **didn't need to say** a word, the look on her face said it all.

Μπορούμε να χρησιμοποιήσουμε το *need* και σαν κανονικό ρήμα. Έχει καταφατικό, ερωτηματικό και αρνητικό τύπο, και χρησιμοποιείται συνήθως στον Present Simple και στον Past Simple. Ακολουθείται από full infinitive.

→ They **need to replace** their old phone lines; they keep getting cut off.

→ I **needed** a long holiday to recharge my batteries.

→ **Do** we **need to request** more time?

Μπορούμε να χρησιμοποιήσουμε *dare* σαν modal κυρίως στους αρνητικούς και ερωτηματικούς τύπους.

→ How **dare** you **interrupt** when I'm on the phone?

→ He **daren't admit** to deleting the files for fear of the consequences.

→ We **dared not discuss** the issue of pay rises.

Σημειώσεις:

Μπορούμε να χρησιμοποιήσουμε το *dare* ή *daresay* να πούμε ότι πιστεύουμε ότι κάτι αληθεύει.

→ It took longer than I expected, but I **daresay** the result will be worth it.

Μπορούμε να χρησιμοποιήσουμε το *dare* και σαν κανονικό ρήμα. Έχει καταφατικό, ερωτηματικό και αρνητικό τύπο, και χρησιμοποιείται συνήθως στον Present Simple και στον Past Simple. Ακολουθείται από full infinitive.

→ How did you **dare (to) read** my emails?

→ Whoever **dared (to) speak** in class used to be punished.

→ He **didn't dare (to) lose** his passwords for fear he'd be locked out of his accounts.

Grammar Exercises

A Complete the sentences with the correct modal verbs.

shall	must have	could have	couldn't have	have to	must	might	should	needn't have	dare

1 You really _____ not have spoken to him like that. He's terribly upset now.

2 He _____ spoken so loudly. We're not deaf!

3 You _____ finished already! You've only just started.

4 I know you've already given me your phone number, but I _____ lost it.

5 I'm starving. Let's go out and have an enormous pizza with all the trimmings, _____ we?

6 Their house is an absolute palace. They _____ paid a fortune for it.

7 How _____ you speak to me in that tone of voice. You should be ashamed of yourself!

8 We _____ do well on this test or our teacher will give us another one next week.

9 The product seems to be discontinued but, then again, it _____ not be. Let's ask the manager.

10 This video is absolutely hilarious. I simply _____ post it on Facebook.

B Complete the second sentence so that it has the same meaning as the first, using the word given.

1 He simply refused to believe I wasn't lying to him.

not

He _____ I was telling him the truth.

2 It wasn't necessary for you to go since you already knew about the method.

need

You _____ if you had already been acquainted with the method.

3 It's possible they have insufficient evidence to convict her.

may

The evidence _____ convict her.

4 I'm cross because you didn't even bother to call me.

could

The least you _____ was call me.

5 I am terrified to contradict him lest he should lose his temper.

dare

I _____ case he loses his temper.

6 Chances are the election results will have far-reaching consequences.

have

The election _____ far-reaching consequences.

7 How in the world are you serious? I wouldn't even entertain the idea.

can't

The idea is completely ludicrous. You _____ serious.

8 Maybe trying to overhaul the entire framework wasn't the best idea in the world.

should

In retrospect, we _____ overhaul the entire framework.

C Circle the correct answer.

1 It's a lovely gift but, honestly, you mustn't / shouldn't have.

2 It's a gorgeous day. You absolutely should / must get out of the house.

3 They're thick as thieves. They can't / must not have just met last week.

4 When you join the military you have to / must get your hair cut whether you want to or not.

5 If you put that pullover in the washing machine it will / should cause shrinkage.

6 Oh no, you can't / mustn't have posted that photo on Facebook. It will go viral!

7 I have no idea what you're on about. Could / Should you possibly elaborate?

8 Under no circumstances should / must you use emoticons in formal letters.

D Complete the paragraph using suitable modal verbs in the correct form. There may be more than one correct answer.

Social media sites have become so common nowadays that we just consider them part of everyone's social network. However, (1) _____ we look at the whole concept of it, it really is a bit strange, isn't it?

First of all, there's the whole idea of 'friends.' This is a baffling turn of phrase since you (2) _____ possibly know all these people with many of them being little more than acquaintances and most total strangers. Yes, it's probably good to know how and what those you love are doing but if you were really all that interested, (3) _____ you just give them a call? So and so went out for dinner at a fancy restaurant and here's a picture of what they ate. Quite frankly, unless I'm invited for dinner, I (4) _____ care less what someone else eats. As for milestones in life, such as getting married or graduating from university–OK, we all wish you the best, but let's face it; we probably don't know you. Then there are those who bombard you with quite inconsequential snippets about having just been to the gym. (Fine, we're all proud of you.) I'm sure it (5) _____ be sheer narcissism. 'Look at me–I'm on holiday.' You may also have just let every thief (a friend of course) know that your house is empty and you (6) _____ be robbed.

When it comes to stating an opinion that the majority disagrees, all probability, you (7) _____ be viciously attacked if you (8) _____ to differ with the masses. People (9) _____ become overtly offensive and say things they (10) _____ dare say to your face.

All in all, it (11) _____ be nothing more than a pleasant pastime–I'm not sure. It does, however, make you wonder about how we keep in the loop nowadays. Maybe we (12) _____ pick up the phone now and again and actually talk to those we care about.

Exam Task

For questions 1–6, complete the second sentence so that it has a similar meaning to the first sentence, using the word given. **Do not change the word given.** You must use between **three** and **eight** words, including the word given.

1 In all likelihood, Jonathan has already uploaded all the new photos on his profile.
   must
   Jonathan _____ on his profile.

2 I wish you had told us that you were going to be so late.
   have
   You _____ delayed.

3 Although she was a very popular girl, she always felt disconnected and lonely.
   but
   She _____ she always felt disconnected and lonely.

4 The board aren't going to embrace the idea, so let's drop it.
   well
   As the board won't _____ drop it.

5 They disassembled the computer, but it wasn't necessary after all.
   needn't
   They _____ apart after all.

6 She wanted to close her Facebook account, but peer pressure prevented her from doing so.
   but
   She _____ for peer pressure.

page 65

5.1 **spawn** (v) /spɔːn/
lay eggs • *Frogs usually spawn in the lake at this time of year.* ➣ spawn (n) ❖ γεννάω αυγά (ωοτοκώ)

Reading
pages 66-67

5.2 **lure** (n) /lʊə(r)/
attractiveness; appeal • *The lure of city life drove her to leave her village.* ➣ lure (v) ❖ γοητεία

5.3 **smattering** (n) /'smætərɪŋ/
a very small amount • *Knowing only a smattering of German, Olga had no intention of going to university in Frankfurt.* ❖ ελάχιστη ποσότητα

5.4 **fire** (v) /'faɪə(r)/
excite or interest sb in sth • *The wildlife documentary fired his interest in travelling to New Guinea.* ❖ εξάπτω, διεγείρω

5.5 **vocation** (n) /vəʊ'keɪʃn/
a chosen profession or job that you feel suits you • *Leo followed his dreams and found his true vocation as a football coach.* ➣ vocational (adj) ❖ ιδανικό επάγγελμα

5.6 **set your sights on sth** (expr) /sət jɔː(r) saɪts ɒn 'sʌmθɪŋ/
be determined to achieve sth • *Roxanne knew she had to study hard as she had set her sights on becoming a doctor.* ❖ βάζω στόχο

5.7 **on the dole** (expr) /ɒn ðə dəʊl/
unemployed and living on state benefits • *How long was she on the dole before she found another job?* ❖ στο ταμείο ανεργίας

5.8 **vicious circle** (expr) /'vɪʃəs 'sɜːkl/
a bad situation that is hard to get out of as one problem leads to another • *They felt trapped in a vicious circle of poverty and unemployment.* ❖ φαύλος κύκλος

5.9 **make your way in life** (expr) /meɪk jɔː(r) weɪ ɪn laɪf/
be successful and make progress • *Betty left home to make her own way in life as soon as she finished her studies.* ❖ προοδεύω στη ζωή

5.10 **aimlessness** (n) /'eɪmləsnəs/
the state of having no plans or idea what to do • *The economic crisis has left so many people out of work with feelings of aimlessness.* ➣ aimless (adj), aimlessly (adv) ❖ έλλειψη στόχου, άσκοπα

5.11 **ritual** (n) /'rɪtʃuəl/
a sequence of actions repeated often in the same way • *Steven was used to the daily ritual of commuting to and from work.* ➣ ritual (adj), ritually (adv) ❖ διαδικασία, το τυπικό

5.12 **surrogate** (adj) /'sʌrəgət/
substituting for sth else which is not available • *Abandoned a few days after birth, the kitten was fortunately adopted and raised happily by its surrogate family.* ➣ surrogate (n) ❖ αναπληρωματικός, θετός

5.13 **camaraderie** (n) /kæmə'rɑːdəri/
the friendly bond between people who work together or are in similar circumstances • *A sense of camaraderie developed among the earthquake victims camped in the park.* ❖ συντροφικότητα

5.14 **inducement** (n) /ɪn'djuːsmənt/
sth given to sb to entice them to do sth • *Unfair taxation systems are no inducement for people to start up a new business.* ➣ induce (v) ❖ παρακίνηση, ενθάρρυνση

5.15 **turn over a new leaf** (expr) /tɜːn 'əʊvə(r) ə njuː liːf/
change the way you behave to be a better person • *Upon his release from prison, Jimmy decided to turn over a new leaf and look for an honest job.* ❖ «γυρνάω σελίδα»

5.16 **grassroots** (n) /grɑːs ruːts/
the ordinary people in a group or society and not their leaders • *At grassroots level, many people are happy to complain, but few are willing to step up and take responsible decisions.* ❖ η βάση, απλοί πολίτες

5.17 **fall through the cracks** (expr) /fɔːl θruː ðə kræks/
not be noticed or dealt with • *Mike had fallen through the cracks of the education system and couldn't read or write until his 20s.* ❖ ξεχασμένος, που παραβλέπεται

5.18 **rehabilitation** (n) /ˌriːəˌbɪlɪ'teɪʃn/
the process of helping sb change to have a healthier or more acceptable lifestyle after a period of illness or addiction, etc. • *Parents of teenage addicts can speak to a counsellor at the drug rehabilitation centre.* ➣ rehabilitate (v) ❖ αποκατάσταση, αποτοξίνωση

5.19 **entrepreneur** (n) /ˌɒntrəprə'nɜː(r)/
sb who opens a new type of business to earn money • *As a budding entrepreneur, he founded his first company at the age of 19.* ➣ entrepreneurial (adj) ❖ επιχειρηματίας

5.20 alluring (adj) /əˈlʊərɪŋ/
attractive and exciting • *The prospect of a free trip to Iceland seemed most alluring.* ➢ allure (v), alluringly (adv) ❖ δελεαστικός

5.21 inherently (adv) /ɪnˈhɪərəntli/
due to the basic nature of sth/sb • *Although Daisy is a charming dog, she is inherently disobedient having had no early training.* ➢ inhere (v), inherent (adj) ❖ εκ φύσεως

5.22 conclusive (adj) /kənˈkluːsɪv/
that proves sth completely • *Without conclusive proof, police cannot arrest the suspected arsonist.* ➢ conclude (v), conclusion (adj), conclusively (adv) ❖ ακλόνητος, αδιάσειστος

5.23 empowerment (n) /ɪmˈpaʊəmənt/
the act of enabling sb to become stronger and have more control over their circumstances • *Having a comfortable private office space gave Sarah a sense of empowerment and confidence in her work.* ➢ empower (v) ❖ ισχύς, κύρος

5.24 downward spiral (expr) /ˈdaʊnwəd ˈspaɪrəl/
a situation that worsens progressively • *The international economy is on a downward spiral, signalling the end of the consumerist era.* ❖ πτωτική τροχιά

5.25 headlong (adv) /ˈhedlɒŋ/
quickly and directly without considering the consequences • *Losing control of her company's budget, she fell headlong into bankruptcy.* ➢ headlong (adj) ❖ ορμητικά

5.26 juvenile detention centre (n) /ˈdʒuːvənaɪl dɪˈtenʃn ˈsentə(r)/
an institute where convicted criminals under 18 years old are imprisoned • *Most of the gang members had already spent a few months in a juvenile detention centre.* ❖ αναμορφωτήριο

5.27 allegiance (n) /əˈliːdʒəns/
loyal support • *The new army recruits had to pledge allegiance to their country.* ❖ πίστη, υποταγή

5.28 thick and fast (expr) /θɪk ənd faːst/
very quickly and in great numbers • *Applications for the job were pouring in thick and fast.* ❖ γρήγορα και σε μεγάλη ποσότητα

5.29 bespectacled (adj) /bɪˈspektəkld/
wearing glasses • *A bespectacled librarian directed me to the reference section.* ❖ με γυαλιά

5.30 prospective (adj) /prəˈspektɪv/
likely to become or do sth • *I sent my CV to dozen of prospective employers.* ➢ prospect (v), prospect (n) ❖ υποψήφιος, μελλοντικός

5.31 lad (n) /læd/
a boy or young man • *A group of lads were hanging around outside the cafe.* ❖ νεαρός

5.32 live wire (n) /laɪv ˈwaɪə(r)/
a very energetic person who is hard to control • *Annabelle's daughter is quite shy, but her son is a real live wire.* ❖ ατίθασο άτομο

5.33 garner (v) /ˈgaːnə(r)/
acquire and gather • *Ted shows off a bit too much in an effort to garner approval from his peers.* ❖ αποκτώ, συλλέγω

5.34 round of applause (expr) /raʊnd əv əˈplɔːz/
a short period of people clapping to show approval • *He received a huge round of applause at the end of his speech.* ❖ χειροκρότημα

5.35 ridicule (n) /ˈrɪdɪkjuːl/
comments made to make sb look stupid • *The prime minister was coming in for a great deal of ridicule from the media.* ➢ ridicule (v), ridiculous (adj), ridiculously (adv) ❖ γελοιοποίηση

5.36 so-called (adj) /ˌsəʊˈkɔːld/
used before a description to show that you don't consider it appropriate • *The so-called 'war on terror' is generating more terrorism than tackling it.* ❖ λεγόμενος, δήθεν

5.37 welfare (n) /ˈwelfeə(r)/
financial or other aid that the government gives to people who are unemployed, poor or have special needs, etc. • *Most people would prefer to have a job than live on welfare.* ❖ κοινωνική πρόνοια

5.38 ghetto (n) /ˈgetəʊ/
a poor area of a city where people of the same background tend to be concentrated • *There was more news of rioting and clashes between gangs and police in the Paris ghetto.* ❖ γκέτο

5.39 benefit (n) /ˈbenɪfɪt/
money that the government pays to people who are unemployed, poor or have special needs, etc. • *Matthew was flat broke when his out-of-work benefit stopped after one year on the dole.* ➢ benefit (v), beneficiary (n), beneficial (adj), beneficially (adv) ❖ επίδομα

5.40 intergenerational (adj) /ˌɪntərˌdʒenəˈreɪʃənl/
including people of different age groups • *The centre offers intergenerational sessions where older people teach skills to unemployed youths.* ❖ μεταξύ διαφόρων γενεών

5.41 rebellion (n) /rɪˈbeljən/
resistance against authority; reluctance to obey and attempts to change accepted rules • *Most children show signs of rebellion against their parents from the age of 12 upwards.* ➢ rebel (v), rebel (n), rebellious (adj), rebelliously (adv) ❖ επανάσταση

5.42 thug (n) /θʌg/
a violent criminal • *The 'friendly' match was cut short when a group of thugs started throwing things at the players.* ➢ thuggery (n), thuggish (adj) ❖ τραμπούκος

5.43 **wannabe** (adj) /ˈwɒnəbi/
trying to behave like sb that you want to be the same as • *Outside the studio were hundreds of wannabe singers awaiting their auditions.*
➢ wannabe (n) ❖ επίδοξος

5.44 **gangster** (n) /ˈɡæŋstə(r)/
a member of a gang of criminals • *The sleazy nightclub was run by a local gangster.*
❖ γκάνγκστερ

5.45 **insight** (n) /ˈɪnsaɪt/
a piece of information or close look that gives you an understanding of sth • *The documentary gave us some insight into the living conditions in Brazilian favelas.*
➢ insightful (adj) ❖ άποψη, αντίληψη

5.46 **veteran** (n) /ˈvetərən/
sb who has had long-term experience in an activity or job • *A Nobel Peace Prize was offered to the veteran singer Bob Dylan.*
❖ βετεράνος

5.47 **twinkle** (n) /ˈtwɪŋkl/
an amused expression in your eyes • *From the slight twinkle in her eye, I knew my friend was about to make a happy announcement.*
➢ twinkle (v), twinkling (adj) ❖ λάμψη στα μάτια

5.48 **specs** (abbrev) /speks/
glasses; abbreviation of *spectacles* • *Ian can't read anything without his specs on.* ❖ γυαλιά

5.49 **get down to business** (expr) /ɡet daʊn tə ˈbɪznəs/
start work on sth seriously • *Let's get down to business before we run out of time to finish this job.* ❖ στρώνομαι στη δουλειά

5.50 **reminisce** (v) /ˌremɪˈnɪs/
think or talk about past experiences or events • *While my parents used to grumble about their boss, they now reminisce about the good times when they had steady jobs.*
➢ reminiscence (n), reminiscent (adj)
❖ αναπολώ

5.51 **transition** (n) /trænˈzɪʃn/
the process of changing from one situation to another • *Adolescence is an interesting transition from childhood to adulthood, which is equally puzzling for parents of teenagers.*
➢ transition (v) ❖ μετάβαση

5.52 **law-abiding** (adj) /lɔː əˈbaɪdɪŋ/
doing everything by the law; never breaking the law • *Even the most law-abiding drivers fail to notice speed restriction limits where the signs are obscured by trees.* ❖ νομοταγής

5.53 **aspiration** (n) /ˌæspəˈreɪʃn/
a strong hope to achieve sth • *With aspirations of fame and fortune, he set out for the bright lights of Broadway.* ➢ aspire (v), aspiring (adj), aspirational (adj) ❖ φιλοδοξία

Attitudes & States: nouns

adversity	fulfilment
aimlessness	ineptness
allegiance	initiative
anguish	irregularity
aspiration	irresolution
attainment	lethargy
awe	lure
backbone	perseverance
camaraderie	prevalence
caste	rebellion
disorientation	recognition
empowerment	stratification
entrepreneur	

Vocabulary pages 68-69-70

5.54 **adversity** (n) /ədˈvɜːsəti/
an extemely difficult situation • *In the face of adversity, she turned to her closest friends for support.* ➢ adverse (adj), adversely (adv)
❖ αντιξοότητα

5.55 **fulfilment** (n) /fʊlˈfɪlmənt/
the achievement of or sense of achieving sth you hoped for • *Seeing her own name above the shop gave Sheila a sense of fulfilment.*
➢ fulfil (v), fulfilling (adj) ❖ εκπλήρωση

5.56 **perseverance** (n) /ˌpɜːsɪˈvɪərəns/
the quality of continuing without giving up until you achieve a goal • *It was no easy hike, but we reached the peak through sheer perseverance.* ➢ persevere (v), persevering (adj) ❖ επιμονή

5.57 **prevalence** (n) /ˈprevələns/
the fact of being noticeably common or occurring frequently in a particular place • *With the increasing prevalence of street gangs in the neighbourhood, we decided it was time to move house.* ➢ prevail (v), prevalent (adj), prevailing (adj) ❖ επικράτηση

5.58 **dogged** (adj) /ˈdɒɡɪd/
persistent • *Mark never gave up his dogged attempts to make it to the top of his profession.*
➢ dog (v) ❖ επίμονος, πεισματάρικος

5.59 **broken home** (n) /ˈbrəʊkən həʊm/
a family with divorced or separated parents • *The concept of coming from a broken home no longer carries the social stigma of the past and has arguably become the new norm.*
❖ διαλυμένο σπίτι

5.60 **fast track** (n) /fɑːst træk/
a quick way to complete or achieve sth • *Hugh's dreams were shattered when he lost the talent contest that he had regarded as a fast track to fame.* ➢ fast-track (v), fast-track (adj) ❖ σύντομος δρόμος

5.61 **rosy** (adj) /ˈrəʊzi/
likely to be a success; over-optimistic • *They retired with hopes of living a rosy life in the countryside.* ❖ ρόδινος

5.62 **crude** (adj) /kruːd/
basic and unrefined (usually in a negative sense); vulgar • *Kate tried to ignore the crude remarks from the group of teenagers on the street.* ➢ crudeness (n), crudely (adv) ❖ άξεστος, κακόγουστος

5.63 **raw** (adj) /rɔː/
natural and uncontrolled (in a positive or negative sense) • *Tears filled his eyes and he could not conceal his raw emotion.* ❖ ωμός

5.64 **gritty** (adj) /ˈɡrɪti/
describing sb who is brave and determined; describing a realistic unpleasant situation • *Only by gritty determination did Vanessa win the tournament.* ➢ grit (n), grittiness (n) ❖ θαρραλέος, τραχύς

5.65 **bleak** (adj) /bliːk/
hopeless; discouraging • *The prospects looked bleak for the housing market with the economic downturn.* ➢ bleakness (n), bleakly (adv) ❖ απογοητευτικός, αποθαρρυντικός

5.66 **harsh** (adj) /hɑːʃ/
severe • *Living on the streets is particularly harsh in winter.* ➢ harshness (n), harshly (adv) ❖ δριμύς, τραχύς, δύσκολος

5.67 **bash** (v) /bæʃ/
hit sb/sth hard • *He slipped on the ice and bashed his head on the pavement.* ➢ bash (n) ❖ κοπανάω

5.68 **dash sb's hopes** (expr) /dæʃ ˈsʌmbədiz həʊps/
destroy sb's hopes • *Louise's hopes of getting the job were dashed when she missed the interview due to the train delay.* ❖ εξανεμίζομαι

5.69 **blunt** (v) /blʌnt/
make sth less sharp; make sth less effective • *Her first month at university had blunted her desire to become a lawyer.* ➢ bluntness (n), bluntly (adv) ❖ αμβλύνω

5.70 **aptitude** (n) /ˈæptɪtjuːd/
a natural talent for doing sth • *All applicants for the post had to sit an aptitude test.* ➢ apt (adj), aptly (adv) ❖ δεξιότητα, ικανότητα

5.71 **backbone** (n) /ˈbækbəʊn/
strength of character • *Nigel didn't have the backbone to face the reporters after his defeat.* ❖ τα κότσια

5.72 **initiative** (n) /ɪˈnɪʃətɪv/
the chance to make a decision quickly and act on sth before sb else does • *Claire took the initiative of designing a new company logo.* ➢ initiate (v), initiation (n) ❖ πρωτοβουλία

5.73 **recognition** (n) /ˌrekəɡˈnɪʃn/
public praise for your actions • *The great artist died in poverty and his masterpieces only received recognition years later.* ➢ recognise (v), recognised (adj), recognisable (adj) ❖ αναγνώριση

5.74 **anguish** (n) /ˈæŋɡwɪʃ/
extreme suffering or distress • *They suffered the anguish of seeing their home destroyed in the war.* ➢ anguished (adj) ❖ οδύνη

5.75 **attainment** (n) /əˈteɪnmənt/
achievement of a goal • *Despite her high level of attainment at school, Agnes preferred farming work to the prospect of university.* ➢ attain (v), attainable (adj) ❖ επίτευγμα

5.76 **ineptness** (n) /ɪˈneptnəs/
lack of ability or skill • *He was fired for his ineptness at handling customer complaints.* ➢ inept (adj), ineptly (adv) ❖ αδυναμία, ανικανότητα
✎ Syn: ineptitude

5.77 **irresolution** (n) /ɪˌrezəˈluːʃn/
the inability or unwillingness to make a decision • *Your irresolution completely blew your chances of winning the contract; you should have made up your mind sooner.* ➢ irresolute (adj), irresolutely (adv) ❖ αναποφασιστικότητα

5.78 **lethargy** (n) /ˈleθədʒi/
tiredness and/or lack of enthusiam • *It took Gary a few weeks to shake off the lethargy brought on by his illness.* ➢ lethargic (adj) ❖ λήθαργος

5.79 **caste** (n) /kɑːst/
a social class, especially in Hindu society • *Only members of the ruling caste are allowed entry to this club.* ❖ κάστα

5.80 **stratification** (n) /ˌstrætɪfɪˈkeɪʃn/
the state of being separated into different levels • *Social stratification was clearly taken into account when they appointed the company director.* ➢ stratify (v) ❖ διαστρωμάτωση

5.81 **irregularity** (n) /ɪˌreɡjəˈlærəti/
sth unacceptable by the usual rules; an error • *The opposition party claimed there had been irregularities during the ballot counts.* ➢ irregular (adj), irregularly (adv) ❖ παρατυπία

5.82 **toughen up** (phr v) /ˈtʌfən ʌp/
become stronger and more resilient • *If you hope to start a business, you'd better toughen up and take some risks.* ❖ σκληραίνω

5.83 **leap at** (phr v) /liːp ət/
accept enthusiastically • *Basil leapt at the chance to go to music school.* ❖ αρπάζω την ευκαιρία

5.84 **fall in with sb** (phr v) /fɔːl ɪn wɪθ 'sʌmbədi/
become friends with ● *He fell in with bad company and began playing truant with them.*
❖ σχετίζομαι με

5.85 **slip up** (phr v) /slɪp ʌp/
make a careless mistake ● *The robber slipped up by calling his friend by his real name, so the whole gang got caught.* ➢ slip-up (n)
❖ κάνω χαζό λάθος

5.86 **get caught up in sth** (exp) /get kɔːt ʌp ɪn 'sʌmθɪŋ/
become unwillingly involved ● *I got caught up in heavy traffic this morning.* ❖ μπλέκομαι σε

5.87 **intern** (n) /'ɪntɜːn/
a student or graduate who has a temporary work experience post in a workplace ● *While studying for his master's degree, Andrew worked as an intern at a local newspaper office.* ➢ internship (n) ❖ εκπαιδευόμενος

5.88 **let go** (phr v) /let gəʊ/
fire; dismiss sb ● *The company had to let half the staff go when sales figures kept dropping.*
❖ διώχνω, απολύω

Phrasal verbs

fall in with sth	slip up
leap at	toughen up
let go	

5.89 **pluck up the courage** (expr) /plʌk ʌp ðə 'kʌrɪdʒ/
manage to feel brave enough to do sth despite the risk involved ● *Stephanie finally plucked up the courage to ask for a pay rise.* ❖ μαζεύω το κουράγιο, βρίσκω το θάρρος

5.90 **down the drain** (expr) /daʊn ðə dreɪn/
wasted ● *Don't buy that old car! It would be just money down the drain.* ❖ «πεταμένα» (χρήματα)

5.91 **throw in the towel** (expr) /θrəʊ ɪn ðə 'taʊəl/
give up trying ● *The course is harder than I expected, but I'm not ready to throw in the towel yet.* ❖ «τα παρατάω»

5.92 **make a go of sth** (expr) /meɪk ə gəʊ əv 'sʌmθɪŋ/
do your best to succeed in sth ● *Despite some teething problems getting started, she's making a go of writing her first novel.* ❖ κάνω προσπάθεια

5.93 **fall short of sth** (expr) /fɔːl ʃɔːt əv 'sʌmθɪŋ/
be below the necessary standard ● *The hotel service fell short of our expectations.*
❖ υστερώ, δεν ανταποκρίνομαι

5.94 **blow your chance** (expr) /bləʊ jɔː(r) tʃɑːns/
do sth that destroys your hope of success ● *He blew his chance at the interview by showing reluctance to do overtime.* ❖ χάνω την ευκαιρία
✎ Syn: blow it

5.95 **not hold out much hope** (expr) /nɒt həʊld aʊt mʌtʃ həʊp/
be pessimistic about sth ● *They didn't hold out much hope of crossing the Atlantic in their small sailing boat.* ❖ τρέφω ελπίδες

5.96 **pick up the pieces** (expr) /pɪk ʌp ðə piːsəz/
recover or help sb to recover to normal after a setback ● *Lindsey avoided criticising her son's choice of partner, but she was around to pick up the pieces after his divorce.* ❖ «μαζεύω τα κομμάτια»

5.97 **be sucked in** (expr) /bi sʌkt ɪn/
become compelled to get involved in ● *I tried not to get sucked into yet another boring discussion about British politics.* ❖ μπλέκω

5.98 **big yourself up** (expr) /bɪg jɔːˈself ʌp/
boast by saying overly positive things about yourself ● *Georgia kept bigging herself up to get voted in as class president.* ❖ παινεύομαι

5.99 **proactive** (adj) /ˌprəʊˈæktɪv/
taking action to make things happen and direct a situation ● *Team members are expected to be proactive and work towards joint solutions to develop this project.* ➢ proactively (adv)
❖ δυναμικός, δραστήριος

5.100 **scam** (n) /skæm/
a devious and illegal way to obtain money from others ● *Jill nearly fell for a phone scam when someone called to say she had won a free holiday to the Caribbean.* ➢ scam (v)
❖ απάτη

5.101 **materialise** (v) /məˈtɪəriəlaɪz/
become a reality; happen as planned ● *The college gave a guarantee that we would all instantly find great jobs after the course, but we are still waiting for them to materialise.* ➢ materialisation (n), material (adj), materially (adv) ❖ πραγματοποιώ, υλοποιώ

5.102 **mercenary** (adj) /ˈmɜːsənəri/
interested in sth for the money ● *He's only working for the NGO for mercenary reasons.* ➢ mercenary (n) ❖ ιδιοτελής

5.103 **in retrospect** (expr) /ɪn ˈretrəspekt/
looking back after the event ● *In retrospect, she regretted not having left her birthplace when she was younger.* ➢ retrospection (n), retrospective (adj), retrospectively (adv)
❖ εκ των υστέρων

5.104 **awe** (n) /ɔː/
a feeling of admiration and wonder ● *They gazed in awe across the magnificent landscape.* ➢ awe (v) ❖ δέος

5.105 **emulate** (v) /ˈemjʊleɪt/
try to do sth in the same way as sb else
• *He hopes to be able to emulate his favourite guitarist's performance one day.* ➣ emulation (n), emulator (n) ❖ μιμούμαι

5.106 **astounded** (adj) /əˈstaʊndɪd/
shocked or surprised at an unlikely achievement • *We were astounded to hear that the dean had been arrested.* ➣ astound (v), astounding (adj), astoundingly (adv) ❖ έκπληκτος

5.107 **at stake** (expr) /ət steɪk/
likely to fail or succeed depending on an action • *The talks went on for hours as the future of the country was at stake.* ➣ stake (v) ❖ διακυβεύεται

5.108 **lucrative** (adj) /ˈluːkrətɪv/
profit-making • *Despite the lucrative salary offered, Eva felt morally obliged to turn down the job in the unscrupulous company.* ➣ lucratively (adv) ❖ επικερδής, προσοδοφόρος

5.109 **deterrent** (n) /dɪˈterənt/
sth that prevents or dissuades sb from doing sth • *The image of a cross section of a smoker's lung was used as a deterrent to teenage smoking.* ➣ deter (v), deterrent (adj) ❖ αποτροπή

5.110 **elevate** (v) /ˈelɪveɪt/
raise sth to a higher position • *His hopes of winning elevated after he won in the quarter finals.* ➣ elevation (n), elevated (adj), elevating (adj) ❖ ανυψώνω

5.111 **escalate** (v) /ˈeskəleɪt/
quickly worsen • *The wave of violence escalated as the word was spread through social media.* ➣ escalation (n), escalator (n) ❖ κλιμακώνω

Grammar **pages 71-72-73**

5.112 **fugitive** (n) /ˈfjuːdʒətɪv/
sb who is running away to avoid capture • *With sniffer dogs on his trail, the fugitive escaped by floating down the river on a log.* ➣ fugitive (adj) ❖ φυγάς

5.113 **volatile** (adj) /ˈvɒlətaɪl/
having a tendency to change suddenly; unstable • *If the housing market weren't so volatile, I'd prefer to sell up immmediately.* ➣ volatility (n) ❖ πτητικός, ευμετάβλητος

Listening **page 74**

5.114 **bucket list** (n) /ˈbʌkɪt lɪst/
a list of things you'd like to do in your lifetime • *Long-distance travel features high on most people's bucket lists.* ❖ λίστα επιθυμιών

5.115 **knock** (v) /nɒk/
criticise • *Don't knock the idea of self-publishing your book; it worked for some of the best-selling writers.* ➣ knock (n) ❖ απαξιώνω

5.116 **have a go at sth** (expr) /həv ə gəʊ at ˈsʌmθɪŋ/
try doing sth • *Harry had a go at sky-diving, but he was too scared to do it a second time.* ❖ επιχειρώ

5.117 **obligatory** (adj) /əˈblɪgətri/
that must be done because of a rule, etc.; compulsory • *A period of army service is obligatory for young men in many countries.* ➣ oblige (v), obligation (n) ❖ υποχρεωτικός

Speaking **page 75**

5.118 **double-edged sword** (expr) /ˈdʌbl edʒd sɔːd/
sth that has both benefits and drawbacks • *Emigration is a double-edged sword that brings new opportunities but presents the challenges of living in another culture as a foreigner.* ❖ δίκοπο μαχαίρι

Expressions

at stake
be inclined to agree
be sucked in
big yourself up
blow your chance
catch sb off guard
cream of the crop
double-edged sword
down the drain
downward spiral
fall short of sth
fall through the cracks
get caught up in sth
get down to business
in retrospect
make a go of sth
make your way in life
not hold out much hope
on the dole
pick up the pieces
pluck up courage
round of applause
set your sights on sth
thick and fast
throw in the towel
turn over a new leaf
vicious circle

Writing
pages 76-77

5.119 cream of the crop (expr) /kriːm əv ðə krɒp/
the best from a group or large number of
things/people • *Naturally, that private school
has a high pass rate since they only accept
applicants who are already the cream of the
crop.* ❖ αφρόκρεμα

5.120 fast-paced (adj) /fɑːst peɪsd/
that happens very quickly • *Amanda sat
peacefully on the station platform reading her
book, ignoring the fast-paced, smartphone-
wielding wannabes sharing her commute.*
❖ σε γρήγορο ρυθμό

5.121 aspirational (adj) /ˌæspəˈreɪʃənl/
full of aspirations to improve your situation
• *Advertisements for the new housing estate
were designed with the aspirational new-
moneyed middle-class customer in mind.*
➢ aspire (v), aspiration (n) ❖ φιλόδοξος

5.122 misguidedly (adv) /ˌmɪsˈɡaɪdɪdli/
wrongly, due to an error of judgement
• *Bradley misguidedly turned to drugs in
search of the excitement that was lacking in
his everyday life.* ➢ misguided (adj)
❖ λανθασμένα

5.123 fertile (adj) /ˈfɜːtaɪl/
that encourages activity or productivity
• *The university campus was fertile ground
for radical groups.* ➢ fertility (n) ❖ εύφορος,
γόνιμος
✎ Opp: unfertile ❖ άγονος

5.124 be inclined to agree (expr) /biː ɪnˈklaɪnd tuː
əˈɡriː/
used to express you have a similar opinion
• *I'm inclined to agree that we shouldn't risk
hiking in this weather.* ❖ τείνω να συμφωνήσω

5.125 forge (v) /fɔːdʒ/
create • *Strong bonds were forged between
the participants on the course.* ➢ forge (n)
❖ σφυρηλατώ

5.126 unscrupulous (adj) /ʌnˈskruːpjələs/
dishonest and immoral • *Unscrupulous
employers have used the job crisis to
exploit their workers by lowering wages
to the minimum.* ➢ unscrupulousness (n),
unscrupulously (adv) ❖ ασυνείδητος
✎ Opp: scrupulous ❖ ευσυνείδητος

5.127 harshly (adv) /ˈhɑːʃli/
strictly; unkindly • *Matilda felt that her tutor
had assessed her essay too harshly because
he held conflicting opinions on the topic.*
➢ harshness (n), harsh (adj) ❖ σκληρά

5.128 small-minded (adj) /smɔːl ˈmaɪndɪd/
intolerant and stubborn; with a narrow set of
rigid views • *Martha relished the anonymity of
the city in stark contrast to the small-minded
village community she had left.* ➢ small-
mindedness (n) ❖ μικρονοϊκός, στενόμυαλος

Attitudes & States: adjectives & adverbs

alluring	lucrative
aspirational	mercenary
astounded	misguidedly
bleak	proactive
crude	prospective
dogged	raw
fast-paced	rosy
fertile	small-minded
gritty	surrogate
harsh	unawares
harshly	unscrupulous
headlong	volatile
intergenerational	wannabe
law-abiding	

Video 5: Surviving Deadly Everest page 78

5.129 crampon (n) /ˈkræmpɒn/
a metal plate with sharp points, which you
attach to the sole of a boot or shoe for climbing
on ice or snow • *We were well-equipped for
the winter hike with crampons attached to our
boots to cross the icy trail.* ❖ κραμπόν

5.130 catch sb off guard (expr) /kætʃ ˈsʌmbədi ɒf
ɡɑːd/
take sb by surprise at a weak moment when
they are unprepared • *A huge wave caught us
off guard and almost capsized our yacht.*
❖ πιάνω απροετοίμαστο

5.131 unawares (adv) /ˌʌnəˈweəz/
unexpectedly; without noticing • *Engrossed in
their fishing, the anglers drifted unawares out
to sea.* ➢ unaware (adj) ❖ απροσδόκητα

5.132 oncoming (adj) /ˈɒnkʌmɪŋ/
approaching • *Blinded by oncoming
headlights, he swerved and crashed into the
ditch.* ❖ επερχόμενος

5.133 altitude (n) /ˈæltɪtjuːd/
the distance above ground level • *The plane
suddenly dropped to a low altitude and
crashed into the mountainside.* ❖ υψόμετρο

5.134 blizzard (n) /ˈblɪzəd/
a heavy snowstorm with strong winds • *Our
car got stuck on the road in a raging blizzard.*
❖ χιονοθύελλα

5.135 disorientation (n) /dɪsˌɔːriənˈteɪʃn/
the confused state of not knowing which
direction to take • *Dennis went through a
period of disorientation upon his return home
following his stay in hospital.* ➢ disorientate
(v), disorientated (adj) ❖ αποπροσανατολισμός

Vocabulary Exercises

A Complete the sentences with the correct form of the words.

1 The economic unrest in Europe is making the _____ of the social classes more pronounced.   **STRATIFY**

2 His _____ may stem from the fact that he has no clear goals for the future.   **RESOLVE**

3 Judy's _____ to become a world-class athlete were crushed in the accident that caused her to walk with a limp for the rest of her life.   **ASPIRE**

4 The rising _____ of teen alcohol consumption is a cause of great concern to parents and teachers.   **PREVAIL**

5 Thomas owes his success to his _____ and hard work; nothing was handed to him on a platter.   **PERSEVERE**

6 All the odds were against him, but he was determined to overcome _____ and make his dream come true.   **ADVERSE**

7 The artist finally got the _____ he craved when one of the largest galleries in London agreed to show his work.   **RECOGNISE**

8 You can't let a minor setback act as a _____ to your plans.   **DETER**

9 We need to iron out a few _____ before we can carry on with the plan.   **REGULAR**

10 No matter what anyone told him, they couldn't shake Nick's confidence in his _____ success.   **COME**

11 Stella is talking with _____ investors to help her expand her business.   **PROSPECT**

12 Kevin used to have a drug problem, but he went into _____ and managed to turn his life around.   **REHABILITATE**

B Choose the best answer.

1 No matter how ___ the future looked to Kelly, she refused to give up hope.
   a rosy   **b** crude   **c** gritty   **d** bleak

2 Alex has a great ___ for mathematics; it's a pity he didn't pursue a career in that field.
   a aptitude   **b** ineptness   **c** attainment   **d** insight

3 It's a disgrace that modern society doesn't treat its war ___ with the respect they deserve.
   a lads   **b** mercenaries   **c** veterans   **d** thugs

4 David lost his job six months ago and has been on the ___ since.
   a dole   **b** benefit   **c** welfare   **d** crampon

5 Being a part of a team and working towards a common goal can help ___ strong friendships that can last a lifetime.
   a spawn   **b** fire   **c** knock   **d** forge

6 It's important to deal with each problem as it comes up, and not allow it to ___ into something that can no longer be fixed.
   a elevate   **b** escalate   **c** magnify   **d** emulate

7 Ever since he was a little boy, Mathew said he knew that teaching was his ___ in life.
   a lure   **b** vocation   **c** grassroots   **d** allegiance

8 Mark was about to drop out of school, but thanks to his friends' ___ he continued his studies and today he is a renowned scientist.
   a smattering   **b** ritual   **c** intervention   **d** camaraderie

9 From the thousands of young ___ pop idols who show up to audition for reality talent shows, very few have any real talent.
   a so-called   **b** dogged   **c** unawares   **d** wannabe

10 He is a(n) ___ businessman, who doesn't care who he may destroy in order to achieve his goals.
   a unscrupulous   **b** aspirational   **c** volatile   **d** proactive

C Complete the expressions with these words.

business   chances   circle   courage   cracks   leaf   life   pieces   retrospect   sights   spiral   towel

1   In _____, it would have been better if I had gone to university.

2   Don't blow your _____ of getting the job by showing up for the interview in shaggy clothes.

3   Sometimes, no matter how much you want something it's just not meant to be. You've got to know when it's time to throw in the _____, and move on to something new.

4   If you really want a chance with Stacy, you've got to pluck up the _____ to ask her out.

5   After his first business venture failed, Mark just picked up the _____ and started all over again.

6   Stop fooling around and let's get down to _____; we have a deadline to meet.

7   The homeless are often caught in a vicious _____; in order to apply for a job they need to give a valid address, but they can't afford to rent a place unless they get a job.

8   Karen had fallen in with a bad crowd when she was young, but she managed to turn over a new _____ and now she is a well-respected business owner and a mother of two wonderful children.

9   School is obligatory up to the age of 16, but with schools so crowded and understaffed it is not uncommon for some children to fall through the _____.

10   Ronda is a very determined young lady, and will achieve anything she sets her _____ on.

11   Alan lost everything he owned when his business went bankrupt, and has been in a downward _____ since.

12   Having lived all his life in a ghetto, it was very hard for Steven to make his way in _____ but thanks to his hard work and perseverance he succeeded.

D Circle the correct word.

1   Coming from a broken / single home himself, George vowed to be a good father if he ever had children.

2   Once he won the television talent show, Ian was on the speedy / fast track to success and fame.

3   When she broke three of her fingers, Lora knew her hopes of becoming a pianist had been dashed / bashed.

4   She grew up in a tough neighbourhood under very raw / harsh conditions.

5   Fresh out of university, Greg landed his first job as an entrepreneur / intern in a large corporation.

6   Everything he had worked for went down the drain / scam when his factory was burned to the ground.

7   When he opened his shop, Jake had no idea it would turn out to be such a lucrative / fertile establishment.

8   Most employers appreciate employees who aren't afraid to take altitude / initiative.

9   I'm sure you would have tried harder, if you had realised that your career was in awe / at stake.

10   His first job after finishing law school was as a law-abiding / surrogate judge.

5 Grammar

5.1 Zero Conditional

If clause	Main clause
Present Simple	Present Simple

Χρησιμοποιούμε το **zero conditional** για να μιλήσουμε για το αποτέλεσμα μιας πράξης ή μιας κατάστασης που ισχύει πάντα. Στη θέση του *if* μπορούμε να χρησιμοποιήσουμε το *when*.
→ *If/When you **emigrate**, it **is** hard to settle down.*

5.2 First Conditional

If clause	Main clause
Present tense	*will, can, could, may, might* + απαρέμφατο χωρίς *to* (bare infinitive)

Χρησιμοποιούμε το **first conditional** για να μιλήσουμε για το αποτέλεσμα μιας πράξης ή μιας κατάστασης που είναι πιθανό να συμβεί τώρα ή στο μέλλον.
→ *If I **find** a better job advertised, I **will apply** for it.*
Μπορούμε επίσης να χρησιμοποιήσουμε προστακτική (imperative) στην κύρια πρόταση.
→ *If you don't understand something, **give** me a call.*

5.3 Second Conditional

If clause	Main clause
Present tense	*will, can, could, may, might* + απαρέμφατο χωρίς *to* (bare infinitive)

Χρησιμοποιούμε το **second conditional** για να μιλήσουμε για κάτι:
που μάλλον δε θα συμβεί τώρα ή στο μέλλον.
→ *If he **left** home, he **wouldn't see** his parents so often.*
που δε θα συμβεί ή που είναι καθαρά υποθετικό στο παρόν ή στο μέλλον.
→ *If I **had** the money, I **would give up** working.*
Μπορούμε να χρησιμοποιήσουμε το second conditional για να δώσουμε συμβουλή.
→ *If I **were** you, I **would forget** about a career in nuclear physics.*

Σημείωση: Συνήθως χρησιμοποιούμε *were* για όλα τα πρόσωπα σε προτάσεις του second conditional.
→ *If the social worker **were** here, she **would advise** us what to do.*

5.4 Third Conditional

If clause	Main clause
Past Perfect	*would, could, might* + *have* + past participle

Χρησιμοποιούμε το **third conditional** για να μιλήσουμε για γεγονότα ή καταστάσεις που θα μπορούσαν να είχαν συμβεί στο παρελθόν, αλλά δε συνέβησαν. Αυτά είναι πάντα υποθετικά γιατί δεν μπορούμε να αλλάξουμε το παρελθόν.
→ *If you **hadn't insulted** him, he **wouldn't have fired** you.*
→ *You **might have stood** a better chance of getting hired if you **had dressed** appropriately.*

5.5 Conditionals without *if*

Μπορούμε να χρησιμοποιήσουμε *provided/providing that, on condition that* και *as long as* στη θέση του *if* σε προτάσεις του first conditional.
→ ***Provided** you keep calm, you will pass the finals with flying colours.*
→ ***As long as** class discrimination exists, the structure of society will remain unfair.*
Μπορούμε να χρησιμοποιήσουμε *unless* σε προτάσεις του first και του second conditional. Σημαίνει *if not*.
→ *She won't attend the conference **unless** the company pays for the fee.*
Μπορούμε να χρησιμοποιήσουμε το *otherwise* αντί για την *if* clause. Σημαίνει *if not*.
→ *Get a haircut, and cover those tattoos before the interview. **Otherwise**, they won't take you seriously.*

Μπορούμε να χρησιμοποιήσουμε το *supposing* σε όλες τις υποθετικές προτάσεις. Η κύρια πρόταση συνήθως είναι ερωτηματική. Σημαίνει 'αν υποθέσουμε' ή 'τι θα γινόταν αν'.

→ **Supposing** *you could start your own business, what would it be?*

Μπορούμε να αντικαταστήσουμε το *if* με προστακτική και να χωρίσουμε τις δύο προτάσεις με *and*.

→ **Do** *that again,* **and** *you'll risk being expelled from school.*

Μπορούμε να χρησιμοποιήσουμε το *if it wasn't for/if it weren't for/if it hadn't been for* + ουσιαστικό να αντικαταστήσουμε το *if*.

→ **If it weren't for** *their children, they would think about emigrating.* (If they didn't have children ...)

→ **If it hadn't been for** *the reference you gave, I wouldn't have got the job.* (If you hadn't given me a good reference ...)

Μπορούμε να χρησιμοποιήσουμε το *but for* στη θέση του *if it wasn't for/if it weren't for/if it hadn't been for*.

→ **But for** *his laziness, he wouldn't have got fired.*

→ **But for** *his tutor's support, he wouldn't have been able to pass the course.*

5.6 Inverted Conditionals

Μπορούμε να χρησιμοποιήσουμε inversion (αντιστροφή) με τους παρακάτω τύπους. Η αντιστροφή είναι πιο επίσημη.

→ **Should you need** *access to the office after hours, please contact the caretaker.* (If you need/should need ...)

→ **Were he to** *lose his position, he would be heartbroken.* (If he were to lose ..., If he lost ...)

→ **Had I** *recognised her, I would have spoken to her.* (If I had recognised ...)

→ **Had he not** *intervened, the situation might have got out of control.* (If he hadn't intervened ...)

5.7 Mixed Conditionals

If clause	Main clause
Past Perfect	*would* + απαρέμφατο χωρίς *to* (bare infinitive)

Έχουμε mixed conditional όταν τα δύο μέρη της υποθετικής πρότασης αναφέρονται σε διαφορετικό χρόνο. Χρησιμοποιούμε mixed conditional για να εκφράσουμε το αποτέλεσμα που έχει στο παρόν ένα υποθετικό γεγονός ή κατάσταση του παρελθόντος. Μπορούμε επίσης να το χρησιμοποιήσουμε για να αναφερθούμε σε μία παρούσα κατάσταση που επεξηγεί ένα γεγονός ή μία κατάσταση του παρελθόντος.

→ *If they* **had had** *more in common, they* **might** *still* **be** *together.*

→ *If he* **weren't** *so worried about losing his job, he* **would have pointed out** *the boss's error.*

5.8 Conditionals with continuous tenses

Μπορούμε να χρησιμοποιήσουμε continuous tenses για να μιλήσουμε για:

μία πράξη διαρκείας

→ *If you're* **going** *shopping,* **will** *you* **buy** *me some bread?*

→ *If he* **had been driving** *more carefully, he* **wouldn't have caused** *the acident.*

μία θέληση

→ *If you* **are planning** *to take time off, you* **should tell** *the manager.*

5.9 *If + going to*

Μπορούμε να χρησιμοποιήσουμε *if + going to* για να μιλήσουμε για:

μία θέληση

→ *If you* **are going to travel** *next week, you should buy your ticket today.*

ένα αποτέλεσμα που είναι φανερό από μία παρούσα κατάσταση

→ *If the local economy* **is going to get** *worse, we'll have to consider emigrating.*

5 Grammar

5.10 *If* + modals

Μπορούμε να χρησιμοποιήσουμε *if* + modals για να εκφράσουμε:

ευγένεια

→ If you **would take** a seat in the waiting room, I will be with you in a minute, Madam.

→ If you **would like** to hold on a moment, I'll check your account details.

→ If I **might be** so bold, could I ask when I'm likely to have a response?

προθυμία

→ If you **will accept** the offer, we will draw up the contract immediately. (Αν δέχεσαι/δεχτείς ...)

απροθυμία

→ If she **won't listen** to me, I will have to take the matter further. (Αν δεν μου δώσει σημασία, ...)

θυμό

→ If he **would pay** attention, I wouldn't have to repeat myself. (Αν πρόσεχε, ...)

→ If you **must play** those games, at least turn the volume off!

Grammar Exercises

A Complete the conditional sentences with the correct form of the verbs in brackets.

1 If Paul's friends _____ (egg) him on to rob the corner shop, he wouldn't have been arrested.

2 If you _____ (finish already) with your homework, you may go out with your friends.

3 If people live below the poverty line, they _____ (not get) much chance of improving their lives.

4 Where does your team practise if it _____ (rain)?

5 She's the best student in her class, so if she failed the exam, it _____ (not do) her self-esteem any good.

6 If he _____ (give) up now, all his efforts to become the top tennis player of his generation would go down the drain.

7 If Carolina _____ (not slip) up and told us what happened, we would never have found the truth about the accident.

8 If Mike hadn't plucked up the courage to move to a new city, he _____ (not land) his dream job.

9 If Nick had been working harder all around the year, he _____ (not fail) the exam.

10 If she had her mother's looks and her father's acting talent, she _____ (able) to make a career in Hollywood.

B Complete the sentences with the words and phrases below.

| otherwise   given   provided   as long as   supposing   what if   on condition   but for   in case   unless   whether |

1 _____ your boss asked you to break the law in exchange for a promotion or higher salary, would you do it?

2 I'll help you finish the project before the deadline _____ you help me with mine next week.

3 _____ that it costs a fortune to travel around the world in style, Nick had few illusions that he'd ever manage to fulfil his dream.

4 You should make sure you're always on time. _____, your position in the company might be at risk.

5 Jeremy wouldn't ask you to do overtime _____ it was absolutely essential to get the project finished before this evening.

6 You don't run the risk of losing your money _____ you invest wisely.

7 It is unclear _____ Kate knew she was breaking the law or not when she made the prank phone call.

8 The judge will probably disregard your misdemeanour _____ that you do community work for a month.

9 'I'll try for the Olympic team.' 'And _____ you fail?'

10 _____ his mentor's advice, Ian would never have succeeded in securing the post of managing director.

C Rewrite sentences 1–10 without *if*. Write all the possible options.

1 If you meet Donna, please tell her the assistant manager is looking for her.

_____

2 If Jasmine hadn't set an example, the children wouldn't have been encouraged to learn more.

_____

_____

_____

3 If the school principal discovered what happened, the students would be suspended from school.

_____

4 If Ismini had texted or called more often, we would have stayed in touch.

_____

5 If you caught anyone cheating in the exam, what would you do?

_____

6 If the arrested teenagers show remorse, their sentence will be reduced to a minimum.

_____

7 If we had suspected that he was stealing the company secrets, we would have had him prosecuted immediately.

_____

8 If his dreams came true, he'd be the happiest man in the world.

_____

9 If so many celebrities hadn't helped out, the charity organisation wouldn't have been able to survive.

_____

_____

_____

10 He would never have achieved such high standards if his teacher hadn't inspired him to do so.

_____

_____

_____

D Match the bold words in sentences 1–8 with their functions a–h.

1 If she **keeps** being rude, the school will be obliged to take measures.
2 If you **would like** to make a donation to our cause, we will happily provide you with further information about tax exemption.
3 If they **were going to rob** the bank, they'd have already been making plans!
4 If you **must wear** those clothes, at least make sure they're clean.
5 If you **would just lend** us a hand here, we might finish before midnight.
6 I'm willing to give you a second chance, if you**'ll pull yourself together**.
7 If **I might ask**, why are you refurbishing your offices?
8 If the children **won't change** their behaviour, we won't take them on the school trip.

a unwillingness
b politeness
c politeness
d willingness
e criticism / anger
f insistence
g anger
h intention

5 Grammar

For questions 1–8, read the text below and think of the word which best fits each space. Use only one word in each space.

Josh will stop at nothing (1) _____ it means he can get what he wants. Sometimes I believe he wouldn't even hesitate to resort to illegal means as (2) _____ as they helped him achieve his goals. His determination to reach the top of the corporate ladder makes him have a (3) _____ at anything that falls in his hands and nothing (4) _____ act as a deterrent to his ambitions. He's rather unscrupulous and I'm (5) _____ to agree with those of his colleagues who dislike and distrust him. He leaps (6) _____ every opportunity he gets to promote himself and at the same time puts down colleagues and friends whom he perceives as threats (7) _____ his career. (8) _____ for the fact that he helped me once when I was starting out in the company, I wouldn't want to have anything to do with him anymore.

6 Made of Money

page 79

6.1 **embed** (v) /ɪmˈbed/
place sth firmly into sth ● *The enemy arrows were embedded on his wooden shield.*
➢ embeddedness (n) ❖ εμφυτεύω

6.2 **shrine** (n) /ʃraɪn/
a place where people visit because it has an important personal or spiritual meaning to them ● *A roadside shrine was erected near the site of the fatal accident.* ➢ enshrine (v)
❖ ναός, ιερό

Reading

pages 80-81

6.3 **precept** (n) /ˈpriːsept/
a principle or general rule ● *She raised her children according to strong moral precepts.*
❖ κανόνας, ηθικό δίδαγμα

6.4 **expenditure** (n) /ɪkˈspendɪtʃə(r)/
the amount of money you spend ● *Excessive expenditure on overstaffed public services has led the country into debt.* ➢ expend (v), expendable (adj) ❖ δαπάνη

6.5 **shilling** (n) /ˈʃɪlɪŋ/
a coin worth 1/20 of one pound used in Britain until 1971 ● *Gran said she only needed a few shillings a day to do all her shopping in the past.* ❖ σελλίνι

6.6 **miserly** (adj) /ˈmaɪzəli/
mean; reluctant to spend money that you have ● *The miserly business owner refused to upgrade the office equipment.* ➢ miser (n), miserliness (n) ❖ τσιγκούνης

6.7 **whereby** (adv) /weəˈbaɪ/
because of which ● *We had to sign a new contract whereby we agreed to work unpaid overtime.* ❖ με το οποίο

6.8 **lustre** (n) /ˈlʌstə(r)/
the quality that makes sth appealing ● *The palace grounds have lost their lustre with the ravages of time.* ➢ lustrous (adj) ❖ λάμψη

6.9 **official** (n) /əˈfɪʃl/
sb in a position of authority in an organisation ● *Tax officials are examining the company's accounts.* ➢ official (adj), officially (adv) ❖ υπεύθυνος

6.10 **parish** (n) /ˈpærɪʃ/
a small geographical area that has its own church and/or elected local government ● *The Sunday morning church bells were heard throughout the parish.* ➢ parishioner (n) ❖ ενορία

6.11 **beadle** (n) /ˈbiːdl/
a minor church officer ● *The beadle made sure the hymn books were all neatly in place before the congregation arrived for the service.* ❖ ενοριακός λειτουργός

6.12 **workhouse** (n) /ˈwɜːkhaʊs/
a place where poor people were sent to live and had to do work ● *In Victorian times, those who could not support their families were often sent to the workhouse and forced to earn their keep there.* ❖ πτωχοκομείο
✎ Syn: poorhouse

6.13 **gloom** (n) /gluːm/
a feeling of hopelessness and sadness; a lack of light ● *An air of gloom and fear hung over the city in the wake of the attacks.* ➢ gloomy (adj), gloomily (adv) ❖ κατήφεια, σκοτεινιά

6.14 **set sth to rights** (expr) /set ˈsʌmθɪŋ tuː raɪts/
correct a situation ● *The newly elected government had promised to set the education system to rights.* ❖ διορθώνω

6.15 **establish** (v) /ɪˈstæblɪʃ/
create sth and make people accept it ● *The first high school in Scotland was established in Dunfermline in 1120.* ➢ establishment (n), established (adj) ❖ ιδρύω

6.16 **periodically** (adv) /ˌpɪəriˈɒdɪkli/
regularly ● *Periodically, the guard walked along the corridors to check up on the prisoners.* ➢ period (n), periodic (adj), periodical (adj) ❖ περιοδικά

6.17 **oatmeal** (n) /ˈəʊtmiːl/
crushed oats used to make food ● *We were offered traditional biscuits made from oatmeal and honey.* ❖ βρώμη

6.18 **gruel** (n) /ˈgruːəl/
a thin porridge; a dish made by boiling oats in water ● *Slaves aboard the ship had nothing but a plate of gruel to sustain them daily.* ➢ gruelling (adj) ❖ χυλός

6.19 **copper** (n) /ˈkɒpə(r)/
a large copper cooking pot ● *The steaming hot soup was served from an old-fashioned copper.* ➢ copper (adj) ❖ χάλκινη χύτρα

6.20 **apron** (n) /ˈeɪprən/
an item of clothing worn over the front of the body to keep clothes clean when you prepare food or do other work ● *The baker's long white apron was covered with flour.* ❖ ποδιά

6.21 **composition** (n) /ˌkɒmpəˈzɪʃn/
a mixture of different things which form sth
• *The composition of the village community is mainly senior citizens with a handful of young families.* ➤ compose (v), composite (adj)
❖ σύσταση, σύνθεση

6.22 **porringer** (n) /ˈpɒrɪŋə(r)/
a small portion of food • *Oliver was refused another porringer of food.* ❖ μικρή μερίδα φαγητού

6.23 **devour** (v) /dɪˈvaʊə(r)/
eat quickly and hungrily • *After devouring its share of the prey, the lion lay down to watch the cubs eat the remains.* ❖ καταβροχθίζω

6.24 **voracious** (adj) /vəˈreɪʃəs/
greedy; eating a lot • *Our long hike had left us with a voracious appetite.* ➤ voracity (n), voraciously (adv) ❖ αδηφάγος, αχόρταγος

6.25 **implicitly** (adv) /ɪmˈplɪsɪtli/
absolutely and without a doubt • *I've known Maria for years and trust her implicitly.*
➤ implicit (adj) ❖ ανεπιφύλακτα

6.26 **cast lots** (expr) /kɑːst lɒts/
choose sth/sb by lot (where each person selects sth from a container whoever gets the different one is chosen) • *Do we really need to cast lots to decide who washes the dishes?*
❖ ρίχνω κλήρο

6.27 **station** (v) /ˈsteɪʃn/
send sb to stand or wait in a particular place; place yourself in a particular place to wait for or watch sth • *A patrol car was stationed at every junction.* ➤ station (n) ❖ σταθμεύω

6.28 **pauper** (n) /ˈpɔːpə(r)/
a very poor person • *The artist died a pauper, which is ironic given the current value of his works.* ❖ άπορος

6.29 **range** (v) /reɪndʒ/
arrange in a certain order • *The photographers ranged themselves along the foot of the stage.* ➤ range (n) ❖ παρατάσσω

6.30 **grace** (n) /greɪs/
a short prayer made before eating a meal
• *After George said a Thanksgiving grace, we tucked in to the turkey dinner.* ➤ grace (v), gracious (adj), graciously (adv) ❖ σύντομη προσευχή πριν το γεύμα

6.31 **commons** (n) /ˈkɒmənz/
a school or college dining hall • *Ron sat at a long table with his classmates for breakfast in the school commons.* ❖ τραπεζαρία σχολείου ή κολλεγίου

6.32 **compassion** (n) /kəmˈpæʃn/
a feeling of sympathy for and urge to help sb/sth that is suffering • *His eyes filled with compassion when he found the abandoned puppies.* ➤ compassionate (adj), compassionately (adv) ❖ συμπόνια, ευσπλαχνία

6.33 **inmate** (n) /ˈɪnmeɪt/
a resident of a prison or other institution which they are not free to leave • *A couple of inmates escaped from the prison by means of a helicopter that suddenly landed in the yard.*
❖ κρατούμενος, τρόφιμος

6.34 **hesitant** (adj) /ˈhezɪtənt/
slow to say or do sth because you are unsure or unwilling • *I'm still hesitant about accepting the job offer as it involves relocating.*
➤ hesitate (v), hesitation (n), hesitantly (adv)
❖ διστακτικός

6.35 **capital punishment** (n) /ˈkæpɪtl ˈpʌnɪʃmənt/
punishment by death • *Capital punishment is still enforced in many states of the USA.*
❖ θανατική ποινή

6.36 **rid sb/sth of sth/sb** (phr v) /rɪd ˈsʌmbədi ˈsʌmθɪŋ əv ˈsʌmbədi/ˈsʌmθɪŋ/
remove the source of a problem from sb/sth
• *Drastic measures are being taken to rid the country of the disease.* ➤ riddance (n)
❖ απαλλάσσω

6.37 **elder** (n) /ˈeldə(r)/
an old and respected member of a tribe or small community • *The village elders met to share air their views I the old square.* ➤ elder (adj), elderly (adj) ❖ γέροντας

6.38 **conspirator** (n) /kənˈspɪrətə(r)/
sb who is involved in a secret plan to do sth damaging • *The conspirators' best tool to bring down the dictator was media propaganda.* ➤ conspire (v), conspiracy (n), conspiratorial (adj) ❖ συνωμότης

6.39 **exploitative** (adj) /ɪkˈsplɔɪtətɪv/
using sb/sth unfairly for your own gain
• *Grossly underpaid and overworked, she took her employers to court over their exploitative terms of service.* ➤ exploit (v), exploitation (n)
❖ καταχρηστικός

6.40 **nudge** (v) /nʌdʒ/
push your elbow against sb beside you to atract their attention • *Dora nudged me and pointed silently towards the snake emerging from the rocks next to us.* ➤ nudge (n)
❖ σκουντώ

6.41 **reckless** (adj) /ˈrekləs/
behaving in careless risk-taking way
• *It was hardly surprising when she crashed off the road since she's always been a reckless driver.* ➤ recklessness (n), recklessly (adv) ❖ απρόσεκτος

6.42 **temerity** (n) /təˈmerəti/
an over-confident outspoken manner that can seem rude • *How dare you have the temerity to speak to me like that!* ❖ θράσος

6.43 **pinion** (v) /ˈpɪnjən/
restrain sb by tying or holding them so that they cannot move • *The kidnappers had pinioned their victim to the chair.* ❖ δένω τα χέρια κάποιου

6.44 **countenance** (n) /ˈkaʊntənəns/
face or facial expression • *Happiness beamed from each child's countenance as they sang.* ❖ όψη, έκφραση

6.45 **distinctly** (adv) /dɪˈstɪŋktli/
easily noticeable or recognisable; clearly
• *I distinctly remember the day we first met.* ➣ distinction (n), distinct (adj) ❖ ευδιάκριτα

6.46 **confinement** (n) /kənˈfaɪnmənt/
the state of being imprisoned or put in a place to limit or restrain your movements • *The prisoner was kept in solitary confinement for six months.* ➣ confine (v) ❖ κράτηση, φυλάκιση

6.47 **apprentice** (n) /əˈprentɪs/
sb who works as a trainee with an experienced worker to learn the skills of a trade • *The plumber arrived with an apprentice carrying his equipment.* ➣ apprentice (v) ❖ μαθητευόμενος

People

apprentice	miser
beadle	official
conspirator	retailer
elder	shareholder
fraudster	street vendor
inmate	tycoon

Vocabulary   pages 82-83-84

6.48 **compensate** (v) /ˈkɒmpenseɪt/
make up for or pay sb back for sth • *He had to work double overtime to compensate for having taken extra leave.* ➣ compensate (v), compensation (n), compensatory (adj) ❖ αποζημιώνω

6.49 **incur** (v) /ɪnˈkɜː(r)/
become liable to pay sth; become subject to sth • *They incurred a massive amount of debt to repay on their credit cards as a result of their reckless spending spree.* ❖ υφίσταμαι, παθαίνω ζημιά

6.50 **reimburse** (v) /ˌriːɪmˈbɜːs/
pay sb back for sth they have lost or paid out
• *The airline reimbursed us for the damage to our suitcases.* ➣ reimbursement (n) ❖ αποζημιώνω

6.51 **squander** (v) /ˈskwɒndə(r)/
spend money carelessly and wastefully
• *He squandered all his spare cash on sports cars and motorbikes and now he's broke.* ➣ squanderer (n) ❖ σπαταλώ

6.52 **retailer** (n) /ˈriːteɪlə(r)/
sb who buys goods from suppliers and sells to consumers • *Many High Street retailers have closed their shops and turned to online selling.* ➣ retail (v), retail (n), retailing (n), retail (adj) ❖ έμπορος λιανικής

6.53 **frenzy** (n) /ˈfrenzi/
a state of fast uncontrolled action • *Supporters cheered in a frenzy of excitement when the winning goal was scored.* ➣ frenzied (adj) ❖ παραλήρημα

6.54 **backtrack** (v) /ˈbæktræk/
go back on a previous decision or statement
• *The moment they came to power, they began to backtrack on their pre-electoral promises.* ❖ πισωγυρίζω, ανακαλώ, οπισθοχωρώ

6.55 **inheritance** (n) /ɪnˈherɪtəns/
the property or money you receive as a legal right from a relative after their death • *Mike's aunt left him a small inheritance in her will.* ➣ inherit (v), inheritor (n), inheritable (adj) ❖ κληρονομιά

6.56 **elaborate** (adj) /ɪˈlæbərət/
complicated but carefully planned • *It must have taken you hours to prepare such an elaborate meal, but it was delicious.* ➣ elaborate (v), elaboration (n), elaborately (adv) ❖ περίτεχνος, περίπλοκος

6.57 **stock exchange** (n) /stɒk ɪksˈtʃeɪndʒ/
the business of buying and selling shares in companies; the building where this activity happens • *There was a flurry of activity on the stock exchange following the announcement of the takeover bid.* ❖ χρηματιστήριο

6.58 **field** (v) /fiːld/
receive and respond to questions or comments
• *I spent half the night fielding comments on my blog.* ❖ απαντώ σε ερωτήσεις ή σχόλια

6.59 **shareholder** (n) /ˈʃeəhəʊldə(r)/
sb who owns shares in a business • *Company shareholders began to sell out when rumours of closure were published.* ❖ μέτοχος

6.60 **margin** (n) /ˈmɑːdʒɪn/
extra amount of sth included to ensure sth is a success; small amount by which sb wins sth
• *The tight schedule left no margin for error.* ➣ marginal (adj), marginally (adv) ❖ περιθώριο

6.61 **merger** (n) /ˈmɜːdʒə(r)/
the act of joining two companies together into one • *The possibility of a merger between two of the country's major banks was ruled out.* ➣ merge (v) ❖ συγχώνευση

6.62 **tycoon** (n) /taɪˈkuːn/
sb who is wealthy and powerful due to success in business • *Aristotle Onassis went from humble beginnings to become a wealthy business tycoon.* ❖ μεγιστάνας

6.63 concession (n) /kən'seʃn/
a cost reduction for people of certain categories • *People over 60 are entitled to travel concessions in the UK.* ➤ concede (v), concessionary (adj) ❖ έκπτωση

6.64 mortgage (n) /'mɔːgɪdʒ/
a repayable amount loaned from a bank or building society to buy property • *Thomas faced the threat of eviction when he couldn't keep up with his mortgage repayments.* ➤ mortgage (v) ❖ στεγαστικό δάνειο

6.65 abuse (n) /ə'bjuːs/
the use or treatment of sth/sb in a harmful or wrong way • *The revolution came about to curb the dictator's abuse of power.* ➤ abuse (v), abusive (adj), abusively (adv) ❖ κατάχρηση

6.66 misuse (n) /ˌmɪs'juːs/
the act of using sth wrongly or dishonestly • *She was fired from the bank after misusing customers' private data for marketing purposes.* ➤ misuse (v) ❖ κακή χρήση

6.67 bribe (n) /braɪb/
an amount of money or other gift illegally offered to sb in exchange for help • *The referee was accused of accepting bribes to sway the result of the match.* ➤ bribe (v), bribery (n) ❖ δωροδοκία

6.68 broke (adj) /brəʊk/
without money; bankrupt • *Could you lend me a few quid till pay day? I'm completely broke.* ❖ χωρίς χρήματα
✎ Also: flat broke = completely broke

6.69 bureaucracy (n) /bjʊə'rɒkrəsi/
the complex system of regulations and ways of processing information in a government department • *You'd think the government could save money and time by reducing the amount of unnecessary bureaucracy involved.* ➤ bureaucrat (n), bureaucratic (adj), bureaucratically (adv) ❖ γραφειοκρατία

6.70 miser (n) /'maɪzə(r)/
sb who hates spending money, even if they are wealtthy • *Scrooge must be the world's most famous miser who never gave anything away until he got scared.* ➤ miserly (adj) ❖ τσιγκούνης, φιλάργυρος

6.71 posh (adj) /pɒʃ/
classy and elegant; expensive and high class • *I'm sure she got the job because of her posh accent, but it's a pity she has nothing interesting to say.* ➤ posh (adv) ❖ καθωσπρέπει, σικ

6.72 skint (adj) /skɪnt/
having no money • *I need a new pair of shoes, but I'm skint so I'll have to make do without them.* ❖ άφραγκος

6.73 backhander (n) /'bækhændə(r)/
a bribe; an illegal payment given secretly in return for special treatment • *The surgeon was caught red-handed accepting a backhander from the patient's family.* ❖ 'λάδωμα'

6.74 tight-fist (n) /taɪt fɪst/
miser • *David was such a tight-fist that he always managed to get out of paying his share of the restaurant bill.* ➤ tight-fisted (adj) ❖ τσιγκούνης

6.75 dosh (n) /dɒʃ/
money • *Let's stop at the ATM; I need to get some dosh for shopping.* ❖ χρήματα

6.76 red tape (n) /red teɪp/
the bureaucratic process that makes it hard to deal with government departments • *Replacing his stolen driving licence involved an incredible amount of red tape.* ❖ γραφειοκρατία

6.77 moneyed (adj) /'mʌnid/
rich • *The well-laid lawns of the moneyed villas were a far cry from the backstreets of the city centre.* ❖ πλούσιος

6.78 extravagant (adj) /ɪk'strævəgənt/
spending more than is necessary or than is affordable • *It seemed extravagant spending so much on a pair of shoes, but at least they were ethically made and so comfortable.* ➤ extravagance (n), extravagantly (adv) ❖ πολυδάπανος, υπερβολικός

6.79 thrifty (adj) /'θrɪfti/
cautious about spending money; not spending more than necessary • *You ought to be a little more thrifty with your pay packet and keep some cash for a rainy day.* ➤ thrift (n) ❖ οικονόμος, λιτός

6.80 lavish (adj) /'lævɪʃ/
luxurious; generous • *Despite their humble home, they always bestow the most lavish hospitality on their guests.* ➤ lavish (v) ❖ πλουσιοπάροχος

6.81 opulent (adj) /'ɒpjələnt/
wealthy; luxurious • *The room was decorated with opulent velvet furnishings.* ➤ opulence (n), opulently (adv) ❖ πολυτελής

6.82 well-heeled (adj) /wel hiːld/
wealthy • *Tim has managed to invest wisely and remain quite well-heeled, so he has a good life.* ❖ εύπορος

6.83 well-to-do (adj) /wel tə duː/
wealthy • *Shirley comes from a well-to-do family and attended the most expensive private schools.* ❖ εύπορος

6.84 aboveboard (adj) /ə'bʌv bɔːd/
honest • *The plumber's estimate was high, but it was completely aboveboard for the extent of repairs required.* ❖ δίκαιος

6.85 **crooked** (adj) /ˈkrʊkɪd/
dishonest • *A special task force was established to weed out crooked public officials.* ➢ crook (n) ❖ ανέντιμος

6.86 **shady** (adj) /ˈʃeɪdi/
suspicious-looking and dishonest • *I'd never buy a car from that shady dealer.* ❖ σκιώδης, ύπουλος

6.87 **stingy** (adj) /ˈstɪndʒi/
mean; miserly • *Contrary to popular belief, the Scots are probably far less stingy than their southern neighbours.* ➢ stinginess (n) ❖ τσιγκούνης

6.88 **spendthrift** (adj) /ˈspendθrɪft/
spending more than necessary • *Their spendthrift gestures gradually put them out of business when they ran out of cash.* ➢ spendthrift (n) ❖ σπάταλος

6.89 **penny-pinching** (adj) /ˈpeni ˈpɪntʃɪŋ/
mean; miserly • *There's a fine line between careful and penny-pinching. What's the point in having money if you can't enjoy it?* ➢ penny-pinching (n) ❖ τσιγκούνης, μίζερος

6.90 **bankruptcy** (adj) /ˈbæŋkrʌptsi/
the state of not having enough money to pay your debts • *Not only have many small firms closed lately, but some large companies have filed for bankruptcy too.* ➢ bankrupt (v), bankrupt (adj) ❖ πτώχευση

6.91 **crack down** (phr v) /kræk daʊn/
make a more serious effort to stop an illegal activity • *Police are cracking down on identity theft.* ➢ crackdown (n) ❖ καταστολή

6.92 **dole sth out** (phr v) /dəʊl ˈsʌmθɪŋ aʊt/
hand out a share of sth, e.g. money, clothes, etc. • *She dropped in at the refugee centre to dole out donations of winter clothing.* ➢ dole (n) ❖ μοιράζω δωρεάν

6.93 **rip sb/sth off** (phr v) /rɪpˈsʌmbədi/ˈsʌmθɪŋ ɒf/
cheat sb/sth • *He realised he'd been ripped off when the so-called nearly-new car broke down on its first run.* ➢ rip-off (n) ❖ κλέβω, κοροϊδεύω

6.94 **shower sb with sth** (phr v) /ˈʃaʊə(r) ˈsʌmbədi wɪθ ˈsʌmθɪŋ/
give sb generous amounts of sth • *The organisation was showered with donations following the TV appeal.* ❖ περιλούζω, κατακλύζω

6.95 **tip off** (phr v) /tɪp ɒf/
warn sb about sth likely to happen • *Police were tipped off that the suspect might be heading for the airport.* ➢ tip-off (n) ❖ ειδοποιώ κρυφά

Adjectives

Rich	Poor
elaborate	broke
posh	indigent
moneyed	skint
well-heeled	wretched
well-to-do	
minted	**Mean**
flush	exploitative
	miserly
Generous	penny-pinching
extravagant	ruthless
lavish	stingy
opulent	thrifty
spendthrift	voracious

Phrasal verbs

come into sth	rid sb/sth of sth/sb
crack down	rip off sb/sth
dole out sth	shower sb with sth
fritter sth away	tip off

6.96 **fraudster** (n) /ˈfrɔːdstə(r)/
sb who pretends to be sb/sth they are not to cheat others out of money • *The gang of fraudsters operated an insurance scam to cheat people out of their savings.* ➢ fraud (n), fraudulent (adj), fraudulently (adv) ❖ απατεώνας

6.97 **come into sth** (phr v) /kʌm ˈɪntə ˈsʌmθɪŋ/
inherit • *Penny came into a fortune when her grandmother passed away.* ❖ κληρονομώ

6.98 **be in a tight corner** (expr) /biː ɪn ə taɪt ˈkɔːnə(r)/
be in a difficult situation that is hard to get out of • *Unemployed, and having a large mortgage to pay off Rita was in a tight corner and could see no way out.* ❖ αδιέξοδο

6.99 **nest egg** (n) /nest eg/
an amount of money saved up over a period of time • *They saved a little bit every month to add to that nest egg which would make retirement more comfortable.* ❖ κομπόδεμα

6.100 **as a last resort** (expr) /əz ə lɑːst rɪˈzɔːt/
when all other options have been tried • *As a last resort, she moved back to her grandparents farm in the countryside.* ❖ ως έσχατη λύση

6.101 **in the fast lane** (expr) /ɪn ðə fɑːst leɪn/
where everything seems exciting and full of action • *As I prefer a quiet life, it's not so much life in the fast lane as life in the bus lane for me!* ❖ συναρπαστικός τρόπος ζωής

6.102 **on the side** (expr) /ɒn ðə saɪd/
as well as your main job • *Stanley works in a bank, but he also designs websites on the side.* ❖ επιπλέον

6.103 **a safe bet** (n) /bet/
sth that is likely to happen • *It's a safe bet that the bank will agree to renegotiate your loan repayment to make things a bit easier.* ➢ bet (v), betting (n) ❖ μεγάλη πιθανότητα

6.104 **in the red** (expr) /ɪn ðə red/
owing more to the bank than you have paid them • *His account was already £2,000 in the red, so the bank refused to lend him any more.* ❖ σε οφειλή / υπερανάληψη

6.105 **bottom line** (n) /ˈbɒtəm laɪn/
the main point to be considered • *The bottom line is that we've reached the end of our savings.* ❖ συμπέρασμα

6.106 **minted** (adj) /ˈmɪntɪd/
very rich • *Look at that car! She must be absolutely minted.* ➢ mint (v), mint (n), mint (adj) ❖ ζάπλουτος

6.107 **flush** (adj) /flʌʃ/
having some money to spare, usually only for a short time • *Having just received her holiday bonus, Angela was feeling quite flush and splashed out on a new hairdo.* ❖ ματσωμένος

6.108 **strapped for cash** (expr) /stræpt fə(r) kaʃ/
short of money • *Theo will be too strapped for cash to go out much until he pays off his car loan.* ❖ «στριμωγμένος» οικονομικά

6.109 **rolling in it** (expr) /ˈrəʊlɪŋ ɪn ɪt/
having a lot of money • *Everyone thinks we're rolling in it because we built our own house, but it took years of effort and we put everything into it.* ❖ «το φυσάω» (το χρήμα)

6.110 **indigent** (adj) /ˈɪndɪdʒənt/
very poor • *Who'd have believed that the former millionaire would ever end up indigent and homeless?* ❖ άπορος

6.111 **born with a silver spoon in your mouth** (expr) /bɔːn wɪθ ə sɪlvə(r) spuːn ɪn jɔː(r) maʊθ/
coming from a rich family • *Being born with a silver spoon in her mouth, she had certainly had a privileged childhood.* ❖ γόνος πλούσιας οικογένειας

6.112 **grit** (n) /grɪt/
determination • *Through sheer grit and personal sacrifice, you should be able to get the business off the ground.* ➢ gritty (adj) ❖ θάρρος

6.113 **frame of mind** (expr) /freɪm əv maɪnd/
a mood • *I'm not in the right frame of mind to sit through a theatre play, so count me out for tonight.* ❖ διάθεση

6.114 **wretched** (adj) /ˈretʃɪd/
extremely bad; awful • *We were shocked to learn just how wretched the conditions are in clothing factories of some supposedly high-end brands.* ➢ wretch (n), wretchedly (adv) ❖ άθλιος

6.115 **on the wrong side of the tracks** (expr) /ɒn ðə rɒŋ saɪd əv ðə træks/
in a poor neighbourhood • *Hamish may have been born on the wrong side of the tracks, but he succeeded in breaking out of the cycle of deprivation that pervaded the district.* ❖ σε φτωχή γειτονιά

6.116 **impetus** (n) /ˈɪmpɪtəs/
a motivating factor; stimulus • *Federer's loss in the first round gave him the impetus to give it his all in the final.* ❖ ώθηση

Expressions

as a last resort
be in a tight corner
born with a silver spoon in your mouth
cast lots
finders keepers (losers weepers)
frame of mind
go the extra mile
in the fast lane
in the red
on the side
on the wrong side of the tracks
rolling in it
set sth to rights
strapped for cash
the haves and have-nots

Grammar　　　　pages 85-86-87

6.117 **tenant** (n) /ˈtenənt/
sb who pays rent to live in a place • *Prospective tenants were expected to pay two months' rent in advance before receiving the keys.* ➢ tenant (v), tenancy (n) ❖ ενοικιαστής

6.118 **fritter sth away** (phr v) /ˈfrɪtə(r) ˈsʌmθɪŋ əˈweɪ/
gradually spend money or time carelessly • *She had frittered away her inheritance within a year.* ❖ σπαταλάω

6.119 **disclose** (v) /dɪsˈkləʊz/
reveal private or secret information • *The doctor was fired when it was disclosed that he had never actually passed a medical degree.* ➢ disclosure (n) ❖ αποκαλύπτω

Listening

page 88

6.120 bitcoin (n) /'bɪtkɔɪn/
a unit of electronic money used for an online trading system • *Just imagine if we all start trading with bitcoins and there would be no need for currency exchange.* ❖ bitcoin, είδος ηλεκτρονικού χρήματος

6.121 hyperinflation (n) /ˌhaɪpərɪnˈfleɪʃn/
a situation of rapidly rising prices which is damaging to a country's economy
• *Hyperinflation during the nineties and early noughties contributed to the world recession.* ❖ υπερπληθωρισμός

6.122 digital currency (n) /'dɪdʒɪtl 'kʌrənsi/
internet-based currency • *One day digital currency may replace banknotes and coins.* ❖ ψηφιακό νόμισμα

6.123 time bank (n) /taɪm bæŋk/
an exchange of work measured in hours or by the hour • *Time banks are a logical concept for people who are able to exchange similar services.* ❖ τράπεζα χρόνου

6.124 legal tender (n) /'li:gl 'tendə(r)/
currency that is valid and legally accepted
• *The old drachma ceased to be legal tender in Greece after the euro was adopted.* ❖ επίσημο νόμισμα

6.125 street vendor (n) /stri:t 'vendə(r)/
sb who sells goods or food directly on the street • *Street vendors were lined up outside the station selling everything from bags and clothes to cheap toys.* ❖ πλανόδιος πωλητής, μικροπωλητής

Verbs

backtrack	embed	range
command	establish	reimburse
compensate	field	salvage
devour	incur	squander
disclose	pinion	station

Speaking

page 89

6.126 finders keepers (losers weepers) (expr)
/'faɪndəz 'ki:pəz ('lu:zəz 'wi:pəz)/
a saying that means sb who finds a lost object has the right to keep it • *If nobody claims the purse you handed in, you'll get it back. So it's a case of finders keepers.* ❖ το να κρατήσει κάποιος ένα αντικείμενο που βρήκε τυχαία

Writing

pages 90-91

6.127 the haves and have-nots (n) /ðə hævs ənd hæv nɒts/
the wealthy and the poor • *Divisions between the haves and have nots appear to be deepening as more people fall into poverty.* ❖ οι πλούσιοι και οι φτωχοί

6.128 looting (n) /'lu:tɪŋ/
the crime of stealing things from shops during or after an emergency, e.g. fire • *During the riots, gangs went on a looting spree in the High Street shops.* ➣ loot (v), loot (n), looter (n) ❖ λεηλασία

6.129 societal (adj) /sə'saɪətl/
of a society and its organisation • *With the Industrial Revolution came societal reforms in Britain as more people moved to live in cities.* ➣ society (n) ❖ κοινωνικός

6.130 windfall (n) /'wɪndfɔːl/
an amount of money that sb gets unexpectedly through a win or a gift • *We received a sudden windfall when our lottery ticket got lucky.* ❖ αναπάντεχα έσοδα/χρήματα

6.131 ruthless (adj) /'ru:θləs/
cruel and heartlessly determined • *He's a ruthless gangster who will stop at nothing to control the streets.* ➣ ruthlessness (n), ruthlessly (adv) ❖ αδίστακτος

6.132 command (v) /kə'mɑːnd/
get sth e.g. rewards because you deserve them • *As a much sought-after speaker, she can command high fees for each public appearance.* ➣ command (n) ❖ απαιτώ αμοιβή

Video 6: Alaskan Money Laundering

page 92

6.133 money laundering (n) /'mʌni 'lɔːndərɪŋ/
transfer money made illegally into banks abroad or a business to make it look legal
• *The company owner was arrested on a charge of money laundering when it was clear he was living beyond his means.* ❖ ξέπλυμα χρήματος

6.134 dollar bill (n) /'dɒlə(r) bɪl/
a US dollar banknote • *The film was a moral tale about a man who found a million dollar bill in the street.* ❖ χαρτονόμισμα δολλαρίου

6.135 charred (adj) /tʃɑːd/
blackened as a result of a fire • *The charred remains of the pine forest extended along the hillside.* ➣ char (v) ❖ απανθρακωμένος

6.136 **distinguishable** (adj) /dɪˈstɪŋgwɪʃəbl/
recognisable • *On the inscription on the base of the statue, the name of the ancient sculptor was still distinguishable.* ➢ distinguish (v), distinguished (adj) ❖ ευδιάκριτος
✎ Opp: indistinguishable ❖ δυσδιάκριτος

6.137 **intact** (adj) /ɪnˈtækt/
complete and undamaged • *You were so lucky the £100 note that was in your shirt pocket remained intact throughout the washing machine cycle!* ❖ άθικτος

6.138 **salvage** (v) /ˈsælvɪdʒ/
save items from a (car/ship/train) wreck or damaged building • *Thousands of pounds worth of jewellery was salvaged from the safety deposit boxes found on the sunken liner.* ➢ salvage (n) ❖ διασώζω

6.139 **stack** (n) /stæk/
a pile • *From the stacks of papers awaiting attention on her desk, I realised it was a bad time to ask Nancy to do me a favour.* ➢ stack (v) ❖ στίβα

6.140 **trooper** (n) /ˈtruːpə(r)/
a state police officer in the USA • *When they broke down on the highway, a state trooper in a patrol car stopped to offer assistance.* ➢ troop (v), troop (n) ❖ πολιτειοφύλακας, εθνοφύλακας (ΗΠΑ)

6.141 **denomination** (n) /dɪˌnɒmɪˈneɪʃn/
a unit of monetary value • *Sharon had a vast collection of coins of different denominations from her international travels.* ➢ denominate (v), denominator (n), denominational (adj) ❖ συνάλλαγμα

6.142 **go the extra mile** (expr) /gəʊ ðə ˈextrə maɪl/
do more than is expected • *While the company's package tours are relatively pricey, they do go that extra mile to offer that holiday-of-a-lifetime experience.* ❖ κάνω μια παραπάνω προσπάθεια

6.143 **bereaved** (adj) /bɪˈriːvd/
having lost a loved one who has recently died • *She went to pay her condolences to her recently bereaved neighbour whose grandfather had passed away.* ➢ bereave (v), bereavement (n) ❖ βαθιά θλιμμένος από απώλεια αγαπημένου προσώπου

Money: nouns

backhander	merger
bankruptcy	miser
bitcoin	money laundering
bribe	mortgage
denomination	nest egg
dollar bill	shilling
dosh	stack
expenditure	stock exchange
inheritance	tight-fist
legal tender	time bank
looting	windfall
margin	

Vocabulary Exercises

A Complete the sentences with the words or phrases given.

> bureaucracy bribed flush frenzy incur maximise reimburse squandered stock exchange tight-fisted

1 Due to the economic crisis, it is difficult not to _____ debt if you don't have adequate savings in the bank.

2 Some traders gamble with our investments on the _____.

3 I shall _____ you the money you spent on the trip as soon as you return.

4 He led a lavish lifestyle and _____ all his inheritance in less than a year.

5 Retailers try to _____ their profits by holding frequent sales and promotions in order to build up a larger customer base.

6 There was a media _____ as to who would win the nomination for the CEO of the large multinational company.

7 Once the company has increased its sales and we are _____ with cash, we will be able to repay the loan and start making a profit.

8 During periods of economic boom house prices tend to soar as speculators are no longer _____ and are prepared to invest heavily now in order to capitalise on their investments in the future.

9 After a great deal of _____ the banker decided to finance the project in view of the positive assessment report.

10 The scrupulous technocrat was aboveboard in his dealings and was obviously incapable of being _____.

B Match to form expressions.

1 in the fast ☐
2 strapped for ☐
3 frame of ☐
4 in the ☐
5 in a tight ☐
6 a last ☐
7 the bottom ☐
8 on the ☐
9 a silver ☐

a cash
b corner
c lane
d line
e mind
f red
g resort
h side
i spoon

C Complete the sentences with the expressions from B.

1 This enterprise is _____ as it owes many creditors and I wonder if it will go bankrupt.
2 Many retirees have had their life savings eroded due to high inflation and they are now _____.
3 _____ is that we have insufficient funds to purchase new equipment to refurbish the factory.
4 I am a bit _____ and I was wondering if you could possibly lend me some money to tide me over until the end of the month.
5 Life _____ requires adequate sources of income to fund one's materialistic lifestyle.
6 As _____, we may have to turn to the bank for a loan in order to keep the firm operational.
7 Many working class families have a second job _____ in order to supplement and augment their incomes.
8 People who are born with _____ in their mouth are privileged financially and are as a result at an advantage over others who lack such good fortune.
9 People have to be in the right _____ to make a success of getting their start-up company off the ground.

D Circle the correct words.

1 Huge corporations are formed by the merger / margin of many smaller companies.
2 The reporter alleged that the corrupt politician had been arrested for abuse / misuse of public funds.
3 People on income support receive special compensation / concession on food and medicine.
4 The billionaire's only heir / inheritance was named during the reading of his will.
5 Having saved up a substantial deposit as a down payment for a house, the young couple were able to secure a backhander / mortgage payable over 25 years.
6 The tycoon / shareholder was informed of severe budget cuts during the shareholder's meeting.
7 During periods of economic stagnation, it is often necessary for families to become thrifty / opulent.
8 He is not penny-pinching / stingy and squanders his salary immediately before the end of the month.
9 Scrooge was renowned for being shady / miserly.
10 It was obvious that the businessman was well-heeled / opulent as he arrived in an expensive imported car.
11 The crooked / extravagant fraudster swindled investors out of their life savings.
12 Homeless people are indigent / thrifty and rely on handouts of food and clothing from charitable aid organisations.

E Complete the sentences with the phrasal verbs in the correct form.

crack down hard on   dole out   rip you off   rob of   shower with   tip off

1 Being an only child, he was _____ expensive equipment.
2 The fraud squad was recently _____ about the accountant who had been falsifying the bank accounts.
3 The wealthy businessman was _____ of his briefcase and laptop in broad daylight.
4 Banks need to regulate unethical rogue traders and _____ stockbrokers who cash in on insider trades.
5 The glib and persuasive salesman will _____ by charging double the amount for the price of the item.
6 Aid organisations _____ rations of food and clothing to those in dire straits.

6 Grammar

6.1 Inversion

Μπορούμε να χρησιμοποιήσουμε ορισμένες λέξεις και φράσεις στην αρχή της πρότασης για να τις δώσουμε έμφαση. Όταν το κάνουμε αυτό, η σειρά των λέξεων αλλάζει. Αυτό ονομάζεται inversion (αντιστροφή).

→ **Never** had they been in such a dire situation.
→ **Not only** did he close the firm, **but** he **also** disappeared without paying the staff.
→ **Under no circumstances** must you reveal the contents of the email.
→ **At no time** did he stop looking for better opportunities.
→ **Little** did he realise the potential consequences of his investment.
→ **Rarely / Seldom** does anyone receive a tax refund.
→ **Not once** did she doubt that her application would be successful.
→ I read the instructions again. **Only then** was I able to assemble the telescope.
→ **So** little cash did the we have that we decided to sell the car.
→ **No sooner** had they heard the good news than they threw a party to celebrate.
→ **Hardly / Scarcely / Barely** had she left the room than the boss summoned her again.
→ **Nowhere** can you find better bargains than at the street market.

Οι εκφράσεις *only after* και *not until* εισάγουν μια φράση ή ένα ουσιαστικό και ακολουθούνται από την αντιστροφή.

→ **Only after / Not until** he graduated did he think about applying for work.

6.2 *So & Such*

Μπορούμε να χρησιμοποιήσουμε *so* και *such* στην αρχή της πρότασης με το ρήμα *to be* για να δώσουμε έμφαση.

→ **So devastating** was the financial crash that the repercussions have been felt for years.
→ **Such** was the devastation created by the financial crash that the repercussions have been felt for years.

6.3 *Wish & If only*

Μπορούμε να χρησιμοποιήσουμε unreal past (μη πραγματικό αόριστο) με *wish* και *if only* για να αναφερθούμε σε επιθυμίες στο παρελθόν, στο παρόν και στο μέλλον.

Χρησιμοποιούμε *wish/if only* + past tense για να μιλήσουμε για το παρόν ή το μέλλον.

→ I **wish** I **lived** in a milder climate.
→ **If only** we **could find** a more economic heating solution.
→ I **wish** we **were given** a tax rebate every year.

Χρησιμοποιούμε *wish/if only* + past perfect για να μιλήσουμε για το παρελθόν.

→ I **wish** I **had had** better grades when I was a student.

Χρησιμοποιούμε *wish/if only* + *would* + bare infinitive (απαρέμφατο χωρίς *to*) για να μιλήσουμε για τις ενοχλητικές συνήθειες των άλλων, ή για να πούμε ότι θα θέλαμε κάτι να αλλάξει στο μέλλον. Το χρησιμοποιούμε για πράξεις και όχι για καταστάσεις.

→ I **wish** he **wouldn't keep** insisting that he has the problem under control when he clearly doesn't.

6.4 *Would rather & Would prefer*

Χρησιμοποιούμε unreal past forms με *would rather* όταν το υποκείμενο του *would rather* και το ρήμα δεν είναι το ίδιο. Όταν το υποκείμενο του *would rather* και το ρήμα είναι το ίδιο, χρησιμοποιούμε το απαρέμφατο χωρίς *to*. Αλλά, μετά από *would prefer* χρησιμοποιούμε το απαρέμφατο με *to*.

→ She **would rather** you **didn't throw away** so much cash on things you don't need.
→ She **would rather** you **hadn't thrown away** so much cash on things you don't need.
→ She **would rather not throw away** so much cash on things she doesn't need.
→ She **would rather not have thrown away** so much cash on things she didn't need.
→ She **would prefer** you **not to throw away** so much cash on things we don't need.
→ She **would prefer** you **not to have thrown away** so much cash on things you don't need.
→ She **would prefer not to throw away** so much cash on things we don't need.
→ She **would prefer not to have thrown away** so much cash on things we didn't need.

6.5 *Had better, It's time*

Χρησιμοποιούμε *It's time* με unreal past forms για να μιλήσουμε για κάτι που έπρεπε να έχει ήδη γίνει ή που πρέπει να γίνει σύντομα.

→ *You can't expect your parents to support you forever.* **It's time you learned to** *manage your own budget.*
→ *You have no control over your spending.* **It's time you cancelled** *your credit card.*

Για να λέμε ότι είναι η σώστη ώρα να κάνουμε κάτι χρησιμοποιούμε *it's time* με το απαρέμφατο με *to*. Συγκρίνετε:

→ **It's time** *to stop work.* (Ήρθε η ώρα να σταματήσουμε.)
→ **It's time** *we stopped work.* (Δουλέψαμε αρκετά.)

Συνήθως χρησιμοποιούμε *had better* + απαρέμφατο χωρίς *to* για να δείξουμε ότι πρέπει να κάνουμε κάτι. Συχνά έχει παρόμοια έννοια με το *it's time* + past simple.

→ *I'd better leave, the bank closes in ten minutes.*
→ *It's time I left, the bank closes in ten minutes.*

Grammar Exercises

A Complete the sentences with the correct words.

| Hardly | Hardly ever | Little | No sooner | Not a single | Not until | Only after | Under no circumstances |

1 _____ had I invested in gold when the market crashed.
2 _____ soul have I seen all day.
3 _____ did he suspect it was a money laundering scheme.
4 _____ he was strapped for cash, did he learn how to budget.
5 _____ penny pinching for years was he able to buy his own house.
6 _____ is dealing with red tape easy. Few civil servants go the extra mile.
7 _____ has he ever lent money to friends. He considers it bad policy.
8 _____ do I get paid than I'm broke again.

B Complete the second sentence so that it has the same meaning as the first, using the word given.

1 It truly is a shame I'm not rolling in it.
 wish
 I _____ rolling in it.
2 Most people consider capital punishment to absolutely barbaric.
 hardly
 Most people _____ capital punishment is justifiable.
3 He's the most tight-fisted person I've ever met in my entire life.
 such
 Never before _____ miserly human being.
4 He drives me crazy with his constant complaining about bureaucracy.
 only
 If _____ about bureaucracy all the time.
5 The expenditure was much higher than we had expected.
 so
 Little did we suspect _____ high.
6 That new restaurant is so trendy it might be a good idea to make a reservation.
 better
 It's such a trendy restaurant that _____ a table.

7 It's a pity you couldn't come. I didn't like being on my own.

   rather

   I _____ so I would have had some company.

8 I'll be able to lavish some money on myself once he reimburses me.

   after

   Only after he pays _____ be a bit more extravagant.

9 You really should call your grandmother. I suspect she'd like to hear from you.

   time

   It's _____ grandmother. She must be wondering how you've been lately.

10 I wouldn't date such a shady character if you paid me all the money in the world.

   circumstances

   Under _____ out with someone of so questionable a reputation.

C Circle the correct answer.

1 You've given me so / such good advice. I really appreciate your help.

2 Little / Only did I realise he was a shareholder in that new investment firm.

3 You'd better / rather take a taxi or you'll be late for the meeting.

4 Not until the phone rang did / could I wake up.

5 It was foolish of him to squander his inheritance. If only / Only if he had known how to budget he wouldn't be broke.

6 In / At no time did he suspect she was so crooked. Well, as they say, 'Love is blind.'

7 I'd actually prefer / rather the blue pullover to the orange one.

8 He had worked himself into such a / so frenzy I didn't know how to calm him down.

D Choose the best answer.

1 He wishes he ___ in gold before the Pound plummeted.

   a would invest   **b** had invested   **c** did invest   **d** will invest

2 Such ___ his state of mind that he attempted suicide.

   a would be   **b** were   **c** is   **d** was

3 So ___ of his achievement that he took up all out to celebrate.

   a proud was he   **b** was he proud   **c** proud he was   **d** was proud he

4 Only ___ the lottery will I be rolling in it. The chances are slim to say the least.

   a should I win   **b** when I win   **c** until I win   **d** if I win

5 Not once ___ his investment was to double within two years.

   a did he imagine   **b** would he imagine   **c** was he to imagine   **d** should he imagine

6 She ___ to go to a warmer climate for Christmas this year instead of skiing in the Alps.

   a would prefer   **b** had better   **c** would rather   **d** prefers going

7 He explains history as if he ___ in WW1. He's such a good storyteller.

   a were   **b** was   **c** had been   **d** will have been

8 I'd rather you ___ her to the party. She talked my ear off all night!

   a don't invite   **b** wouldn't invite   **c** shouldn't invite   **d** hadn't invited

9 Scarcely ___ when the students rushed out of class.

   a did the bell ring   **b** had the bell rung   **c** would the bell ring   **d** the bell rang

10 He's all doom and gloom. If only ___ be a bit more optimistic.

   a would he   **b** he should   **c** he would   **d** could he

For questions 1–8, complete the second sentence so that it has a similar meaning to the first sentence. Do not change the word given. You must use between three and eight words, including the word given.

1 He didn't realise he'd been ripped off until he got home.

   got

   Not until _____ been overcharged.

2 'You shouldn't accept presents from the public under any circumstances,' his supervisor warned him.

   should

   'Under _____ from the public,' his supervisor warned him.

3 If I were you, I'd hire an accountant to help me with the books.

   better

   You _____ with the books.

4 I wish my husband hadn't made such a heavy investment in stocks and shares.

   invested

   If _____ in stocks and shares.

5 The bitcoin met with such huge success that it became the currency in several official transactions.

   was

   So _____ became the currency in several official accounts.

6 I would prefer it if you didn't borrow any money from the loan shark.

   rather

   I would _____ to lend you any money.

7 Susan hardly knew that she was due to be laid off.

   know

   Little _____ about to be laid off.

8 We're really late in implementing a new financial policy.

   about

   It's _____ financial policy.

page 95

7.1 **glow-worm** (n) /ˈgləʊ wɜːm/
a kind of insect, the female of which produces a green light at the end of its tail ● *At night, we could see the flickering lights of glow-worms in the bushes outside our tent.* ❖ πυγολαμπίδα

7.2 **shimmer** (v) /ˈʃɪmə(r)/
shine brightly, esp on the surface of sth moving ● *Moonlight shimmered on the ripples of the lake.* ➢ shimmer (n) ❖ λαμπυρίζω

Reading

pages 96-97

7.3 **detox** (v) /ˈdiːtɒks/
detoxify; cleanse your body of harmful substances by following a certain diet and routine ● *After the excesses of Christmas parties, Neil felt he had to detox from meats and sweets to get back in shape.* ➢ detoxify (v), detox (n), detoxification (n) ❖ κάνω αποτοξίνωση

7.4 **prosperity** (n) /prɒˈsperəti/
success and wealth ● *The country's prosperity depends on the tourism sector.* ➢ prosper (v), prosperous (adj), prosperously (adv) ❖ ευημερία
✎ Syn: affluence

7.5 **detrimental** (adj) /ˌdetrɪˈmentl/
damaging ● *Plans for the construction of a hotel complex on the beach were opposed on the grounds that it would be detrimental to the environment.* ➢ detriment (n), detrimentally (adv) ❖ επιζήμιος, επιβλαβής

7.6 **take the plunge** (expr) /teɪk ðə plʌndʒ/
decide to do sth risky despite being nervous about it ● *They finally took the plunge and signed up for the Himalayan trek.* ❖ το παίρνω απόφαση

7.7 **off the beaten track** (expr) /ɒf ðə ˈbiːtən træk/
in an isolated spot ● *I stopped for the night a backpackers hostel off the beaten track in the Scottish Highlands.* ❖ έξω από την πεπατημένη

7.8 **answer for** (phr v) /ˈɑːnsə(r) fə(r)/
admit responsibility for sth; make up for doing sth ● *When the tiny island of Spinalonga became overrun with tourists, the locals felt the TV series filmed there had a lot to answer for.* ❖ είμαι υπόλογος

7.9 **simplistic** (adj) /sɪmˈplɪstɪk/
making sth appear simpler than it is ● *The government's plan to tax hotels even further is far too simplistic and will reduce revenues in the long term.* ➢ simplify (v), simplification (n), simplistically (adv) ❖ απλοϊκός

7.10 **hear sth on the grapevine** (expr) /hɪər ˈsʌmθɪŋ ɒn ðə ˈgreɪpvaɪn/
hear a piece of news from informal sources, through gossip ● *I heard on the grapevine that the area is to become a designated nature reserve, but I'm not sure if it's true.* ❖ μαθαίνω κάτι από κουτσομπολιό, κυκλοφορούν φήμες

7.11 **pristine** (adj) /ˈprɪstiːn/
very clean and well maintained ● *The white steps leading to the village church were kept in pristine condition.* ❖ άσπιλος

7.12 **seething** (adj) /ˈsiːðɪŋ/
moving energetically in a large number ● *The watermelon skin left on the beach was covered by a seething swarm of wasps.* ➢ seethe (v) ❖ ξαναμμένος

7.13 **begrudge** (v) /bɪˈgrʌdʒ/
resent that sb has sth which you feel they don't deserve ● *You shouldn't begrudge him taking a long holiday since he's been working so hard for years.* ➢ begrudgingly (adv) ❖ φθονώ

7.14 **trappings** (n) /ˈtræpɪŋz/
physical signs or decoration usually associated with sth ● *The resort has all the trappings of a traditional British seafront town with its promenade and colourful beach huts.* ❖ στολίδια

7.15 **sensibilities** (n) /ˌsensəˈbɪlətiz/
sensitive feelings ● *Detracting from the historic significance of the site, the tacky souvenir shops offended the sensibilities of the more discerning visitors.* ➢ sensible (adj), sensibly (adv) ❖ ευαισθησίες

7.16 **trickle down** (phr v) /ˈtrɪkl daʊn/
move very slowly from the top to the lower levels ● *Little of the income generated from high-end cruise ships has trickled down to the local ecomony.* ➢ trickle (n) ❖ καταλήγω σταδιακά

7.17 **make a dent in sth** (expr) /maɪk ə dent ɪn ˈsʌmθɪŋ/
make a difference by reducing the amount of sth ● *The mild winter made a dent in the takings at the ski resort as there was no snow on the slopes for weeks.* ❖ επηρεάζω μειώνοντας

7.18 haggle (v) /ˈhægl/
try to reach an agreement over a price ● *After haggling over the extortionate taxi fare, the driver finally accepted the reasonable amount we offered.* ❖ παζαρεύω

7.19 novelty (adj) /ˈnɒvlti/
unusual or out of the ordinary ● *As the passengers disembarked, street sellers laden with novelty items awaited at the port.* ➢ novelty (n), novel (adj) ❖ καινοτομία, νεωτερισμός

7.20 measly (adj) /ˈmiːzli/
disapprovingly small or insignificant ● *The minimum wage was reduced to a measly three euros per hour.* ❖ μηδαμινός, ευτελής

7.21 add insult to injury (expr) /æd ˈɪnsʌlt tə ˈɪndʒəri/
make a bad situation worse ● *Our train was delayed by six hours, and to add insult to injury, the station cafe had closed, so there were no refreshments available.* ❖ «σαν να μη φτάνει αυτό»

7.22 put one over on sb (expr) /pʊt wʌn ˈəʊvə(r) ɒn ˈsʌmbədi/
fool (sb); deceive ● *I'm sure the taxi driver put one over on us by taking us by the longest route to the museum.* ❖ ξεγελάω

7.23 voluntourism (n) /ˌvɒlənˈtʊərɪz(ə)m/
a type of tourism that allows travellers to do voluntary work in countries they want to visit ● *Voluntourism has attracted foreign visitors to assist with wildlife projects, such as the sea turtle rescue project in Greece.* ➢ voluntourist (n) ❖ συνδυασμός τουρισμού και εθελοντισμού

7.24 goodwill (n) /ˌɡʊdˈwɪl/
helpful intentions towards others ● *In a spirit of goodwill, Sue offered the homeless man a bottle of water and a sandwich.* ❖ καλή θέληση, καλή διάθεση

7.25 exacerbate (v) /ɪɡˈzæsəbeɪt/
worsen a bad a situation ● *That cream will only exacerbate your sunburn; try some yoghurt instead.* ➢ exacerbation (n) ❖ ερεθίζω, χειροτερεύω

7.26 secluded (adj) /sɪˈkluːdɪd/
in a place far away or sheltered from other people ● *What had formerly been a secluded beach on our previous visits had been transformed into an exclusive spa complex.* ➢ seclude (v), seclusion (n) ❖ απομονωμένος

7.27 spew (v) /spjuː/
emit in large amounts ● *Black smoke spewed out from the huge funnel of the ship.* ❖ ξερνώ

7.28 cargo (n) /ˈkɑːɡəʊ/
things transported in a ship or plane ● *The precious cargo of antiquities was recovered from the shipwreck.* ❖ φορτίο

7.29 soapbox (n) /ˈsəʊpbɒks/
a box or platform you stand on to declare your views in public ● *Vicky's on her soapbox again about immigration.* ❖ Αγγλικός όρος για κιβώτιο όπου στέκεται ομιλητής

7.30 imperialistic (adj) /ɪmˌpɪəriəˈlɪstɪk/
supporting the attitude that one country is inferior to another ruling power ● *The Inuit are still up against the imperialistic notion that they all live in igloos.* ➢ imperialism (n), imperialist (n) ❖ ιμπεριαλιστικός

7.31 discrepancy (n) /dɪsˈkrepənsi/
a difference between things that should be the same ● *The passenger was detained by police when the check-in staff noticed a discrepancy on his passport.* ❖ διαφορά, ασυμφωνία

7.32 lax (adj) /læks/
not strict ● *We hastily exited the smoke-filled restaurant, appalled at the lax attitude to the anti-smoking laws.* ❖ χαλαρός, αμελής

7.33 ivory (n) /ˈaɪvəri/
the hard whitish substance that forms the tusks of elephants and some other animals ● *Melinda refused to touch her grandma's old piano, disgusted that the keys were made of real ivory.* ❖ ελεφαντόδοντο

7.34 turn a blind eye to (expr) /tɜːn ə blaɪnd aɪ tuː/
pretend you don't notice sth ● *Unwilling to turn a blind eye to animal abuse, Irene posted a video of the cruel donkey driver on her blog which went viral.* ❖ «κάνω τα στραβά μάτια»

7.35 crackpot (adj) /ˈkrækpɒt/
unusual or crazy ● *Brian's latest crackpot idea is to go swimming with whales.* ➢ crackpot (n) ❖ εκκεντρικός, παλαβός, λοξός

7.36 commendable (adj) /kəˈmendəbl/
worthy of praise ● *The hotel facilities and service were highly commendable; our stay was worth every penny.* ➢ commend (v), commendation (n), commendably (adv) ❖ αξιέπαινος

7.37 implicit (adj) /ɪmˈplɪsɪt/
indirectly suggested ● *Her ongoing support was implicit from the tone of her voice.* ➢ imply (v), implication (n), implicitly (adv) ❖ υπονοούμενος, σιωπηλός

7.38 blare (v) /bleər/
make a very loud noise ● *Music blared from the nearby nightclub till the small hours of the morning.* ➢ blare (n) ❖ ηχώ δυνατά, ουρλιάζω

7.39 souk (n) /suːk/
a traditional Arab market ● *We purchased an assortment of spices and a colourful rug at the souk.* ❖ σουκ (παραδοσιακή Αραβική αγορά, παζάρι)

Places

brink	province
enclave	souk
foothill	

Vocabulary   pages 98-99-100

7.40 **oddity** (n) /ˈɒdəti/
sth/sb that appears strange • *If the Tower of Pisa is ever returned to a vertical position, it could cease to become the oddity that attracts millions of visitors.* ➢ odd (adj), oddly (adv)
❖ παραδοξότητα, μοναδικότητα

7.41 **rarity** (n) /ˈreərəti/
sth that's rare • *Asian restaurants were once a rarity in Greece, but now they are becoming more commonplace.* ➢ rare (adj), rarely (adv)
❖ σπανιότητα

7.42 **deciding** (adj) /dɪˈsaɪˌdɪŋ/
that affects a result more than other things
• *The weather forecast will be the deciding factor in their choice of destination for their winter beak.* ➢ decide (v), decision (n), decisive (adj), decidedly (adv), decisively (adv)
❖ αποφασιστικός, καθοριστικός

7.43 **desired** (adj) /dɪˈzaɪəd/
wanted • *The tour operator's advertising campaign had the desired effect and bookings began to pour in.* ➢ desire (v), desire (n), desirability (n), desirable (adj), desirous (adj), desirably (adv) ❖ ζητούμενος, επιδιωκόμενος

7.44 **dim** (adj) /dɪm/
vague; unclear • *Brad had a dim recollection of visiting the Parthenon twenty years earlier.* ➢ dim (v), dimly (adv) ❖ αμυδρός

7.45 **educated guess** (n) /ˈedʒukeɪtɪd ges/
a guess likely to be correct based on existing knowledge • *Making an educated guess, I'd say the kittens are about two months old.*
❖ καλή εκτίμηση

7.46 **narrow escape** (n) /ˈnærəʊ ɪˈskeɪp/
a situation where you only just avoid danger
• *We had a very narrow escape when the plane almost crash landed on the trees close to the runway.* ❖ «την γλυτώνω φτηνά»

7.47 **prime** (adj) /praɪm/
major; typical • *The temple was a prime example of sixth-century Greek architecture.* ➢ prime (v), prime (n) ❖ εξαίρετος

7.48 **enclave** (n) /ˈenkleɪv/
a small area of a city or country where the community has a unique culture • *Women are not allowed to visit the monastic enclave on the rocky peninsula.* ❖ θύλακας

7.49 **unsettling** (adv) /ʌnˈsetlɪŋ/
worrying • *Seeing how the island's economy had deteriorated so drastically was an unsettling experience.* ➢ unsettle (v)
❖ ανησυχητικός

7.50 **influx** (n) /ˈɪnflʌks/
the arrival of people or goods, etc. in large numbers • *Apart from the weekly influx of cruise passengers on their day trip, business has been very quiet on the island this year.*
❖ εισροή

7.51 **injection** (n) /ɪnˈdʒekʃn/
a large amount of money put in to support a business, etc. • *Despite the injection of grants to develop tourism, small businesses have become unviable due to tax measures.*
➢ inject (v) ❖ ένεση

7.52 **short-sighted** (adj) /ˌʃɔːt ˈsaɪtɪd/
not considering the possible consequences of sth • *It was a very short-sighted decision to turn up in the city without making a prior hotel booking.* ➢ short-sightedness (n) ❖ μυωπικός

7.53 **cautionary** (adj) /ˈkɔːʃənəri/
giving a warning • *His travel blog gave a cautionary tale explaining the hazards of travelling alone in the area.* ➢ caution (v), caution (n), cautious (adj), cautiously (adv)
❖ προειδοποιητικός

7.54 **unbridled** (adj) /ʌnˈbraɪdld/
uncontrolled and excessive • *The children's eyes shone with unbridled enthusiasm at the prospect of visiting Disneyland.* ❖ αχαλίνωτος

7.55 **buzz** (n) /bʌz/
a strong and enjoyable feeling of excitement
• *Motorcycle racing gives Richard a real buzz.*
➢ buzz (v) ❖ εξιτάρομαι, αναστατώνομαι ευχάριστα

7.56 **out of this world** (expr) /aʊt əv ðɪs wɜːld/
amazing; impressive • *The view from our terrace at sunset was out of this world.*
❖ εκπληκτικός, εξωκόσμιος

7.57 **out of the ordinary** (expr) /aʊt əv ðə ˈɔːdnri/
strange or different • *The concept of an underwater hotel is somewhat out of the ordinary.* ❖ ασυνήθιστος, σπάνιος

7.58 **drive (sb/sth) out** (phr v) /draɪv ˈsʌmbədi/ ˈsʌmθɪŋ aʊt/
compel sb/sth to leave a place • *The last remaining villagers were driven out in the 1960s when the area was designated an archaeological site.* ❖ διώκω, εκτοπίζω

7.59 **wipe out** (phr v) /waɪp aʊt/
destroy completely • *The emperor ordered the destruction of the temples to wipe out traces of the ancient polytheist religion.* ❖ εξαφανίζω

7.60 **dawn on** (phr v) /dɔːn ɒn/
finally begin to understand • *It suddenly dawned on us that we had missed the last bus to our hotel, so we hitched a lift from a kindly fellow tourist.* ❖ σταδιακή διαπίστωση

7.61 **itinerary** (n) /aɪˈtɪnərəri/
a plan and schedule for a journey • *The five-day itinerary includes a tour of UNESCO sites.* ❖ δρομολόγιο

7.62 **stumble upon** (phr v) /ˈstʌmbl ʌpɒn/
find by chance • *They happened to stumble upon the ruins of an ancient sanctuary when hiking in the wild cross country.* ❖ βρίσκω κατά τύχη
✎ Also: stumble across

Phrasal verbs

answer for	drive (sb/sth) out
cling on to	stumble upon
come in for	trickle down
dawn on	wipe out

7.63 **tranquillity** (n) /trænˈkwɪləti/
the state of undisturbed quiet and peacefulness • *The tranquillity of the pine forest was shattered by a blast of loud music blaring from a parked camper van.* ➣ tranquillise (v), tranquilliser (n), tranquil (adj) ❖ γαλήνη

7.64 **sparsely** (adv) /ˈspɑːsli/
with only small numbers or amounts of sth in a large area • *The holiday apartment was sparsely furnished, offering only the basic facilities.* ➣ sparseness (n), sparse (adj) ❖ αραιά

7.65 **vaccine** (n) /ˈvæksiːn/
a chemical put into the body to protect from disease • *Unfortunately, there is no vaccine to protect against mosquito-borne diseases such as dengue, which is prevalent in Asia and South America.* ➣ vaccinate (v), vaccination (n) ❖ εμβόλιο

7.66 **phenomenal** (adj) /fəˈnɒmɪnl/
very large or impressive • *A phenomenal range of souvenirs and other local goods were on sale in the souk.* ➣ phenomenon (n), phenomenally (adv) ❖ πρωτοφανής

7.67 **devastate** (v) /ˈdevəsteɪt'/
destroy completely • *The tsunami had devastated the island within minutes.* ➣ devastation (n), devastating (adj), devastatingly (adv) ❖ ερημώνω, καταστρέφω εντελώς

7.68 **wreak** (v) /riːk/
cause sth bad to happen • *Wildfires invariably wreak destruction across the country in the dry season.* ❖ προκαλώ, επιβάλλω

Look!

Προσέξτε ότι το ρήμα **wreak** είναι ανώμαλο.

*The hurricane **wrought** havoc.*

*Havoc was **wrought** with the power supply as a result of the storm.*

7.69 **province** (n) /ˈprɒvɪns/
an area of a country not including the capital city • *Life can appear idyllic in the provinces so long as adequate facilities, such as medical care, are close at hand.* ➣ provincial (adj), provincially (adv) ❖ επαρχία

7.70 **wham** (excl) /wæm/
used to denote a loud sound or sudden event • *A lightning bolt struck the tower – wham! – right in front of us.* ❖ μπαμ (ξαφνικός κρότος ή γεγονός)

7.71 **whim** (n) /wɪm/
a spontaneous desire to do sth that may not be necessary or practical • *They set off to explore the underwater caves on a whim.* ➣ whimsical (adj), whimsically (adv) ❖ ιδιοτροπία

7.72 **play it by ear** (expr) /pleɪ ɪt baɪ ɪə(r)/
decide what to do as a situation develops without a forward plan • *The ski slopes may not be open, but let's just head for Parnassos and play it by ear when we arrive.* ❖ «βλέποντας και κάνοντας»

7.73 **the tip of the iceberg** (expr) /ðə tɪp əv ðə ˈaɪsbɜːg/
the smallest visible part of a larger problem • *The online review represents only the tip of the iceberg as only a handful of people bothered to complain about the service.* ❖ η άκρη του παγόβουνου

7.74 **a drop in the ocean** (expr) /ə drɒp ɪn ðə ˈəʊʃn/
an insignificant amount, not large enough to change a situation • *Though the food packages were welcome, they were just a drop in the ocean compared to the number of starving homeless.* ❖ σταγόνα στον ωκεανό

7.75 **on the spur of the moment** (expr) /ɒn ðə spɜː əv ðə ˈməʊmənt/
without forward planning • *On a cold winter's night in Aberdeen, we decided on the spur of the moment to book a holiday in New Zealand.* ❖ απόφαση της στιγμής

7.76 **a riot of (sth)** (expr) /ə ˈraɪət əv ˈsʌmθɪŋ/
a mass of different types of the same thing • *The trees were a riot of orange hues in late autumn.* ❖ μεγάλος αριθμός από ποικιλίες του ιδίου πράγματος

7.77 **a stone's throw** (expr) /ə stəʊnz θrəʊ/
a short distance away • *Their bungalow was just a stone's throw from a secluded beach.*
❖ κοντινός

Expressions

a drop in the ocean
a riot of (sth)
a stone's throw
add insult to injury
make a dent in sth
off the beaten track
on the spur of the moment
out of the ordinary
out of this world
play it by ear
put one over on sb
take the plunge
the tip of the iceberg
turn a blind eye to

7.78 **microclimate** (n) /ˈmaɪkrəʊklaɪmət/
a small geographic area whose climate differs from the surrounding area • *Casablanca has its own microclimate which tends to be cooler than the rest of Morocco.* ❖ μικροκλίμα

7.79 **microcopy** (n) /ˈmaɪkrəˈkɒpi/
the short-form text used in apps and transactions • *Microcopy shows up in online error boxes explaining what users should do.*
❖ μικρά γράμματα που χρησιμοποιούνται σε εφαρμογές κινητής τηλεφωνίας κτλ.

7.80 **microcosm** (n) /ˈmaɪkrəʊkɒzəm/
sth that includes all the elements of sth much larger • *The island was a microcosm of the whole country.* ➢ microcosmic (adj), microcosmically (adv) ❖ μικρόκοσμος

7.81 **peculiar (to)** (adj) /pɪˈkjuːliə/
belonging to • *This particular species of fish is peculiar to the lake at Prespes.* ❖ ενδημικό ή χαρακτηριστικό συγκεκριμένης περιοχής

7.82 **embark** (v) /ɪmˈbaːk/
get on a ship; start out doing sth • *We said our final goodbyes and left our friends to embark on the ferry.* ➢ embarkation (n)
❖ επιβιβάζομαι, ξεκινώ
✎ Opp: disembark ❖ αποβιβάζομαι

7.83 **embody** (v) /ɪmˈbɒdi/
represent the concept of sth • *The Olympic Games embody the spirit of international peace and cooperation.* ➢ embodiment (n)
❖ ενσωματώνω

7.84 **come in for** (phr v) /kʌm ɪn fə(r)/
be subject to • *The local authority has come in for a lot of criticism about the state of the beaches.* ❖ υφίσταμαι

7.85 **cling on to** (phr v) /klɪŋ ɒn tuː/
be unwilling to give sth up • *Sadie clung on to the dream that one day she would be able to travel to every continent.* ❖ προσκολλώμαι

7.86 **brag** (v) /bræg/
show off; boast arrogantly • *He bragged to his gang about stealing the car.* ➢ brag (n)
❖ κομπάζω, καυχιέμαι

7.87 **gloat** (v) /gləʊt/
express pleasure at sth you succeeded in at sb else's expense • *It's time the new government stopped gloating over their victory and started putting their pre-election promises into action.* ➢ gloating (adj) ❖ εκφράζομαι χαιρέκακα

7.88 **swagger** (v) /ˈswægə(r)/
walk in an exaggerated, overtly proud way • *The victor swaggered off the court, waving to his fans and brandishing his trophy.*
➢ swagger (n) ❖ κορδώνομαι, περπατώ με κομπασμό

7.89 **concurrently** (adv) /kənˈkʌrəntli/
at the same time as sth else • *The photography and art courses run concurrently, so you can't attend both in the same term.*
➢ concur (v), concurrence (n), concurrent (adj) ❖ ταυτόχρονα

7.90 **recurrently** (adv) /rɪˈkɜːrəntli/
repeatedly • *She had the same dream recurrently for several nights in a row.* ➢ recur (v), recurrence (n), recurrent (adj), recurring (adj) ❖ επαναλαμβανόμενα

7.91 **concurringly** (adv) /kənˈkʌrɪŋli/
with the same opinion as sth else • *The department heads agreed concurringly to close the office for two weeks during the holiday season.* ➢ concur (v), concurrence (n), concurring (adj) ❖ συμπίπτοντας

7.92 **cursively** (adv) /ˈkɜːsɪvli/
in a manner with the letters joined together • *It is a rarity to read script written cursively in our digital age.* ➢ cursive (adj) ❖ συνεχής (ενωμένη, ρέουσα) γραφή

7.93 **explicitly** (adv) /ɪkˈsplɪsɪtli/
openly and directly • *Reception staff are explicitly instructed to be courteous to guests.*
➢ explicitness (n), explicit (adj) ❖ ρητά

7.94 **extravagantly** (adv) /ɪkˈstrævəgəntli/
in an excessive way • *The building was extravagantly decorated with gold-trimmed wall paintings.* ➢ extravagance (n), extravagant (adj) ❖ πολυδάπανα, υπερβολικά

Nouns: states

microclimate	resilience
microcosm	sensibilities
oddity	tranquillity
paradox	trappings
prosperity	whim
rarity	

Grammar pages 101-102-103

7.95 somewhat (adv) /ˈsʌmwɒt/
rather • *I always feel somewhat relieved when my suitcase appears in the baggage reclaim area.* ❖ κάπως

7.96 utterly (adv) /ˈʌtəli/
absolutely • *Sean was utterly exhausted after the long-haul flight.* ➤ utter (adj) ❖ εντελώς

7.97 virtually (adv) /ˈvɜːtʃuəli/
almost • *There were virtually no hotels operating in the low season in the area.* ➤ virtual (adj) ❖ πρακτικά

7.98 resilience (n) /rɪˈzɪliəns/
the strength and ability to withstand difficult situations • *Their climbing equipment showed great resilience, having stood the tests of time.* ➤ resilient (adj) ❖ αντοχή

7.99 predator (n) /ˈpredətə(r)/
an animal that hunts and eats other animals • *Some species of fish have a sting to protect them from predators.* ➤ predatory (adj) ❖ αρπακτικό, θηρευτής

7.100 foothill (n) /ˈfʊthɪl/
a small hill on the lower slopes of a mountain • *The village lies in the foothills of the Alps.* ❖ πρόποδας

7.101 brink (n) /brɪŋk/
a situation where sth exciting or dangerous is very close to happening • *I believe the company is on the brink of bankruptcy.* ❖ χείλος

7.102 poaching (n) /ˈpəʊtʃɪŋ/
illegal hunting • *Poaching, which all too often goes unpunished, is one of the major hazards endangering elephants.* ➤ poach (v), poacher (n) ❖ λαθροθηρία

7.103 sedate (v) /sɪˈdeɪt/
use a drug to cause sth/sb to become calm or sleep • *The dog was so agitated that it had to be sedated before the vet could examine it.* ➤ sedation (n), sedative (n), sedate (adj), sedative (adj), sedately (adv) ❖ ναρκώνω

7.104 inhumane (adj) /ˌɪnhjuːˈmeɪn/
extremely cruel and uncaring • *Stealing the blanket from the homeless man was an unforgivable inhumane act.* ➤ inhumanity (n), inhumanely (adv) ❖ απάνθρωπος
✎ Opp: humane ❖ ανθρώπινος

7.105 quack (n) /kwæk/
sb who makes false claims to have medical skills or knowledge; slang term for doctor • *Don't believe everything that quack tells you; get a second opinion from a more reputable doctor.* ❖ ψευτογιατρός, κομπογιαννίτης

Adverbs

abundantly	extravagantly
concurringly	somewhat
cursively	utterly
explicitly	virtually

Listening page 104

7.106 fracking (n) /ˈfrækɪŋ/
the process of using liquid at high pressure to force open natural cracks in the earth to extract oil or gas • *Conservationists are concerned that fracking will cause irreversible damage to the environment.* ❖ χρήση υγρού σε υψηλή πίεση για την εξόρυξη υδρογονανθράκων μέσω θραύσης πετρωμάτων

7.107 upcycling (n) /ˈʌpsaɪklɪŋ/
the process of treating used objects/ materials to create sth more valuable than the original object • *The imposing statues were constructed by upcycling empty aluminium cans.* ➤ upcycle (v), upcycled (adj) ❖ αξιοποίηση ανακύκλωσης για τη δημιουργία αντικειμένων πρόσθετης αξίας

7.108 understatement (n) /ˈʌndəsteɪtmənt/
a statement that makes sth sound less serious or important than it is • *Light rain? That is an understatement; there's thunderstorm on the way.* ➤ understate (v) ❖ όταν μετριάζουμε ή ωραιοποιούμε την πραγματικότητα

7.109 foregone conclusion (n) /ˈfɔːgɒn kənˈkluːʒn/
a result that is certain to happen • *It's a foregone conclusion that marine species will continue to die out if sea pollution is not stopped.* ❖ αναπόφευκτο

Speaking
page 105

7.110 **vibrant** (adj) /ˈvaɪbrənt/
energetic and lively; bright • *The carnival floats were decorated with colours as vibrant as the festive atmosphere.* ➤ vibrantly (adv)
❖ ζωηρός

Writing
pages 106-107

7.111 **indigenous** (adj) /ɪnˈdɪdʒənəs/
native to an area • *He played a musical instrument similar to the didgeridoo that is peculiar to the indigenous people of Australia.*
❖ εγχώριος, ενδογενής, ντόπιος

7.112 **deplete** (v) /dɪˈpliːt/
cause the supply of sth to reduce • *Earth's natural resources are fast being depleted.*
➤ depletion (n) ❖ εξαντλώ, μειώνω, απεμπλουτίζω

7.113 **foster** (v) /ˈfɒstə(r)/
encourage the development of sth • *The conference aimed to foster greater cooperation between nations on the issue of sea pollution.*
❖ ενθαρρύνω

7.114 **complement** (v) /ˈkɒmplɪment/
add sth extra to improve sth else • *They were served several side dishes to complement the main course.* ➤ complement (n), complementary (adj) ❖ συμπληρώνω

7.115 **abundantly** (adv) /əˈbʌndəntli/
to a great extent; extremely • *It was abundantly clear that the turtle had been injured by a ship's propeller.* ➤ abound (v), abundance (n), abundant (adj) ❖ σε μεγάλο βαθμό

7.116 **paradox** (n) /ˈpærədɒks/
sth that has strangely contrasting features • *Robin Williams was a sad paradox – the funny man who suffered from depression.*
➤ paradoxical (adj), paradoxically (adv)
❖ παράδοξο

7.117 **sprawling** (adj) /ˈsprɔːlɪŋ/
spreading over a wide area • *The sprawling concrete mass of the city stretches in all directions around the Acropolis hill.* ➤ sprawl (v), sprawl (n) ❖ πολύ εξαπλωμένος

7.118 **overrun** (v) /ˌəʊvəˈrʌn/
crowd out a place in large numbers • *The beaches are overrun with local and foreign visitors in the summer months.* ❖ κατακλύζω

7.119 **albeit** (conj) /ˌɔːlˈbiːɪt/
although it was • *It was a fulfilling, albeit tiring, hike around the mountain.* ❖ αν και

7.120 **by the same token** (conj) /baɪ ðə seɪm ˈtəʊkən/
for the same reason; by the same logic • *There was no guarantee the hotel would make a profit, but by the same token, the season had not been a complete disaster.*
❖ με τον ίδιο τρόπο, με το ίδιο σκεπτικό

7.121 **inasmuch as** (conj) /ˌɪnəzˈmʌtʃ əz/
used to add a justification for sth already mentioned • *They were utterly worn out, inasmuch as they'd just completed a 25 km walk.* ❖ καθόσον, δεδομένου

7.122 **notwithstanding** (conj) /ˌnɒtwɪθˈstændɪŋ/
despite sth • *Notwithstanding Paul's knowledge of Spanish, he hadn't a clue what the villagers were trying to tell him.*
➤ notwithstanding (adv) ❖ παρ' όλο που, μολονότι, παρά

Video 7: Reef Cleaner
page 108

7.123 **entanglement** (n) /ɪnˈtæŋglmənt/
the state of being caught or trapped in sth • *Loggerhead turtles are prone to injury through entanglement in fishing nets.*
➤ entangle (v) ❖ παγίδευση, εμπλοκή
✎ Opp: disentanglement ❖ διάσπαση, απεμπλοκή

7.124 **barge** (n) /bɑːdʒ/
a long, flat-bottomed boat • *Colourful gondolas and barges were lined up along the side of the canal.* ❖ μαούνα, ποταμόπλοιο

7.125 **utilise** (v) /ˈjuːtəlaɪz/
make use of • *The hikers utilised a piece of wood to support their injured companion's broken leg until they reached the refuge.*
➤ utilisation (n) ❖ χρησιμοποιώ

7.126 **brutalise** (v) /ˈbruːtəlaɪz/
treat sb/sth in a violent way ● *The slaves were brutalised and kept in appalling conditions.*
➤ brutality (n), brutal (adj), brutally (adv)
❖ φέρομαι με ακραία βίαιο και απάνθρωπο τρόπο

7.127 **snag** (v) /snæg/
get sth caught and torn on a sharp object
● *I couldn't avoid snagging my trousers on the thorny bushes which we had to walk through.*
➤ snag (n) ❖ μπλέκω

7.128 **shears** (n) /ʃɪəz/
a garden tool like large heavy scissors
● *Mildred was snipping away at her garden hedge with a pair of stainless steel shears.*
➤ shear (v) ❖ μεγάλο ψαλίδι, συνήθως για χρήση στον κήπο

7.129 **biodegradable** (adj) /ˌbaɪəʊdɪˈɡreɪdəbl/
that can be naturally decomposed ● *It's ironic that many supposedly environmentally friendly vegetables are sold wrapped in plastic which is not biodegradable.* ➤ biodegrade (v)
❖ βιοδιασπώμενος
✎ Opp: non-biodegradable ❖ μη βιοδιασπώμενος

Vocabulary Exercises

A Replace the phrases in bold with phrases from the box in the correct form.

> a stone's throw away   just a drop in the ocean   off the beaten track   on the grapevine   on the spur of the moment
> out of this world   put one over   take the plunge   the tip of the iceberg   turn a blind eye to

1 I don't like to spend my holidays in cosmopolitan places; I much prefer secluded areas that are **not visited by many people** _____ .

2 Although George was terrified of heights, he decided to **take the risk** _____ and try skydiving.

3 The village was not in any tour guides, but I heard about it **from people who were talking about it** _____.

4 The travel agent tried to **fool** _____ me by showing me photoshopped pictures of the area, but I had done my research on the internet and knew it wasn't really as idyllic as he was presenting it.

5 It's disgraceful how the local authorities **ignore** _____ the damage some unscrupulous hotel owners do to the environment, just so they can make a little more money from the people who will visit.

6 We hadn't been planning to go on holiday, but when we saw the brochure, we decided **there and then** _____ that we just had to go.

7 You have got to try the local cuisine; their food is **incredible** _____!

8 We discovered a lovely beach that is clean and fairly quiet, and it's only **a short drive** _____ from our home.

9 We were shocked to see how many products made from ivory and other parts of endangered animals were sold on the market – and to think that this is only **a small part of the problem** _____.

10 Voluntourists are repairing the old school in the village, but that's **very little help** _____ compared to the problems the area is facing.

B Choose the best answer.

1 ___ the objections of the local residents, they went ahead with the building of the resort.
   a albeit   **b** in as much as   **c** what with   **d** notwithstanding

2 They regretted letting the travel writer include their town in his guide, as it was soon ___ with tourists.
   a overrun   **b** snagged   **c** brutalised   **d** spewed

3 He's very proud of his home town and is always ___ that it has the best scenery.
   a swaggering   **b** bragging   **c** gloating   **d** haggling

4 It is a very popular holiday destination and sees a great ___ of visitors every year.
   a influx   **b** injection   **c** enclave   **d** input

5 The huge resorts, with their spas and swimming pools, ___ the island of its sparse water resources, leaving very little clean water for the locals to use.
   a sedate   **b** foster   **c** deplete   **d** devastate

6 The environmental protection laws in the area are very ___ making it easy for poachers to sell what they catch.
   a dim   **b** wham   **c** lax   **d** simplistic

7 Just imagine, you can enjoy all this beauty for a(n) ___ sum of money.
   a measly   **b** unbridled   **c** prime   **d** desired

8 When we booked the holiday, we ___ asked for a room with a sea view, but all we can see is the parking area.

   a concurrently   **b** recurringly   **c** utterly   **d** explicitly

9 I must admit that the surroundings are very serene, but I find it ___ unnerving that we are alone in the woods.

   a cursively   **b** extravagantly   **c** virtually   **d** somewhat

10 The local craftsmen have a reputation for their skill in the ___ of old furniture and other used items.

   a fracking   **b** upcycling   **c** sprawling   **d** poaching

C Complete the text with the correct form of the words.

Voluntourists

Kenneth and Patty were thinking of doing something different this summer, so they decided to give voluntourism a try. In today's society it may be considered somewhat of a(n) **(1)** _____ to want to spend your holiday time helping people you have never met, but that is exactly what they wanted to do. They felt that they couldn't bear to spend one more summer in a city **(2)** _____ with noisy tourists, people pushing them in the streets and music **(3)** _____ from loudspeakers at every street corner.

ODD

SEETHE
BLARE

They were fascinated by the **(4)** _____ of the idea that they would not only be experiencing the **(5)** _____ that only unspoilt nature can offer, but that they would also have the opportunity to meet people with similar to their own social **(6)** _____ and work with them to help the local communities.

NOVEL
TRANQUIL
SENSIBLE

However, before they could be allowed to **(7)** _____ on their journey, there were several things they needed to do. First of all, they needed to choose a credible agency. Given the risks involved in such a(n) **(8)** _____, they needed to be able to trust their guide **(9)** _____.

EMBARKATION

UNDERTAKE
IMPLICIT

Once that was taken care of, they would still have to spend several weeks training for their expedition. They would need to learn how to survive in the wilderness, and how to **(10)** _____ the resources they could find themselves for survival. As the areas they would be visiting are often very **(11)** _____ populated, it may take hours or even days before help could reach them in an emergency. All of the agencies they had spoken with stressed the importance of this training, and gave them **(12)** _____ warning that it is the arrogance of people towards nature, that makes it a dangerous place.

UTILITY
SPARSE

CAUTION

D Circle the correct words.

1 The specific tree can only be found in those woods due to the microclimate / microcosmos of the area.

2 The weather will be the deciding / desired factor when we choose our next holiday destination.

3 Visitors are not allowed to walk unaccompanied in the enclosure, as many of the animals living there are on the foothill / brink of extinction.

4 We found her idea of touring the Mediterranean in a hired yacht rather abundant / extravagant.

5 To say that the view from the top of the mountain is beautiful would be a(n) understatement / foregone conclusion – it is absolutely breathtaking.

6 They had no reason to believe that the building of the resort would disrupt the local villagers way of life but, by the same token / paradox, they couldn't say for sure that it wouldn't either.

7 The trade the tourist industry brings to an area adds to the discrepancy / prosperity of the local community.

8 Before travelling to an exotic destination, travellers may be required to get a number of vaccines / itineraries.

9 If you drive around the countryside, you will often stumble upon / dawn on some of the most beautiful, albeit little-known spots for a picnic.

10 The local producers need to start using stainless steel / biodegradable packaging for their products.

11 They came in for / clung on to a great disappointment when they saw their hotel room – it was nothing like the picture in the brochure the agent had shown them.

12 When travelling abroad, we like to try the delicacies indigenous / peculiar to the countries we are visiting.

7 Grammar

7.1 Gradable & ungradable adjectives

Τα επίθετα που περιγράφουν ποιότητα και έχουν comparative form (συγκριτικό βαθμό) και superlative form (υπερθετικό βαθμό) είναι gradable (διαβαθμίσιμος). Αυτό σημαίνει ότι αυτός ή αυτό που περιγράφεται από το επίθετο μπορεί να έχει το χαρακτηριστικό που αναφέρεται σε μεγαλύτερο ή μικρότερο βαθμό. Τα gradable επίθετα μπορούν να είναι strong (δυνατά) ή weak (αδύνατα). Τα δυνατά gradable επίθετα έχουν ήδη την έννοια *very* + weak gradable adjective. Για παράδειγμα, το δυνατό επίθετο *astonished* σημαίνει *very surprised* (πολύ έκπληκτος).
Τα strong gradable και ungradable adjectives μπορούν να προσδιοριστούν με επιρρήματα όπως *absolutely, totally,* και *completely,* ενώ Τα weak gradable adjectives μπορούν να προσδιοριστούμε επιρρήματα όπως *fairly, very, rather* κλπ.

gradable (weak) adjectives
➜ They were **rather shocked** at the state of the beach.
gradable (strong) adjectives
➜ They were **totally disgusted** at the state of the beach.
ungradable adjectives
➜ The price was **absolutely extortionate**.

7.2 *Quite*

Η έννοια του επιρρήματος *quite* αλλάζει ανάλογα με το επίθετο που τροποποιεί.
Σημαίνει *fairly* αν τροποποιεί ένα weak gradable adjective.
➜ They were **quite shocked** at the state of the beach.
Σημαίνει *extremely* αν τροποποιεί ένα strong gradable adjective.
➜ They were **quite disgusted** at the state of the beach.

7.3 *Too, Only too, None too*

Too σημαίνει ότι υπάρχει περισσότερο από κάτι από όσο είναι απαραίτητο. Συνήθως έχει αρνητική έννοια. Όταν θέλουμε να εκφράσουμε μια θετική ή ουδέτερη ιδέα, συνήθως χρησιμοποιούμε *very*.
➜ The consumer society has gone **too far** and now we're facing the consequences.
➜ Reaching the South Pole was **too difficult** and they failed.
➜ Reaching the South Pole was **very difficult**, but they succeeded.
Only too σημαίνει *very*, για να δείξουμε ότι θέλουμε να κάνουμε κάτι.
➜ I would be **only too happy** to take you on a guided tour.
Only too δείχνει επίσης ότι θα θέλαμε μία κατάσταση να είναι διαφορετική.
➜ She knows **only too well** the risks involved in travelling solo.
None too σημαίνει *not at all*.
➜ I was **none too surprised** to hear that you felt homesick.

7.4 Modifying adverbs

Μερικά επίθετα και επιρρήματα χρησιμοποιούνται για να τονίσουν συναισθήματα.
➜ The campaign to reduce the use of fossil fuels was an **utter** failure.
➜ Their efforts to cut down on the use of fossil fuels were **utterly** hopeless.
➜ The **pathetic** warning signs about fire hazards proved ineffective.
➜ The warning signs about fire hazards proved **pathetically** ineffective.

7.5 *Hardly, barely, scarcely* vs *almost, virtually, practically*

Τα επιρρήματα *hardly, barely* και *scarcely* είναι ευρεία αρνητικά. Αυτό σημαίνει ότι κάνουν μια δήλωση σχεδόν εντελώς αρνητική.
➜ They **scarcely** had time to reach safety when the tsunami struck.
➜ There was **hardly** any hope of finding survivors.
Αντί για αυτά τα ευρεία επιρρήματα, μπορούμε να χρησιμοποιήσουμε *almost, virtually* ή *practically* τα οποία ακολουθούνται από μια αρνητική λέξη όπως *no, never, nowhere* κλπ. ή ένα ρήμα με αρνητική έννοια.
➜ They had **virtually lost** all hope of being rescued.
➜ The rescue team **had almost given up** hope of finding them.

7 Grammar

7.6 Position of adjectives & adverbs

Τα περισσότερα επίθετα τοποθετούνται πριν από ένα ουσιαστικό. Μερικά επίθετα όπως *alone, alive, asleep, afraid, ill* και *well* χρησιμοποιούνται μετά από ένα ουσιαστικό και ένα ρήμα όπως *be, seem, look, remain* κλπ.

→ The **scared** cubs would not come in the open.
→ The cubs were **afraid** to come out in the open.
→ A **lone** tiger was seen crossing the bridge.
→ The tiger seen crossing the bridge was **alone**.

Τα επίθετα τοποθετούνται μετά από τις αντωνυμίες όπως *someone, anyone, everywhere* και *nothing*.

→ There was **something quite strange** about her.
→ Encountering a group of poachers is **nothing unusual** in this area.

7.7 Adjectives which change meaning according to position

Μια μικρή ομάδα επιθέτων έχουν άλλη έννοια μπροστά από ένα ουσιαστικό και άλλη όταν τοποθετούνται μετά από το ουσιαστικό.

→ **Concerned** members of the community complained to their local MP. (the worried members)
→ The members of the community **concerned** met with their MP. (the members whom the matter concerns)
→ The MPs explanation was rather long and **involved**. (the explanation was complicated)
→ An explanation was given by the MP **involved**. (the MP who was responsible for dealing with the matter)
→ The **present** situation is getting out of control. (the situation now)
→ He refused to discuss the matter with the reporters **present**. (the reporters in attendance)
→ They should have had **proper** instructions on emergency procedures. (correct instructions)
→ When the storm started **proper**, we were still at sea. (a real storm)
→ Those **responsible** for littering the beach will be fined. (those who are to blame)
→ Any **responsible** citizen would pick up their own litter. (any decent/sensible citizen)

Grammar Exercises

A Circle the correct words.

1 It was slightly / absolutely chilly last night so we lit the fireplace.
2 Gerald Durrell, the famous zoologist and conservationist, was totally / fairly dedicated to his life's work.
3 The very / absolutely breathtaking view makes the trek to the top worth the visitor's while.
4 The scientists were completely / very taken aback at the unexpected results of the experiment.
5 Mina, who's a fairly / rather competent speaker of Japanese, acted as our interpreter on our business trip to Kyoto.
6 He was quite / a bit convinced that one of the reasons for the climate change was the extensive use of air-conditioning around the world.
7 Ian was a bit / completely concerned with the impact of the new golf course on the local water resources.
8 The Presidential candidate was rather / totally annoyed at the questions addressed to him over environmental policies.
9 I'm completely / rather surprised at the ignorance and indifference of people about environmental issues.
10 Simon and Sonia were quite / slightly upset by the way the locals treated stray animals.

B Complete with words and phrases from the box. In some cases, more than one answer is possible.

| only too | none too | utter | bitterly | astonishingly | hardly | barely | scarcely | almost | virtually | practically |

1 The portions at the restaurant were tiny and to add insult to injury the food was _____ uncooked.
2 Unfortunately, the firefighters put out the fire _____ late to save the habitat of the last remaining animals of the species.
3 The law protecting the forests around the city was passed _____ soon. About half the forest areas have already been logged.

4 Jennifer was _____ disappointed to have failed in her mission to rescue the silver-backed gorillas in the area.

5 We were shocked by the _____ devastation the mining company caused to the area.

6 The smoke and ash from the volcano were so thick we were _____ blind.

7 They _____ made it out of the building alive after the earthquake.

8 Keisha could _____ believe her eyes when she saw the products made from endangered species on sale at the market.

9 The offer is _____ too good to be true – if I were you, I'd proceed with care.

10 _____, the species survived despite the extensive destruction of its habitat.

C Rearrange the words and phrases to make sentences.

1 want / alone. / I / to / on / go / trip / don't / the

_____

2 the / The / baby / weren't / was / and / we / asleep / allowed / to / giraffe / enclosure. / visit

_____

3 child / It / a / that / was / the / alive / was / after / found / days / three / in / the / forest. / miracle / spending

_____

4 experienced / No one / has / for / applied / post / the / of / head keeper / enough / at / zoo. / the

_____

5 long / My / well / aunt / to / follow / enough / us / the / the / trek / on / through / forest. / wasn't

_____

6 refused / The / to / deer / looked / and / very / eat / ill. / baby

_____

7 available / There / was / to / drowning / us / help / rescue / animal. / the / nobody

_____

8 are / that / Conservationists / the / insect / future / of / is / species / the / newly-discovered / bleak. / afraid

_____

9 happened / Nothing / has / for / new / quest / in / fuels. / non-polluting / the

_____

10 but / was / She / around, / looked / her / there / clean / nowhere / for / to / sit / down.

_____

D Complete the sentences with the modifying adverbs and adjectives in brackets.

1 The _____ about the factory waste pollution incident filed a report at the police station. **(concerned / citizens)**

2 The _____ about this matter staged a protest. **(concerned / citizens)**

3 He gave us (an) _____ which I'm not sure I can believe. **(involved / explanation)**

4 The _____ in the factory pollution scandal was forced to resign. **(involved / politician)**

5 All the _____ at the conference expressed their concerns about the case. **(present / people)**

6 The _____ requires taking immediate measures to reverse the damage done. **(present / situation)**

7 We expect the _____ for the cover up to face disciplinary measures. **(responsible / officials)**

8 We need to have _____ who have environmental pollution at heart. **(responsible / officials)**

7 Grammar

For questions 1–8, read the text below and decide which answer (A, B, C or D) best fits each gap.

Baby elephant finds friend

In Zululand, South Africa, a(n) (**1**) ___ unlikely pair have become best friends: a baby elephant and a large dog.

After his herd rejected him due to his (**2**) ___ serious health problems, Ellie, the baby elephant would most likely have died in the wild. Luckily for her, she was discovered by the Thula Thula Rhino Orphanage in South Africa. Ellie arrived at the rhino orphanage (**3**) ___ too soon as she was critically (**4**) ___ and had few chances of survival.

The charity organisation usually rehabilitates baby rhinos, but it is also (**5**) ___ in the care of other African wildlife babies. When Ellie the elephant first arrived, her concerned rescuers (**6**) ___ thought she would make it, but they nursed her day and night. She (**7**) ___ didn't make it, but when Duma the dog was introduced into the picture the two became inseparable, Ellie took an interest in life and started recovering fast. Her rescuers were (**8**) ___ astonished when she made a recovery.

1	**a**	rather	**b**	absolutely	**c**	almost	**d**	slightly
2	**a**	totally	**b**	completely	**c**	quite	**d**	virtually
3	**a**	all	**b**	none	**c**	barely	**d**	only
4	**a**	ill	**b**	sick	**c**	diseased	**d**	patient
5	**a**	responsible	**b**	present	**c**	concerned	**d**	involved
6	**a**	virtually	**b**	hardly	**c**	utterly	**d**	almost
7	**a**	almost	**b**	scarcely	**c**	hardly	**d**	practically
8	**a**	slightly	**b**	fairly	**c**	absolutely	**d**	very

8 Knowledge is Power

8.1 **slate** (n) /sleɪt/
a small sheet of dark grey stone that was used to write on in schools in the past • *What a long way school notebooks have come in a century – from slates to tablets!* ➣ slate (v)
❖ σχιστόλιθος

Reading

8.2 **Mickey Mouse** (adj) /ˈmɪkiː maʊs/
fake; of poor quality • *Tom took some surprising good photos, considering he only has a cheap Mickey Mouse camera.* ❖ «της πλάκας», ευτελές

8.3 **snob** (n) /snɒb/
sb who acts as if they are better than others because they know more or have different tastes • *Carol is too much of a snob to join her friends at the backstreet café; she prefers a more high class venue.* ➣ snobbery (n), snobbish (adj), snobbishly (adv) ❖ σνομπ

8.4 **land a job** (expr) /lænd ə dʒɒb/
obtain a job • *How did he manage to land a prime job at the embassy?* ❖ βρίσκω δουλειά

8.5 **hands-on** (adj) /hændz ɒn/
being practically involved in doing sth
• *The final year of the course involves work placements for students to gain hands-on experience.* ❖ πρακτική προσέγγιση

8.6 **sick (and tired) of sth/sb** (expr) /sɪk (ənd ˈtaɪəd) əv ˈsʌmθɪŋ/ˈsʌmbədi/
fed up with sth/sb • *I'm sick and tired of being bombarded with marketing phone calls.* ❖ έχω βαρεθεί / έχω σιχαθεί

8.7 **subject sb to sth** (phr v) /səbˈdʒekt ˈsʌmbədi təˈsʌmθɪŋ/
make sb endure sth unpleasant • *Maria was subjected to ridicule by her classmates when she expressed her wish to study at Oxfordbridge University.* ➣ subject (n), subject (adj) ❖ υφίσταμαι (κάτι)

Look!
Προσέξτε την διαφορά στην προφορά μεταξύ του ρήματος και του ουσιαστικού **subject**. Το ρήμα προφέρεται /səbˈdʒekt/ (sub*ject*), ενώ το ουσιαστικό /ˈsʌbdʒɪkt/ (*sub*ject).

8.8 **undertaking** (n) /ˌʌndəˈteɪkɪŋ/
an important task • *The new university is a joint undertaking between the old technical college and a private investor.* ➣ undertake (v) ❖ επιχείρηση

Look!
Θυμηθείτε ότι το ουσιαστικό **undertaker** σημαίνει εργολάβος κηδειών, τελετών.

8.9 **critical thinking** (n) /ˈkrɪtɪkl ˈθɪŋkɪŋ/
the process of considering information carefully to judge it objectively • *Students are encouraged to develop the skill of critical thinking to process information analytically.* ❖ κριτική σκέψη

8.10 **vocational** (adj) /vəʊˈkeɪʃənl/
relating to the skills and knowledge required for a particular job • *In order to become an electrician, Ken attended a one-year vocational training course.* ➣ vocation (n) ❖ επαγγελματικός

8.11 **state of affairs** (expr) /stɪət əv əˈfeəz/
a situation • *The government can no longer turn a blind eye to the shocking state of affairs in the public education system.* ❖ κατάσταση

8.12 **snobbery** (n) /ˈsnɒbəri/
the attitude of people who act as though they are superior to others • *Although he was offered a place at Cambridge, Terry opted for a local university to avoid the risk of facing class snobbery.* ➣ snob (n), snobbish (adj), snobbishly (adv) ❖ ακαταδεξία

8.13 **pale in comparison** (expr) /peɪl ɪn kəmˈpærɪsn/
seem less significant • *This light shower pales in comparison to the hurricanes coming in across the Atlantic.* ❖ ωχρώ σε σύγκριση

8.14 **bastion** (n) /ˈbæstiən/
an institute or group that holds onto a certain way of life that it represents • *Ancient Athens was one of the first bastions of democracy.* ❖ προπύργιο

8.15 **superiority** (n) /suːˌpɪəriˈɒrəti/
the state of being better or in a stronger position than others • *Although she had only just passed her degree with a minimum of study, the fact that it was from St Andrews University gave her an air of superiority.* ➣ superior (n), superior (adj) ❖ υπεροχή

8.16 **hail from** (phr v) /heɪl frɒm/
originally come from or have been born in
• *Marios hails from Crete, but he's been living
in Patra for years.* ❖ κατάγομαι από

8.17 **hallowed** (adj) /ˈhæləʊd/
respected • *Open-air theatrical performances
are one of Greece's hallowed traditions.*
❖ καθαγιασμένος

8.18 **red-brick university** (n) /red brɪk
ˌjuːnɪˈvɜːsəti/
a university built in the late 19th to early 20th
century as opposed to older established
ones (e.g. Oxford, Cambridge) • *The original
red-brick universities specialised in science
and engineering, but have now branched
out into other fields of study.* ❖ Βρετανικά
πανεπιστήμια του 19ου ή 20ου αιώνα

8.19 **in sync with** (expr) /ɪn sɪnk wɪθ/
in line with; in agreement with • *Coming from
a totally different cultural background, Ivan's
ideas were not quite in sync with those of his
British colleagues.* ❖ σε συγχρονισμό / σε
κοινή αντίληψη

8.20 **classics** (n) /ˈklæsɪks/
the study of ancient Greek and Latin language
and literature • *Anyone who has studied
classics will be familiar with the works of
Homer.* ➢ classical (adj), classic (adj)
❖ κλασικοί συγγραφείς

8.21 **take offence** (expr) /teɪk i əˈfens/
feel insulted or hurt by a remark • *Most people
would take offence at being called an upper-
class twit, but Graham took it as a joke.*
❖ προσβάλλομαι, παρεξηγούμαι

8.22 **mockingly** (adv) /ˈmɒkɪŋli/
in a way that ridicules sb/sth • *Tina mockingly
referred to her teacher's accent as 'Grenglish'.*
➢ mock (v), mocking (n), mocking (adj)
❖ χλευαστικά

8.23 **rigorous** (adj) /ˈrɪgərəs/
that has to be done according to strict rules/
standards • *The exam was supervised with
rigorous security standards.* ➢ rigour (n),
rigorously (adv) ❖ αυστηρός

8.24 **placement** (n) /ˈpleɪsmənt/
a temporary period spent gaining practical
experience in a workplace • *To complete her
social work qualification, Helen had to spend
parts of her course on placement in both state
and voluntary organisations.* ➢ place (v)
❖ πρακτική άσκηση

8.25 **have the last laugh** (expr) /həv ðə læst lɑːf/
be more successful than others expected;
prove others to be wrong • *Anthony had the
last laugh when his better qualified friends,
who were unemployed, came to him for their
car repairs.* ❖ «γελάει καλύτερα όποιος γελάει
τελευταίος» / δικαιώνομαι

8.26 **tuition** (n) /tjuˈɪʃn/
teaching fees • *University education is
definitely not accessible for everyone as tuition
fees are on the increase.* ❖ δίδακτρα

8.27 **applied** (adj) /əˈplaɪd/
that can be used practically rather than only in
theory • *William is studying applied linguistics
at Cambridge with a view to becoming a
teacher.* ➢ apply (v) ❖ εφηρμοσμένος

8.28 **a means to an end** (expr) /ə miːnz tə ɒn
end/
sth of little importance in itself which will lead
to sth better • *Liz regarded English language
teaching as a means to an end as it served
as an internationally marketable skill.* ❖ απλό
μέσο που οδηγεί σε κάτι καλύτερο

8.29 **cry out for** (expr) /kraɪ aʊt fɜː(r)/
demand; require very much • *The country is
crying out for workers with practical skills and
creative talent rather than more philosophers
and lawyers.* ❖ έχω μεγάλη ανάγκη από

8.30 **joblessness** (n) /ˈdʒɒbləsnəs/
the number of people out of work;
unemployment • *The rate of joblessness has
grown to around 50% among young people,
which is a tragic state of affairs.* ➢ jobless
(adj) ❖ ανεργία

8.31 **practicality** (n) /ˌpræktɪˈkæləti/
the quality of being suitable and of realistic
or practical use • *Becoming a design
engineer involves combining practicality with
imagination.* ➢ practical (adj), practically (adv)
❖ πρακτικότητα

Vocabulary pages 112-113-114

8.32 **acknowledgement** (n) /əkˈnɒlɪdʒmənt/
acceptance that sth is right • *Harry
received a bonus from his employer as an
acknowledgement of his contribution to the
company's success.* ➢ acknowledge (v)
❖ αναγνώριση

8.33 **appendix** (n) /əˈpendɪks/
an additional section giving supplementary
information at the end of a book, etc. • *You
can check out the rules in the grammar
appendix of your student's book.* ➢ append
(v), ❖ παράρτημα
✎ Plural: appendices

8.34 **bibliography** (n) /ˌbɪbliˈɒgrəfi/
a list of books, articles, etc. that you have
referred to in a piece of writing • *Don't forget
to include your bibliography quoting your
sources at the end of your thesis.*
➢ bibliographer (n), bibliographical (adj)
❖ βιβλιογραφία

8.35 **criteria** (n) /kraɪˈtɪəriə/
the standards by which sth is assessed or categorised ● *Do you think exams are the best criteria to assess a student's progress?*
❖ κριτήριο
✎ Singular: criterion

8.36 **fundamental** (adj) /ˌfʌndəˈmentl/
basic; most important ● *Thorough research providing statistics is fundamental to back up your report.* ➢ fundamentally (adv)
❖ θεμελιώδης

8.37 **hypothesis** (n) /haɪˈpɒθəsɪs/
an idea that you believe to be correct based on a guess or assumption ● *Her argument is pure hypothesis, so she needs to expand with a few hard facts to make it hold water.*
➢ hypothesise (v), hypothetical (adj), hypothetically (adv) ❖ υπόθεση
✎ Plural: hypotheses

8.38 **indicator** (n) /ˈɪndɪkeɪtə(r)/
a sign that shows how sth is now or likely to be ● *Exam results are not always an accurate indicator of a person's ability.* ➢ indicate (v), indication (n), indicative (adj) ❖ δείκτης

8.39 **plagiarism** (n) /ˈpleɪdʒərɪz(ə)m/
the act of copying sb's ideas, especially in written works ● *A simple internet search confirmed the editor's suspicions of several instances of plagiarism within the book.*
➢ plagiarise (v), plagiarist (n) ❖ λογοκλοπή

8.40 **dissertation** (n) /ˌdɪsəˈteɪʃn/
a piece of academic writing on a certain subject ● *Pauline had to sacrifice her social life to produce her 5,000-word dissertation for her course assessment.* ❖ διατριβή

8.41 **adhere to** (v) /ədˈhɪə tuː/
follow a set of rules, etc.● *You'd better adhere to the school rules or you may be expelled.*
➢ adherence (n), adherent (adj) ❖ τηρώ

8.42 **dean** (n) /diːn/
sb in charge of a university department ● *The graduates filed onto the stage one by one to receive their degrees from the dean.*
❖ πρύτανης

8.43 **faculty** (n) /ˈfæklti/
a department of study in a university; all the teachers in a university department
● *Professor Higgins became dean of the Faculty of Science in 2010.* ❖ σχολή

8.44 **formidable** (adj) /ˈfɔːmɪdəbl/
impressively powerful or worthy of respect
● *Renia's CV with her formidable list of work experience highly impressed the interview panel.* ➢ formidably (adv) ❖ δεινός, τρομερός

8.45 **intellect** (n) /ˈɪntəlekt/
the ability to reason and understand advanced concepts ● *Marie Curie was considered a woman of outstanding intellect.* ➢ intellectual (adj), intellectually (adv) ❖ νοημοσύνη

8.46 **rationalise** (v) /ˈræʃnəlaɪz/
find a logical reason why sth/sb does sth
● *Bob's parents tried to rationalise why their older son had turned into the school bully in his first year at primary school.*
➢ rationalisation (n), rational (adj), rationally (adv) ❖ αιτιολογώ

8.47 **append** (v) /əˈpend/
add sth on to the end of a written work
● *A list of photo credits were appended at the back of the book.* ➢ appendix (n)
❖ προσαρτώ, προσθέτω

8.48 **supplementary** (adj) /ˌsʌplɪˈmentri/
given in addition to sth else ● *For extra practice, supplementary exercises were added to the online version of the course.*
➢ supplement (v), supplement (n)
❖ συμπληρωματικός

8.49 **posit** (v) /ˈpɒzɪt/
put forward a hypothesis as a basis for argument ● *Whoever posited the unscientific theory of mass poisoning through the use of chemtrails has a lot to answer for.*
➢ position (n) ❖ θέτω

8.50 **surmise** (v) /səˈmaɪz/
deduce ● *We surmised that the tutor had given us the wrong test paper since the questions were far too easy.* ➢ surmise (n)
❖ συμπεραίνω, συνάγω

8.51 **inexplicable** (adj) /ˌɪnɪkˈsplɪkəbl/
unable to be explained ● *For some inexplicable reason, Frances dropped out of the course when she was doing very well.*
➢ inexplicably (adv) ❖ ανεξήγητος
✎ Opp: explicable ❖ που εξηγείται

8.52 **intelligible** (adj) /ɪnˈtelɪdʒəbl/
that can be understood ● *The phone line was so faint that her voice was barely intelligible.*
➢ intelligibly (adv) ❖ κατανοητός
✎ Opp: unintelligible ❖ ακατανόητος

8.53 **apply yourself** (v) /əˈplaɪ jɔːˈself/
work very hard to achieve sth ● *If you want to get better grades, you'll have to start applying yourself to your studies till the final exams are over.* ❖ αφοσιώνομαι

8.54 **assign** (v) /əˈsaɪn/
give sb a particular task to do or role to carry out ● *The invigilator was assigned the task of collecting the papers at the end of the exam.*
➢ assignment (n) ❖ αναθέτω

8.55 **apparatus** (n) /ˌæpəˈreɪtəs/
a set of equipment for a specific task
● *Oxygen tanks and other diving apparatus lined the walls of the water sports centre.*
❖ εξοπλισμός

8.56 **paraphernalia** (n) /ˌpærəfəˈneɪliə/
a collection of objects used for an activity
• *Ian carries a bag of spare tubes, spanners and other paraphernalia whenever he goes long-distance cycling.* ❖ σύνεργα

8.57 **rationale** (n) /ˌræʃəˈnɑːl/
the main reason behind a particular idea
• *I don't understand the rationale behind the revised school curriculum.* ➢ rationalise (v), rational (adj), rationally (adv) ❖ αιτιολογία

8.58 **scope** (n) /skəʊp/
a range of things that sth/sb deals with; opportunity to do sth • *There is little scope for expansion in our specialised line of business.* ❖ περιθώριο, πεδίο δράσης

8.59 **sphere** (n) /sfɪə(r)/
an area of interest or focus • *More women are coming to the forefront in the sphere of international politics.* ➢ spherical (adj) ❖ σφαίρα

Education: nouns

acknowledgement	joblessness
apparatus	mentorship
appendix	placement
bastion	plagiarism
bibliography	practicality
classics	rapport
compilation	rationale
crammer	red-brick university
criteria	referral
critical thinking	scope
dean	slate
dissertation	sphere
faculty	superiority
hypothesis	tuition
indicator	tutor
intellect	

8.60 **omen** (n) /ˈəʊmən/
a sign that sth might happen • *The prime minister lives in hope of finding a positive omen for the country's economic future.* ❖ οιωνός

8.61 **drift off** (phr v) /drɪft ɒf/
fall asleep • *Arthur had stayed up all night studying and was so tired he almost drifted off during the exam.* ❖ με παίρνει ο ύπνος

8.62 **keep at sth** (phr v) /kiːp æt ˈsʌmθɪŋ/
continue doing sth without stopping • *If you keep at it, you'll finish your dissertation in no time.* ❖ συνεχίζω, επιμένω

8.63 **mount up** (phr v) /maʊnt ʌp/
increase over time • *Their debts kept mounting up until they admitted they could no longer afford private school fees.* ❖ συσσωρεύομαι

8.64 **take sth in** (phr v) /teɪk ˈsʌmθɪŋ ɪn/
comprehend sth completely • *The news came as such a shock that it took me a few minutes to take it all in.* ❖ καταλαβαίνω, κατανοώ

8.65 **on the face of it** (expr) /ɒn ðə feɪs əv ɪt/
based on a first impression • *On the face of it, she seems like the best person for the job, but only time will tell.* ❖ κατά πρώτη εκτίμηση, κατά τα φαινόμενα

8.66 **in a nutshell** (expr) /ɪn ə ˈnʌtʃel/
in a few words; succinctly • *In a nutshell, there are not so many job opportunities for forensic scientists in our town.* ❖ εν ολίγοις

8.67 **on the threshold** (expr) /ɒn ðə ˈθreʃhəʊld/
about to enter a new situation • *On the threshold of a major political decision, John suddenly resigned from his post and walked out.* ❖ στο κατώφλι

8.68 **know the ropes** (expr) /nəʊ ðə rəʊps/
be familiar with or experienced in how to do sth • *Having been in the retail business for years, he certainly knows the ropes.* ❖ έχω πείρα και γνώση

8.69 **be on the same page** (expr) /biː ɒn ðə seɪm peɪdʒ/
be in agreement about what to do • *Most adolescents believe that their parents are never on the same page as them.* ❖ σε συμφωνία, στο ίδιο μήκος κύματος

8.70 **drop the subject** (expr) /drɒp ðə ˈsʌbdʒɪkt/
stop a discussion on a particular issue
• *I confess I deserved to fail the exam as I didn't study for it, so let's just drop the subject.* ❖ αλλάζω θέμα συζήτησης

8.71 **saved by the bell** (expr) /seɪvd baɪ ðə bel/
relieved of doing sth you don't want to do because of an interruption • *My maths teacher just rang to cancel today's lesson. Saved by the bell!* ❖ γλυτώνω ή απαλλάσσομαι από κάτι που δεν θέλω να κάνω

8.72 **learn the hard way** (expr) /lɜːn ðə hɑːd weɪ/
find out how to do sth through your own experience or mistakes • *Maggie had no support from her parents when she left home; they made her learn the hard way.* ❖ μαθαίνω μόνος μου

8.73 **hit the books** (expr) /hɪt ðə bʊks/
study hard • *Summer's over guys! It's time to hit the books again to get through this course with flying colours.* ❖ το ρίχνω στο διάβασμα

8.74 **read between the lines** (expr) /riːd bɪˈtwiːn ðə laɪnz/
look for an implicit meaning in sth • *Reading between the lines, I think he want to leave his job.* ❖ καταλαβαίνω από τα συμφραζόμενα

8.75 **by the book** (expr) /baɪ ðə bʊk/
according to the rules ● *We were surprised at Mandy's use of plagiarism as she had always done everything by the book.* ❖ σεβόμενος τους κανόνες

8.76 **cite** (v) /saɪt/
make reference to sth as an example ● *Can you cite any examples to support your theory?* ➣ citation (n) ❖ παραθέτω, μνημονεύω

8.77 **referral** (n) /rɪˈfɜːrəl/
the act of sending sb to a person or place they need to go to, e.g. for help ● *The head teacher recommended the child's referral to a speech therapist.* ➣ refer (v), referee (n), reference (n) ❖ παραπομπή

8.78 **compilation** (n) /ˌkɒmpɪˈleɪʃn/
a collection of things, e.g. music or written works ● *His first book was a compilation of short stories.* ➣ compile (v) ❖ συλλογή, σύνθεση, ανθολογία

8.79 **curricular** (adj) /kəˈrɪkjələ(r)/
connected with a school curriculum ● *The village school's core curricular subjects were reading, writing and maths.* ➣ curriculum (n) ❖ διδακτέας ύλης
✎ Opp: extra-curricular ❖ εξωσχολικός

8.80 **exemplify** (v) /ɪgˈzemplɪfaɪ/
be a clear example of sth ● *The statues exemplified the style of the famous sculptor, Praxiteles.* ➣ example (n), exemplary (adj) ❖ αποτελώ παράδειγμα

8.81 **assimilate** (v) /əˈsɪməleɪt/
allow sb to become an integral part of a place, group, etc. ● *Since the 1990s, a whole generation of Balkan immigrants have become assimilated into Greek society.* ➣ assimilation (n) ❖ αφομοιώνω

Expressions with verbs

be on the same page
cry out for
drop the subject
have the last laugh
hit the books
know the ropes
land a job
learn the hard way
pale in comparison
read between the lines
take offence

Grammar pages 115-116-117

8.82 **vehemently** (adv) /ˈviːəməntli/
very strongly; forcefully ● *Karl is vehemently opposed to private education, maintaining that everyone should have an equal chance in life.* ➣ vehement (adj) ❖ έντονα, με όλη μου τη δύναμη

8.83 **absent-minded** (adj) /ˌæbsənt ˈmaɪndɪd/
forgetful ● *Professor Jackson pretends to be absent-minded by forgetting the end of a formula just to make sure his students know the answer.* ➣ absent-mindedness (n), absent-mindedly (adv) ❖ αφηρημένος

8.84 **crammer** (n) /ˈkræmə(r)/
a short course to help students prepare quickly for exams ● *George had to spend his two-month summer break on a crammer to prepare for his final year exams at high school.* ➣ cram (v) ❖ σύντομο αλλά εντατικό μάθημα

8.85 **tailor-made** (adj) /ˈteɪlə eɪd/
designed specifically to suits sb's needs ● *They offer tailor-made courses with a flexible schedule and content to suit individual requirements.* ❖ φτιαγμένο στα μέτρα

8.86 **disciplined** (adj) /ˈdɪsəplɪnd/
trained to behave according to the rules ● *Catherine was impressed that her first group of Chinese students were so disciplined in comparison with their Mediterranean counterparts.* ➣ discipline (v), disciplinary (adj) ❖ πειθαρχημένος
✎ Opp: undisciplined ❖ απειθάρχητος

8.87 **offspring** (n) /ˈɒfsprɪŋ/
a person's child; the young of an animal ● *While the majority of parents want the best for their offspring, it's not that easy to work out what 'the best' is.* ❖ απόγονος, γόνος

8.88 **fend for yourself** (phr v) /fend fɜː jɔːˈself/
look after yourself ● *The children were left to fend for themselves for an hour or so after school before their parents got back from work.* ❖ τα καταφέρνω μόνος μου

Phrasal verbs

drift off	mount up
fend for yourself	subject sb to sth
hail from	take sth in
keep at sth	

Listening

8.89 **enhance** (v) /ɪnˈhɑːns/
improve the quality, appearance, value, etc. of sth/sb ● *Mum's taking an Open University course in computing to enhance her job prospects.* ➢ enhancement (n) ❖ επαυξάνω, βελτιώνω

8.90 **accelerate** (v) /əkˈseləreɪt/
make sth happen or go faster ● *The learning process is accelerated when learners are personally motivated.* ➢ acceleration (n) ❖ επιταχύνω

8.91 **facilitate** (v) /fəˈsɪlɪteɪt/
make sth happen more easily ● *Smaller class groups will facilitate student participation.* ➢ facilitation (n) ❖ διευκολύνω

8.92 **reinforce** (v) /ˌriːɪnˈfɔːs/
make sth stroonger ● *The influx of immigrants has reinforced the stress on the country's education budget.* ➢ reinforcement (n) ❖ ενισχύω

8.93 **hinder** (v) /ˈhɪndə(r)/
make it difficult for sth/sb to progress ● *Bullying might be a contributing factor which hinders a child's progress at school.* ➢ hindrance (n) ❖ δυσχεραίνω, εμποδίζω

Education: verbs

accelerate	facilitate
adhere to	fulfil
append	hinder
apply yourself	posit
assign	rationalise
assimilate	reinforce
cite	renovate
enhance	stray
exemplify	surmise

Speaking

page 119

8.94 **renovate** (v) /ˈrenəveɪt/
repair or redecorate sth to improve its appearance and condition ● *Barbara bought an old farm cottage and had it renovated.* ➢ renovation (n) ❖ ανακαινίζω

8.95 **soundproof** (v) /ˈsaʊndpruːf/
condition sth so that sound cannot get into or out of it ● *Ria and Al have soundproofed the walls of their spare room by covering them with empty cardboard egg boxes!* ➢ soundproof (adj) ❖ ηχομονώνω

8.96 **extracurricular** (adj) /ˌekstrəkəˈrɪkjələr/
outside the usual school curriculum ● *Mary's kids take part in so many extracurricular activities that they have no time left for free play.* ❖ εξωσχολικός

Expressions

a means to an end	on the threshold
by the book	saved by the bell
in a nutshell	sick (and tired) of sth/sb
in its entirety	
in sync with	state of affairs
on the face of it	

Writing

pages 120-121

8.97 **novel** (adj) /ˈnɒvl/
new and imaginative ● *The theatre group had devised a novel approach to encourage audience participation.* ➢ novelty (n) ❖ νέος

8.98 **in its entirety** (expr) /ɪn ɪts ɪnˈtaɪərəti/
as a whole ● *In its entirety, the play lasted for three hours with only a short interval.* ➢ entire (adj), entirely (adv) ❖ στο σύνολό του

8.99 **parallel** (n) /ˈpærəlel/
a similar feature or situation, etc. ● *Although the variables have changed, it is still possible to draw parallels between the conflicts between nations in the past with those of the present.* ➢ parallel (v), parallel (adj) ❖ παραλληλισμός

8.100 **accessible** (adj) /əkˈsesəbl/
easily understood ● *His books are both accessible and enjoyable to people of all ages.* ➢ access (v), access (n) ❖ προσιτός, προσβάσιμος

8.101 **tutor** (n) /ˈtjuːtə(r)/
a teacher, especially one who teaches individuals or small groups ● *Adrian supplements his teaching salary by working as a private tutor in evening classes.* ➢ tutor (v), tuition (n) ❖ δάσκαλος σε μικρές ομάδες μαθητών/φοιτητών ή σε ένα μαθητή/φοιτητή

8.102 **steer sth/sb** (v) /stɪə(r) ˈsʌmθɪŋ/ˈsʌmbədi/
guide sb/sth ● *Ellen always manages to steer the topic of discussion towards animal abuse whenever we eat out together.* ❖ κατευθύνω

8.103 **stray** (v) /streɪ/
wander off the topic and start talking about sth else ● *His essay was fairly well-written, but for the fact that he had strayed off topic in the final paragraph.* ➢ stray (n), stray (adj), astray (adv) ❖ εκτρέπομαι

8.104 **competent** (adj) /ˈkɒmpɪtənt/
capable of doing sth to the required standard ● *I'd recommend Thelma as a competent accountant with an aptitude for problem solving.* ➢ competence (n), competently (adv) ❖ ικανός
✎ Opp: incompetent ❖ ανίκανος

8.105 **rapport** (n) /ræˈpɔː(r)/
a friendly, understanding relationship • *She developed an instant rapport with her students through making them feel their opinions were valued.* ❖ συμπάθεια, αρμονική σχέση

8.106 **harmonious** (adj) /hɑːˈməʊniəs/
peaceful and friendly • *Relations between the two countries have never been harmonious, so the possibility of war could become a reality.*
➢ harmonise (v), harmony (n), harmoniously (adv) ❖ αρμονικός

Adjectives

absent-minded	hands-on
accessible	harmonious
applied	inexplicable
competent	intelligible
curricular	Mickey Mouse
disciplined	novel
extracurricular	rigorous
formidable	supplementary
fundamental	tailor-made
hallowed	vocational

Video 8: Environmental Theme Park
page 122

8.107 **mentorship** (n) /ˈmentəʃɪp/
a helping process where sb experienced assists sb with less experience of sth • *The school's mentorship programme worked well in its experimental stages.* ➢ mentor (v), mentor (n) ❖ καθοδήγηση

8.108 **remedy** (v) /ˈremədi/
give a solution to a problem • *To remedy the problems facing unemployed teenagers, the centre runs a drop-in counselling service as well as support groups.* ➢ remedy (n), remedial (adj) ❖ αντιμετωπίζω

8.109 **fulfil** (v) /fʊlˈfɪl/
satisfy • *In an overcrowded classroom setting with students of mixed ability, teachers feel frustrated that they are unable to fulfil their own potential.* ➢ fulfilment (n), fulfilling (adj) ❖ εκπληρώνω, πραγματοποιώ

Vocabulary Exercises

A Complete the table.

Adjective	Noun
1 absent-minded	
2 accessible	
3 competent	
4 curricular	
5 disciplined	
6 fundamental	
7 harmonious	
8 inexplicable	
9 intelligible	
10 rigorous	
11 supplementary	
12 vocational	

B Complete the sentences with the verbs in the correct form.

adhere append apply assign assimilate cite exemplify posit rationalise surmise

1 Students have to _____ to a strict study programme in order to achieve the required grades necessary to get into a prestigious university.

2 Young students are eager to explore new concepts, philosophies and ideas in order to _____ and make sense of the world they live in.

3 The PhD student was advised by her supervisor to _____ the survey responses and additional material at the end of her dissertation.

4 Many scientists and academics _____ that each country will need to develop its own particular mix of energy sources, focusing on cleaner renewable energy as a substitute for fossil fuels.

5 Not having been adequately prepared for the exam, John _____ that he would have to burn the midnight oil and study very hard to achieve his goal of attaining high grades.

6 The teacher _____ a history project to the student and the due date for submission was at the end of the semester.

7 Having procrastinated and fallen behind in her work, Helen was reprimanded and advised to _____ herself more to attain satisfactory grades.

8 Graduate students are required to _____ secondary sources to support and justify their theoretical arguments.

9 This novel _____ the current trend towards minimalism in literature.

10 The information age necessitates that we are able to _____ vast amounts of information rapidly and sufficiently so as to apply the knowledge gleaned in a relevant way.

C Complete the sentences using the expressions in the correct form.

be on the same page by the book drop the subject in a nutshell know the ropes
learn the hard way on the face of it on the threshold read between the lines saved by the bell

1 _____ Emma appears to be a very self-confident student; however in reality she struggles with low self-esteem.

2 Learning is a complex process but _____ it is all about exploring ideas and assimilating new knowledge and experiences to the full.

3 In the field of education we are currently _____ of clarifying how learning takes place at the neurological level.

4 The young teacher took a while to adapt to the new curriculum but eventually she felt that she _____.

5 At the beginning of the term the lecturer and students _____ as the lecturer couldn't convey his ideas succinctly and his lectures were as a result incomprehensible.

6 The pupil struggled to answer the question and was fortunately _____ when the head master called the teacher out of the classroom for consultation.

7 He _____ that staying up all night was not conducive to memorising facts and preparing for an exam.

8 In the middle of his first year he _____ he felt that he was weakest in and devoting all his efforts to passing the other subjects.

9 The teacher gave ambiguous instructions, so all the students had to _____ to understand what was really required of them in order to complete the task.

10 Anne was penalised for minor errors as the teacher was going _____ regarding the correct style and layout of the essay.

D Complete the words to match the definitions.

1 It refers to other books that have been written on the same subject, which you have quoted or used information from in a text.

   b _ _ _ _ _ _ _ _ _ _

2 It refers to who supplied the photographs or helped with special research.

   a _ _ _ _ _ _ _ _ _ _ _ _ _

3 This refers to a group of departments in a college or university that specialises in a particular group of subjects, for example, engineering.

   f _ _ _ _ _ _

4 This refers to research and work completed to satisfy the requirements for a doctoral degree, whereas a thesis refers to the requirements for a Masters degree.

   d _ _ _ _ _ _ _ _ _ _ _

5 It gives extra information about something and often occurs at the end of a book, thesis, etc.

   a _ _ _ _ _ _ _

6 It shows what a situation or status of something is like and it functions to measure the level of something.

   i _ _ _ _ _ _ _

7 They are standards against which we judge something when we are evaluating or testing it.

   c _ _ _ _ _ _ _

8 This is what happens when you copy somebody else's work and claim that it is your own.

   p _ _ _ _ _ _ _ _ _

9 This is an explanation based on limited evidence that is posited in order to serve as a starting point for further investigation and research.

   h _ _ _ _ _ _ _ _

10 This person is the head of a university department.

   d _ _ _

8 Grammar

8.1 Reported Speech

Όταν μεταφέρουμε τον ευθύ λόγο (direct speech) σε πλάγιο (reported speech), οι χρόνοι που χρησιμοποιεί ο ομιλητής συνήθως αλλάζουν ως εξής:

Present Simple	Past Simple
*'He **teaches** maths,' she said.*	*She said (that) he **taught** maths.*
Present Continuous	**Past Continuous**
*'He **is teaching** the sixth form,' she said.*	*She said (that) he **was teaching** the sixth form.*
Present Perfect Simple	**Past Perfect Simple**
*'She **has taken** the exam twice,' he said.*	*He said (that) she **had taken** the exam twice.*
Present Perfect Continuous	**Past Perfect Continuous**
*'You **have been working** hard,' she said.*	*She said (that) they **had been working** hard.*
Past Simple	**Past Perfect Simple**
*'She **answered** all the questions,' he said.*	*He said (that) she **had answered** all the questions.*
Past Continuous	**Past Perfect Continuous**
*'She **was studying**,' he said.*	*He said (that) she **had been studying**.*

Άλλες αλλαγές στους τύπους των ρημάτων:

can	could
*'He **can** work fast,' she said.*	*She said (that) he **could** work fast.*
may	*might*
*'She **may** become a teacher,' he said.*	*He said (that) she **might** become a teacher.*
must	*had to*
*'You **must** do your utmost,' she said.*	*She said (that) we **had to** do our utmost.*
will	*would*
*'They **will** succeed,' he said.*	*He said (that) they **would** succeed.*

Σημείωση:
1 Τα ρήματα *say* και *tell* χρησιμοποιούνται συχνά στον reported speech. Το ρήμα *tell* ακολουθείται από αντικείμενο (object).
→ *My teacher **said** (that) I could become a lawyer.*
→ *My teacher **told me** (that) I could become a lawyer.*
2 Μπορούμε να παραλείψουμε τη λέξη *that*.
→ ***She said that** she had done her best.*
→ ***She said** she had done her best.*
3 Θυμηθείτε να αλλάξετε τις αντωνυμίες και τα κτητικά επίθετα όταν χρειάζεται.
→ *'**I'm** going to the library,' she said.*
→ *She said (that) **she** was going to the library.*
→ *'That's **your** book,' he said.*
→ *He said (that) that was **my** book.*
4 Οι παρακάτω χρόνοι και λέξεις δεν αλλάζουν στον reported speech:
Past Perfect Simple, Past Perfect Continuous, *would, could, might, should, ought to, used to, had better*, καθώς και *must/mustn't* όταν αναφέρονται σε συμπέρασμα.

8.2 Reported Speech: Changes in time and place

Όταν μεταφέρουμε τον ευθύ λόγο σε πλάγιο, συχνά αλλάζουμε και κάποιες λέξεις που δηλώνουν χρόνο και τόπο.

Direct speech	Reported speech
'He's writing his essay **now**,' she said.	She said he was writing his essay **then**.
'She's sitting the exam **today**,' he said.	He said she was sitting the exam **that day**.
'We can't go out **tonight**,' he said.	He said they couldn't go out that **night**.
'I missed the lesson **yesterday**,' he said.	He said he had missed the lesson **the previous day** / **the day before**.
'He left school **last year**,' she said.	She said he had left school **the previous year** / **the year before**.
'I'll finish the assignment **tomorrow**,' he said.	He said he would finish the assignment **the next day** / **the following** day.
'He's graduating **next week**,' she said.	She said he was graduating **the following week**.
'**This** is our head teacher's office,' she said.	She said **that** was their head teacher's office.
'The exam finished an hour **ago**,' he said.	He said the exam had finished an hour **before**.
'He's having an interview **at the moment**,' she said.	She said he was having an interview **at that moment**.
'Your tablet is **here** on the desk,' she said.	She said my tablet was **there** on the desk.

8.3 Reporting Verbs

Εκτός από τα ρήματα *say*, *tell* και *ask*, μπορούμε να χρησιμοποιήσουμε και άλλα ρήματα για να μεταφέρουμε με μεγαλύτερη ακρίβεια τα λόγια κάποιου. Προσέξτε τους διαφορετικούς τρόπους σύνταξης.

verb + full infinitive	
agree	'Yes, I'll help you with your research' she said. She **agreed to help** me with my research.
claim	'I'm the best student in the class,' she said. She **claimed to be** the best student in the class.
decide	'I think I'll take a break from studying,' she said. She **decided to take** a break from studying.
refuse	'I won't write the dissertation again,' she said. She **refused to write** the dissertation again.
offer	'Shall I write the dissertation again?' she asked. She **offered to write** the dissertation again.
promise	'Don't worry, I'll write the dissertation again,' she said. She **promised to write** the dissertation again.

verb + object + full infinitive	
advise	'If I were you, I wouldn't go to university,' he said. He **advised me not to go** to university.
encourage	'Come on, you can get into to university if you study hard,' he said. He **encouraged me to study hard**.
order	'Switch off your phones!' he told them. He **ordered them to switch** off their phones.
persuade	'You should apply for the scholarship,' he said. You're right,' I said. He **persuaded me to apply** for the scholarship.
remind	'Remember to keep away from hooligans,' he said. He **reminded me to keep** away from hooligans.
warn	'Don't be late for class again! You'll be have to resit the course,' he said. He **warned me not to be** late for class again.

forbid	'Do not speak during the exam,' she said. She **forbade them to speak** during the exam.

verb + gerund (-ing)

admit	'I took your book,' she said. She **admitted taking** my books.
deny	'No, I didn't take your books,' she said. She **denied taking** my books.
recommend	'You should get a new tablet,' she said. She **recommended getting** a new tablet.
suggest	'Let's go to the library,' she said. She **suggested going** to the library.
mention	'By the way, I wrote that article yesterday,' he said. He **mentioned writing** the article the day before.
describe	'I was so nervous before the exam,' she said. She **described feeling** nervous before the exam.

verb + preposition + gerund (-ing)

apologise for	'I'm sorry I didn't bring your book,' he said. He **apologised for not bringing** my book.
complain of	'I had to rewrite the whole dissertation!' he said. He **complained of having** to rewrite the whole dissertation.
insist on	Of course I'll rewrite the whole dissertation,' he said. He **insisted on rewriting** the whole dissertation.
admit to	I'm afraid I've taken your book by mistake,' she said. She admitted to taking my book by mistake.

verb + object + preposition + gerund (-ing)

accuse sb of	'I'm sure you took my book, he said. He **accused me of taking** his book.
congratulate sb on	'You got into university! Well done!' he said. He **congratulated me on getting** into university.

verb + that

announce	'I'm going to drop out of the course,' she said. She **announced that** she was going to drop out of the course.
complain	'I don't have time to write the essay,' she said. She **complained that** she didn't have time to write the essay.
demand	'You must help me to write the essay,' she said. She **demanded** that I help her to write the essay.
mention	By the way, we're getting a new teacher,' he said. He **mentioned that** we were getting a new teacher.

verb + object + that

inform	'The lesson begins at 9:30am,' she said. She **informed me that** the lesson began at 9:30am.
warn	'This course is very demanding!' she said. She **warned (them) that** the course was very demanding.
assure	'You'll pass no problem,' she said. She **assured me that** I would pass no problem.

verb + that + (should) + bare infinitive

insist	'You really should take a break,' he said. He **insisted that** I (should) take a break.
propose	'We could take a break,' he said. He **proposed that** they (should) take a break'.

recommend	The curriculum should be revised,' she said. She **recommended that** the curriculum (should) be revised.
demand	'Give me your exam papers,' he said. He **demanded that** we (should) give him our exam papers.
urge	'You have to study harder,' the tutor said. The tutor **urged that** we (should) study harder.

8.4 Reported Questions

Όταν μεταφέρουμε ερωτήσεις από τον ευθύ στον πλάγιο λόγο (reported speech), οι αλλαγές στους χρόνους, στις αντωνυμίες, στα κτητικά επίθετα, στο χρόνο και στον τόπο είναι όπως και στις καταφατικές προτάσεις του πλαγίου λόγου. Στις ερωτήσεις στον πλάγιο λόγο, το ρήμα ακολουθεί το υποκείμενο όπως στον ευθύ λόγο και δε χρησιμοποιούμε ερωτηματικό.

Όταν η άμεση ερώτηση περιέχει ερωτηματική λέξη, χρησιμοποιούμε αυτή τη λέξη και στην πλάγια ερώτηση.
➔ '**When** did you join the course?' he asked.
➔ He asked **when** I had joined the course.

Όταν η άμεση ερώτηση δεν περιέχει ερωτηματική λέξη, χρησιμοποιούμε if ή *whether* στην πλάγια ερώτηση.
➔ 'Is the course as difficult as you expected?' she asked.
➔ She asked **if/whether** the course was as difficult as I had expected.

Χρησιμοποιούμε *whether or not* για να προτείνουμε εναλλακτικές πιθανότητες.
➔ 'Did you apply for the course or didn't you?' she asked.
➔ 'Did you apply for the course or not?' she asked.
➔ She asked **whether or not** I had applied for the course.

Grammar Exercises

A Complete the sentences to report what was said.

1 'You may want to book ahead. That restaurant is all the rage nowadays.'
   She suggested _____

2 'If you like, I can help you with your CV and you'll be sure to land the job.'
   She offered _____

3 'What do you think about studying this weekend?'
   She proposed hitting _____

4 'I give you my word. I won't tell a soul about your plans.'
   She promised _____

5 'Come on — you can do it if you really try.'
   She encouraged _____

6 'You simply must stick to the criteria or your work will not be accepted.'
   She insisted _____

7 'I know it's a sad state of affairs but it will all work out in the end.'
   She assured _____

8 'You'd better apply yourself or you'll be in big trouble with your teacher.'
   She warned _____

8 Grammar

B Complete the sentences using direct speech. Do not repeat the reporting verb.

1 The government announced they would raise taxes next year.
'Taxes _____

2 She promised to help me with my homework if I let her use my notes from the lecture.
'Only if _____

3 She regretted not going to university in her youth.
'I wish _____

4 He apologised for his inexplicable behaviour.
'I'm _____

5 She complained about the cost of tuition fees and didn't know where she would find the money.
'It's terrible _____

6 The teacher forbade him to use a calculator in the exam.
'Using a calculator _____

C Circle the correct reporting verb.

1 He admitted / mentioned committing the robbery to the police.
2 She demanded /suggested that I adhere to the rules or there would be dire consequences.
3 He adamantly refused / denied drifting off during his wife's graduation ceremony.
4 She congratulated / informed him that he had passed his exam with flying colours.
5 She finally persuaded / advised him to get a new computer.

D Complete the sentences with a suitable reporting verb from C.

1 She _____ the other day that she hailed from Yorkshire. I'd thought she was Irish.
2 She _____ him on his receiving the Nobel Prize for literature.
3 We _____ that he should get hands-on experience by volunteering before studying to become a nurse.
4 She absolutely _____ to subject herself to studying Classics.
5 The careers counselor _____ me that there was a crying out for technicians in the medical field.

E Complete the second sentence so that it has the same meaning as the first, using the word given.

1 'You do remember that your dissertation is due at the end of the month, don't you?'
reminded
She _____ hand in my dissertation at the end of the month.

2 'Don't you think we would all benefit from more critical thinking in education?'
proposed
She _____ thinking be addressed more in education.

3 'I simply will not do that for you. You have to learn to fend for yourself.'
refused
She _____ insisting I had to learn to do things on my own.

4 'I am sick and tired of picking up your dirty socks! Next time they're going in the trash.'
complained
She _____ dirty socks and threatened to throw them away.

5 'I rather doubt you wrote this on your own.'
accused
The teacher _____ plagiarism.

6 'How dare you insinuate I am a snob! That is a complete fallacy.'
denied
He vehemently _____ and took offence that I would even suggest such a thing.

7 'Can you possibly defeat so formidable an opponent?'

asked

She _____ a formidable opponent.

8 'Well done! Everyone else's work pales in comparison.'

congratulated

She _____ work.

Exam Task

For questions 1–8, read the text below. Use the word given in capitals at the end of some of the lines to form a word that fits in the space in the same line.

The Montessori concept

The Montessori (**1**) _____ approach was developed by Italian physician and educator Maria Montessori based on her extensive research with 'special needs' children and characterized by an emphasis on (**2**) _____, freedom within limits, and respect for a child's natural (**3**) _____, physical and social development.

EDUCATE

DEPEND
PSYCHOLOGY

She advocated the use of mixed-age classrooms, student choice of activity from within a prescribed range of options, (**4**) _____ blocks of work time, ideally for at least three hours, a constructivist or "discovery" model, where students learn different (**5**) _____ from working with materials, rather than by direct instruction, specialized materials developed by Montessori and her collaborators, freedom of movement within the classroom and a trained Montessori teacher.

INTERRUPT

CONCEIVE

Montessori education is (**6**) _____ a model of human development, and the approach is based on that model. Based on her observations, Montessori believed that children who are at liberty to choose (**7**) _____ activities and act freely within an environment prepared according to her model, would act spontaneously for optimal development.

FUNDAMENT

CURRICULUM

Maria Montessori observed various developmental changes in children as they grew up, and created a classroom environment, lessons and materials to respond to their new (**8**) _____.

CHARACTER

9 Flying the Nest

Reading

9.1 milestone (n) /ˈmaɪlstəʊn/
a significant event in your life • *Emigrating to New Zealand was a significant milestone in Athena's life.* ❖ ορόσημο

9.2 disproportionately (adv) /ˌdɪsprəˈpɔːʃənətli/
in a way that is unevenly divided • *Magda spends a disproportionately large amount of time on her work.* ➢ disproportion (n), disproportionate (adj) ❖ δυσανάλογος

9.3 manifestation (n) /ˌmænɪfeˈsteɪʃn/
a fact or action that shows something is true or exists • *The demonstration was a clear manifestation of support for the opposition party.* ➢ manifest (v), manifest (n), manifest (adj), manifest (adv) ❖ εκδήλωση

9.4 perpetuate (v) /pəˈpetʃueɪt/
cause a situation to continue • *Their dependency on private education simply perpetuates the cycle of class inequality.* ➢ perpetuation (n), perpetual (adj), perpetually (adv) ❖ διαιωνίζω

9.5 discrimination (n) /dɪˌskrɪmɪˈneɪʃn/
the act of treating people differently on basis of their gender, race, age, etc. • *Returning to work at 40, Jane faced age discrimination at every turn; being told she was too old for most jobs.* ➢ discriminate (v), discriminating (adj), discriminatory (adj) ❖ διάκριση, προκατάληψη

9.6 mortality (n) /mɔːˈtæləti/
the number of deaths during a period of time • *Infant mortality is disproportionately high in poor countries.* ➢ mortal (n), mortal (adj), mortally (adv) ❖ θνησιμότητα
✎ Opp: immortality ❖ αθανασία

Look!

Προσέξτε ότι η λέξη **mortality** σημαίνει και θνητότητα.

Watching the funeral procession made me contemplate my own mortality.

9.7 legitimate (adj) /lɪˈdʒɪtɪmət/
accepted by law; justifiable • *Their decision to dismiss Nick was perfectly legitimate as he had been colluding with a rival firm.* ➢ legitimise (v), legitimacy (v), legitimately (adv) ❖ νόμιμος, θεμιτός
✎ Opp: illegitimate ❖ παράνομος

9.8 maturity (n) /məˈtʃʊərəti/
the state of being completely developed • *Amal was forced into an arranged marriage before she had reached maturity.* ➢ mature (v), mature (adj), maturely (adv) ❖ ωριμότητα
✎ Opp: immaturity ❖ ανωριμότητα

9.9 deference (n) /ˈdefərəns/
polite respect • *The books were censored in deference to the culture of the country.* ➢ defer (v), deferential (adj), deferentially (adv) ❖ σεβασμός, υποχώρηση

9.10 legislative (adj) /ˈledʒɪslətɪv/
related to law-making procedures • *Legislative changes regarding sex discrimination were introduced in the UK in 1975.* ➢ legislate (v), legislation (n), legislator (n) ❖ νομοθετικός

9.11 enforcement (n) /ɪnˈfɔːsmənt/
the act of putting a law into practice so it is obeyed • *Despite the Greek no-smoking law, its enforcement is lax or non-existent in most areas.* ➢ enforce (v), enforceable (adj) ❖ επιβολή, εφαρμογή

9.12 burden (n) /ˈbɜːdn/
a heavy or stressful responsibility • *In Mediterranean societies, the burden of elderly care usually falls on the family.* ➢ burden (v) ❖ βάρος, επιβάρυνση, φορτίο

9.13 revere (v) /rɪˈvɪə(r)/
respect and admire to a great extent • *Revered as a great peacemaker, a day of mourning was declared on his death.* ➢ reverence (n), reverent (adj), reverently (adv) ❖ σέβομαι, τιμώ

9.14 ranks (n) /ræŋks/
the status of frontline soldiers rather than army officers; the ordinary members of a group rather than the leaders • *Out of business and out of luck, she was forced to join the ranks of the unemployed.* ➢ rank (v), rank (n) ❖ μη-βαθμοφόρος στρατιώτης

9.15 sacred (adj) /ˈseɪkrɪd/
of religious importance; very important and highly respected • *Several animals, such as cows and monkeys, are regarded as sacred in Hindu culture and are not to be harmed.* ➢ sacredness (n) ❖ ιερός

9.16 excruciating (adj) /ɪkˈskruːʃieɪtɪŋ/
extremely painful • *The prisoners were subject to the most excruciating forms of torture.* ➢ excruciatingly (adv) ❖ ανυπόφορος

9.17 **initiation** (n) /ɪˌnɪʃiˈeɪʃn/
an act of making sb part of a group; an act of introducing sb to an activity • *His first book was a flop, but served as a lesson in his initiation as an author.* ➢ initiate (v), initiative (n), initiator (n) ❖ μύηση

9.18 **venomous** (adj) /ˈvenəməs/
poisonous • *The painful sting of the venomous jellyfish took me weeks to get over.* ➢ venom (n) ❖ δηλητηριώδης

9.19 **hallucination** (n) /həˌluːsɪˈneɪʃn/
an illusion that sb imagines, usually due to the effect of an illness or drug • *The painkillers were so strong that Greg was suffering hallucinations.* ➢ hallucinate (v), hallucinatory (adj) ❖ παραίσθηση

9.20 **come to** (phr v) /kʌm tuː/
recover consciousness • *When the sailor came to, he realised he was shipwrecked on an island.* ❖ επανακτώ τις αισθήσεις μου

9.21 **agitated** (adj) /ˈædʒɪteɪtɪd/
behaving nervously or anxiously • *He began to get agitated as he awaited the test results.* ➢ agitate (v), agitation (n), agitating (adj), agitatingly (adv) ❖ ταραγμένος

9.22 **raring** (adj) /ˈreərɪŋ/
eager; enthusiastic about sth • *We were all packed and raring to go.* ❖ ανυπόμονος

9.23 **readiness** (n) /ˈredinəs/
the state of being prepared for sth • *She donned her wedding gown in readiness for the ceremony.* ➢ ready (adj), readily (adv) ❖ ετοιμότητα

9.24 **span** (n) /spæn/
a length of time that sth lasts • *Young children have a relatively short attention span.* ➢ span ❖ διάρκεια

9.25 **impediment** (n) /ɪmˈpedɪmənt/
an obstacle • *Omar's nationality was an impediment in his quest to find a job in Italy.* ➢ impede (v) ❖ εμπόδιο

9.26 **consent** (n) /kənˈsent/
permission to do sth • *Under 18-year-olds cannot marry without parental consent in most European countries.* ➢ consent (v), consenting (adj) ❖ συγκατάθεση

9.27 **feat** (n) /fiːt/
an act that demands great strength or skill • *Herakles was revered for achieving great feats of courage and ingenuity.* ❖ κατόρθωμα

9.28 **fortitude** (n) /ˈfɔːtɪtjuːd/
the courage shown under extreme difficulty • *The boys endured the pain of the poisonous stings with great fortitude.* ❖ γενναιότητα, σθένος

9.29 **diminish** (v) /dɪˈmɪnɪʃ/
become weaker or less • *His savings rapidly diminished as did the chances of finding work.* ➢ diminished (adj) ❖ ελαττώνω, μειώνω

9.30 **provoke** (v) /prəˈvəʊk/
cause sth to happen; create a certain reaction • *His sudden movement provoked the bear's attack.* ➢ provocation (n), provocative (adj), provocatively (adv) ❖ προκαλώ

9.31 **ageist** (adj) /ˈeɪdʒɪst/
discriminatory against people on grounds of age • *Despite laws to the contrary, ageist attitudes prevail in the job market where employers hire younger staff on lower pay.* ➢ ageism (n) ❖ αυτός που κάνει ηλικιακές διακρίσεις

Adjectives

accomplished	legitimate
ageist	mediocre
agitated	raring
autonomous	sacred
conscientious	sovereign
emancipated	spontaneous
excruciating	upfront
instrumental	venomous
legislative	

Vocabulary pages 128-129-130

9.32 **eviction** (n) /ɪˈvɪkʃn/
the act of making sb leave a house on legal grounds • *If we can't keep up with the rent, we'll soon be facing eviction.* ➢ evict (v) ❖ έξωση

9.33 **lease** (n) /liːs/
an official contract for the use of a property or vehicle for a period of time • *Their landlord will demand a rent increase when their three-year lease expires.* ➢ lease (v) ❖ μίσθωση

9.34 **let** (v) /let/
rent a house • *We found a small apartment to let in the suburbs.* ❖ νοικιάζω

9.35 **sublet** (v) /ˌsʌbˈlet/
rent out a property that you rent from sb else • *The Watsons have sublet their spare room temporarily to a student who is on a work placement.* ❖ υπενοικιάζω

9.36 **tenancy** (n) /ˈtenənsi/
the period during which you rent a property; the right to occupy a property you rent • *They let the house under a one-year tenancy agreement.* ➢ tenant (n), tenanted (adj) ❖ ενοικίαση, μίσθωση

9.37 upfront (adj) /ˌʌpˈfrʌnt/
in advance • *There was an upfront deposit of a month's rent for the flat.* ➣ upfront (adv)
❖ προκαταβολικά, εκ των προτέρων

9.38 utilities (n) /juːˈtɪlətiz/
public services such as power or water supplies • *The building had been derelict for years and all the utilities had been disconnected.* ➣ utilise (v) ❖ υπηρεσίες κοινής ωφελείας (ΔΕΗ, ΕΥΔΑΠ, ΟΤΕ κλπ.)

9.39 testify (v) /ˈtestɪfaɪ/
make a statement that sth is true • *I can write you a reference to testify to your work experience with the company.* ➣ testament (n)
❖ επιβεβαιώνω, μαρτυρώ

9.40 retain (v) /rɪˈteɪn/
keep sth • *Ivana has to apply for a permit every year to retain the right to stay in the country.* ➣ retention (n), retainer (n), retaining (adj) ❖ διατηρώ

9.41 tender (v) /ˈtendə(r)/
officially submit sth • *The company tendered an estimate for internal repairs required before the building can be occupied.* ➣ tenderness (n), tender (n), tender (adj), tenderly (adv)
❖ καταθέτω επίσημη προσφορά / πρόταση / εκτίμηση

9.42 relieve sb of sth (phr v) /rɪˈliːv ˈsʌmbədi əv ˈsʌmθɪŋ/
remove a responsibility or role from sb • *As a result of his cowardice, William was relieved of his position as captain.* ➣ relief (n)
❖ απαλλάσσομαι

9.43 give sb their marching orders (expr) /gɪv ˈsʌmbədi ðeə ˈmaːtʃɪŋ ˈɔːdəz/
oder sb to leave a job or place • *Caught stealing from the cash register, Simon was given his marching orders.* ❖ απολύω

9.44 paternity leave (n) /pəˈtɜːnəti liːv/
a period of time that a father is allowed to take off work to care for his newborn child • *Paul chose to take a few months paternity leave to look after the baby when his wife resumed work.* ❖ άδεια πατρότητας

9.45 delegate (v) /ˈdelɪgeɪt/
assign work or part of your responsibilities to sb else • *There was too much work for one person, so Cynthia delegated the more time-consuming parts to her assistant.*
➣ delegate (n), delegation (n) ❖ αναθέτω, εξουσιοδοτώ

9.46 nominate (v) /ˈnɒmɪneɪt/
officially put forward sb's name for an important role, award, etc. • *Bob was nominated for a Nobel Peace Prize in 2016.*
➣ nomination (n) ❖ προτείνω κάποιον επισήμως

9.47 downtime (n) /ˈdaʊn.taɪm/
a period of time when sb stops working to relax; a period of time when sth is not working • *You look as if you need some downtime; it's months since you've had a break.* ❖ διάλειμμα

9.48 flexitime (n) /ˈfleksitaɪm/
a system of flexible working hours • *Working flexitime means that Karen can start work at the office as soon as the kids leave for school at 7:30 and go home at 15:30.* ❖ ελαστικό ωράριο

9.49 autonomous (adj) /ɔːˈtɒnəməs/
independent • *West Papua became an autonomous province in 2003.* ➣ autonomy (n), autonomously (adv) ❖ αυτόνομος

9.50 emancipated (adj) /ɪˈmænsɪpeɪtɪd/
freed from some type of restriction • *Women in western society are more emancipated than their counterparts around the globe due to the effects of political activism in the 20th century.*
➣ emancipate (v), emancipation (n)
❖ χειραφετημένος

9.51 enfranchise (v) /ɪnˈfræntʃaɪz/
give sb the right to vote or to have citizenship • *As a result of the women's Suffrage movement, women were first enfranchised to a limited extent by an act of Parliament in 1918 in the UK.* ➣ enfranchisement (n)
❖ χειραφετώ, απελευθερώνω
✎ Opp: disenfranchise ❖ υποβαθμίζω

9.52 liberate (v) /ˈlɪbəreɪt/
free a person or country from sth/sb that controls or restricts them • *New legislation was introduced to liberate slaves.* ➣ liberation (n) ❖ απελευθερώνω

9.53 sovereign (adj) /ˈsɒvrɪn/
self-governing • *The Kingdom of Scotland was an independent sovereign state until 1707.*
➣ sovereign (n) ❖ κυρίαρχος

9.54 monasticism (n) /məˈnæstɪsɪz(ə)m/
the way of life related to monks or nuns in a monastery • *Buddhist monasticism remains customary in some South-east Asian countries, such as Thailand.* ➣ monastic (adj)
❖ μοναστικός βίος

9.55 hierarchy (n) /ˈhaɪəraːki/
the people who hold controlling power in a country or organisation; a system where people are ranked in levels of importance • *She joined the hierarchy, having been elected as a member of parliament in the 1980s.* ➣ hierarchical (adj) ❖ ιεραρχία

9.56 mediocre (adj) /ˌmiːdiˈəʊkə(r)/
of ordinary standard or quality, not exceptional • *In view of the team's mediocre performance this season, it's unlikely they will make it to the final rounds.* ➣ mediocrity (n) ❖ μέτριος

9.57 **conscientious** (adj) /ˌkɒnʃi'enʃəs/
giving attention to deal and correctness
• *Amelia has always been a conscientious student who consistently completes her assignments to exceptional standards.*
➢ conscience (n), conscientiousness (n), conscientiously (adv) ❖ ευσυνείδητος

9.58 **tribunal** (n) /traɪ'bjuːnl/
a court specialising in a particular type of legal issues • *The decision to strip him of his rank due to unprofessional conduct was taken at a military tribunal.* ❖ δικαστήριο

9.59 **saddle sb with sth** (phr v) /'sædl 'sʌmbədi wɪθ 'sʌmθɪŋ/
give sb responsibility for doing sth unpleasant
• *Richard got saddled with the job of cleaning the camp toilets.* ❖ αγγαρεύω

9.60 **stand in** (phr v) /stænd ɪn/
replace sb at work, etc. • *Our dentist was on leave, so his partner was standing in for him at the surgery.* ➢ stand-in (n) ❖ αντικαθιστώ

9.61 **step down** (phr v) /step daʊn/
resign from a position of power• *The party leader stepped down the day after the referendum.* ❖ παραιτούμαι

9.62 **lay sb off** (phr v) /leɪ 'sʌmbədi ɒf/
make sb redundant • *When the pit became flooded, hundreds of mine workers were laid off.* ➢ lay-off (n) ❖ απολύω

9.63 **lean on sb/sth** (phr v) /liːn ɒn 'sʌmbədi/ 'sʌmθɪŋ/
depend on sb/sth for support • *Although now in her 20s, she still leans on her family for financial support.* ❖ βασίζομαι για υποστήριξη σε κάποιον ή κάτι

9.64 **strike out** (phr v) /straɪk aʊt/
start doing sth new • *Disillusioned with the job market, Kevin struck out on his own and opened a bicycle repair shop.* ❖ ξεκινώ κάτι καινούργιο

Verbs

concede	nominate
delegate	perpetuate
deposit	provoke
diminish	retain
enfranchise	revere
let	sublet
liberate	tender
merge	testify

Phrasal verbs

come to	saddle sb with sth
lay sb off	stand in
lean on sb/sth	step down
relieve sb of sth	strike out

9.65 **pull your weight** (expr) /pʊl jɔː weɪt/
work hard to the best of your abilities • *You'd better start pulling your weight if you expect to get a pay rise.* ❖ εργάζομαι σκληρά και όσο καλύτερα μπορώ

9.66 **burn the midnight oil** (expr) /bɜːn ðə 'mɪdnaɪt ɔɪl/
work or study long hours into the night
• *Her sleep patterns were totally out of sync after months of burning the midnight oil before the exams.* ❖ εργάζομαι ή μελετώ μέχρι πολύ αργά

9.67 **be thrown in at the deep end** (expr) /biː θrəʊn ɪn æt ðə diːp end/
be made to start sth difficult, often without experience • *Tracy was thrown in at the deep end and left in charge of the office when the manager went off sick.* ❖ πέφτω στα βαθειά (ξεκινώ κάτι δύσκολο και καινούργιο)

9.68 **leave sb to their own devices** (expr) /liːv'sʌmbədi tə ðeə əʊn dɪ'vaɪsɪz/
let sb decide what to do on their own • *While their parents were out at work, the twins were left to their own devices for an hour or so after school.* ❖ αφήνω κάποιον να αποφασίσει και να πράξει μόνος του και χωρίς βοήθεια

9.69 **be wet behind the ears** (exp) /biː wet bɪ'haɪnd ðə ɪəz/
be inexperienced • *She has just started her apprenticeship, so she's still a bit wet behind the ears.* ❖ άπειρος

9.70 **free hand** (n) /friː 'hænd/
the right to make your own decisions on what to do • *Since he seemed quite capable, the school owner gave David a free hand in designing the course.* ❖ ελευθερία στις αποφάσεις και πράξεις

9.71 **of your own accord** (expr) /əv jɔː əʊn ə'kɔːd/
without being made to do sth • *Fiona left the company of her own accord, having received a better offer.* ❖ από μόνος μου, οικειοθελώς

9.72 **see fit** (expr) /siː fɪt/
consider sth appropriate to do • *I can give you my opinion, but at the end of the day, you should just do whatever you see fit.* ❖ κρίνω ότι είναι το σωστό ή πρέπον

9.73 **be at liberty to do sth** (expr) /biː æt tə duː 'sʌmθɪŋ/
have permission or the right to do sth • *You are at liberty to express your own opinions.* ❖ ελεύθερος να πω ή να κάνω κάτι

9.74 **at will** (expr) /æt wɪl/
any time you like • *Hospital visiting times are restricted, so relatives and friends are not allowed to remain in the wards at will.* ❖ όποτε θέλω

9.75 **batch** (n) /bætʃ/
a group of things dealt with together; an amount of a product made at the same time • *Taxi drivers hovered outside the airport, waiting for the next batch of passengers to arrive.* ➣ batch (v) ❖ φουρνιά, παρτίδα

9.76 **a bundle of nerves** (expr) /ə 'bʌndl əv nɜːvz/
extremely nervous about sth • *He was a bundle of nerves waiting to hear the outcome of the interview.* ❖ σε μεγάλη αγωνία

9.77 **bale** (n) /beɪl/
a large amount of material collected together and tied up • *Bales of hay lay in neat rows in the fields ready for collection.* ➣ bale (v) ❖ μπάλλα, δέμα

9.78 **deed** (n) /diː/
an intentional act • *Rescuing the child from the blaze was a brave and heroic deed.* ❖ πράξη, κατόρθωμα

9.79 **be no mean feat** (expr) /biː nəʊ miːn fiːt/
be sth difficult to do • *Running a company and keeping it sustainable is no mean feat.* ❖ δεν είναι μικρό πράγμα

9.80 **pull strings** (expr) /pʊl strɪŋs/
use your influence to get an advantage • *Rosemary's friend managed to pull some strings to help her get a scholarship.* ❖ «κινώ τα νήματα»

9.81 **pull the plug on sth** (expr) /pʊl ðə plʌg ɒn 'sʌmθɪŋ/
stop sth from proceeding • *The government has pulled the plug on student grants.* ❖ σταματώ, καταργώ

9.82 **pull the punches** (expr) /pʊl ðə pʌntʃɪz/
say sth bad in a polite way to avoid upsetting people • *The reporter certainly didn't pull any punches; he was quite offensive and prying.* ❖ λέω κάτι άσχημο ή προσβλητικό με ευγενικό τρόπο

9.83 **pull up stakes** (expr) /pʊl ʌp steɪks/
move house and go to live elsewhere (US Eng) • *Nicola's family recently pulled up stakes and emigrated to Canada for a more secure future.* ❖ μετοικώ
✎ Also: pull up sticks (Br Eng)

Expressions

a bundle of nerves

at will
of your own accord

be at liberty to do sth
be no mean feat
be thrown in at the deep end
be wet behind the ears
burn the midnight oil
give sb their marching orders
leave sb to their own devices
pull strings
pull the plug on sth
pull the punches
pull up stakes
pull your weight
see fit
tied to sb's apron strings

Grammar pages 131-132-133

9.84 **deposit** (n) /deposit/
a down payment made in advance • *Malcolm has been saving up for a deposit to buy a flat.* ➣ deposit (v) ❖ προκαταβολή

9.85 **orientation** (n) /ˌɔːriən'teɪʃn/
a period of preparatory training • *We haven't started lessons yet as we're having a week of orientation to get used to university life.* ➣ orientate (v) ❖ προσανατολισμός
✎ Opp: disorientation ❖ αποπροσανατολισμός

Listening page 134

9.86 **tied to sb's apron strings** (expr) /taɪd tə 'sʌmbədiz 'eɪprən strɪŋz/
dependent on sb, especially your mother • *Isn't it time you got a place of your own, son? You can't stay tied to my apron strings forever!* ❖ εξαρτημένος από κάποιον, συνήθως τη μητέρα

9.87 **etiquette** (n) /'etɪket/
the rules of polite culturally acceptable behaviour • *Before travelling abroad, it's wise to read up on the local etiquette to avoid embarrassing moments.* ❖ ετικέτα, εθιμοτυπία, πρωτόκολλο

9.88 **manoeuvre** (n) /mə'nuːvə(r)/
a movement to control the position or direction of sth • *Our pilot carried out some skilful manoeuvres to avoid flying into the eye of the storm.* ➣ manoeuvre (v) ❖ ελιγμός, μανούβρα

9.89 **squatter** (n) /ˈskwɒtə(r)/
sb who moves into sb else's property and lives there without paying • *The abandoned factory has been taken over by squatters.* ➤ squat (v)
❖ καταπατητής

9.90 **dress code** (n) /dres kʊəd/
the rules that state which clothes are appropriate • *Teachers and students are expected to respect the school dress code.*
❖ ενδυμασία

9.91 **explicitly** (adv) /ɪkˈsplɪsɪtli/
in a clear and direct way • *The students were explicitly told to submit their assignments by the end of the month.* ➤ explicit (adj) ❖ ρητώς
✎ Opp: implicitly ❖ άρρητα

9.92 **spontaneous** (adj) /spɒnˈteɪniəs/
doing things suddenly without prior planning; done without prior planning • *The manager was stunned at Timothy's spontaneous resignation.* ➤ spontaneity (n), spontaneously (adv) ❖ αυθόρμητος

Adverbs

disproportionately   explicitly

Speaking page 135

9.93 **concede** (v) /kənˈsiːd/
admit that sb else is correct or sth is true
• *Elena conceded that learning to drive was not as easy as it seemed.* ➤ concession (n)
❖ παραδέχομαι, αναγνωρίζω

9.94 **adulthood** (n) /ˈædʌlthʊd/
the state of being an adult • *At what age do you consider a child has reached adulthood?*
❖ ενηλικίωση

Writing pages 136-137

9.95 **accomplished** (adj) /əˈkʌmplɪʃt/
highly skilled and having achieved a lot
• *Once the naughty boy of the class, he had grown up to become a calm and accomplished young man.* ➤ accomplish (v), accomplishment (n) ❖ τέλειος, επιτυχημένος

9.96 **rose-coloured glasses** (n) /rəʊz ˈkʌləd glaːsiz/
an unrealistic over-optimistic view of life
• *He's rather naïve and tends to view the world through rose-coloured glasses.*
❖ το να τα βλέπει κανείς όλα ρόδινα

9.97 **merge** (v) /mɜːdʒ/
blend together with other things so the differences are not clear; join two or more things to form one • *Feelings of anxiety merged with happy excitement as he approached his sold home.* ➤ merger (n)
❖ συγχωνεύω, ενώνω

9.98 **anecdote** (n) /ˈænɪkdəʊt/
a short amusing or interesting story about an experience or other event • *In the staff room, teachers exchanged amusing anecdotes about their students.* ➤ anecdotal (adj) ❖ σύντομο και διασκεδαστικό περιστατικό

9.99 **instrumental** (adj) /ˌɪnstrəˈmentl/
having a key influence • *Her aunt was instrumental in getting her the job.*
➤ instrument (n) ❖ καθοριστικός

9.100 **disposable income** (n) /dɪˈspəʊzəbl ˈɪnkʌm/
the money you have available after making tax payments, etc. • *Many families are struggling to make ends meet as their disposable income has shrunk in the recent years.* ❖ διαθέσιμο εισόδημα

9.101 **eye-opener** (n) /ˈaɪˌəʊpnə(r)/
a surprising experience or information that makes you understand more about sth
• *Helping out at the soup kitchen for the first time was a real eye-opener.* ➤ eye-opening (adj) ❖ κάτι αποκαλυπτικό

9.102 **facet** (n) /ˈfæsɪt/
one part of sth • *The article covered the most important facets of academic life.* ❖ πτυχή

Compound nouns

disposable income   rose-coloured glasses
dress code   tree ring
eye-opener
paternity leave

Video 9: Best Job Ever! page 138

9.103 **calcite** (n) /ˈkælsaɪt/
an opaque or clear carbonate mineral that forms part of major rocks • *A phosphorescent light glowed from some of the calcites on the cave walls in the cavers' torchlight.* ➤ calcify (v), calcification (n) ❖ ασβεστίτης

9.104 **deposit** (v) /dɪˈpɒzɪt/
leave behind a layer of a substance on the surface of sth • *The retreating floods had deposited a layer of mud and gravel on the town streets.* ➤ deposit (n) ❖ αφήνω ως ίζημα

9.105 **remains** (n) /rɪˈmeɪnz/
parts of sth left when the rest has been used or removed ● *They uncovered the remains of an ancient warrior while excavating the sanctuary.* ➢ remain (v), remainder (n), remaining (adj) ❖ λείψανα, απομεινάρια

9.106 **remoteness** (n) /rɪˈməʊtnəs/
the state of being far away from inhabited areas ● *The geographical remoteness of the island makes import costs high.* ➢ remote (adj), remotely (adv) ❖ απομακρυσμένη θέση

9.107 **tree ring** (n) /triː rɪŋ/
the circular lines visible in wood when a tree is cut horizontally across the trunk ● *As well as calculating the age of a tree, scientists can use old tree rings to detect the effects of weather patterns throughout the centuries.* ❖ οι κύκλοι που διαγράφονται στον κορμό ενός δέντρου

Nouns

adulthood	hallucination
anecdote	impediment
bale	initiation
batch	lease
burden	manifestation
calcite	manoeuvre
consent	maturity
deed	milestone
deference	monasticism
deposit	mortality
discrimination	orientation
downtime	ranks
enforcement	readiness
etiquette	remains
eviction	remoteness
facet	span
feat	squatter
flexitime	tenancy
fortitude	tribunal
free hand	utilities

Vocabulary Exercises

A Choose the best answer.

1 Very often teenage boys are willing to be put through difficult challenges and ___ pain in order to prove they are brave enough to be accepted in a gang.

  a legitimate   **b** excruciating   **c** agitated   **d** raring

2 Being accepted into one of the country's best university was no mean ___.

  a feat   **b** span   **c** rank   **d** batch

3 In most countries you need your parents' ___ in order to get married before the age of 18.

  a maturity   **b** deference   **c** initiation   **d** consent

4 When she turned 18, Lucy decided to get a job because she didn't want to be a(n) ___ on her parents any longer.

  a burden   **b** impediment   **c** fortitude   **d** bale

5 I am three months in arrears with my rent, and my landlord is threatening me with ___.

  a mortality   **b** lease   **c** eviction   **d** tenancy

6 Sonia realised she had no future with Arthur as he was still tied to his mother's ___ strings.

  a saddle   **b** apron   **c** dress   **d** facet

7 Kevin was so proud when he finally managed to save enough money to put down a(n) ___ on his first car.

  a squatter   **b** etiquette   **c** calcite   **d** deposit

8 My father was in the army, so, when I was young, we were often forced to pull ___.

  a the plug   **b** strings   **c** the punches   **d** up stakes

9 Karen is such an optimist; she sees everything through ___ glasses.

  a disposable   **b** rose-coloured   **c** accomplished   **d** eye-opener

10 There is no way I can pay my rent on my own, so I have decided to ___ my flat.

  a let   **b** tender   **c** sublet   **d** retain

B Replace the phrases in bold with these words or phrases in the correct form.

> a bundle of nerves   a free hand   at liberty   burn the midnight oil   give (sb) their marching orders
> leave (sb) to their own devices   of your own accord   pull your own weight   pull some strings
> step down   throw in at the deep end   wet behind the ears

1 If you want to share a flat with some of your friends, you have to each **do your own share of the housework and pay your share of the bills** _____.

2 Ever since I was a student I have never been a morning person; on the contrary, I prefer to **work late into the night** _____ when everyone else is asleep and there is peace and quiet.

3 My boss likes to **give** all new employees **difficult assignments** _____ on their very first day at work to see how well they can cope.

4 It's difficult for many parents to learn to **let** their children **work on their own** _____ to solve their problems.

5 You can't expect Steven to never make any mistakes; he's still **so young and inexperienced** _____.

6 When I went to work with my father at his firm, he decided to give me **complete independence** _____ to run the business as I wanted.

7 Nobody forced James to leave school and get a job. He did it **because he wanted to** _____.

8 I had to **ask for some favours from people I know** _____, but I managed to get a grant for my research.

9 Tessa was **extremely nervous** _____ as she waited for a reply to her application for a scholarship.

10 Martin will definitely be **fired** _____ when the manager realises he lied on his CV about speaking three foreign languages fluently.

11 I called the personnel department to ask who had got the job I was denied, but they told me they were not **allowed** _____ to disclose that information.

12 When his daughter got her master's degree and announced she was coming to work with him, Robert decided it was time that he **resigned** _____ and left the running of the company to her.

C Complete the text with the correct form of the words.

1 When young people think about leaving home they often only think about the rent they will need to pay; they don't realise that _____ such as electricity, water, etc. often cost more than the rent.   **UTILISE**

2 Unfortunately, the cost of living alone in a city these days is _____ high compared to the salaries young people can hope to earn.   **PROPORTION**

3 Refusing to deal with an unpleasant situation can only serve to _____ it.   **PERPETUAL**

4 When you work in a company, you need to respect the _____ and do as you are told by your superiors.   **HIERARCHICAL**

5 The first week in college is often an _____ week to help students become acquainted with the new environment.   **ORIENTATE**

6 My contract states _____ that I am allowed four weeks paid holiday a year.   **EXPLICIT**

7 When you are very young you are prone to make _____ decisions, without thinking about the consequences.   **SPONTANEITY**

8 He never learnt to be responsible with his money, because he comes from an affluent family and has always had _____ money made available to him.   **DISPOSE**

9 It is important for a manager to know how to _____ responsibility and not try to do everything himself.   **DELEGATION**

10 Young people today are far more _____ than their parents ever were.   **EMANCIPATE**

D Circle the correct word.

1   It's important for young children to have some downtime / flexitime in the course of the day.

2   I work for a company that has a downtime / flexitime system, so I can choose my own working hours.

3   It's hard to believe there are still countries today where women have not yet been enfranchised / nominated.

4   She was the first woman to ever be enfranchised / nominated as chairman of the company.

5   You can never be truly liberated / autonomous until you have got your own job and have moved out of your parents' house.

6   Everyone considers her a(n) liberated / autonomous woman because she chose to pursue a career and not have children.

7   They are an equal opportunity employer and make no manifestation / discrimination against applicants based on their age, sex or race.

8   He refuses to see that his parents are trying to control him, and believes their interfering manner is just a manifestation / discrimination of their love.

9   Putting your own interests aside and performing selfless deeds / feats to help others is a sign of maturity.

10 He has been a great asset to the company and performed remarkable deeds / feats of organisation since he was hired.

9 Grammar

9.1 Relative Clauses

Οι relative clauses (αναφορικές προτάσεις) δίνουν περισσότερες πληροφορίες για το υποκείμενο ή το αντικείμενο μιας πρότασης. Εισάγονται με τις παρακάτω λέξεις:
• *who* για πρόσωπα
• *which* για πράγματα
• *whose* για να δείξουμε κτήση ή ιδιοκτησία
• *when* για χρόνο
• *where* για τοποθεσίες

9.2 Defining Relative Clauses

Μια προσδιοριστική αναφορική πρόταση (defining relative clause) μας δίνει πληροφορίες που είναι απαραίτητες ώστε να καταλάβουμε για ποιο πρόσωπο ή ποιο πράγμα μιλάμε. Δεν χρησιμοποιούμε κόμμα για να τη χωρίσουμε από την υπόλοιπη πρόταση. Μπορούμε να χρησιμοποιήσουμε *that* αντί για *who* και *which* στις προσδιοριστικές αναφορικές προτάσεις.

➔ That's the building **which/that his office is in**.

Όταν το *who*, *which* ή το *that* είναι αντικείμενο της προσδιοριστικής αναφορικής πρότασης, μπορούμε να παραλείψουμε την αναφορική αντωνυμία.

➔ **He's** the man **(who)** rented the flat to her.
➔ **Its** the flat **(which)** Liz rented.

9.3 Non-defining Relative Clauses

Μια μη-προσδιοριστική πρόταση (non-defining relative clause) μας δίνει παραπάνω πληροφορίες που όμως δεν είναι απαραίτητες για να καταλάβουμε το νόημα της κύριας πρότασης. Χρησιμοποιούμε κόμμα για να τη χωρίσουμε από την υπόλοιπη πρόταση.

➔ Charlotte, **who is out of work**, finds it hard to pay the rent.

9.4 Prepositions in Relative Clauses

Η αναφορική αντωνυμία μπορεί να αναφέρεται στο αντικείμενο της πρόθεσης. Όταν το ύφος είναι ανεπίσημο, η πρόθεση μπαίνει μετά από το ρήμα. Όταν έχουμε επίσημο ύφος, η πρόθεση μπορεί να μπει πριν από την αναφορική αντωνυμία. Μετά από πρόθεση δεν μπορούμε να χρησιμοποιήσουμε την αναφορική αντωνυμία *that*.

➔ The shop **that** Maisie works **in** is open 24/7.
➔ The shop **in which** Maisie works is open 24/7.
➔ The students **who** I shared the flat **with** are at technical college.
➔ The students **with whom** I shared the flat are at technical college.

9.5 Relative pronouns with quantifiers

Στις μη-προσδιοριστικές προτάσεις, μπορούμε να χρησιμοποιήσουμε τις αναφορικές αντωνυμίες με ποσοδείκτες όπως *most of, both of, the minority of* και αριθμούς κλπ.

➔ The tenants, **most of whom** are students, are behind with their rent.

Οι αριθμοί μπορούν επίσης να ακολουθούν την αναφορική αντωνυμία.

➔ The tenants, **of whom two are students**, are moving out next month.
➔ The tenants, **two of whom are students**, are moving out next month.

9.6 Participle Clauses

Υπάρχουν δύο είδη participles (μετοχές). Η present participle – ενεργητική μετοχή (verb + *-ing*), και η past participle – παθητική μετοχή (verb + *-ed* ή άλλος ανώμαλος τύπος ρήματος).
Μπορούμε να χρησιμοποιήσουμε participles σε participle clauses (μετοχικές προτάσεις) ώστε να κάνουμε μια πρόταση συντομότερη. Μπορούν να αντικαταστήσουν το υποκείμενο και το ρήμα σε μια πρόταση, όταν το υποκείμενο της κύριας και της δευτερεύουσας πρότασης είναι το ίδιο. Χρησιμοποιούμε present participle όταν το ρήμα είναι ενεργητικό (active), και past participle όταν το ρήμα είναι παθητικό (passive).

➔ Before **applying for** the job, I asked my tutor to give me a reference.
➔ **Given** a good reference from his tutor, he stood a better chance of getting the job.

Μπορούμε να χρησιμοποιήσουμε μετοχή για να αντικαταστήσουμε την αναφορική αντωνυμία και το ρήμα.
→ *The staff **who were made** redundant were furious.*
→ *The staff **made redundant** were furious.*
→ *The people **who live** next door have a huge mortgage.*
→ *The people **living** next door have a huge mortgage.*

Μπορούμε επίσης να χρησιμοποιήσουμε μια μετοχή (participle) για να αντικαταστήσουμε το conditional.
→ *If she were employed as an accountant, she would do her own tax returns.*
→ ***Employed** as an accountant, she would do her own tax returns.*

Μπορούμε επίσης να χρησιμοποιήσουμε μια μετοχή (participle) μετά από μια πρόθεση.
→ ***Before becoming** an accountant, she didn't do her own tax returns.*
→ ***Before having become** an accountant, she didn't do her own tax returns.*

Μπορούμε επίσης να χρησιμοποιήσουμε μια μετοχή (participle) για ταυτόχρονες πράξεις.
→ ***Entering** the bank, she realised she'd left her bag at home. (As she entered the bank, she realised …)*

Μπορούμε επίσης να χρησιμοποιήσουμε μια μετοχή (participle) για μια αιτία.
→ ***Having left** her bag at home, she didn't have any ID with her. (Because she had left her bag at home …)*

Μπορούμε επίσης να χρησιμοποιήσουμε perfect participle (μετοχή αορίστου), δηλαδή having + past participle για να ενώσουμε δύο προτάσεις που έχουν το ίδιο υποκείμενο.
Αυτό το κάνουμε:
όταν μια πράξη έχει ολοκληρωθεί πριν από μια άλλη πράξη.
→ ***He withdrew** all his savings and then paid his rent.*
→ ***Having withdrawn** all his savings from the bank, he paid his bills.*
όταν μια πράξη συνεχιζόταν για ένα χρονικό διάστημα πριν αρχίσει μια άλλη πράξη.
→ ***He had been working** in the company for years and he was entitled to a large redundancy payment.*
→ ***Having been working** in the company for years, he was entitled to a large redundancy payment.*

Χρησιμοποιούμε την perfect participle στην ενεργητική και στην παθητική φωνή.
ενεργητική φωνή (active voice): *having* + past participle
→ ***Having asked** the accountant to fill in her tax return, she waited in the office.*
παθητική φωνή (passive voice): *having been* + past participle
→ ***Having been asked** to fill in her tax return, the accountant did so immediately.*

9.7 Clauses of Reason

Μπορούμε να ξεκινήσουμε μια πρόταση με τις παρακάτω λέξεις για να δείξουμε την αιτία μιας συγκεκριμένης κατάστασης: *so, because of, for, because, owing to, due to, as, since, seeing that/as, with, what with.*
→ ***Since** we're already in so much debt, we can't afford a new car.*
→ *They had to sell their car **owing to** the fact that they owed so much.*
→ ***What with** so many expenses, they had nothing left at the end of the month.*
→ *Why don't you downsize your car, **seeing that/as** it would mean a tax saving?*

9.8 Clauses of Purpose & Result

Μπορούμε να ξεκινήσουμε μια πρόταση με τις παρακάτω λέξεις για να δείξουμε τον σκοπό μιας συγκεκριμένης κατάστασης: *so that, in order to, so as to, for* και το full infinitive (απαρέμφατο με *to*).
→ *We can sell the car **in order to** / **so as to** pay off the mortgage.*
→ *Rental agreements are required **to state** / **for stating** the terms of the lease.*

Μπορούμε να ξεκινήσουμε μια πρόταση με τις παρακάτω λέξεις για να το αποτέλεσμα μιας συγκεκριμένης κατάστασης: *so, such a(n), so many, so much, so few, so little, too/not enough + to.*
→ *The employees were **too low paid** / **not well paid enough** that they felt exploited.*
→ *The employees were **so low paid** that they felt exploited.*

9.9 Clauses of Contrast

Μπορούμε να εκφράσουμε αντίθεση με τις παρακάτω λέξεις: *despite, in spite of, despite the fact that, in spite of the fact that, however, nevertheless, although, though, even though, whereas, while, not that, much as.*

→ *He would love to study astronomy.* **Not that** *he has the qualifications to be accepted.*

→ **Much as** *he would love to study astronomy, he doesn't have the qualifications to be accepted.*

Grammar Exercises

A Complete the sentences with a word or short phrase.

1 Tomas is the man _____ we owe our freedom!

2 Kate, _____ selfless sacrifice helped our cause, was a true hero!

3 My friends, most _____ I've known since childhood disagreed with my decision.

4 The laws, the majority _____ were passed over a century ago, were meant to protect children.

5 The house _____ Kostas Varnalis, the poet, lived until the end of his life is in Pangrati.

6 The time _____ politicians could do whatever they wanted unheeded, has passed since the advent of the social media.

7 The room _____ the political prisoners were kept was heavily guarded.

8 Her aim of becoming independent, _____ she had dreamed _____ as a child, became unattainable after she lost her job.

9 Bob's resignation, _____ he handed _____ yesterday, hasn't been accepted by his boss.

10 There were many protestors in the rally, some _____ carried banners and posters with them.

B Rewrite the sentences starting with a participle clause.

1 After Paul had lived alone for years, he found it difficult to share the house with his grown-up children.

_____

2 The bridge which had been built in the early 19th century sustained a lot of damage in the war.

_____

3 The CEO who had been hired to run the company was laid off without any explanation.

_____

4 If Jenny had been shown how to be independent as a child, she wouldn't have turned out to be such a needy adult.

_____

5 As Tamara heard the song, she remembered the happy times she had shared with her family at that cottage.

_____

6 Because the enemy had grown impatient, they decided to attack the besieged city.

_____

7 Before they declared themselves a sovereign country, they checked the international law.

_____

8 When Pauline was asked to pay her share of the rent, she pretended she didn't hear.

_____

9 The new recruit who tried to show he could pull his weight at every opportunity, made a total mess of the project.

_____

10 As Matina was new to the surroundings, she took her time to learn the ropes.

_____

C Complete the sentences with words from the box. In some sentences more than one option is possible.

| since   due   what with   seeing that   as   in order to   so as to   for   too   so   as a result   to |

1 There are frequent power cuts on the island _____ of the lack of service to the electricity factory machinery.
2 _____ the other tasks he had to complete, John neglected to pay his rent on time.
3 I won't invite Maurine to my party, _____ she didn't invite me to hers.
4 The peace talks were put off _____ to the rigid stance of the parties involved.
5 We need to arrange a meeting _____ reach a compromise.
6 _____ I couldn't afford to live on my own, I decided to get a room in a flat share.
7 A lot of politicians nowadays use the social media _____ propaganda purposes.
8 We offer all our new students an orientation programme _____ help them with settling in before the actual lessons start.
9 The tenants took excellent care of the property _____ lose their deposit.
10 The university course was _____ expensive for me to do.

D Circle the correct words.

1 He grew up in a privileged neighbourhood. Although / Despite this fact, he's chosen to live and work in one of the most underprivileged areas of the town.
2 Although / In spite he hadn't done a day's work before starting his own company, he's pulled through exceptionally well.
3 Much as / Whereas I would like to help you, my hands are tied, unfortunately.
4 While / Not that Bettina professes to be my best friend, she's never backed me up in a difficult situation.
5 Theo and Janine decided to rent a flat, in spite of / nevertheless knowing only too well they couldn't afford it.
6 During my first year at university, I never asked for my parents help even though / while I faced lots of problems.
7 Terry is a really independent and mature child, whereas / though his twin brother is the exact opposite.
8 He hasn't done much to deserve such an honour. Nevertheless / Although, he's been made chair of the department.

For questions 1–6, complete the second sentence so that it has a similar meaning to the first sentence, using the word given. Do not change the word given. You must use between three and eight words, including the word given.

1 Samantha was relieved of her duties when she was caught stealing money.

   laid

   Having _____ off.

2 Although Al is very new at this job, he's managed to turn this company around.

   wet

   Despite _____, Al has managed to turn this company around.

3 Before our boss allowed Joe to do whatever he wanted, he passed him through rigorous tests.

   free

   Before _____, our boss passed him through rigorous tests.

4 Our landlord, who Sheila had spoken badly to some days ago, refused to renew our lease.

   rude

   Our landlord to _____ some days ago, refused to renew our lease.

5 After Simon realised what a difficult task he was given, he felt overwhelmed by it.

   saddled

   After _____, Simon felt overwhelmed by the task.

6 Although my employer claimed that he wanted me to take it easy, he asked me to do overtime.

   despite

   My employer had me _____ that he wanted me to take it easy.

Reading

pages 140-141

10.1 **billboard** (n) /'bɪlbɔːd/
a large board where advertisements are posted on a building or on a roadside
• *Thanks to local activists, most of the unsightly billboards which festooned the national roads have been removed by law.*
❖ διαφημιστική πινακίδα

10.2 **juggernaut** (n) /'dʒʌgənɔːt/
a very large organisation which has overwhelming power • *Independent films cannot easily compete with the Hollywood juggernaut.* ❖ πολύ μεγάλος και ισχυρός οργανισμός ή αντικείμενο

10.3 **platform** (n) /'plætfɔːm/
an opportunity to make your ideas or beliefs known publicly • *She uses Facebook as a platform to air her personal views.*
❖ πλατφόρμα (μέσον) επικοινωνίας και προβολής

10.4 **cut-throat** (adj) /kʌt θrəʊt/
aggressively competitive • *She could not afford any bad press that might destroy her name in the cut-throat world of modelling.*
❖ άκρως ανταγωνιστικός

10.5 **sitcom** (n) /'sɪtkɒm/
a TV comedy series based on the same group of characters in funny situations • *Wendy never misses an episode of the sitcom Absolutely Fabulous reruns.* ❖ κωμική σειρά

10.6 **endorsement** (n) /ɪn'dɔːsmənt/
a statement made by sb to show they support sth • *Sales of the scent have increased since its endorsement from the popular actor.*
➢ endorse (v) ❖ υποστήριξη, επιδοκιμασία

10.7 **foray** (n) /'fɒreɪ/
an effort to become involved in a different area of activity • *He made a short-lived foray into the business world before becoming an author.*
❖ σύντομη ενασχόληση

10.8 **replete** (adj) /rɪ'pliːt/
full with sth • *The article was replete with factual errors.* ❖ γεμάτος

10.9 **falsehood** (n) /'fɔːlshʊd/
the state of being untrue • *They set up an experiment to test whether the advertising claims reading the shampoo were truth or falsehood.* ➢ falsify (v), false (adj), falsely (adv) ❖ ψεύδος

10.10 **pseudo-** (prefix) /'suːdəʊ/
false; pretending to be true • *The pseudo-celebrity regularly appears on breakfast TV chat shows.* ❖ ψεύδο-

10.11 **medication** (n) /ˌmedɪ'keɪʃn/
a form of medicine • *You should avoid driving whilst taking certain medications.* ➢ medicate (v), medicated (adj) ❖ φάρμακο

10.12 **mandatory** (adj) /'mændətəri/
compulsory by law • *It is mandatory for food companies to list ingredients on the labels of their products.* ➢ mandate (v), mandate (n) ❖ υποχρεωτικός, επιτακτικός

10.13 **mindful** (adj) /'maɪndfl/
aware; conscious • *Mindful of the risks involved, he decided not to attempt the climb alone.* ➢ mindfulness (n) ❖ προσεκτικός

10.14 **go down** (phr v) /gəʊ daʊn/
be received or remembered in a particular way
• *The film went down well with the critics.*
❖ ικανοποιώ, αρέσω

10.15 **gushing** (adj) /'gʌʃɪŋ/
over-enthusiastic in an insincere way • *Her gushing endorsement of the washing powder left viewers unconvinced.* ➢ gush (v), gush (n) ❖ υπερβολικά ενθουσιώδης

10.16 **disclaimer** (n) /dɪs'kleɪmə(r)/
a statement which shows that a person or organisation, etc. rejects responsibility for sth
• *The packaging included a disclaimer that the supplements were not recognised as having medicinal value.* ➢ disclaim (v) ❖ αποποίηση ευθύνης

10.17 **semblance** (n) /'sembləns/
an outward appearance of sth which may not be a reality • *The advertisement bore no semblance of truth whatsoever.* ❖ ίχνος

10.18 **authenticity** (n) /ˌɔːθen'tɪsəti/
the quality of being genuine • *The authenticity of their claims are open to question.*
➢ authenticate (v), authentication (n), authentic (adj), authentically (adv)
❖ αυθεντικότητα

10.19 **intimacy** (n) /'ɪntɪməsi/
closeness between people • *The blogger developed an intimacy with her followers which helped promote her website.* ➢ intimate (v), intimate (adj), intimately (adv) ❖ οικειότητα

10.20 **trim** (adj) /trɪm/
slim and fit-looking • *When we saw him perform live, he looked nothing like the photoshopped trim figure from the profile image.* ➢ trimness (n) ❖ κομψός και λεπτός

10.21 **infusion** (n)) /ɪn'fjuːʒən/
a hot drink made from herbs or fruit • *A soothing chamomile infusion will assist relaxation.* ➢ infuse (v) ❖ αφέψημα

10.22 gruelling (adj) /ˈgruːəlɪŋ/
extremely difficult and tiring ● *It was a gruelling eight-hour flight made worse by the extra delay.* ❖ εξαντλητικός

10.23 dismantle (v) /dɪsˈmæntl/
take sth to pieces ● *The computer had to be completely dismantled to replace the part.*
➢ dismantling (n) ❖ αποσυναρμολογώ, αποσυνθέτω

10.24 credibility (n) /ˌkredəˈbɪləti/
the quality that makes sb appear trustworthy and respectable ● *The scandal destroyed his credibility as a politician.* ➢ credit (v), credible (adj), credibly (adv) ❖ αξιοπιστία

10.25 attainable (adj) /əˈteɪnəbl/
that can be achieved or reached ● *You would be more self-content if you set more realistically attainable goals instead of wearing yourself out.* ➢ attain (v), attainment (n)
❖ εφικτός

10.26 vouch for sb/sth (phr v) /vaʊtʃ fɔː ˈsʌmbədi/ ˈsʌmθɪŋ/
state that you can verify the good character of sb/sth ● *Can you vouch for Judy's work experience?* ❖ εγγυώμαι γιά κάποιον ή κάτι

10.27 rub off (phr v) /rʌb ɒf/
have an influence on sb/sth else so that it adopts some of the same qualities, beliefs, etc. ● *His optimism never fails to rub off on his companions.* ❖ επηρεάζω

10.28 sneaky (adj) /ˈsniːki/
secretive or deceptive ● *That was a sneaky trick you pulled on your brother.* ➢ sneak (v)
❖ ύπουλος

10.29 camouflage (v) /ˈkæməflɑːʒ/
cover the appearance of sth to make it look like sth else ● *His natural looks are well camouflaged by hairpieces and botox.*
➢ camouflage (n) ❖ καμουφλάρω

10.30 suspend (v) /səˈspend/
stop an activity ● *Authorities have finally suspended the search for the missing plane.*
➢ suspension (n), suspended (adj)
❖ διακόπτω, αναστέλλω

10.31 snappy (adj) /ˈsnæpi/
witty and easily remembered ● *T-shirts bearing snappy slogans hung outside the souvenir shop.* ❖ έξυπνος και ευκολομνημόνευτος

10.32 pepper sth with sth (expr) /ˈpepə(r) ˈsʌmθɪŋ wɪθˈ sʌmθɪŋ/
include large quantities of sth repeatedly in sth ● *Her Twitter feed is peppered with quotes from others more famous than she will ever be.* ➢ pepper (n) ❖ κατάμεστος

10.33 plug (v) /plʌg/
give words of praise to promote sth ● *In his cookery book, the chef avoided reference to specific brands in order to avoid plugging them.* ➢ plug (n) ❖ διαφημίζω

10.34 efficacy (n) /ˈefɪkəsi/
the ability to have the desired effect
● *Exhaustive tests have been carried out to assess the efficacy of the medication.*
➢ efficacious (adj) ❖ αποτελεσματικότητα

10.35 manipulation (n) /məˌnɪpjuˈleɪʃn/
the act of controlling sb/sth by making them behave in a certain way ● *Political campaigners are adept at the manipulation of public opinion.* ➢ manipulate (v), manipulative (adj) ❖ χειραγώγηση, «μαγείρεμα»

10.36 candid (adj) /ˈkændɪd/
(of photos) taken unexpectedly while the subject is behaving naturally; open and direct
● *The magazine was full of candid shots of celebrities, supposedly caught unawares as they went about their daily lives.* ➢ candour (n), candidly (adv) ❖ στιγμιαίος, αυθόρμητος

10.37 unwitting (adj) /ʌnˈwɪtɪŋ/
unaware of what is happening ● *She became the unwitting victim of a telephone scam.*
➢ wit (n), unwittingly (adv) ❖ ανυποψίαστος

10.38 disclosure (n) /dɪsˈkləʊʒə(r)/
the act of revealing sth that was previously unknown ● *She took the publishers to court over the public disclosure of her letters.*
➢ disclose (v) ❖ αποκάλυψη

10.39 versus (prep) /ˈvɜːsəs/
used to compare two different things ● *A child can figure out the difference between hearsay versus facts.* ❖ έναντι, μεταξύ

10.40 get into hot water (expr) /get ɪntə hɒt wɔːtə/
get into trouble ● *You're liable to get into hot water if you put too much personal information for the whole world to see on social media.*
❖ βρίσκω μπελά

10.41 take a dim view of sth (expr) /teɪk ə dɪm vjuː əvˈsʌmθɪŋ/
disapprove of sth ● *Our science teacher took a dim view of being called a geek.*
❖ δεν εγκρίνω

10.42 from scratch (expr) /frɒm skrætʃ/
from the beginning ● *When I realised my essay was off topic, I had to start writing it from scratch again.* ❖ ξεκινώ από την αρχή

10.43 rake in sth (phr v) /reɪk ɪn ˈsʌmθɪŋ/
collect sth, especially money, in large amounts
● *That actor must be raking it in from the coffee ads.* ❖ συγκεντρώνω μεγάλη ποσότητα (συνήθως χρημάτων)

10.44 tantalising (adj) /ˈtæntəlaɪzɪŋ/
tempting ● *The tantalising view of the tropical beach beckoned to them from the glossy ad.*
➢ tantalise (v), tantalisingly (adv)
❖ δελεαστική

10.45 **make money hand over fist** (expr) /meɪk
mʌni hænd əʊvə fɪst/
make a lot of money very quickly • *The skilled
hacker has been making money hand over fist
from online gaming.* ❖ βγάζω πολλά χρήματα
πολύ γρήγορα

10.46 **staggering** (adj) /ˈstæɡərɪŋ/
very surprising • *She has a staggering number
of followers who read her blogs on social
media.* ➣ stagger (v) ❖ εντυπωσιακός

10.47 **overt** (adj) /əʊˈvɜːt/
publicly open • *Pay no attention to their overt
claims that using a credit card will solve your
problems.* ❖ φανερός

10.48 **fall foul of sth** (expr) /fɔːl faʊəv ˈsʌmθɪŋ/
do sth wrong or illegal often without intending
to • *The film fell foul of the censorship board.*
❖ παραβαίνω κανόνες ανοικειοθελώς

10.49 **explicit** (adj) /ɪkˈsplɪsɪt/
open and direct • *The reasons why the post
were deleted should be made explicit.*
➣ explicitly (adv) ❖ ρητός, σαφής

10.50 **monetary** (adj) /ˈmʌnɪtri/
related to money • *How can they market
goods of little monetary value at such
extortionate prices?* ❖ χρηματικός

10.51 **egocentric** (adj) /ˌeɡəʊˈsentrɪk/
self-centred and not considering the needs of
others • *Who has time to read through all the
egocentric messages and photos on social
media?* ➣ ego (n), egoism (n), egoist (n)
❖ εγωκεντρικός

10.52 **effusive** (adj) /ɪˈfjuːsɪv/
appearing to be overly emotional • *I didn't
know quite how to respond to her effusive
welcome since we were practically strangers.*
➣ effusion (n), effusively (adv) ❖ διαχυτικός

Expressions

fall foul of sth
from scratch
get into hot water
make money hand over fist
take a dim view of sth

Nouns: marketing

asset	infomercial
benchmark	infusion
billboard	jingle
consumerism	juggernaut
desolation	materialism
disclaimer	medication
disclosure	merchandising
endorsement	momentum
epitome	platform
falsehood	recession
foray	saturation
franchise	semblance
immediacy	sitcom

Vocabulary pages 142-143-144

10.53 **infomercial** (n) /ˌɪnfəʊˈmɜːʃl/
an extended advertisement that emulates
documentary style • *Until the last scene of
the infomercial, we'd made several guesses
what it was advertising.* ❖ εκτενής διαφήμιση
συγκαλυμμένη ως ντοκυμανταίρ

10.54 **jingle** (n) /ˈdʒɪŋɡl/
a short piece of music used in an
advertisement • *You know you've been
watching too much TV when you start
humming the jingles.* ➣ jingle (v)
❖ μουσική από διαφήμιση

10.55 **materialism** (n) /məˈtɪəriəlɪz(ə)m/
the way of life that puts money and
possessions over everything else • *The
economic downturn has led us to question
the ethics of materialism.* ➣ materialist (n),
materialistic (adj) ❖ υλισμός

10.56 **merchandising** (n) /ˈmɜːtʃəndaɪzɪŋ/
the activity or process of advertising and
marketing goods • *The trashy novel and film
became a box office success only through
clever merchandising.* ➣ merchandise (v),
merchandise (n) ❖ η προώθηση πωλήσεων
αγαθών μέσω μάρκετινγκ, διαφήμισης και
άλλων τεχνικών

10.57 **momentum** (n) /məˈmentəm/
a moving object's (or similar metaphor's)
retention of kinetic energy • *Support for the
leading candidate began to lose momentum
as the election day drew near.* ➣ momentous
(adj), momentously (adv) ❖ ορμή

10.58 franchise (n) /ˈfræntʃaɪz/
an agreement between a company and sb who wants to market its products or services using its brand name in a given place • *Airport baggage handling services are run through a private business franchise.* ➣ franchise (v), franchisee (n) ❖ franchise, δικαιοχρησία

10.59 discern (v) /dɪˈsɜːn/
understand the meaning of or notice sth • *It was difficult to discern the source of the misinformation.* ➣ discernible (adj), discernibly (adv) ❖ διακρίνω

10.60 vanity (n) /ˈvænəti/
extreme pride in your own appearance or abilities • *Are compulsive selfies acts of vanity or a sign of insecurity?* ➣ vain (adj), vain (adv) ❖ ματαιοδοξία

10.61 typographical (adj) /ˌtaɪpəˈgræfɪkl/
related to typing and the preparing of written material for print • *His bank statement showed a staggering balance, as a result of a typographical error.* ➣ typography, typographer (n), typographically (adv) ❖ τυπογραφικός
✎ Syn: typographic

10.62 promotional (adj) /prəˈməʊʃənl/
related to advertising • *They sent out a promotional email to all their customers.* ➣ promote (v), promotion (n), promoter (n) ❖ διαφημιστικός

Adjectives

attainable	overt
candid	promotional
cut-throat	replete
effusive	snappy
egocentric	sneaky
explicit	staggering
gruelling	tantalising
inescapable	trim
mandatory	typographical
mindful	unwitting

10.63 classified (adj) /ˈklæsɪfaɪd/
a small advertisement in a newspaper or website placed by people who want to buy or sell goods or services, etc. • *They sold their old car through an online classified ad.* ❖ αγγελία

10.64 market share (n) /ˈmaːkɪt ʃeə(r)/
the relative number of sales of a product that one company has compared with sales of all companies selling the same thing • *He claims to have a 60 % share of the international publishing market.* ❖ μερίδιο αγοράς

10.65 leaflet drop (n) /ˈliːflət drɒp/
a distribution of large numbers of advertising leaflets to homes, etc. • *As a student, he earned some cash by doing leaflet drops for a promotional company.* ❖ διανομή φυλλαδίων

10.66 trade paper (n) /treɪd ˈpeɪpə(r)/
a newspaper with news exclusively related to a particular type of business • *The latest word in the trade papers is that a merger of the telecommunication giants is imminent.* ❖ εξειδικευμένη κλαδική εφημερίδα, οικονομική εφημερίδα

10.67 cajole (v) /kəˈdʒəʊl/
persuade sb to do sth through kind words • *She had to be cajoled into doing the interview.* ❖ καλοπιάνω

10.68 coax (v) /kəʊks/
encourage; persuade • *Len tried to coax his father into buying him a car.* ➣ coaxing (n), coaxing (adj) ❖ πείθω με καλόπιασμα και παρότρυνση

10.69 entice (v) /ɪnˈtaɪs/
attract or persuade sb to do sth • *Promises of cash rewards are used to entice clients to change their phone providers.* ➣ enticement (n), enticing (adj), enticingly (adv) ❖ δελεάζω

10.70 hype (v) /haɪp/
exaggerate the qualities of sth to attract attention to it • *Stunning landscape images were used to hype up the hotel's location.* ➣ hype (n) ❖ υπερβάλλω τα προσόντα ώστε να προκαλέσω ενδιαφέρον και προσοχή

10.71 induce (v) /ɪnˈdjuːs/
cause sth to happen; persuade sb to do sth • *Even the offer of a bonus could not induce her to stay another moment in the job.* ➣ inducement (n), induction (n) ❖ προκαλώ, προτρέπω

10.72 pitch (v) /pɪtʃ/
promote a product; put forward (an idea) • *The energy bars are pitched as a healthy snack despite containing harmful additives.* ➣ pitch (n) ❖ προάγω προϊόν ή ιδέα

10.73 sway (v) /sweɪ/
cause sth to change; cause sb to change an opinion • *Currency rates began to sway dramatically when the election result was known.* ➣ sway (n) ❖ επηρεάζομαι, ταλαντεύομαι

10.74 tout (v) /taʊt/
try to persuade people to buy sth • *Street vendors touted their wares at every corner.* ➣ tout (n) ❖ διαλαλώ (το εμπόρευμα)

10.75 woo (v) /wuː/
try to persuade sb to support sth • *Targeted offers of cut-price vouchers are aimed to woo customers to overpriced restaurants.* ❖ προσπαθώ να προσελκύσω

10.76 equate (v) /iˈkweɪt/
regard sth as the same as sth else • *High earnings do not equate with happiness, but they might help make life more comfortable.* ➢ equation (n), equality (n), equal (adj), equally (adv) ❖ ισοδυναμώ με

10.77 gear sth to/towards sb/sth (phr v) /gɪə ˈsʌmθɪŋ tuː/təˈwɔːdz ˈsʌmθɪŋ/ˈsʌmbədi/
adapt sth to make it suitable for a particular purpose • *The ad for snack bars was clearly geared towards working parents.*
❖ προσαρμόζω προς συγκεκριμένη χρήση

10.78 saturation (n) /ˌsætʃəˈreɪʃn/
the point where sth cannot be added to because there is already an abundance • *The best way to avoid saturation coverage of news events is to switch off the TV and media threads.* ➢ saturate (v) ❖ κορεσμός

10.79 restraint (n) /rɪˈstreɪnt/
sth that prevents sth increasing • *Those annoying marketing calls keep coming without restraint.* ➢ restrain (v), restraining (adj)
❖ συγκράτηση

10.80 charisma (n) /kəˈrɪzmə/
the quality to charm and impress others • *She lacked the charisma and finesse of her parents.* ➢ charismatic (adj) ❖ χάρισμα

10.81 hypocrite (n) /ˈhɪpəkrɪt/
sb who pretends to believe in or support sth that they don't • *He's always recommending products he's never used himself. What a hypocrite!* ➢ hypocrisy (n), hypocritical (adj), hypocritically (adv) ❖ υποκριτής

10.82 acquire (v) /əˈkwaɪə(r)/
obtain by buying or receiving as a gift; gain by your own efforts • *Miranda has acquired a reputation as film director.* ➢ acquisition (n), acquired (adj) ❖ αποκτώ

10.83 compliment (n) /ˈkɒmplɪmənt/
a comment or gesture that expresses admiration or praise • *It was a great compliment to be invited to dinner by the mayor.* ➢ compliment (v), complimentary (adj) ❖ κομπλιμέντο, φιλοφρόνηση

10.84 fraud (n) /frɔːd/
a crime of cheating a person or organisation out of money • *The gang were involved in large-scale internet fraud, cheating small companies out of cash.* ➢ fraudulent (adj)
❖ απάτη

10.85 wear sb down (phr v) /weə ˈsʌmbədi daʊn/
tire sb out so they agree to do sth • *The sales staff's approach is to wear customers down with repeated phone calls until they give in and buy something. It's water-on-a-stone tactics.*
❖ πείθω μέσω συνεχούς πίεσης και επανάληψης

10.86 suck sb/sth in (phr v) /sʌk ˈsʌmbədi/ˈsʌmθɪŋ ɪn/
make sb get involved in sth • *Don't get sucked in to pyramid marketing schemes; the only one who profits is the company owner.*
❖ παρασύρομαι

10.87 splash out (phr v) /splæʃ aʊt/
spend a lot of money at once • *With discounts that were almost too good to be true, she splashed out and treated herself to a couple of new outfits.* ❖ ξοδεύω πολλά χρήματα σε σύντομο χρονικό διάστημα

10.88 flick through sth (phr v) /flɪk θruː ˈsʌmθɪŋ/
look quickly through written material, photos, information, etc. • *In search of a housewarming gift for his friend, Andy flicked through the pages of the brochure from that well-known Swedish furniture outlet.*
❖ ξεφυλλίζω

10.89 vacant (adj) /ˈveɪkənt/
unresponsive as though devoid of thought • *My enquiry about the comparative technical specs of the various TVs on sale was met with a shrug and a vacant look from the sales assistant.* ➢ vacate (v), vacancy (n), vacantly (adv) ❖ κενός

10.90 persistence (n) /pəˈsɪstəns/
the act of continuing to try to do sth in a determined way despite difficulties • *My persistence paid off when the company finally agreed to give me a refund for the faulty printer.* ➢ persist (v), persistent (adj), persistently (adv) ❖ εμμονή, επιμονή

10.91 strive (v) /straɪv/
try very hard • *The shop strives to retain its existing customers through loyalty incentives.* ➢ strife (n) (adv) ❖ αγωνίζομαι, προσπαθώ σκληρά

10.92 inescapable (adj) /ˌɪnɪˈskeɪpəbl/
that cannot be avoided; unavoidable • *Counting their losses, they came to the inescapable conclusion that it was time to close the business.* ➢ inescapably (adv)
❖ αναπόφευκτος

10.93 tank (v) /tæŋk/
fail by reaching a point with no hope of growth • *When Greece's economy tanked, it translated into the closing of numerous family businesses.* ➢ tank (n), tanker (n)
❖ πέφτω σε αξία, τιμή, κτλ.

10.94 recession (n) /rɪˈseʃn/
an economic period when trade and production levels are at a low, resulting in high unemployment • *The world economy has been in deep recession for the past decade.* ➢ recede (v), recess (n), recessive (adj), recessively (adv) ❖ ύφεση

10.95 **scorn** (n) /skɔːn/
an attitude towards sb/sth that you regard as stupid or inferior • *His suggestion was met with scorn from the store manager.* ➢ scorn (v), scornful (adj), scornfully (adv) ❖ καταφρόνηση

10.96 **satire** (n) /ˈsætaɪə(r)/
a form of criticism through humour often to exaggerate weaknesses in an amusing way • *Aristophanes masterfully addressed social issues through satire in ancient time.* ➢ satirise (v), satirical (adj), satirically (adv) ❖ σάτυρα

10.97 **sarcasm** (n) /ˈsɑːkæzəm/
the use of comments that have an opposite meaning to what they say to criticise or make fun of sb • *'So the dog ate your homework again,' said the teacher with more than a hint of sarcasm.* ➢ sarcastic (adj), sarcastically (adv) ❖ σαρκασμός

10.98 **asset** (n) /ˈæset/
anything of value which a person or company owns • *After the company declared bankruptcy, its assets were sold off.* ❖ περιουσιακό στοιχείο

10.99 **benchmark** (n) /ˈbentʃmɑːk/
a standard used to draw comparisons against • *The country's national health service was seen as a benchmark for the rest of Europe.* ➢ benchmark (v) ❖ σημείο αναφοράς, μέτρο

10.100 **intimidate** (v) /ɪnˈtɪmɪdeɪt/
frighten sb into doing sth you want them to • *The bank tried to intimidate them into settling our debts out of court.* ➢ intimidation (n), intimidating (adj) ❖ εκφοβίζω

10.101 **fracture** (v) /ˈfræktʃə(r)/
break sth; split sth into pieces so it can't function • *The ranks of the opposition party fractured after their electoral defeat.* ➢ fracture (n), fractious (adj) ❖ διασπώ

10.102 **repression** (n) /rɪˈpreʃn/
the use of force to restrict a group of people • *Greeks suffered religious and other forms of repression during the Ottoman rule.* ➢ repress (v), repressive (adj), repressively (adv) ❖ καταστολή

10.103 **desolation** (n) /ˌdesəˈleɪʃn/
the feeling of loneliness and sadness; the state of a place that has been abandoned or destroyed • *He lived with a constant sense of desolation during the long period of unemployment.* ➢ desolate (v), desolate (adj) ❖ απόγνωση, ερήμωση

Nouns: behaviour & attitude

authenticity	persistence
charisma	repression
compliment	restraint
credibility	sarcasm
hypocrite	satire
inferiority	scorn
intimacy	vanity
manipulation	fraud

Phrasal verbs

butt in	rake in sth
flick through sth	rub off
gear sth to/towards sb/sth	splash out
	suck sb/sth in
go down	vouch for sb/sth
pepper sth with sth	wear sb down

Speaking page 149

10.104 **butt in** (phr v) /bʌt ɪn/
interrupt rudely • *Sorry to butt in, but I've just had some serious news.* ❖ διακόπτω αγενώς

10.105 **consumerism** (n) /kənˈsjuːmərɪz(ə)m/
the idea that people should buy and use goods in large quantities for a society to progress • *The family got into extreme debt due to excessive consumerism.* ➢ consume (v), consumer (n), consumption (n) ❖ καταναλωτισμός

10.106 **status symbol** (n) /ˈsteɪtəs ˈsɪmbəl/
sth that people believe to show high social status and wealth • *Large cars, once a status symbol, have simply become a tax burden for most.* ❖ σύμβολο κύρους

Compound nouns

leaflet drop	status symbol
market share	trade paper
raw material	

Writing pages 150-151

10.107 **blight** (v) /blaɪt/
destroy or damage sth • *The country has been blighted by public sector redundancies and company closures.* ➢ blight (n) ❖ καταστρέφω

10.108 raw material (n) /rɔː məˈtɪəriəl/
the basic untreated components used to make sth • *China imports a number of raw materials from Australia for use in manufacturing.*
❖ πρώτη ύλη

10.109 swell (v) /swel/
increase in size • *Due to the heavy rains, the river began to swell and burst its banks.*
➢ swell (n), swelling (n), swollen (adj)
❖ φουσκώνω

10.110 sparingly (adv) /ˈspeərɪŋli/
using sth carefully in small amounts
• *Use inverted form sparingly in your text.*
➢ spare (v), spare (n), sparing (adj)
❖ με οικονομία, με φειδώ

10.111 immediacy (n) /ɪˈmiːdiəsi/
the direct importance and resulting urgency
• *Texting lacks the immediacy of face-to-face discussion.* ➢ immediate (adj), immediately (adv) ❖ αμεσότητα

10.112 epitomise (v) /ɪˈpɪtəmi/
be an accurate example of sth • *His books epitomised the living conditions in post-war Britain.* ➢ epitome (n) ❖ ενσαρκώνω

10.113 epitome (n) /ɪˈɪˈpɪtəmi/
an accurate example of sth • *Materialism was regarded as the epitome of success.*
➢ epitomise (v) ❖ επιτομή

10.114 inferiority (n) /ɪnˌfɪəriˈɒrəti/
the state of being less important or of lower quality than sth/sb else • *The book goes a long way to debunk the myth of racial inferiority.* ➢ inferior (adj) ❖ κατωτερότητα

Video 10: Skateboards from Trash
page 152

10.115 repurpose (v) /ˌriːˈpɜːpəs/
adapt sth to make it suitable for another purpose • *He repurposed his great-grandmother's old sewing machine to make a stylish table.* ❖ προσαρμόζω κάτι ώστε να έχει διαφορετική χρήση

Vocabulary Exercises

A Choose the correct answers.

1 The advertising agency promoted the new innovative technological product using a(n) ___.
   a compliment   **b** saturation   **c** pitch   **d** infomercial

2 Advertising companies spend a great deal of time and effort to ___ the product.
   a blight   **b** franchise   **c** hype   **d** woo

3 Consumers are often ___ to buy products when they listen to catchy jingles on air.
   a enticed   **b** intimidated   **c** induced   **d** promoted

4 The glib salesman used an ___ approach to persuade the consumer to purchase the large item by offering a substantial discount.
   a implicit   **b** explicit   **c** effusive   **d** overt

5 When a business increases its ___, this indicates that it is doing better compared to its competitors.
   a market share   **b** leaflet drop   **c** classified ads   **d** trade papers

6 In the age of consumerism and status symbols, customers purchase products that appeal to their ___.
   a restraint   **b** efficacy   **c** benchmark   **d** vanity

7 During times of financial austerity consumers experience severe hardship and feelings of ___.
   a repression   **b** desolation   **c** persistence   **d** materialism

8 Jane doubted the ___ of the leather handbag as there were so many fake and imitation brands of goods being sold on the black market.
   a authenticity   **b** credibility   **c** merchandising   **d** intimacy

B Choose the correct words or phrases.

1 Many a falsehood / camouflage is propagated through social media because these platforms don't have adequate vetting procedures in place to filter out such misleading news content.

2 This fake environmentally friendly product has tantalising / staggering potential to capitalise on the gullibility of consumers.

3 Celebrities endorse products via the social media; however, they aren't always candid / attainable in their assessment of its efficacy.

4 Customers take a dim view / get into hot water if they are exploited by misleading or ambiguous adverts.

5 The content of the advertising leaflet contained a promotional / typographical error concerning the price of the item and it misquoted it as being much more expensive.

6 It is not effective to employ sarcasm / satire in an advertisement as it could patronise and insult consumers.

7 The cosmetics and fashion industries collude in appealing to young girls' unwitting / egocentric desires to purchase their products in order to beautify themselves.

8 As I turned on the radio, I tapped my fingers on the table in rhythm to the catchy sound of the jingle / billboard.

9 The salesman's hard sell technique raked me in / sucked me in and I felt weary from the pressure to buy.

10 Mary's marketing expertise proved to be an invaluable endorsement / asset to the fledgling company.

C Complete the sentences with the words from the box.

charisma   disclosure   foray   fraud   hypocrite   infusion   momentum   recession   semblance   scorn

1 Now that the sales have picked up _____, store owners anticipate a substantial profit.

2 _____ of industrial secrets to a competitor is often termed as industrial espionage.

3 The general manager of the tobacco company was a _____ as he promoted sales of tobacco while not being a smoker himself for health reasons.

4 An advertising campaign stands a greater chance of success if it uses actors who have _____.

5 The company embarked on a _____ into emerging markets in South-East Asia.

6 The corrupt managing director of the company was convicted of _____ and embezzlement after a protracted trial that was heavily publicised in the media regarding the environmental inefficacy of the company's product.

7 After the scandal the director poured _____ on its competitor's products for fraudulent practice.

8 During times of economic _____ companies tend to downsize their operations and make their employees redundant in order to maximise profits.

9 When the stock market crashed the government stepped in and imposed regulatory controls in an effort to re-establish a _____ of financial stability.

10 According to the government, the crisis was narrowly averted due to an _____ of vast amounts of cash into the stricken economy.

D Complete the sentences using the verbs in the correct form.

acquire   discern   equate   flick   fracture   gear   splash   strive   sway   tout   tank   wear

1 Advertisers bombard us with advertisements via the media to _____ to increase their market share.

2 Companies _____ out on sleek and fancy advertising campaigns to coax us into buying their products.

3 Consumers _____ their personal success with living life in the fast lane.

4 Luxury items such as designer clothes, fancy sports cars and expensive wrist watches or mobile phones are often _____ as status symbols to flaunt a wealthy lifestyle.

5 Advertisements specifically aimed at children are _____ towards persuading their parents to purchase items under feelings of pressure and guilt.

6 Constant and persistent advertising using implicit messages in the media can _____ even the hardiest of consumers down.

7 In the need for instant gratification as well as the need to _____ newer and faster electronic goods or updates for computers, it will become ever more difficult to dispose of or recycle them.

8 Implicit messages in advertisements appeal to the vanity of wealthy consumers, who feel they are better able to _____ the true value of an expensive item.

9 Numerous companies have proliferated ever since the market _____ into smaller market sectors.

10 Most customers feel _____ by peer pressure and buy new products whether they need them or not.

11 In bookshops people often just browse around and _____ through the pages of a book or magazine.

12 The marketing campaign _____ abysmally because it failed to appeal to the younger generation.

10 Grammar

10.1 Countable & Uncountable nouns

Τα ουσιαστικά στα Αγγλικά είναι countable (αριθμήσιμα) ή uncountable (μη αριθμήσιμα), και μερικά όπως *paper, wood, work* μπορούν να είναι είτε countable ή uncountable με διαφορετική έννοια. Τα uncountable nouns έχουν μόνο ένα τύπο και δεν τα χρησιμοποιούμε με αριθμούς ή το αόριστο άρθρο (*a/an*).

Χρησιμοποιούμε *an amount of, a piece of, a great deal of* κλπ. για να μιλήσουμε για ένα ποσοστό.
→ She gave us **a great deal of advice** before we set up the campaign.
→ She gave us **a piece of advice** before we set up the campaign.
→ They received **a large amount of money** as a research grant.

Χρησιμοποιούμε *a number of* για να μιλήσουμε για countable nouns.
→ We've had **a number of requests** for help.

Χρησιμοποιούμε *a lot of* και με τα δύο είδη ουσιαστικών.
→ There's been **a lot of publicity** about homelessness lately.

Χρησιμοποιούμε *few* και *fewer* με countable nouns και *(a) little* και *less* με uncountable nouns.
→ They made **a few complaints** about the noise.

Συνηθισμένα uncountable nouns είναι *research, homework, money, information, advice*.

10.2 Indefinite Pronouns

Υπάρχουν δύο είδη indefinite pronouns (αόριστες αντωνυμίες). Η πρώτη κατηγορία περιλαμβάνει αντωνυμίες που αναφέρονται σε αόριστα ουσιαστικά (non-specific nouns). Τέτοιες αντωνυμίες είναι οι: *anybody, anyone, anything, everyone, everybody, everything, nobody, no one, none, nothing, somebody, someone, something*.
→ Simon remembers **everyone** from university but **no one** from the old neighbourhood.
→ I haven't talked to **anyone** about the incident.

Μπορούμε να τα χρησιμοποιήσουμε σε συνδυασμό με else για να αναφερθούμε σε άλλο άτομο, πράγμα ή τόπο.
→ Have you told **anyone else** about the incident?

Η δεύτερη κατηγορία περιλαμβάνει αντωνυμίες που αναφέρονται σε συγκεκριμένο ουσιαστικό (specific noun), του οποίου η έννοια είναι εύκολα κατανοητή είτε γιατί είχε αναφερθεί προηγουμένως είτε γιατί την αποσαφηνίζουν οι λέξεις που ακολουθούν την αόριστη αντωνυμία. Αυτές οι αντωνυμίες είναι *all, any, each, few, neither, some, another, both, either, many, one, several*.
→ **Many** of the reporters asked questions, but **few** of them got the answers they hoped for.
→ **Any** objections? Put them in writing if you have **any**.

10.3 Demonstrative Pronouns

Οι demonstrative pronouns (δεικτικές αντωνυμίες) είναι *this, that, these* και *those*. Τις χρησιμοποιούμε για να αναφερθούμε σε ένα ή περισσότερα πράγματα που βρίσκονται κοντά ή μακριά.
→ Did you read **that**?
→ Take a look at **these** here.

Χρησιμοποιούμε demonstrative pronouns επίσης για να αναφερθούμε και σε πρόσωπα.
→ Hi, **this** is Bryony speaking. Is **that** Sam?

10.4 Reciprocal Pronouns

Οι reciprocal pronouns (αλληλοπαθείς αντωνυμίες) αναφέρονται σε ουσιαστικά πληθυντικού αριθμού ή σε δύο ή περισσότερα ουσιαστικά. Χρησιμοποιούμε reciprocal pronouns όταν μιλάμε για μια αμοιβαία πράξη ή ένα αμοιβαίο συναίσθημα.
→ Friends often give gifts to **each other**.

Οι reciprocal pronouns έχουν και κτητικό τύπο.
→ Journalists often plagiarise **one another's** stories.

10.5 Reflexive Pronouns

Οι reflexive pronouns (αυτοπαθείς αντωνυμίες) αναφέρονται στο υποκείμενο μιας πρότασης. Χρησιμοποιούνται:
για να δώσουμε έμφαση στο υποκείμενο (subject).
→ *The actor **herself** would never wear the perfume.*
όταν το υποκείμενο (subject) και το αντικείμενο (object) είναι ίδια.
→ *I allow **myself** to buy a few small treats every month.*
μετά από πρόθεση όταν το υποκείμενο και το αντικείμενο ταυτίζονται.
→ *Fred can think for **himself** without asking for his parents opinion.*

10.6 Articles

Χρησιμοποιούμε το definite article *(the):*
για να μιλήσουμε γενικά και επίσημα.
→ *Advertising focuses on **the brand** rather than **the cost**.*
με μερικά επίθετα που αναφέρονται σε ομάδες ανθρώπων.
→ *The club is frequented by **the rich and famous**.*
με επίθετα στον υπερθετικό βαθμό.
→ *He is **the highest paid actor** in the business.*
με συγκεκριμένα ουσιαστικά.
→ *He produced **the documentary** about the star.*
με ουσιαστικά που τα θεωρούμε μοναδικά.
→ *He'd give **the Earth** for a new scoop.*

Χρησιμοποιούμε το indefinite article *(a/an)* για να:
μιλήσουμε για κάτι μη συγκεκριμένο, με την έννοια 'one'.
→ *They have **a special offer** on **a smart TV**.*
μιλήσουμε επίσημα για γενικά πράγματα.
→ ***A customer** entering the shop for the first time usually turns to the right.*
αναφέρουμε κάτι για πρώτη φορά.
→ *I read **an article** about marketing trends.*

Χρησιμοποιούμε το zero article για να:
μιλήσουμε για singular uncountable nouns (μη αριθμήσιμα ουσιαστικά στον ενικό αριθμό).
→ ***Generosity** is priceless commodity.*
μιλήσουμε για plural countable και uncountable nouns (αριθμήσιμα και μη αριθμήσιμα ουσιαστικά στον πληθυντικό αριθμό).
→ ***Children** are attracted to bright colours.*

Grammar Exercises

A Complete the sentences with these words and phrases.

little   a little   less   lots of   a lot of   a few   fewer   quite a bit of
a huge amount of   a great deal of   a piece of   all

1 To make that pudding you'll need _____ sugar. Personally, it's too sweet for my liking.

2 It seems that _____ people have any faith in the mainstream media nowadays.

3 Several MSM broadcasts have lost _____ credibility and people are turning to alternative news sites.

4 The price of placing a classified ad was _____ than I had expected.

5 Yes, you can use _____ cinnamon in the cake but use it sparingly or it will taste bitter.

6 I have _____ faith in the Pound since it tanked after the vote. It will recover but the question is when.

7 I've got _____ free time nowadays so I've decided to take up funambulism, otherwise known as tightrope walking.

8 There was _____ dissent when the economy could not get out of recession.

9 There is _____ hypocrisy in the cut-throat industry of advertising.

10 They published a disclaimer on their label after having received _____ complaints from the public.

11 Only _____ shops will let you flick through their magazines before buying.

12 Let me give you _____ advice. Don't count your chickens before they hatch.

B Circle the correct words.

1 a His personal hygiene leaves something / everything to be desired.

   b I know. Someone / Anyone should tell him but it's such a delicate subject to broach.

2 a He did everything / anything in his power to promote his book.

   b Yes, few / a few are his connections in the publishing field so he had to find alternatives.

3 a The absent-minded professor thought he was being clear as a bell, but somebody / nobody had a clue what he was talking about.

   b Quite frankly, few / each of the students could barely stay awake let alone assimilate any of what he said.

4 a He makes less / fewer annual income than I do.

   b That's fair because, in fact, he has less / fewer responsibility than you do.

5 a He does everything / something by the book.

   b I know. He really should learn it's OK to make a few / all exceptions.

C Choose the best answers.

1 I splashed out yesterday and bought ___ new baggage for my trip.
   a a few   b some   c a little   d a great deal of

2 I tried to get ___ information out of him but he dropped the subject.
   a any   b little   c some   d all

3 Could you please give me ___ advice on which platform is the best for online lessons?
   a a bit of   b a number of   c several   d much

4 I can't read ___ paper now because he has spilled coffee all over it.
   a no   b the   c a   d anything

5 Well, ___ chili is really spicy at this restaurant. I don't think you'll enjoy it.
   a the   b all   c a   d some

6 I haven't heard ___ from Frank these days. Wonder what he's up to.
   a something   b a little   c all   d anything

7 I have ten students in that class. ___ of them is a genius.
   a Every   b Each   c All   d Some

8 You're such a hypochondriac! I'm sure there's ___ wrong with you.
   a something   b a little   c everything   d nothing

9 I know it's a difficult problem but does ___ at all know the answer?
   a no-one   b someone   c anyone   d everyone

10 She made a couple of scrumptious cakes for the annual bazaar, ___ of which sold within seconds.
   a none   b all   c each   d both

D Write the correct article where necessary.

1 Necessity is _____ mother of _____ invention.

2 When _____ going gets tough, _____ tough get going.

3 _____ pen is mightier than _____ sword.

4 _____ broken clock is right twice _____ day.

5 _____ haste makes _____ waste.

6 _____ bird in _____ hand is worth two in _____ bush.

7 Every cloud has _____ silver lining.

8 It's not over until _____ fat lady sings.

For questions 1–8, read the text below and think of the word which best fits each space. Use only one word in each space.

Love shopping?

Ever gone to the grocery shop for a carton of milk and come back with bags full of groceries? Ever bought 'buy two, get one free' products because they were on sale when (**1**) ___ just needed one? Ever thought you couldn't live without this absolutely perfect (and useful) gadget, bought it and never used it – or used it just once?

If you've answered yes to just (**2**) ___ of these questions, rejoice, you're like the rest of us humans. But if you've answered yes to (**3**) ___ three and could go on to give a great (**4**) ___ more examples of how you buy things impulsively, then you're in trouble.

If you believe you're a shopaholic, you shouldn't try to face this problem by (**5**) ___. You need to seek assistance from a specialist. However, if you're looking for ways to keep things under control, take heed of (**6**) ___ following advice. Leave your credit cards at home. Paying in cash makes you more aware of how much an item costs than just swiping a piece of plastic. (**7**) ___ also physically limits how much you can buy or pay for (**8**) ___.

11 Say Cheese!

Reading

pages 156-157

11.1 **entity** (n) /'entəti/
sth that exists independently in its own right
• *His company is no longer a separate entity since its acquisition by the corporation.*
❖ οντότητα

11.2 **fringe** (n) /frɪndʒ/
the outer area of sth • *The magazine remains on the fringe of mainstream media.* ➤ fringe (v), fringe (adj) ❖ περιθώριο

11.3 **telephoto lens** (n) /ˌtelifəʊtəʊ 'lenz/
a camera lens that adjusts to produce large images of distant subjects • *Through the telephoto lens, he captured every detail of the nesting eagle on top of the rock.* ❖ τηλεφακός

11.4 **scourge** (n) /skɜːdʒ/
sth/sb that causes terrible damage • *The recession has been the scourge of the decade.* ➤ scourge (v) ❖ μάστιγα

11.5 **poignant** (adj) /'pɔɪnjənt/
emotionally moving • *The empty shops were a poignant reminder of the economic situation.* ➤ poignancy (n), poignantly (adv) ❖ καυστικός

11.6 **convict** (v) /kən'vɪkt/
officially declare that sb is guilty of a crime
• *They were convicted of murder and sentenced to life imprisonment.* ➤ convict (n), convicted (adj) ❖ καταδικάζω

Look!
Προσέξτε την διαφορά στη προφορά μεταξύ του ρήματος και του ουσιαστικού *convict*. Το ρήμα προφέρεται /kən'vɪkt/ (con<u>vict</u>), ενώ το ουσιαστικό /'kɒnvɪkt/ (<u>con</u>vict).

11.7 **stumble** (v) /'stʌmbl/
walk in an awkward uncontrolled way
• *Hearing the alarm, he stumbled out of bed still half asleep.* ➤ stumble (n) ❖ παραπατώ, σκοντάφτω, σκουντουφλώ

11.8 **paparazzo** (n) /ˌpæpə'rætsəʊ/
a press photographer who follows famous people to photograph them • *Despite her valiant attempts to stay out of the press, one paparazzo was particularly persistent and snapped her on the patio in her pyjamas.*
❖ παπαράτσι
✎ Plural: paparazzi

11.9 **documentarian** (n) /ˌdɒkjumen'teəriən/
sb who makes documentaries • *Debbie took on a new role as a documentarian portraying social issues after being made redundant when the newspaper closed down.*
➤ document (v), document (n), documentation (n) ❖ παραγωγός ντοκυμαντέρ

11.10 **bureau** (n) /'bjʊərəʊ/
organisation that collects and provides information • *You can see what jobs are available at the employment bureau.*
➤ bureaucrat (n), bureaucracy (n), bureaucratic (adj) ❖ γραφείο, υπηρεσία

11.11 **decimate** (v) /'desɪmeɪt/
seriously damage sth • *His career was decimated by the company closure.*
➤ decimation (n) ❖ καταστρέφω, αποδεκατίζω

11.12 **gripping** (adj) /'grɪpɪŋ/
very interesting and exciting • *The film was a gripping tale of courage and endurance.*
➤ grip (v), grip (n) ❖ συναρπαστικός

11.13 **hard-hitting** (adj) /hɑːd 'hɪtɪŋ/
openly and honestly critical • *Deeply offended by the interviewer's hard-hitting questions, he got up and walked out of the studio.*
❖ δυναμικός, σκληρός

11.14 **scratch the surface** (expr) /skrætʃ ðə 'sɜːfɪs/
uncover only a small part of an issue • *The documentary was interesting, but was lacking in detail and clearly only scratched the surface of the main problem.* ❖ αποκαλύπτω μικρό μέρος από κάτι

11.15 **delve into sth** (phr v) /delv ɪntə'sʌmθɪŋ/
research sth thoroughly • *Detectives delved into his personal correspondence and found evidence of his dirty dealings.* ❖ εμβαθύνω, ερευνώ

11.16 **subgenre** (n) /'sʌbˌʒɒ̃rə/
a type of media, literature, etc. that differs from the others within the same category • *Hard rock is considered a subgenre of rock music in the wider sense.* ❖ υπο-είδος μουσικής, λογοτεχνίας κλπ.

11.17 **proverbially** (adv) /prə'vɜːbiəli/
in a way that is widely known and understood
• *The reporters were proverbially dogged in their pursuit of a scoop.* ➤ proverb (n), proverbial (adj) ❖ όπως είναι πασίγνωστο

11.18 **fly on the wall** (expr) /flaɪ ɒn ðə wɔːl/
sb who listens to others without being seen
• *I'd love to be a fly on the wall to see her reaction when she finds out what happened.*
❖ «να είμαι από μια μεριά» (για να δω κρυφά)

11.19 **impartially** (adv) /ˌɪmˈpɑːʃəli/
objectively; without taking sides • *Not enough of the news seems to be presented completely impartially, as so many journalists have their own political agenda.* ➤ impartiality (n), impartial (adj) ❖ αμερόληπτα

11.20 **strike a chord** (expr) /straɪk ə kɔːd/
arouse interest by saying sth that people can relate to • *The documentary on bullying struck a chord within the education sector.* ❖ απηχώ, θίγω την «ευαίσθητη χορδή» κάποιου

11.21 **discreet** (adj) /dɪˈskriːt/
careful not to reveal sth secret • *She was always very discreet about her family background.* ➤ discretion (n), discreetly (adv) ❖ διακριτικός

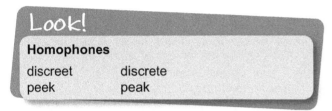

Look!

Homophones

| discreet | discrete |
| peek | peak |

11.22 **peek** (n) /piːk/
a quick, sometimes secretive, look at sth • *I took a quick peek at the clock, hoping that the interview would end soon.* ➤ peek (v) ❖ κρυφοκοίταγμα, γρήγορη ματιά

11.23 **insatiable** (adj) /ɪnˈseɪʃəbl/
not able to be satisfied • *Underlying her insatiable need for attention, lies an inferiority complex.* ➤ insatiably (adv) ❖ ακόρεστος

11.24 **perception** (n) /pəˈsepʃn/
the way sth is regarded • *The hard-hitting documentary changed the public perception of milk production.* ➤ perceive (v), perceptible (adj), perceptibly (adv) ❖ αντίληψη

11.25 **stalk** (v) /stɔːk/
follow and observe sb without their permission • *She was sick of being stalked by the paparazzi.* ➤ stalker (n) ❖ ακολουθώ και παρατηρώ κάποιον χωρίς την άδειά του

11.26 **door stepping** (n) /dɔː ˈstepɪŋ/
watching sb's home • *Tired of reporters and their door stepping, he moved house to a secret location registered under a pseudonym.* ➤ doorstep (n) ❖ συστηματική / συνεχής παρακολούθηση της κατοικίας κάποιου

11.27 **have it both ways** (expr) /hæv ɪt bəʊθ weɪz/
benefit in an impossible way from two contrasting approaches • *How can you stay out of the public eye if you want to be famous? You can't have it both ways.* ❖ έχω και τα δύο, «το έχω δίπορτο»

11.28 **emphatically** (adv) /ɪmˈfætɪkli/
forcefully stressing a point • *The politician emphatically denied any connection with the off-shore bank.* ➤ emphasise (v), emphasis (n), emphatic (adj) ❖ εμφατικά

11.29 **unflattering** (adj) /ʌnˈflætərɪŋ/
making sb/sth look less attractive than they are or would prefer to be seen • *The press photographers just lap up unflattering shots of celebrities without their make-up on.* ❖ μη κολακευτικό

11.30 **seedier** (adj) /ˈsiːdiə(r)/
less pleasant, often linked with immoral activities • *He prefers to keep quiet about the seedier side of his extramarital relationships.* ➤ seediness (n) ❖ ελεεινότερος

11.31 **drive sth home** (expr) /draɪvˈsʌmθɪŋ həʊm/
strongly get a point across; forcefully convey a meaning • *She drove home the point that the tax payers were entitled to know how their money was being spent.* ❖ γίνομαι απολύτως κατανοητός

11.32 **hint** (n) /hɪnt/
a very small amount of sth • *There was more than a hint of sarcasm in her voice.* ➤ hint (v) ❖ υπαινιγμός

11.33 **symbolic** (adj) /sɪmˈbɒlɪk/
important in terms of an idea implied • *He removed the sweeping statement from his blog as a symbolic gesture of apology.* ➤ symbolise (v), symbol (n), symbolically (adv) ❖ συμβολικός

11.34 **compliant** (adj) /kəmˈplaɪənt/
easily obeying particular rules; very willing to agree with sth/sb • *The editor became less compliant to the journalist's suggestion to include the article when he received a call from the prime minister's office.* ➤ comply (v), compliance (n) ❖ υπάκουος, συνεργάσιμος

11.35 **skyrocket** (v) /ˈskaɪrɒkɪt/
rise or increase rapidly • *Sales of the newspaper skyrocketed with the exclusive report.* ❖ ταχεία αύξηση

11.36 **adrenaline** (n) /əˈdrenəlɪn/
a hormone that increases the heart-rate and energy level • *The prospect of capturing the couple together on film got the photographer's adrenaline flowing.* ❖ αδρεναλίνη

11.37 **sb's/sth's days are numbered** (expr) /ˈsʌmbədɪz/ˈsʌmθɪŋz deɪz ɑː ˈnʌmbəd/
sb/sth will not continue or be successful much longer • *Her days as an award-winning author are numbered as she seems to be running out of ideas.* ❖ οι ημέρες (του) είναι μετρημένες

11.38 **superficial** (adj) /ˌsuːpəˈfɪʃl/
only considering the obvious aspects of sth • *His report gave only a superficial analysis of the political problem.* ➤ superficiality (n), superficially (adv) ❖ επιφανειακός

Vocabulary   pages 158-159-160

11.39 lampoon (v) /læmˈpuːn/
criticise in an amusing way ● *The cartoonist has a talent for hilariously lampooning celebrities.* ➣ lampoon (n) ❖ σατιρίζω

11.40 recluse (n) /rɪˈkluːs/
sb who chooses to live alone and avoids company ● *The former star now prefers to live as a recluse in the company of her pets.* ➣ reclusive (adj) ❖ ερημίτης

11.41 scoop (n) /skuːp/
an important news story that is the first to be published on the topic ● *The tabloid scoop revealed that the ageing star was suffering from a serious illness.* ➣ scoop (v) ❖ σημαντική είδηση που εμφανίζεται πρώτη φορά

11.42 slander (n) /ˈslaːndə(r)/
a spoken statement which gives false information aiming to damage sb's reputation ● *She took the talk show host to court for slander.* ➣ slander (v) ❖ συκοφαντία

11.43 conman (n) /ˈkɒnmæn/
sb who deceives sb to gain money ● *The elderly widow was cheated out of her savings by a conman.* ➣ con (v), con (n) ❖ απατεώνας

11.44 buffoonish (adj) /bəˈfuːnɪʃ/
silly; clownish ● *His clumsy denial of the claims came across as buffoonish rather than convincing.* ➣ buffoon (n) ❖ γελοίος

11.45 undeterred (adj) /ˌʌndɪˈtɜːd/
not put off from doing sth ● *Undeterred by the slanderous accusations against her, she continued her campaign to expose the media mogul.* ❖ απτόητος

11.46 deranged (adj) /dɪˈreɪndʒd/
incapable of normal, rational thinking ● *The accusations were so absurd that they appeared to be the product of a deranged mind.* ➣ derangement (n) ❖ διαταραγμένος

11.47 cement (v) /sɪˈment/
make something, such as an agreement, stronger ● *The treaty was drawn up to cement relations between the ruling powers after the war.* ➣ cement (n) ❖ ενισχύω, δυναμώνω

11.48 blackmail (n) /ˈblækmeɪl/
the crime of threatening to reveal information about sb unless they pay you to keep quiet ● *Digging deep into the victim's past, the detective uncovered a web of corruption and blackmail involving respected figures.* ➣ blackmail (v) ❖ εκβιασμός

11.49 excerpt (n) /ˈeksɜːpt/
a short part of a larger text, film, etc. ● *He read a short excerpt from his new novel at the press conference.* ➣ excerpt (v) ❖ απόσπασμα

11.50 exile (n) /ˈeksaɪl/
the state of being forced to leave one's country to live elsewhere ● *After the revolt, the royal family were sent into exile.* ➣ exile (v) ❖ εξορία

11.51 libel (n) /ˈlaɪbl/
the act of publishing a statement about sb that is untrue and damaging to their reputation ● *The newspaper produced evidence that their claims were actually true and not just libel.* ➣ libel (v), libellous (adj) ❖ λίβελλος, δυσφήμιση

11.52 memoir (n) /ˈmemwaː(r)/
a personal written account of sb's life experience ● *Not being literary minded, he hired a shadow writer to produce his best-selling memoirs.* ❖ απομνημόνευμα

11.53 obscurity (n) /əbˈskjʊərəti/
the state of being long forgotten or unknown ● *The actor rose from obscurity as a plumber to become an Oscar winner.* ➣ obscure (adj), obscurely (adv) ❖ αφάνεια

11.54 aristocracy (n) /ˌærɪˈstɒkrəsi/
the upper class ● *The party claims to represent the working classes rather than the aristocracy.* ➣ aristocrat (n), aristocratic (adj), aristocratically (adv) ❖ αριστοκρατία

11.55 news outlet (n) /njuːz ˈaʊtlet/
a source where news can be obtained ● *Social media sites alone are not always reliable as news outlets as they tend to recycle the same old, often unfounded stories.* ❖ πηγή ειδήσεων

11.56 leak (n) /liːk/
the disclosure of secret information to the public ● *The journalist went into hiding after admitting responsibility for the leak of top secret information to the media.* ➣ leak (v), leaky (adj) ❖ διαρροή

11.57 discrete (adj) /dɪˈskriːt/
separate and distinct from others of the same kind ● *Fiction can be divided into several discrete subgenres.* ➣ discreteness (n), ❖ χωριστός

11.58 correspondent (n) /ˌkɒrəˈspɒndənt/
a news reporter who covers a particular subject or region ● *The public were horrified to learn of the torture of foreign correspondents at the front line.* ➣ correspond (v), correspondence (n), corresponding (adj) ❖ ανταποκριτής

Nouns: crimes

blackmail	libel	slander

Nouns: people

aristocracy	persona
conman	recluse
correspondent	toddler
paparazzo	

11.59 **credible** (adj) /ˈkredəbl/
believable • *Given her gentle public image, it did not seem credible that she could have been so cruel to her children.* ➢ credit (v), credibility (n), credible (adv) ❖ αξιόπιστος
✎ Opp: incredible ❖ αναξιόπιστος

11.60 **immortal** (adj) /ɪˈmɔːtl/
famous and likely to be remembered for a long time • *A toast was raised to the bard's immortal memory.* ➢ immortalise (v), immortal (adj), immortality (n) ❖ αθάνατος

11.61 **fabled** (adj) /ˈfeɪbld/
legendary • *Our itinerary included a visit to the fabled Sanctuary of Eleusis.* ➢ fable (n) ❖ μυθικός

11.62 **Z-list** (adj) /ˈzedlɪst/
indicating those who are only slightly famous • *Daytime TV is peppered with Z-list celebrities, known for nothing more than seasonal chat shows.* ❖ λίγο γνωστός ή διάσημος

11.63 **illustrious** (adj) /ɪˈlʌstriəs/
renowned and greatly admired • *The awards ceremony was attended by illustrious guests from the world of literature.* ❖ επιφανής

11.64 **limelight** (n) /ˈlaɪmlaɪt/
the focal point of publicity • *Patrick never enjoyed being in the limelight offstage.* ❖ δημοσιότητα

11.65 **string** (n) /strɪŋ/
a series of • *After a string of hits as a teenage star, he withdrew into obscurity.* ➢ string (v) ❖ σειρά από (π.χ. γεγονότα)

11.66 **the big time** (n) /ðə bɪg taɪm/
a successful point in a chosen career • *He never thought he would make the big time until he landed the part of the villain in a James Bond film.* ❖ «πιάνω την καλή»

11.67 **destined** (adj) /ˈdestɪnd/
having a certain, predetermined future • *Not fitting the image of the slim beautiful heroine, she was destined to play the dispensable victim and sundry supporting roles.* ➢ destiny (n), destination (n) ❖ προορισμένος

11.68 **banal** (adj) /bəˈnɑːl/
dull and unimportant • *Even the non-stop action with striking visual images and sound effects could not compensate for the banal dialogue and storyline.* ➢ banality (n) ❖ μπανάλ, τετριμμένος, κοινός

11.69 **stardom** (n) /ˈstɑːdəm/
the state of being famous as a performer • *As a child actress in E.T., Drew seemed destined for stardom.* ❖ δόξα, διασημότητα

11.70 **one-hit wonder** (n) /wʌn hɪt ˈwʌndə(r)/
sb who makes one successful piece of music or performance but no others thereafter • *The band produced a catchy tune that stormed the charts in the 80s, but it was just a one-hit wonder.* ❖ καλλιτέχνης με μία μόνο μεγάλη επιτυχία

11.71 **discernible** (adj) /dɪˈsɜːnəbl/
that can be discerned or recognised • *There was no discernible difference between the two brands.* ➢ discern (v), discernibly (adv) ❖ ευδιάκριτος

11.72 **high-end** (adj) /haɪ end/
high-class and expensive • *Judging from their prices, the clothes are obviously aimed at the high-end market.* ❖ ακριβός, υψηλού επιπέδου

11.73 **be at odds** (expr) /biː æt ɒdz/
be in disagreement • *The films gushing opening reviews were completely at odds with the reactions from the bored audience.* ❖ είμαι σε αντίθεση

11.74 **persona** (n) /pəˈsəʊnə/
the traits of a person's character as shown to others • *His public persona was a dreadful façade, designed to disguise his heartless self.* ❖ (δημόσιο) πρόσωπο, εικόνα

11.75 **be in good/bad taste** (expr) /biː ɪn gʊd/bæd teɪst/
be appropriate and inoffensive / be inappropriate and offensive • *We were unimpressed as most of his jokes were in very bad taste.* ❖ καλόγουστος / κακόγουστος

11.76 **bogus** (adj) /ˈbəʊgəs/
false and pretending to be genuine • *Nobody believed the bogus report about the discovery of a giant's bones.* ❖ ψευδής

11.77 **abuzz** (adj) /æˈbʌz/
filled with constant noise, excitement, etc. • *The media was abuzz with rumours of their divorce.* ❖ γεμάτος

11.78 **upwards of** (prep) /ˈʌpwədz əv/
more than • *Upwards of a million copies of their album have been sold around the world.* ❖ περισσότερο από

11.79 **over the top** (expr) /əʊvə(r) ðə tɒp/
exaggerated • *Her accent was completely over the top and destroyed an otherwise enjoyable play.* ❖ υπερβολικός

11.80 **aspiring** (adj) /əˈspaɪərɪŋ/
hoping to do or become sth • *Dozens of aspiring young hopefuls applied to audition for the role.* ➢ aspire (v), aspiration (n) ❖ επίδοξος

11.81 **in the name of sth** (expr) /ɪn ðə neɪm əv ˈsʌmθɪŋ/
in order to be or achieve sth; for the sake of
• *How many hours do you expect to work in the name of success?* ❖ για χάρη του / στο όνομά του

11.82 **partial** (adj) /ˈpɑːʃl/
subjective; showing support in favour of one side of sth • *His side of the story is definitely partial as he knows the suspect.* ➢ partiality (n), partially (adv) ❖ μεροληπτικός
✎ Opp: impartial ❖ αμερόληπτος

11.83 **disseminate** (v) /dɪˈsemɪneɪt/
distribute or spread news, etc. • *The dictator used the online news channel to disseminate propaganda.* ➢ dissemination (n) ❖ διαδίδω, διασπείρω

Grammar **pages 161-162-163**

11.84 **there's no accounting for taste** (expr) /ðeəz nəʊ əˈkaʊntɪŋ fə teɪst/
used to show you do not agree with sb's choice; there's no way to explain why people like different things, especially those that seem unappealing • *I can't understand why she feels the need to have tattoos – there's no accounting for taste.* ❖ ο καθένας με τα γούστα του

11.85 **the proof of the pudding (is in the eating)** (expr) /ðə pruf əv ðə ˈpʊdɪŋ (ɪz ɪn ðə ˈiːtɪŋ)/
you can only judge sth by personal experience, not from theory • *The book doesn't sound worth reading, but the proof of the pudding is in the eating, so I'll give it a go.* ❖ φαίνεται στην πράξη

11.86 **reprimand** (v) /ˈreprɪmɑːnd/
officially tell sb off for doing sth • *Students were reprimanded for using Instagram during the class.* ➢ reprimand (n) ❖ επιπλήττω

11.87 **speculate** (v) /ˈspekjuleɪt/
make a judgement based on an educated guess or assumption • *We could only speculate as to whether the takeover rumours were true until we heard more.* ➢ speculation (n) ❖ υποθέτω, κάνω εικασίες

11.88 **toddler** (n) /ˈtɒdlə(r)/
a child who has just learnt to walk and moves unsteadily • *A small group of toddlers played with their toys as their nursery teachers kept a watchful eye on them.* ➢ toddle (v) ❖ νήπιο

11.89 **fluff your lines** (expr) /flʌf jɔː laɪnz/
make a mistake when you are reciting a script • *The director made them rerecord the scene where the leading actor fluffed his lines.* ❖ μπερδεύω τα λόγια μου (π.χ. στο θέατρο)

11.90 **flattering** (adj) /ˈflætərɪŋ/
that makes sb/sth appear more attractive • *White is not the most flattering colour to match your pale complexion; it makes you look tired and grey.* ➢ flatter (v), flattery (n) ❖ κολακευτικός
✎ Opp: unflattering ❖ διόλου κολακευτικός

11.91 **leap** (n) /liːp/
a significant change or improvement • *We've witnessed a huge leap in sales since we ran the TV ad.* ➢ leap (v) ❖ πρόοδος, αύξηση

11.92 **utter** (v) /ˈʌə(r)/
say sth • *He listened patiently, without uttering a word until his son finished making his excuses.* ➢ utterance (n), utter (adj), utterly (adv) ❖ αρθρώνω, ξεστομίζω

11.93 **mishear** (v) /ˌmɪsˈhɪə(r)/
misunderstand sth you hear which sounded like sth else • *I was sure she said her name was Mabel, but I must have misheard her.* ❖ παρακούω, ακούω λάθος

11.94 **scrutinise** (v) /ˈskruːtənaɪz/
examine sth closely • *The judges scrutinised the photo for signs of digital enhancement.* ➢ scrutiny (n) ❖ διερευνώ, εξετάζω λεπτομερώς

11.95 **transmission** (n) /trænsˈmɪʃn/
the act of broadcasting information or other data • *Signal fires were often used for the transmission of news across the ancient world.* ➢ transmit (v), transmitter (n) ❖ μετάδοση

Expressions

be at odds
be in good/bad taste
drive sth home
fluff your lines
fly on the wall
have it both ways
in the name of sth
over the top
play to the camera
sb's/sth's days are numbered
scratch the surface
strike a chord
the proof of the pudding (is in the eating)
there's no accounting for taste
warts and all

Listening **page 164**

11.96 **dumb sth down** (phr v) /dʌm ˈsʌmθɪŋ daʊn/
make sth less challenging • *The plot of the film had been dumbed down in the remake.* ❖ απλοποιώ

11.97 **warts and all** (expr) /wɔːts ənd ɔːl/
including imperfections • *She promised to love him as he was, warts and all.*
❖ με τα μειονεκτήματα

11.98 **play to the camera** (expr) /pleɪ tə ðə ˈkæməræ/
act differently in the presence of cameras • *He's normally so shy, but when he gets hold of a microphone, he can certainly play to the camera.* ❖ αλλάζω συμπεριφορά μπροστά σε φακό/κάμερα

11.99 **unscripted** (adj) /ʌnˈskrɪptɪd/
without a plan • *Their apparently random street interviews were not completely unscripted as volunteers had been selected in advance.* ❖ αυτοσχέδιος

11.100 **cringeworthy** (adj) /ˈkrɪndʒwɜːði/
causing embarrassment or upset • *The film's title is cringeworthy, as was most of the inane dialogue.* ➣ cringe (v), cringe (n) ❖ πολύ χαμηλής ποιότητας

11.101 **misnomer** (n) /ˌmɪsˈnəʊmə(r)/
an inappropriate or misleading name • *'Seafront hotel' was bit of a misnomer since it was five miles from the shore.* ❖ εσφαλμένο όνομα

11.102 **humiliate** (v) /hjuːˈmɪlieɪt/
make sb feel stupid or humble • *Even though Ted knew his friend was wrong, he didn't want to humiliate him by pointing it out in front of others.* ➣ humiliation (n), humility (n), humiliating (adj) ❖ ταπεινώνω, εξευτελίζω

Verbs

cement	reprimand
channel	scrutinise
convict	skyrocket
decimate	speculate
delve into sth	spiral
dumb sth down	stalk
glean	stumble
humiliate	unfold
lampoon	unleash
mishear	utter
ponder	

Speaking
page 165

11.103 **memorabilia** (n) /ˌmemərəˈbɪliə/
a collection of old things that remind sb of sth/sb which they are connected with • *His entire room was filled with childhood memorabilia, giving the impression that he could be described as a 'kidult'.* ➣ memorable (adj), memorably (adv) ❖ αναμνηστικά

11.104 **convention** (n) /kənˈvenʃn/
a large meeting of people involved with a common field • *Hundreds of delegates attended the sales convention.* ➣ convene (v), conventional (adj), conventionally (adv) ❖ συνέδριο

Adjectives

archival	fabled	reminiscent
aspiring	flattering	seedier
banal	gripping	sheer
bogus	hard-hitting	stardom
buffoonish	high-end	superficial
compliant	illustrious	symbolic
credible	immortal	undeterred
cringeworthy	insatiable	unflattering
deranged	mesmerising	unscripted
destined	partial	Z-list
discernible	poignant	

Writing
pages 166-167

11.105 **mesmerising** (adj) /ˈmezməraɪzɪŋ/
hypnotic; having a strongly attractive quality that holds sb's attention • *The sound effects were utterly mesmerising.* ➣ mesmerise (v) ❖ μαγευτικός

11.106 **meteorically** (adv) /ˌmiːtiˈɒrɪkəli/
in a rapidly developing way • *She rose meteorically to the halls of fame.* ➣ meteoric (adj) ❖ ραγδαία

11.107 **unfold** (v) /ʌnˈfəʊld/
develop • *As the plot unfolds, we realise that all is not as bright as it seems.* ❖ ξετυλίγω

11.108 **unleash** (v) /ʌnˈliːʃ/
release • *The fans unleashed their disappointment with offensive chants.* ❖ εξαπολύω, απελευθερώνω

11.109 **archival** (adj) /ɑːˈkaɪvəl/
retrieved from old archives • *We found some old views of the area as it was 100 years ago among some archival photo in the library.* ➣ archive (n) ❖ αρχειακό

11.110 **footage** (n) /ˈfʊtɪdʒ/
part of a film showing an event • *We found some old footage of the band's performance on YouTube.* ❖ οπτικοακουστικό υλικό

11.111 **indictment** (n) /ɪnˈdaɪtmənt/
an indication of sth negative • *The need for food banks is a sad indictment of our society.* ➣ indict (v), indictable (adj) ❖ ένδειξη ότι κάτι είναι σε κακή κατάσταση και αξίζει να καταδικαστεί

11.112 **spiral** (v) /ˈspaɪrəl/
increase rapidly • *The economy has been spiralling downward for years.* ➣ spiral (n), spiral (adj) ❖ αυξάνομαι, μειώνομαι

11.113 ponder (v) /ˈpɒndə(r)/
consider slowly • *He pondered the question for a moment before replying.* ➢ ponderous (adj), ponderously (adv) ❖ ζυγιάζω, μελετώ

11.114 biopic (n) /ˈbaɪəʊpɪk/
a biographical film • *Meryl Streep was chosen for the leading role in the biopic about the life of Margaret Thatcher.* ❖ βιογραφική ταινία

11.115 glean (v) /gliːn/
find information, with difficulty, from a variety of limited sources • *From what we are able to glean from historic accounts, he must have been an important figure.* ❖ περισυλλέγω, σταχυολογώ

11.116 channel (v) /ˈtʃænl/
direct sth towards a particular aspect or area, etc. • *He channelled all his energy into his music.* ➢ channel (n) ❖ διοχετεύω

11.118 sheer (adj) /ʃɪə(r)/
absolute; used to emphasise the size or amount of sth • *It was sheer folly to attempt the expedition alone.* ➢ sheer (v), sheer (adv) ❖ απόλυτος

11.119 reminiscent (adj) /ˌremɪˈnɪsnt/
that reminds you of sth • *The villagers took part in ritual dances reminiscent of years gone by.* ➢ reminiscence (n) ❖ που θυμίζει

Adverbs

emphatically	meteorically
impartially	proverbially

Other nouns

adrenaline	hint	perception
biopic	indictment	scoop
bureau	leak	scourge
carcass	leap	stardom
convention	limelight	string
door	memoir	subgenre
stepping	memorabilia	telephoto
entity	news outlet	lens
excerpt	obscurity	the big time
exile	one-hit	transmission
footage	wonder	
fringe	peek	

Video 11: A Polar Picture
page 168

11.117 carcass (n) /ˈkɑːkəs/
the dead body of an animal • *The carcass of a fox lay by the roadside.* ❖ κουφάρι, πτώμα

Vocabulary Exercises

A Match the two halves of the sentences.

1 Some celebrities have to realise that they can't **have it both ways** ☐

2 He always writes in-depth stories of all current affairs ☐

3 That documentary really **drives home** the message that ☐

4 Sometimes I wish I could be a **fly on the wall** in the house of some of the rich and famous ☐

5 When the actress spoke up against discrimination in her acceptance speech at the Oscar Awards Ceremony, ☐

6 The new reality show's ratings have been dropping continuously since it first aired - ☐

7 Jerry was so nervous on the opening night ☐

8 Despite the low quality illustrations and the bad writing, this magazine is bought by thousands of readers – ☐

9 The article tries to paint an accurate picture of the prime minister ☐

10 Most people on so-called reality shows are just **playing to the cameras** ☐

a something must be done immediately if we want to avoid an ecological disaster in the near future.

b so what we see is actually a far cry from reality.

c they will either keep their private life private, or they will have the newspapers writing about them.

d that he completely **fluffed his lines.**

e I guess **there's no accounting for taste.**

f so that I could see what their everyday life is really like.

g unlike most news reporters nowadays, who merely **scratch the surface** of the events.

h as he really is – **warts and all**.

i it really **struck** a responsive **chord** with minority groups everywhere.

j it's obvious that **its days** on the channel are **numbered**.

B Complete the sentences with the correct form of the words.

1 Stella is studying in a reputable school for media studies and aspires to become a famous _____ one day.   DOCUMENTARY

2 The film tells a(n) _____ tale of passion and deceit.   GRIP

3 The public seem to have a(n) _____ appetite for news about the lives of their favourite celebrities.   SATIATE

4 The young actress is threatening to sue the magazine for posting such _____ pictures of her.   FLATTER

5 The TV presenter's contract clearly states that he is to stick to his script at all times and is forbidden to make any _____ comments whatsoever.   SCRIPT

6 Most celebrities have accepted the fact that they will be constantly _____ for how they dress and what they say in every public appearance they make.   SCRUTINY

7 Clothes, personal items and other _____ of famous people can go for thousands of pounds in an auction.   MEMORY

8 He has played many successful parts, but it was the role of Martin, a crafty _____, that won him his first Academy Award.   CON

9 Her first job on television was as a war _____ for a national news channel.   CORRESPOND

10 The stories you read in gossip magazines can hardly be considered _____.   CREDENCE

C Choose the best answers.

1 The documentary attempts to make people aware of the ___ of poverty in our times.
   a fringe   **b** entity   **c** scourge   **d** bureau

2 The famous singer asked for police protection because she believed she was being ___ by an admirer.
   a stalked   **b** lampooned   **c** convicted   **d** reprimanded

3 The politician claimed that the evidence the reporter based her article against him on was ___.
   a partial   **b** bogus   **c** abuzz   **d** banal

4 The DVD contains extra ___ that had not been included in the original film.
   a carcass   **b** footage   **c** outlet   **d** excerpt

5 A reporter needs to be sure about his sources before he prints something about another person or else he may be sued for ___.
   a blackmail   **b** obscurity   **c** libel   **d** misnomer

6 Didn't you think some of the speeches at the opening ceremony were a bit ___?
   a upwards   **b** at odds   **c** big time   **d** over the top

7 The young model is very attractive and has the most ___ blue eyes I have ever seen.
   a mesmerizing   **b** archival   **c** reminiscent   **d** sheer

8 When the events involve people close to you, it's very difficult to be objective and report the news ___.
   a meteorically   **b** impartially   **c** proverbially   **d** emphatically

9 Every time there is a scandal in show biz, sales of tabloid newspapers ___.
   a cement   **b** speculate   **c** skyrocket   **d** stumble

10 After he had retired, the award-winning actor decided to write his ___.
   a stardom   **b** biopic   **c** scoop   **d** memoir

D Complete the sentences with these words in the correct form.

door stepping indictment leap lens limelight peek
persona recluse libel string subgenre transmission

1 Due to the strike of the technicians, there may be interruptions in the _____ of the programme today.

2 Signing with the large music label was a great _____ for her singing career.

3 In her private life she is very shy and timid – nothing at all like her TV _____.

4 Having lived all his life in the _____, Tom couldn't handle it when the media suddenly stopped being interested in him.

5 When the magazine printed that the lead actress behaved abusively towards the other members of the cast, she sued them for _____.

6 Since he retired, the former star has become a(n) _____, and refuses to give interviews to anyone.

7 Ever since news of her divorce has come out, the well-loved television show presenter has had to go stay at her parents' house to avoid the _____ by the paparazzi.

8 The paparazzo used a strong telephoto _____ to manage to get photos of the young starlet in the privacy of her own back yard.

9 Negative utopia is a _____ of science fiction, which describes a seemingly perfect, but in reality deeply troubled, future society.

10 Fans were standing outside the theatre for hours in hope of catching a _____ at the singer as she was entering the building.

11 He had a _____ of hits in the beginning of the 90s, but has since disappeared.

12 The troubled young actress will have to face trial, following her arrest and _____ for shoplifting.

11 Grammar

11.1 Gerunds

Για να σχηματίσουμε το gerund (γερούνδιο) προσθέτουμε την κατάληξη -ing σε ένα ρήμα. Μπορούμε να χρησιμοποιήσουμε ένα gerund:
ως ουσιαστικό.
→ **Appearing** on reality shows is not for everyone.
μετά από πρόθεση.
→ She was criticised **for insulting** the reporters.
μετά από το ρήμα go όταν μιλάμε για δραστηριότητες.
→ He **goes hunting** for new stories every week.

Μπορούμε επίσης να χρησιμοποιήσουμε gerund μετά από κάποια ρήματα και φράσεις:
admit, avoid, be used to, can't help, can't stand, deny, dislike, (don't) mind, enjoy, fancy, feel like, finish, forgive, hate, have difficulty, imagine, involve, it's no good, it's no use, it's (not) worth, keep, like, love, miss, practise, prefer, prevent, regret, risk, spend time, suggest.
→ **It's no use asking** them to stop following you, they'll just keep door-stepping.
→ Hannah **regretted giving up** her singing career.

11.2 Infinitives

Active / Ενεργητική	Passive / Παθητική
Present (παρόν)	(to) take (to) be taken
Perfect (παρελθόν)	(to) have taken (to) have been taken

→ A professional photographer will **take** her photo.
→ Her photo will **be taken** by a professional photographer.

11.3 Full Infinitives

Σχηματίζουμε full infinitive με to και το ρήμα. Χρησιμοποιούμε full infinitive:
για να εξηγήσουμε το σκοπό μιας πράξης.
→ The paparazzo went backstage **to catch** the actor unawares.
μετά από επίθετα όπως afraid, scared, happy, glad, pleased, sad κλπ.
→ I was **pleased to be given** a ticket for the performance.
μετά από τις λέξεις too και enough.
→ The acting was too poor **to win** an award.
→ His singing wasn't good **enough to impress** the judges.

Χρησιμοποιούμε επίσης full infinitive μετά από συγκεκριμένα ρήματα και φράσεις:
afford, agree, allow, appear, ask, begin, choose, decide, expect, fail, forget, hope, invite, learn, manage, need, offer, persuade, plan, prepare, pretend, promise, refuse, seem, start, want, would like.
→ He **refused to give** an interview with the press.
→ He **has agreed to endorse** the product.

Χρησιμοποιούμε επίσης full infinitive μετά από συγκεκριμένα ουσιαστικά.
→ A successful actor must have the **self-discipline to avoid** excessive behaviour.
→ She won a **ticket to see** her favourite band.

11.4 Bare Infinitives

Χρησιμοποιούμε bare infinitive (απαρέμφατα χωρίς to) μετά από:
modal verbs.
→ We **could buy** tickets for the opening night.
had better για να δώσουμε συμβουλή.
→ You **had better book** early for the opening night.
would rather για να εκφράσουμε προτίμηση.
→ I **would rather listen** to his music at home than pay so much to see him live.

11 Grammar

Σημείωση: Χρησιμοποιούμε *let* + αντικείμενο + bare infinitive όταν κάποιος έχει την άδεια να κάνει κάτι, και χρησιμοποιείται μόνο στην ενεργητική φωνή. Στην παθητική μπορούμε να χρησιμοποιήσουμε *be allowed to*.

→ They **wouldn't let** the audience **enter** the backstage area.
→ The audience **wasn't allowed to enter** the backstage area.

Χρησιμοποιούμε *make* + αντικείμενο + bare infinitive για να πούμε πως κάποιος αναγκάζεται να κάνει κάτι. Στην παθητική (passive voice) χρησιμοποιούμε full infinitive.

→ The security staff **made** the photographers **move** well away from the stage.
→ The photographers **were made to stay** well away from the stage.

11.5 Gerund or Infinitive?

Ορισμένα ρήματα ακολουθούνται από gerund ή *to* + infinitive χωρίς να αλλάζει η σημασία τους. Τέτοια ρήματα είναι *begin, bother, continue, hate, like, love* και *start*.

→ Anna didn't bother **rehearsing / to rehearse** before she went on stage.

Υπάρχουν άλλα ρήματα που ακολουθούνται από gerund ή *to* + infinitive, αλλά αλλάζει η σημασία τους. Τα πιο συνηθισμένα από αυτά είναι *forget, go on, regret, remember, stop* και *try*.

→ I **regret paying** so much for a ticket. It wasn't worth it. (I shouldn't have paid so much.)
→ We **regret to announce** that the main act has been cancelled. (We are sorry to announce ...)
→ I **remember seeing** her debut performance. (I have memory of it.)
→ I **remembered to record** the CD. (First I remembered it and then I did it.)
→ They **stopped performing** live ago. (They no longer do it.)
→ We **stopped to watch** the street performers. (We stopped what we were doing to do something else.)

Grammar Exercises

A Complete the sentences with words from the box and the correct form of the verbs in brackets.

can't help	have the ability	look forward	be afraid	be eager	fancy	go	admit	object	pretend

1 A lot of celebrities _____ (follow) around by paparazzi.

2 My son _____ (meet) his idol, but was completely let down when the footballer turned out to be superficial and egotistical.

3 The politician _____ (answer) questions which showed him in a flattering light.

4 Margaret _____ (believe) what the conspiracy theorist was telling her – she kept nodding her head in agreement.

5 The boots looked so wonderfully luxurious, I _____ (splurge out) for them without a second thought.

6 '_____ (go out) for a coffee during our break?' he asked me.

7 Petros Markaris is a writer who _____ (depict) modern Greek society in acute detail in his books.

8 Socialites _____ (shop) for clothes and accessories. Most such stuff is thrown upon them in the hope they'll endorse it and provide free publicity.

9 After the scandal broke out, she _____ (get out) of the house for fear of having her photo taken.

10 The photographer _____ (take) the actor's pictures without his consent.

B Complete the sentences with the correct form of the verbs in brackets.

1 He's thought _____ (involve) in a huge financial scandal.

2 By the end of the 21st century, traditional print media will _____ (take over) by internet news sites.

3 Paparazzi may camp outside celebrities' houses for days on end, with the sole aim _____ (get) exclusive photos of them.

4 The journalist was conscientious enough _____ (report) both sides of the story.

5 Many aspiring actors will go to any length in an effort _____ (become) more widely known.

6 Yes, tickets may still _____ (buy) at the box office, but everybody books them online.

7 Nothing more can _____ (do) to remedy the situation. It's too late now.

8 After her inflammatory comments on a live show, she seems _____ (disappear) off the face of the earth!

9 We've arranged for the parcel _____ (pick up) by a courier.

10 After the raving reviews he received, Paul's acting career was expected _____ (catapult) all the way to the top.

C Rewrite the sentences starting with the words given.

1 All foreign correspondents have to report to the headquarters on a daily basis.
The headquarters make _____

2 They may let you attend the press conference if you have the right credentials.
You may _____

3 Young artists looking to be in the limelight should focus on producing original work.
Young artists looking to be in the limelight ought _____

4 It seemed that Kate had the talent to achieve stardom, but her hopes fell through.
Kate seemed _____

5 Jonathan would prefer to visit the museum rather than watch the new musical.
Jonathan would rather _____

6 If I were you, I'd be very careful about my appearance in seedy bars across town.
You had _____

7 Perhaps the reviewer didn't actually read the whole book before writing his scathing review.
The reviewer may _____

8 She wanted to go out for the evening dressed scantily, but her mother made her change outfits.
She wanted to go out for the evening dressed scantily, but she was _____

9 Only accredited journalists may attend this interview with the president.
Only accredited journalists are _____

10 I wasn't allowed to publish the article without making significant changes to it first.
The editor _____

D Circle the best answers.

1 Do you remember ____ that Z-list celebrity at Martin's party?
   a to see   b seeing

2 Please remember ____ the new issue of National Geographic.
   a to buy   b buying

3 I'll never forget ____ the president's hand! It was the highlight of my visit in Washington D.C.
   a to have shaken   b having shaken

4 He keeps bragging about his money and fame, but he seems to have forgotten ____ from his friends and being penniless at the beginning of his career.
   a to borrow   b borrowing

5 There was a sudden hush in the room and everybody stopped ____ and turned towards the door.
   a to talk   b talking

6 The politician stopped ____ to his supporters on his way to the podium.
   a to shake hands and talk   b shaking hands and talking

7 Have you tried ____ this new site? It's got the most juicy gossip!
   a to use   b using

8 She tried ____ the party pretending she was invited but she was turned away.
   a to crash   b crashing

9 I regret ____ you that your application for the post has been turned down.
   a to tell   b telling

10 I deeply regret ____ Martha that the film she acted in was an utter flop.
   a to tell   b telling

11 William went on ___ about his acting career even though his listeners were clearly bored.

    a to blab   **b** blabbing

12 The eminent professor finished her lecture and went on ___ questions from the public.

    a to answer   **b** answering

Exam Task

For questions 1–8, read the text below and think of the word which best fits each space. Use only one word in each space.

Today's eminence

What is it about today's celebrities that attracts us? It's no **(1)** _____ trying to solve the puzzle. People obsess about social media celebrities, personas whose only asset is their looks and the appearances they make on the red carpet or some 'in' clubs or restaurants. They haven't got the **(2)** _____ to sing or act or even be funny or witty, and yet here we are reading avidly about them in the tabloids and on the latest gossip blogs. They demand, and if I **(3)** _____ say so, receive the recognition that was previously reserved for a Hitchcock, a Garbo and a Kallas. Their sole reason of existence is **(4)** _____ be in the limelight, but they don't have anything to offer to society in order to justify all this attention. In a different era they'd be hardly **(5)** _____ talking about. However, they are part of a system that feeds them and feeds off them to go **(6)** _____ producing useless items that would never **(7)** _____ needed under different circumstances – it's these no-name, Z-list celebs who artificially create a need for products **(8)** _____ expensive for the common person to buy and who boost consumerism to new extremes.

12 Culture Shock

12.1 **conical** (adj) /ˈkɒnɪkl/
shaped like a cone • *The Apache tents have a conical shape with a gap at the top for smoke to come out.* ➢ cone (n), conically (adv)
❖ κωνικός

12.2 **wet market** (n) /wet ˈmɑːkɪt/
a market selling fresh meat and produce, and not durable goods such as cloth and electronics • *Lee sold his goats at the wet market.* ❖ κρεοπωλεία και μανάβικα

Reading
pages 170-171

12.3 **sophistication** (n) /səˌfɪstɪˈkeɪʃn/
the quality of having a lot of experience and knowledge of the culture and other socially important issues • *Having a well-stocked bookcase gave the room an atmosphere of sophistication.* ➢ sophisticate (n), sophisticated (adj) ❖ φινέτσα

12.4 **worldliness** (n) /ˈwɜːldlinəs/
the quality of having a lot of life experience and thus being broad-minded • *Having been brought up by German parents in Asia, Kim had an air of worldliness in the eyes of her English collleagues.* ➢ worldly (adj)
❖ κοσμικότητα

12.5 **establishment** (n) /ɪˈstæblɪʃmənt/
a business or other organization, or the place where an organization operates • *The university is a well-respected establishment.* ➢ establish (v), established (adj) ❖ ίδρυμα

12.6 **platter** (n) /ˈplætə(r)/
a large flat serving dish • *The restauranteur brought a huge platter of starters before the main meal.* ❖ πιατέλα

12.7 **culinary** (adj) /ˈkʌlɪnəri/
related to cookery • *He participate in a reality show to present his culinary skills.*
❖ μαγειρικός, γαστρονομικός

12.8 **yield** (v) /jiːld/
provide • *Our trees yield several kilos of olives annually.* ➢ yield (n) ❖ αποδίδω, παράγω

12.9 **domesticate** (v) /dəˈmestɪkeɪt/
begin cultivating a plant for human use
• *Domesticating a stray cat can be a difficult task lasting several months.* ➢ domestication (n), domesticated (adj) ❖ εξημερώνω

12.10 **lineage** (n) /ˈlɪniːɪdʒ/
ancestry • *Judging from his clothes, he appeared to be of noble lineage.* ❖ καταγωγή, γενεαλογία

12.11 **taxonomy** (n) /tækˈsɒnəmi/
the branch of science dealing with the classification of things • *Chromosomes are useful in the taxonomy of living things.*
➢ taxonomist (n), taxonomic (adj)
❖ ταξονομία

12.12 **derivative** (n) /dɪˈrɪvətɪv/
sth which is based on sth else • *Certain products which sold as 'chocolate' in other countries are referred to as 'chocolate derivatives' in Italy.* ➢ derive (v), derivate (adj)
❖ παράγωγο

12.13 **hieroglyph** (n) /ˈhaɪərəglɪf/
an ancient Egyptian symbol used to represent a word, sound or syllable • *Archaeologists have managed to decipher the meaning of the Egyptian hieroglyphs on the wall of the king's tomb.* ➢ hieroglyphics (n), hieroglyphic (adj)
❖ ιερογλυφικό

12.14 **rudimentary** (adj) /ˌruːdɪˈmentri/
basic; undeveloped • *I have only a rudimentary knowledge of Polish – just enough to utter polite responses.* ➢ rudiments (n)
❖ στοιχειώδης, βασικός

12.15 **ferment** (v) /fəˈment/
cause sth to undergo a chemical change through the action of yeast or bacteria • *Most fruits and some vegetables can be fermented to make wine.* ➢ fermentation (n) ❖ προκαλώ ζύμωση

12.16 **vessel** (n) /ˈvesl/
a container • *They used coconut shells as drinking vessels to serve the cocktails.*
❖ δοχείο

12.17 **tribute** (n) /ˈtrɪbjuːt/
a gift from one country or tribe to another as a peace offering • *In agricultural societies, peasants had to pay tribute to the ruling power to defend their land from enemies.*
➢ tributary (adj) ❖ φόρος, εισφορά

12.18 **ruse** (n) /ruːz/
a trick used to obtain sth by cheating
• *So-called discount offers are simply a ruse to attract more customers.* ❖ τέχνασμα, κόλπο

12.19 **counterfeit** (adj) /ˈkaʊntəfɪt/
sth that has been made to look like a genuine article • *Keith was horrified when the shopkeeper refused to accept the €100 note upon discovering that it was counterfeit.*
❖ πλαστός

12.20 **worthless** (adj) /ˈwɜːθləs/
not worth anything; useless • *The shares had become worthless by the time the company went bankrupt.* ➢ worth (n), worthy (adj)
❖ άχρηστος, χωρίς αξία, ευτελής

12.21 **hull** (n) /hʌl/
the leafy outer covering of a seed or plant; husk • *She deftly scooped out the flesh of the avocado from its hull.* ❖ φλοιός, κέλυφος

12.22 **symbolically** (adv) /sɪmˈbɒlɪkli/
in a symbolic way; as a symbol • *The statue symbolically represented the nation's independence.* ➢ symbolise (v), symbolism (n), symbolic (adj) ❖ συμβολικά

12.23 **etymology** (n) /ˌetɪˈmɒlədʒi/
the origin of a word and its meaning • *The history and etymology of many English words dates back to ancient Greek.* ➢ etymologist (n) ❖ ετυμολογία

12.24 **hybrid** (n) /ˈhaɪbrɪd/
sth that is produced by a blend of two or more things • *The fruit of the tree was a hybrid of an apple and a pear.* ➢ hybrid (adj) ❖ υβρίδιο

12.25 **alkali** (n) /ˈælkəlaɪ/
a chemical substance which causes acids to neutralise or effervesce • *As it is an alkali, adding soda to citrus fruit juice will cause it to effervesce.* ➢ alkalise (v), alkaline (adj) ❖ αλκάλιο

12.26 **pungent** (adj) /ˈpʌndʒənt/
strong smelling or tasting • *The pungent aroma of orange blossoms filled the night air.* ➢ pungency (n), pungently (adv) ❖ δριμύς, οξύς

12.27 **lavender** (n) /ˈlævəndə(r)/
a sweet-scented plant with pale purple flowers • *Before packing away her winter woollies, she leaves small bunches of lavender to keep them fresh and ward off insects.* ❖ λεβάντα

12.28 **divine** (adj) /dɪˈvaɪn/
connected with a god • *It was the divine right of kings to receive tributes from their subjects.* ➢ divinity (n), divinely (adv) ❖ θεϊκός

12.29 **palatable** (adj) /ˈpælətəbl/
with a pleasant taste • *The murky brown soup was, fortunately, much more palatable than it looked; in fact it was quite tasty.* ➢ palate (n) ❖ εύγευστος, νόστιμος

12.30 **fraudulent** (adj) /ˈfrɔːdjələnt/
deceptively made to cheat sb, usually to make money • *The company was taken to court for fraudulent advertising.* ➢ fraudulence (n), fraud (n), fraudulently (adv) ❖ απατηλός

Food-related words

Nouns	salt cellar	palatable
alkali	vessel	pungent
fare		
hull	**Adjectives**	**Verbs**
hybrid	culinary	ferment
karavai	divine	
platter	intoxicating	

Vocabulary pages 172-173-174

12.31 **heritage** (n) /ˈherɪtɪdʒ/
a country's history and long-standing traditions regarded as an integral part of its character • *The Olympic Games are a symbol of Greece's national heritage.* ➢ heritable (adj) ❖ κληρονομιά

12.32 **mannerism** (n) /ˈmænərɪz(ə)m/
a subconscious habit or way of behaving • *She has the annoying mannerism of constantly looking at her phone in the middle of a conversation.* ➢ manner (n), manners (n), mannered (adj) ❖ μανία, ιδιομορφία

12.33 **reluctant** (adj) /rɪˈlʌktənt/
unwilling; not keen to do sth • *He was reluctant to discuss his wartime experience as it evoked painful memories.* ➢ reluctance (n), reluctantly (adv) ❖ απρόθυμος

12.34 **age-old** (adj) /ˈeɪdʒˈəʊld/
sth that has existed for many years; traditional • *The age-old tradition of bullfighting is fast losing its popularity in Spain.* ❖ παλαιός, από παλιά

12.35 **quaint** (adj) /kweɪnt/
attractive with an old-worldly quality • *The upbeat resort was once a quaint fishing village on the coast of Cornwall.* ➢ quaintness (n), quaintly (adv) ❖ γραφικός, ιδιαίτερος

12.36 **old-time** (adj) /ˈəʊldˌtaɪm/
associated with an earlier period • *His great-grandfather was a banjo player in an old-time music hall.* ➢ old-timer (n) ❖ παλιός

12.37 **ever-present** (adj) /ˈevə ˈpreznt/
constanty remaining • *Around the souk, the ever-present aroma of spices filled the air.* ❖ πανταχού παρών, διαρκής

12.38 **long-standing** (adj) /lɒŋ ˈstændɪŋ/
that has existed for many years • *It is a long-standing Hawaiian tradition to offer visitors a garland of flowers as a greeting.* ❖ μακροχρόνιος, παλαιός

12.39 **paternal** (adj) /pəˈtɜːnl/
from the father's side of the family • *Nancy's paternal grandmother comes from Sparta.* ➢ paternity (n), paternally (adv) ❖ πατρικός

12.40 **nomadic** (adj) /nəʊˈmædɪk/
with a lifestyle that involves moving as a group from place to place • *Many Bedouins have now abandoned their nomadic lifestyle in favour of urban life.* ➢ nomad (n) ❖ νομαδικός

12.41 **time-honoured** (adj) /taɪm ˈɒnəd/
respected as having existed for many years • *In the time-honoured tradition, the flame was carried all the way from Olympia around the world to the venue of the Games.* ❖ καθιερωμένος, σεβαστός

12.42　**the Renaissance** (n) /ðə rɪˈneɪsns/
the period during the 14th to 16th centuries when art and literature were influenced by a revived interest in classical ancient Greek and Roman culture • *The Renaissance began in Florence with the influx of Greek scholars fleeing the Ottoman conquest.*
❖ η Αναγέννηση

12.43　**dowry** (n) /ˈdaʊri/
the custom of giving money or property to a woman or her husband by the woman's family to support her when she marries
• *Until a couple of centuries ago, dowries were still commonly provided to a husband by his bride's father in western society.* ❖ προίκα

12.44　**legacy** (n) /ˈlegəsi/
a situation that is a result of past actions or events • *We are now having to endure the legacy left by the consumerist era of the 80s and 90s.* ➢ legacy (adj) ❖ κληρονομιά

12.45　**vestige** (n) /ˈvestɪdʒ/
a small trace of sth that has remained over time • *The castle ruins remain as the last vestige of 13th century Frankish rule.*
➢ vestigial (adj) ❖ ίχνος

12.46　**residue** (n) /ˈrezɪdjuː/
a small amount of a substance left after a process is complete • *They were obviously tea drinkers, from the brown residue around the inside of their cups.* ➢ residual (adj)
❖ υπόλειμμα

12.47　**heirloom** (n) /ˈeəluːm/
an object that has been handed down the generations in a family • *This old teapot is a family heirloom which belonged to my great-aunt's mother.* ➢ heir (n), heiress (n), heirloom (adj) ❖ οικογενειακό κειμήλιο

12.48　**relic** (n) /ˈrelɪk/
an object or custom, etc. surviving from the past • *The display case contained pieces of Bronze Age kitchenware and other such relics.*
❖ κειμήλιο

12.49　**chronicle** (n) /ˈkrɒnɪkl/
a written account of events in chronological order • *Pausanias the traveller's chronicles have shed much light on the history of ancient Greece up to the 2nd century AD.* ➢ chronicle (v), chronicler (n) ❖ χρονικό

12.50　**memorial** (n) /məˈmɔːriəl/
sth built to remember a famous historic event or figure • *It is customary for people to lay wreaths around the war memorial to honour the victims of war on Remembrance Day.* ➢ memorial (adj) ❖ μνημείο

12.51　**revival** (n) /rɪˈvaɪvl/
the process of regaining strength or sth's improving prospects • *The tourist industry is beginning to show some signs of revival after years of recession.* ➢ revive (v) ❖ αναβίωση

12.52　**recite** (v) /rɪˈsaɪt/
say sth out loud which you have learnt by heart, e.g. a poem or piece of prose • *On 25th January, Scots get together to celebrate the birthday of their national poet, Robert Burns, by reciting some of his best-loved works whilst enjoying traditional food and drinks.*
➢ recitation (n), recital (n), recitative (adj)
❖ απαγγέλω

12.53　**oral** (adj) /ˈɔːrəl/
spoken • *Angela did very well in the oral exam and turned the whole thing into a natural conversation with the examiner, gaining top marks for speaking fluently.* ➢ oral (n), orally (adv) ❖ προφορικός

12.54　**vocal** (adj) /ˈvəʊkl/
loudly voicing your opinions; generally connected with the voice • *The proposal to do away with the national holiday met with resistance from a vocal majority.* ➢ vocal (n), vocally (adv) ❖ φωνητικός, ομιλητικός

12.55　**aural** (adj) /ˈɔːrəl/
generally connected with hearing • *We did a listening comprehension test to measure our aural skills.* ➢ aurally (adv) ❖ ακουστικός

12.56　**phonetic** (adj) /fəˈnetɪk/
using symbols from a special alphabet to denote different sounds; generally connected with sounds • *This book includes phonetic symbols to assist in pronunciation.*
➢ phonetics (n), phonetically (adv)
❖ φωνητικός

12.57 **deviance** (n) /ˈdiːviəns/
an act of doing sth differently from the normal way • *The tribe have retained their old ways and are resistant to any deviance from their social norms.* ➢ deviate (v), deviant (n), deviant (adj), deviantly (adv) ❖ αποκλίνουσα συμπεριφορά

12.58 **primitive** (adj) /ˈprɪmətɪv/
simple and unsophisticated • *Some native Australian animals, including the platypus and marsupials, are among the most primitive species in existence.* ➢ primitively (adv) ❖ πρωτόγονος

12.59 **sit tight** (expr) /sɪt taɪt/
stay where you are and wait or don't move • *The train had just pulled out of the station, so all we could do was sit tight and wait for the next one.* ❖ παραμένω καθιστός

12.60 **hold fast** (expr) /həʊld fæst/
keep believing in sth despite them being questioned or threatened • *Despite a series of setbacks, he held fast to his original business plan until the company eventually took off.* ❖ επιμένω, παραμένω σταθερός

12.61 **esteemed** (adj) /ɪˈstiːmd/
highly regarded or respected • *The esteemed professor was our guest speaker at the medical convention.* ➢ esteem (n) ❖ αξιότιμος

12.62 **stay put** (expr) /steɪ pʊt/
stay where you are • *Though many of their compatriots had emigrated due to the financial crisis, they decided to stay put and try to weather the storm.* ❖ παραμένω

12.63 **integrate** (v) /ˈɪntɪgreɪt/
mix well and become part of a social group • *It takes a couple of generations for foreign incomers to become truly integrated in another culture.* ➢ integration (n), integral (adj), integrally (adv) ❖ εντάσσω, αφομοιώνω

12.64 **defy** (v) /dɪˈfaɪ/
refuse to obey an order; go against a rule • *Oliver did not dare to defy Fagin, for fear of being beaten.* ➢ defiance (n), defiant (adj), defiantly (adv) ❖ αψηφώ, προκαλώ

12.65 **ostracise** (v) /ˈɒstrəsaɪz/
exclude sb from a social group and refuse to converse with them • *He was ostracised by the village community for questioning their religious beliefs.* ➢ ostracism (n) ❖ εξοστρακίζω

12.66 **reverent** (adj) /ˈrevərənt/
respectful • *A reverent silence fell as the priest entered the temple.* ➢ revere (v), reverence (n), reverently (adv) ❖ ευλαβής
✎ Opp: irreverent ❖ ασεβής

12.67 **veil** (n) /veɪl/
a covering worn to conceal the face • *The bride wore a traditional lace veil of her face.* ➢ veil (v), veiled (adj) ❖ βέλο, πέπλο

12.68 **cremate** (v) /krəˈmeɪt/
burn a corpse, usually as part of a funeral ceremony • *As a dying wish, the angler requested that his body was to be cremated and the ashes scattered in the river.* ➢ cremation (n), crematorium (n) ❖ αποτεφρώνω

12.69 **adorn** (v) /əˈdɔːn/
decorate • *The temple was adorned with scented flowers and colourful statues.* ➢ adornment (n) ❖ κοσμώ, στολίζω

12.70 **frond** (n) /frɒnd/
a long thin leaf • *Through the palm fronds, we could make out a cruise ship on the horizon.* ❖ φύλλο

12.71 **sane** (adj) /seɪn/
logical; of sound mind • *In my view, anyone who takes such foolhardy risks in the name of sport is not entirely sane.* ➢ sanity (n) ❖ λογικός, συνετός
✎ Opp: insane ❖ παράλογος

12.72 **undercurrent** (n) /ˈʌndəkʌrənt/
a hidden feeling which has a noticeable effect on sth • *An undercurrent of envy prevented them from developing a closer relationship.* ❖ υποβόσκων

12.73 **accomplishment** (n) /əˈkʌmplɪʃmənt/
achievement • *The stadium was one of the architects greatest accomplishments.* ➢ accomplish (v), accomplished (adj) ❖ πραγματοποίηση, εκπλήρωση

12.74 **blow your own trumpet** (expr) /bləʊ jɔː ʊən ˈtrʌmˌpət/
boast about your success • *Though Steve has never been one to blow his own trumpet, he is rather proud of winning the trophy for Tang Soo Do.* ❖ περιαυτολογώ, καυχιέμαι

12.75 **decipher** (v) /dɪˈsaɪfə(r)/
discover the meaning of sth difficult to understand • *He deciphered the enemy's signal code just in time to help plan a counter attack.* ➢ decipherable (adj) ❖ αποκρυπτογραφώ, βγάζω νόημα

12.76 **fondness** (n) /ˈfɒndnəs/
affection • *The British fondness for a nice cup of tea is a legacy of their empirical past.* ➢ fond (adj), fondly (adv) ❖ προτίμηση

12.77 **fit** (n) /fɪt/
a short-lasting uncontrollable state of an extreme emotion, e.g. laughter, crying, etc. • *The class burst into fits of laughter at the English teacher's attempts to speak Greek.* ❖ κρίση, παροξυσμός

12.78 **bout** (n) /baʊt/
a short period of sth, especially illness
• *A bout of gastric flu caused her to lose quite a bit of weight.* ❖ αγώνας, πάλη

Expressions

blow your own trumpet
hold fast
sit tight
stay put

Grammar   pages 175-176-177

12.79 **blight** (n) /blaɪt/
a disease that detroys a crop; sth that sth/sb badly • *The blight of fungus destroyed the vines before the grapes had ripened.* ➢ blight (v) ❖ καταστροφή, εμπόδιο

12.80 **creole** (adj) /ˈkriːəʊl/
the language of sb of mixed racial roots, especially in the southern states of the USA and West Indies • *On our visit to the West Indies, we adored the spicy creole cuising, but could not understand much of the creole language.* ❖ κρεολός

12.81 **karavai** (n) /kəreəˈvaɪ/
a round loaf of traditional Russian bread
• *Karavai is a type of decorated bread, traditionally served at Russian weddings to symbolise fertility.* ❖ καρβέλι

12.82 **salt cellar** (n) /sɔlt ˈselə(r)/
a small container which salt is poured
• *Could you pass the salt cellar and pepper pot please? This sauce needs a little seasoning.* ❖ αλατιέρα

12.83 **embroidered** (adj) /ɪmˈbrɔɪdəd/
decorated with patterns made by stitching with coloured threads • *The woman at the market stall tried to persuade us to buy her embroidered tablecloths.* ➢ embroider (v), embroidery (n) ❖ κεντημένος

12.84 **folklore** (n) /ˈfəʊklɔː(r)/
the traditional stories of a country • *There's usual a moral ending in tales from ancient folklore.* ❖ λαϊκή παράδοση, λαογραφία

Nouns

Feelings & Actions	
accomplishment	fondness
deviance	installation
endurance	mannerism
establishment	ruse
fit	sophistication
	worldliness

Listening   page 178

12.85 **indescribable** (adj) /ˌɪndɪˈskraɪbəbl/
so unusual that sth cannot be described
• *Terrorism in this country caused indescribable suffering to its people.*
❖ απερίγραπτος
✎ Opp: describable ❖ που περιγράφεται

Speaking   page 179

12.86 **long-winded** (adj) /lɒŋ ˈwɪndid/
that goes into a lot of detail and takes too long to get to the point • *Although some of her points were valid, her speech about racial inequality was too long-winded.*
❖ μακροσκελής

12.87 **installation** (n) /ˌɪnstəˈleɪʃn/
the act of placing sth in a position so that it can be used • *The installation of the new heating system only took a couple of days.* ➢ install (v) ❖ εγκατάσταση

Writing   pages 180-181

12.88 **teething problems** (n) /ˈtiːðɪŋ ˈprɒbləms/
problems faced in the initial stages of doing sth new • *Opening a restaurant was a good idea, but we faced a number of teething problems before getting off the ground.*
❖ αρχικά προβλήματα

12.89 **ordinarily** (adv) /ˈɔːdnrəli/
usually; normally • *Ordinarily, he never attends religious ceremonies, but he made an exception out of respect to his wife's family.*
➢ ordinary (adj) ❖ συνήθως

12.90 **gem** (n) /dʒem/
sth with a uniquely desirable quality • *The peninsula is a hidden gem, with unspoilt beaches and towering cliffs.* ❖ κόσμημα

12.91 **haunt** (n) /hɔːnt/
a place that many people visit • *Visiting his old university campus, Dad took me round some of his old haunts in the city.* ➢ haunt (v), haunted (adj) ❖ στέκι

12.92 **veritable** (adj) /ˈverɪtəbl/
used to emphasise or qualify a metaphor or exaggeration • *The dinner was a veritable disaster; everything went wrong that could go wrong!* ❖ πραγματικός

12.93 **fare** (n) /feə(r)/
produce on sale, especially food • *As we passed each stall, we were offered samples of the traditional fare on sale.* ❖ προϊόντα

12.94 **intoxicating** (adj) /ɪnˈtɒksɪkeɪtɪŋ/
making you feel excited as though overpowered • *The intoxicating smell of cooking filled the air.* ➢ intoxicate (v), intoxication (n) ❖ μεθυστικός, διεγερτικός

12.95 unqualified (adj) /ˌʌnˈkwɒlɪfaɪd/
complete • *The fundraiser was an unqualified success.* ❖ απόλυτος, πλήρης

12.96 gleefully (adv) /ˈɡliːfəli/
happily; in a very pleased way • *She gleefully agreed to prepare the food for the wedding feast.* ➤ glee (n), gleeful (adj)
❖ με πολλή χαρά / ευθυμία

Video 12: Rite of Passage
page 182

12.97 rite of passage (n) /raɪt əv ˈpæsədʒ/
a traditional ritual that symbolises an important stage in sb's life • *The mother prepared her daughter's gown for her rite of passage upon her coming of age.* ❖ εορτασμός σημαντικής στιγμής στη ζωή, όπως η γέννηση, εφηβεία, γάμος, τεκνοποίηση κλπ.

12.98 clay (n) /kleɪ/
a kind of soft mud used in making ceramic dishes • *The potter skilfully moulded the clay into a gorgeous vase with a few muntes, then placed it in the kiln to harden.* ❖ πηλός

12.99 endurance (n) /ɪnˈdjʊərəns/
the ability to withstand great difficulty • *The ordeal put the girls through both physical and psychological endurance.* ➤ endure (v) ❖ δοκιμή αντοχής

12.100 womanhood (n) /ˈwʊmənhʊd/
the state of being a woman • *The ceremony denoted that the girls had reached womanhood and were ready to find a husband.* ❖ ενηλικίωση, γυναικεία φύση

12.101 tepee (n) /ˈtiːpiː/
a large conical tent traditional to Native Americans in the past • *Most Native Americans now live in towns or cities and few would contemplate the prospect of a nomadic life in a tepee that their ancestors had.*
❖ ινδιάνικη σκηνή

Other nouns

blight	gem	tribute
bout	lavender	undercurrent
clay	lineage	wet market
derivative	revival	womanhood
etymology	taxonomy	

Vocabulary Exercises

A Complete the sentences with the correct form of the words.

1 The jeweller designed a highly intricate necklace composed of numerous spherical and _____ beads. **CONE**

2 Since ancient times the bonds of matrimony helped to forge bonds between powerful dynastic leaders in order to perpetuate their _____. **LINE**

3 Ancient tribes often led a _____ existence, regularly uprooting their dwellings and moving their livestock in search of greener and fresher pastures. **NOMAD**

4 The addition of a piquant flavor to any cuisine always makes the food more _____. **PALATE**

5 Since time _____ conflicts have existed between nations and states and between groups and individuals. **MEMORIAL**

6 People from isolated communities who have had little or no contact with modern technological developments tend to lack _____ and sophistication. **WORLD**

B Circle the correct words.

1 In certain societies it is still expected that a wife should bring a dowry / heirloom to her future spouse as a condition of marriage.

2 Young people sometimes integrate / ostracise a member of their peer group because they dislike their mannerisms or social backgrounds.

3 A reverent / esteemed crowd of mourners paid their last respects to the deceased president at his funeral.

4 Many North American communities still enjoy listening to old-time / age-old music at festivals where musicians play fiddles, guitars and banjoes as well as singing country songs and dancing to folk dances.

5 The young activists were very oral / vocal in their criticism of the new legislation as it would curtail their personal liberties in society.

6 There has been a(n) long-standing / ever-present dispute in classicist circles concerning the extent to which ancient Minoan civilisation was influenced by Egyptian or Mesopotamian civilisations.

C Complete the expressions with the words from the box.

fast   put   rites   teething   tight   trumpet   traditions   wet

1 People from all over the world have held onto time-honoured _____ as a means of defending their culture and way of life against the inroads of globalisation.

2 Evolving urban cultures are characterised by people who don't just sit _____ but rather adapt to and assimilate new trends in technology.

3 Milestones in any society, such as birth, puberty, adulthood and marriage are considered as _____ of passage, as they are essential to connect young people with their communities and foster social growth.

4 Anne's grandmother still prefers to purchase fresh produce at a _____ market rather than going to shops selling durable goods and electronic items.

5 Emma is justified in blowing her own _____ as she has accomplished so much for her disadvantaged community in such a short space of time.

6 Modern society runs the risk of staying _____ if it doesn't adapt to changing cultural norms and technological developments.

7 It is to be expected that there are always _____ problems when one re-evaluates new codes of conduct and norms of behavior.

8 Many traditional community leaders hold _____ to their religious and historical beliefs and won't be swayed by outside influences or values promoted by globalisation.

D Complete the sentences with the adjectives from the box.

aural   counterfeit   culinary   phonetic   primitive   pungent   quaint   reluctant   rudimentary   veritable

1 People who neither have fashion sense nor are culture vultures merely possess _____ knowledge of the latest trends.

2 During the performance of the Christmas play, all the festive lights were switched on, transforming the theatre into a _____ winter wonderland.

3 Averse to becoming a slave to fashion, Mandy was _____ to follow the dictates of fashion promoted by fashion houses through the media.

4 The Greek language is based on a _____ system, whereby the symbol is represented by the actual sound; however, English is based on phonics where vowel combinations and diphthong blends can represent different sounds.

5 The ticket tout tried to pass off the _____ concert tickets as genuine in an attempt to make some money illegally.

6 Each society promotes its traditional style of _____ arts, in terms of how the food is prepared, cooked and presented.

7 The _____ smell of fried onions dipped in garlic sauce wafted through air and assailed my nostrils as I entered the restaurant.

8 I still prefer _____ picturesque country houses in small villages rather than the severe Brutalist style of architecture portrayed by many severe-looking commercial buildings.

9 Nowadays in modern cities we all suffer from an overload of _____ stimuli, constantly bombarded by sounds of music, power-driven DIY and gardening tools, and barking dogs, to name but a few.

10 _____ societies based on close ancestral bonds still flourish in some parts of the world today untainted by modern technological developments or lifestyles.

E Complete the sentences with one word in each gap.

chronicle   etymology   establishment   frond   legacy   mannerism   relic   residue   revival   vestige

1 What a terrible _____ will modern society leave its children and their offspring unless it tackles the problems associated with the profligate burning of fossil fuels and climate change?

2 Throughout the ages the _____ of the original words and their precise associated semantic meanings have changed and evolved to assimilate neologisms created in modern culture.

3 In any social group there always exists a privileged elite group of politicians or powerful leaders known as the _____, who exercise control over others with similar values.

4 The last _____ of the primitive Amazonian tribe were lost as a result of the destruction of their habitat caused by the unabated logging of trees.

5 Each and every culture possesses distinctive and unique characteristics, gestures or _____ to express meaning and their feelings.

6 The high fashion boutique specialised in making exquisite leather jackets with _____ embellishments.

7 A _____ of many people's lives and personal events can be found stored on their social media pages.

8 There has been a new _____ of *avant garde* art inspiring architectural designs which are modern, innovative and radical in shape.

9 After the deceased person's taxes had been paid to the state, the _____ was bequeathed to her only surviving heir.

10 An ancient artefact or _____ of great historical significance was found lying amongst the remains of the disintegrating shipwreck lying on the seabed.

12 Grammar

12.1 Cleft Sentences

Χρησιμοποιούμε τις cleft sentences για να δώσουμε έμφαση. Μοιάζουν με τις relative clauses. Cleft structures συμπεριλαμβάνουν φράσεις όπως: *the reason why, the thing that, the person/people who, the place where, the day when* και προτάσεις με το *what-* και *all* με το *is* ή *was*.

→ **The reason (why)** they endured so much pain **was** to prove their manhood.
→ **The people who** profit from tourism most **are** the cruise operators.
→ **The place where he felt most relaxed was** near the stream in the forest.
→ **The one thing** the Spanish have in common with Mexico **is** their language.
→ **What the English love most** is a good cup of tea.
→ **What they were doing in the middle of the jungle** is anyone's guess.
→ **What's happening now** is that communities are becoming more diverse.
→ **What surprised us most** were the sophisticated building techniques used in the construction.
→ **All that these countries can agree on is** the need to avoid a major war.

Οι cleft sentences χρησιμοποιούνται επίσης με προθέσεις και επιρρήματα.
→ **It was after the ceremony** that the wedding feast began.
→ The wedding ceremony went on for hours. It was **then** that the feast began.
→ **It was slowly but surely** that the use of chocolate became popular.

Σημείωση: Δεν χρησιμοποιούμε cleft sentences με τα stative verbs.

Grammar Exercises

A Rewrite the sentences starting with the given words and using the words in bold.

1 Ethiopia was the country where, around 800 BC, nomads combined beans and animal fat to take with them as food on long trips.

   in

   It _____

2 As for Colombia, we are not sure how coffee actually arrived there.

   how

   What _____

3 The first shipment of coffee wasn't exported from Colombia to the United States until 1835.

   only

   It _____

4 It took three decades for coffee to become the main export of Colombia.

   later

   It _____

5 Colombia now comes second in the world in coffee production.

   biggest

   It _____

6 Coffee tariffs became the primary source of revenue for the government.

   this

   Coffee tariffs were imposed and it _____

7 Forming the Colombian Coffee Federation was the reason for Colombian coffee expanding to global markets.

   caused

   It _____

8 At the end of the 1950s prices for Colombian coffee tanked owing to an overabundance of coffee on the global market.

led

What _____

9 Colombians decided to address the problem by raising awareness of the importance of origin in quality of coffee.

did

What _____

10 So Colombians were the first to strategically market their product and differentiate itself.

marketed

It _____

B Rewrite these sentences using standard word order.

1 It is cultural heritage that unifies people.

_____

2 It is integration that helps people strongly identify with another culture.

_____

3 It is cross cultural awareness of mannerisms that facilitates effective communication.

_____

4 It was in the Early Bronze Age when the first hieroglyphics were written.

_____

5 It was from Greek the word 'phonetics' derived.

_____

6 It is etymology that tells us the origin of a word.

_____

7 It is rudimentary knowledge of a local language that leads to social integration.

_____

8 It is one of Shakespeare's legacies that he coined many words and phrases in English.

_____

C Match 1–8 with a–h to describe some Chinese New Year traditions.

1 What they do before the New Year's celebration is ☐
2 What they avoid doing is ☐
3 What housewives also do is ☐
4 All they use for decorations is ☐
5 What people wear is ☐
6 What tourists attending the celebration should do is ☐
7 It is ☐
8 It is the lantern festival that ☐

a traditional Chinese dress in red or gold.
b is a highlight of the celebration.
c avoid wearing black as it symbolises death.
d clean their homes thoroughly.
e display bowls of fruit or treats in the house.
f by setting off loud firecrackers that evil spirits are driven away.
g cleaning afterwards to keep the good luck in.
h red ornaments often made out of paper.

D Choose the best answers.

1 What he did _____ was blow his own trumpet, which didn't go down well with anybody.

  a do   **b** make   **c** have   **d** know

2 Dear me. _____ I did was ask him how he was and I got this long-winded monologue.

  a The only   **b** Nothing   **c** All   **d** What

3 The Beatles made a catchy little tune called, '_____ You Need is Love,' which is often true.

  a Do   **b** Everything   **c** That   **d** All

4 ___ she is talented at is restoring heirlooms, not design.

   a What   **b** It's   **c** The one   **d** All

5 I don't know what his problem is. ___ I did was ask him how his day went and he almost had a fit.

   a All   **b** What   **c** That   **d** The only

6 It ___ his courage I doubt–it's his sanity.

   a wasn't   **b** isn't   **c** can't be   **d** hasn't

7 How on Earth do you know how to get there? What I ___ is a GPS app on my phone.

   a want   **b** did   **c** do   **d** have

8 She wasn't just slightly annoyed. What she ___ was irate.

   a did   **b** had   **c** was   **d** saw

Exam Task

For questions 1–8, read the text below and decide which answer (A, B, C or D) best fits each gap.

Culture Shock

Moving from a big city to a tiny village or vice versa, or moving abroad for work or study may cause you to experience what is called culture shock. (**1**) ___ you first move to a new place, it is with enthusiasm that you face every new experience. You fall in love with the language and the people, you admire the landscape and you find (**2**) ___ little corners everywhere you turn your head. However, this mood of discovery, called the Honeymoon Stage eventually fades away and the next stage, (**3**) ___ of Frustration sets in. What happens is this: you get used to seeing all your new environment through rose-tinted glasses and you start noticing (**4**) ___ those things that spoil it or are different from what you've been accustomed to and make your life difficult–litter in the street, inconvenient shopping hours or a public transport system that isn't as efficient as the one you left back home. It is during this stage that a lot of people decide to move back to their familiar environment as (**5**) ___ of depression caused by the frustration set in. If you manage to get passed this stage, you can move on to Adjustment, the stage (**6**) ___ you learn to adjust to your new surroundings and situation and manage to acclimatise and feel more (**7**) ___ of the new culture. Finally, though it may take weeks, months or in some cases even years, you reach the final stage of culture shock: Acceptance. It is at this stage when you feel at ease in your new environment, which brings you peace of mind as you realise you don't need to (**8**) ___ understand the new culture to be able to live and thrive in it.

1 **a** Unless   **b** When   **c** While   **d** Before
2 **a** quaint   **b** strange   **c** weird   **d** graphic
3 **a** it   **b** what   **c** this   **d** that
4 **a** such   **b** all   **c** every bit of   **d** the sum of
5 **a** sets   **b** groups   **c** bouts   **d** bursts
6 **a** why   **b** which   **c** where   **d** that
7 **a** fond   **b** appreciative   **c** affectionate   **d** delightful
8 **a** fully   **b** totally   **c** absolutely   **d** utterly

Alphabetical Word List

An alphabetical list of all the words that appear in the Companion follows. The number next to the entry shows where the word appears.

A

a bundle of nerves   9.76
a drop in the ocean   7.74
a means to an end   8.28
a pain in the neck   1.152
a riot of (sth)   7.76
a safe bet   6.103
a slap in the face   1.141
a stone's throw   7.77
aberrant   1.74
abnormal   1.75
abolish   3.122
abolition   3.121
aboveboard   6.84
absent-minded   8.83
abstain   3.134
abundantly   7.115
abuse   6.65
abuse   3.87
abuzz   11.77
accelerate   8.90
accessible   8.100
accomplished   9.95
accomplishment   12.73
acknowledgement   8.32
acquaintance   1.25
acquire   10.82
activism   3.38
adamant   1.77
add insult to injury   7.21
address   3.47
adhere to   8.41
adolescence   1.55
adolescent   1.54
adorn   12.69
adrenaline   11.36
adulthood   9.94
advent   2.91
adversely   1.199
adversity   5.54
advocate   3.82
aesthetically   2.76
affluent   3.73
aftershock   3.127
against all odds   1.19
against your will   1.159
ageist   9.31
age-old   12.34
agitated   9.21
ahead of the curve   2.90
aimlessness   5.10
alarm   3.85

albeit   7.119
alert   4.110
alkali   12.25
allegiance   5.27
alluring   5.20
altitude   5.133
altruism   3.41
altruistic   3.64
amiable   1.93
analogy   4.57
anecdote   9.98
anguish   5.74
annoyance   1.185
answer for   7.8
anticipate   2.133
apathetic   1.85, 3.95
appallingly   1.112
apparatus   8.55
append   8.47
appendix   8.33
applicable   4.14
applied   8.27
apply yourself   8.53
apprentice   6.47
apron   6.20
aptitude   5.70
archival   11.109
aristocracy   11.54
arouse   1.102
as a last resort   6.100
asking price   2.29
aspiration   5.53
aspirational   5.121
aspiring   11.80
assault   3.86
assert   1.103
asset   10.98
assign   8.54
assimilate   8.81
associate   1.165
astounded   5.106
asylum seeker   3.128
at a loss   1.73
at arm's length   1.143
at ease   1.162
at heart   1.157
at stake   5.107
at will   9.74
at your fingertips   2.85
attainable   10.25
attainment   5.75
attention-seeking   4.96
attribute   1.50

attribute   1.166
aural   12.55
austerity   3.21
authenticity   10.18
authority   1.63
automated   2.143
autonomous   9.49
avatar   4.49
aviation   2.46
awe   5.104

B

back and forth   2.97
back sb up   1.174
back to front   2.98
backbone   5.71
backhander   6.73
backtrack   6.54
baffle   1.61
bale   9.77
banal   11.68
band together   3.50
bankruptcy   6.90
banner   3.152
bare   1.2
barge   7.124
bash   5.67
bastion   8.14
batch   9.75
be at liberty to do sth   9.73
be at odds   11.73
be beside yourself   1.154
be in a tight corner   6.98
be in good/bad taste   11.75
be in sb's bad books   1.156
be in tune with   1.153
be inclined to agree   5.124
be no mean feat   9.79
be on good terms   1.155
be on the same page   8.69
be on the same wavelength   1.158
be sucked in   5.97
be thick as thieves   4.45
be thrown in at the deep end   9.67
be wet behind the ears   9.69
beadle   6.11
beanie   2.23
begrudge   7.13
behind sb's back   1.148
benchmark   10.99
benefactor   3.57

beneficially   1.198
beneficiary   3.60
benefit   5.39
benevolent   3.98
bereaved   6.143
bespectacled   5.29
biased   3.117
bibliography   8.34
big yourself up   5.98
billboard   10.1
bio   4.50
biodegradable   7.129
biofluorescence   2.151
biopic   11.114
bitcoin   6.120
bite your tongue   1.149
bitterly   1.179
blackmail   11.48
blare   7.38
blast   1.11
blatant   4.95
blatantly   3.83
bleak   5.65
blight   12.79
blight   10.107
blizzard   5.134
blow your chance   5.94
blow your own trumpet   12.74
blunt   5.69
board   4.27
bogus   11.76
bombard   4.99
born with a silver spoon in your mouth   6.111
bottom line   6.105
boundary   1.209
bout   12.78
boycott   3.88
brag   7.86
branding   4.1
breach   2.81
breadwinner   3.126
breed   1.105
brew   2.123
bribe   6.67
brigade   4.31
brim   2.19
bring out the best in sb   3.112
brink   7.101
broke   6.68
broken home   5.59
brutal   3.101
brutalise   7.126

doom 2.139

door stepping 11.26

dosh 6.75

double-edged sword 5.118

down the drain 5.90

downfall 2.13

downtime 9.47

downward spiral 5.24

dowry 12.43

draw the line 1.204

dread 2.126

dress code 9.90

drift apart 1.126

drift off 8.61

drive (sb/sth) out 7.58

drive sth home 11.31

drone 2.147

drop the subject 8.70

dumb sth down 11.96

durable 2.42

dynamite 1.10

dynasty 4.38

dysfunctional 1.70

E

educated guess 7.45

eel 2.154

efficacy 10.34

effluent 3.74

effusive 10.52

egg (sb) on 1.135

ego 1.142

egocentric 10.51

elaborate 6.56

elaborate 4.15

elated 1.81

elder 6.37

element 2.33

elevate 5.110

eliminate 1.64

eloquent 1.97

emancipated 9.50

embark 7.82

embed 6.1

embody 7.83

embrace 4.89

embroidered 12.83

emigrate 3.77

eminent 2.49

emit 2.51

emoticon 4.53

emotive 4.108

empathetic 1.52

empathy 3.79

emphatically 11.28

empirical 4.8

empowerment 5.23

emulate 5.105

enclave 7.48

encompass 1.65

encounter 4.111

endorsement 10.6

endurance 12.99

enforcement 9.11

enfranchise 9.51

engage in sth 1.202

enhance 8.89

enrich 3.148

entail 2.62

entanglement 7.123

entertain 4.6

entice 10.69

entity 11.1

entourage 4.32

entrepreneur 5.19

envisage 2.125

epileptic 1.27

epitome 10.113

epitomise 10.112

equate 10.76

eradicate 2.58

erode 2.57

escalate 5.111

essence 4.25

establish 6.15

establishment 12.5

esteemed 12.61

ethically 1.51

etiquette 9.87

etymology 12.23

ever-present 12.37

eviction 9.32

exacerbate 7.25

exceed 2.138

excerpt 11.49

excessive 1.201

excruciating 9.16

exemplify 8.80

exert 1.107

exile 11.50

exit 1.17

expenditure 6.4

explicit 10.49

explicitly 7.93, 9.91

exploitative 6.39

exponentially 2.118

extracurricular 8.96

extravagant 6.78

extravagantly 7.94

extrovert 1.189

eye-opener 9.101

F

fabled 11.61

façade 3.10

facet 9.102

facilitate 8.91

faction 4.29

faculty 8.43

fake 3.132

fall back on 3.105

fall foul of sth 10.48

fall in with sb 5.84

fall on deaf ears 3.113

fall short of sth 5.93

fall through the cracks 5.17

falsehood 10.9

familiarity 1.110

fare 12.93

far-reaching 4.88

fascination 1.60

fast track 5.60

fast-paced 5.120

feat 9.27

feminist 3.125

fend for yourself 8.88

ferment 12.15

fertile 5.123

fictitious 3.55

field 6.58

finders keepers (losers weepers) 6.126

fire 5.4

fission 2.60

fit 12.77

fit in 1.127

flag 2.117

flattering 11.90

flattery 2.11

flexitime 9.48

flick through sth 10.88

flourish 1.57

fluff your lines 11.89

flush 6.107

fly on the wall 11.18

folklore 12.84

follow in sb's footsteps 3.146

fondness 12.76

food bank 3.6

footage 11.110

foothill 7.100

foray 10.7

foregone conclusion 7.109

foreman 1.9

foremost 3.48

forge 5.125

fork out 2.38

formative 4.90

formidable 8.44

forthcoming 2.140

fortitude 9.28

foster 7.113

fracking 7.106

fracture 10.101

frame of mind 6.113

framework 4.83

franchise 10.58

fraternity 4.33

fraud 10.84

fraudster 6.96

fraudulent 12.30

free hand 9.70

frenzy 6.53

fringe 11.2

fritter sth away 6.118

from scratch 10.42

frond 12.70

frontal lobe 1.31

frontier 2.121

fugitive 5.112

fulfil 8.109

fulfilment 5.55

fundamental 8.36

fungi 2.107

furnace 2.45

fusion 2.61

G

gangster 5.44

garner 5.33

gathering 1.184

gear sth to/towards sb/sth 10.77

gelada 1.1

gem 12.90

generic 2.10

genie pants 2.22

genome 2.109

gesture 1.212

get along famously 4.46

get behind sth 3.114

get caught up in sth 5.86

get down to business 5.49

get hold of sb 4.67

get into hot water 10.40

get sth off your chest 1.146

ghastly 2.88

ghetto 5.38

give sb the elbow 1.151

give sb their marching orders 9.43

glean 11.115

gleefully 12.96

glimpse 1.221

gloat 7.87

globalisation 4.65

gloom 6.13

glow-worm 7.1

go back 1.128

go down 10.14

go the extra mile 6.142

goatherd 4.3

going forward 4.109

goodwill 7.24

grace 6.30

grain 2.106

grasp 1.219

grassroots 5.16

gripping 11.12

grit 6.112

gritty 5.64

make money hand over fist 10.45

make your mark 3.147

make your way in life 5.9

maladjusted 1.72

mandatory 10.12

manifestation 9.3

manipulation 10.35

mannerism 12.32

manoeuvre 9.88

margin 6.60

marginalise 3.144

market share 10.64

mask 3.40

materialism 10.55

materialise 5.101

matter-of-fact 3.137

maturity 9.8

measly 7.20

measure up 2.25

medication 10.11

mediocre 9.56

medium 4.97

melatonin 2.52

meme 4.54

memoir 11.52

memorabilia 11.103

memorial 12.50

mentality 4.17

mentally 1.23

mentorship 8.107

mercenary 5.102

merchandising 10.56

merciful 3.100

merge 9.97

merger 6.61

mesmerising 11.105

meteorically 11.106

meticulous 1.84

Mickey Mouse 8.2

microclimate 7.78

microcopy 7.79

microcosm 7.80

micro-organism 2.70

middleman 3.22

milestone 9.1

mimic 2.84

mind you 2.15

mind-boggling 4.5

mindful 10.13

minimalist 2.5

minted 6.106

miraculous 1.8

misanthrope 1.76

miser 6.70

miserly 6.6

misguidedly 5.122

mishear 11.93

misnomer 11.101

misspent 1.68

mistaken 1.188

misuse 6.66

mob 1.168

mockingly 8.22

momentum 10.57

monasticism 9.54

monetary 10.50

money laundering 6.133

moneyed 6.77

monocultural 4.91

monsoon 3.131

more or less 2.100

mortality 9.6

mortgage 6.64

mosaic 1.46

mount 3.89

mount up 8.63

multitude 1.66

mutation 2.110

mutually 3.26

N

nanofibre 2.136

narcissism 3.39

narcissistic 4.102

narrow escape 7.46

needless to say 3.142

neglect 1.71

negligence 2.92

neon 2.150

nest egg 6.99

neuroscience 1.7

neurotic 1.90

news outlet 11.55

newsfeed 4.100

NGO 3.2

no big deal 3.140

nomadic 12.40

nominate 9.46

non-confrontational 1.208

non-verbal 4.94

norm 4.104

not be fussed (about sth) 2.18

not hold out much hope 5.95

notoriously 4.92

notwithstanding 7.122

nourish 4.76

novel 8.97

novelty 7.19

novice 1.183

nudge 6.40

O

oatmeal 6.17

obedience 3.116

obligatory 5.117

obliterate 3.124

obnoxious 1.92

obscurity 11.53

obsessive 1.91

obsolete 2.73

obstinate 1.80

occupy 3.90

oddity 7.40

of your own accord 9.71

off the beaten track 7.7

official 6.9

offspring 8.87

old-time 12.36

omen 8.60

on cloud nine 1.161

on edge 1.163

on the cards 2.130

on the dole 5.7

on the face of it 8.65

on the side 6.102

on the spur of the moment 7.75

on the threshold 8.67

on the wrong side of the tracks 6.115

oncoming 5.132

one-hit wonder 11.70

one-sided 4.48

oppress 3.68

optimal 1.49

opulent 6.81

oral 12.53

ordeal 3.130

ordinarily 12.89

orientation 9.85

originate 2.113

orphanage 3.25

ostracise 12.65

out of character 1.164

out of the ordinary 7.57

out of this world 7.56

outburst 1.177

outdated 2.74

outrage 3.151

outright 1.215

outsider 1.181

outweigh 2.44

over the top 11.79

overexpose 2.28

overhaul 4.81

overjoyed 1.83

overrun 7.118

overt 10.47

overwhelm 1.187

P

painstaking 2.78

palatable 12.29

pale in comparison 8.13

paparazzo 11.8

paradox 7.116

parallel 8.99

paraphernalia 8.56

parish 6.10

parlour game 4.11

partial 11.82

paternal 12.39

paternity leave 9.44

pauper 6.28

peculiar (to) 7.81

peek 11.22

peer 1.56

peer pressure 1.113

penny-pinching 6.89

pepper sth with sth 10.32

perception 11.24

periodically 6.16

perpetuate 9.4

persecute 3.71

perseverance 5.56

persevere 2.95

persistence 10.90

persona 11.74

phenomenal 7.66

philanthropist 3.36

philosophical 1.121

phonetic 12.56

physically 1.22

physiologically 2.156

pick up the pieces 5.96

picket 3.91

pinion 6.43

pitch 10.72

pixel 2.1

placement 8.24

plagiarism 8.39

plantation 4.113

platform 10.3

platonic 1.122

platoon 4.39

platter 12.6

play it by ear 7.72

play to the camera 11.98

pleasurable 1.69

pluck up the courage 5.89

plug 10.33

poaching 7.102

pocket 3.9

poignant 11.5

poised 1.95

polio 2.59

polling station 3.120

ponder 11.113

popularise 4.10

porringer 6.22

posh 6.71

posit 8.49

posse 4.43

post-traumatic 1.29

posture 1.223

power plant 3.149

practicality 8.31

precede 2.34

precedent 2.94

precept   6.3
precursor   4.12
predator   7.99
prejudiced   3.103
prep   3.52
pretence   3.13
prevalence   5.57
prevalent   3.42
primary   4.116
prime   7.47
primitive   12.58
principled   1.98
pristine   7.11
privileged   3.118
proactive   5.99
proceed   2.112
progenitor   2.108
prominently   3.34
promotional   10.62
prone (to)   1.178
propel   1.16
prosecute   3.72
prospective   5.30
prosperity   7.4
proverbially   11.17
province   7.69
provoke   9.30
proximate   4.62
pseudo-   10.10
pull strings   9.80
pull the plug on sth   9.81
pull the punches   9.82
pull up stakes   9.83
pull your weight   9.65
pungent   12.26
put one over on sb   7.22
put sb down   1.139
put sth into perspective   2.149
put your foot in it   1.150

Q

quack   7.105
quaint   12.35
quantum theory   2.89

R

radical   2.8
radioactivity   2.71
rake in sth   10.43
rally   3.93
randomly   4.9
range   6.29
ranks   9.14
rapport   8.105
raring   9.22
rarity   7.41
rationale   8.57
rationalise   8.46
raw   5.63

raw material   10.108
read between the lines   8.74
readiness   9.23
reap the benefit   3.49
rear its (ugly) head   1.210
rebellion   5.41
recession   10.94
recipient   3.24
reciprocal   1.117
recite   12.52
reckless   6.41
recluse   11.40
recognition   5.73
recurrently   7.90
red tape   6.76
red-brick university   8.18
redeem   3.59
redefine   1.217
redistribution   3.27
referral   8.77
rehabilitation   5.18
reimburse   6.50
reinforce   8.92
relic   12.48
relief   3.3
relieve sb of sth   9.42
reluctant   12.33
reluctantly   2.145
remains   9.105
remedy   8.108
reminisce   5.50
reminiscent   11.119
remoteness   9.106
render   2.9
renovate   8.94
repel   1.214
replete   10.8
repression   10.102
reprimand   11.86
repulse   1.222
repurpose   10.115
resemblance   1.225
residue   12.46
resilience   7.98
resounding   2.127
restraint   10.79
retailer   6.52
retain   9.40
revere   9.13
reverent   12.66
revival   12.51
revolt   3.67
rid sb/sth of sth/sb   6.36
ridicule   5.35
ridicule   1.203
rigorous   8.23
rip sb/sth off   6.93
rite of passage   12.97
ritual   5.11
roadblock   3.154

rod   1.12
rolling in it   6.109
rose-coloured glasses   9.96
rosy   5.61
round of applause   5.34
round up   3.53
rub off   10.27
rudimentary   12.14
run up against   3.106
run-down   3.8
ruse   12.18
ruthless   6.131

S

sacred   9.15
saddle sb with sth   9.59
safe and sound   2.101
salt cellar   12.82
salvage   6.138
sane   12.71
sarcasm   10.97
satire   10.96
saturation   10.78
saved by the bell   8.71
sb's/sth's days are numbered   11.37
scam   5.100
scoff   2.35
scoop   11.41
scope   8.58
scorn   10.95
scourge   11.4
scratch the surface   11.14
scrupulous   1.99
scrutinise   11.94
scrutiny   2.80
secluded   7.26
sedate   7.103
see fit   9.72
seedier   11.30
seething   7.12
seizure   1.28
self-absorbed   4.101
self-awareness   1.34
self-content   1.170
self-esteem   1.172
selfless   3.20
self-satisfaction   1.171
self-sufficiency   1.173
semblance   10.17
semicomatose   1.21
seminal   2.12
sensibilities   7.15
sensor   2.56
sentiment   3.19
serene   1.96
serenity   2.153
set sth to rights   6.14
set your sights on sth   5.6
settle down   1.130

shady   6.86
shareholder   6.59
shawl   3.15
shears   7.128
shed light on   2.115
sheer   11.118
shilling   6.5
shimmer   7.2
short-sighted   7.52
shower sb with sth   6.94
shrine   6.2
shrinkage   4.63
shudder   4.105
sick (and tired) of sth/sb   8.6
sift   2.116
signee   3.35
simplistic   7.9
sit tight   12.59
sitcom   10.5
skew   4.106
skint   6.72
skull   1.18
skyrocket   11.35
slander   11.42
slap   1.140
slate   8.1
sleek   2.7
slew   2.6
slip up   5.85
slogan   3.153
small talk   4.86
small-minded   5.128
smattering   5.3
snag   7.127
snappy   10.31
snare   3.1
sneaky   10.28
snob   8.3
snobbery   8.12
soapbox   7.29
so-called   5.36
societal   6.129
sold on sth   2.36
solely   3.58
solid   1.35
solidarity   3.133
somewhat   7.95
sophistication   12.3
sorrow   1.220
sought-out   1.38
souk   7.39
soul-crushing   3.32
soundproof   8.95
soup kitchen   3.7
sovereign   9.53
span   9.24
spare no effort   3.115
sparingly   10.110
sparsely   7.64
spawn   5.1